Innovation and Continuity in English Studies

Bamberger Beiträge zur Englischen Sprachwissenschaft

University of Bamberg Studies in English Linguistics

Herausgegeben von/edited by Wolfgang Viereck

Bd./Vol. 44

Peter Lang

Frankfurt am Main · Berlin · Bern · New York · Oxford · Wien

Herbert Grabes (ed.)

Innovation and Continuity in English Studies

A Critical Jubilee

Die Deutsche Bibliothek - CIP-Einheitsaufnahme

Innovation and continuity in English studies : a critical jubilee / ed. by Herbert Grabes. - Frankfurt am Main ; Berlin ; Bern ; Bruxelles ; New York ; Oxford ; Wien : Lang, 2001
(University of Bamberg studies in English linguistics ; Vol. 44)
ISBN 3-631-38372-X

ISSN 0721-281X
ISBN 3-631-38372-X
US-ISBN 0-8204-5427-3

Printed in Germany 1 2 4 5 6 7

www.peterlang.de

Dedicated to the Founders of IAUPE

Contents

A Note from the Editor

When the request to edit this volume reached me it was rather late – in fact, too late, in my own experience and that of the colleagues whom I asked for advice. On the other hand, I shared the view of the president and the secretary of IAUPE, and the chairman of the International Committee, that the fiftieth anniversary should not pass without a jubilee volume to document our joint endeavour. All that the time remaining permitted me to do was to undertake the effort required to gather enough contributions to represent both the scope and quality of the work done in IAUPE.

Given this aim, the first and most difficult task was to decide which of our many members I was to ask to contribute, and this decision clearly had to be made in close cooperation with those who officially represent our Association. And here the long list of those I wish to thank for their substantial help already begins; without the suggestions made by our president Wolfgang Viereck, our secretary Ian Kirby and the chairman of the International Committee, Ihab Hassan, I would surely not have known what to do.

Next a title had to be chosen, and I hope its present form will do justice to the efforts of IAUPE and serve as an adequate frame for the various contributions to this volume. These contributions had to be written and submitted under severe time constraints, and I would like to express my sincere gratitude to all those colleagues who were willing to put aside other obligations in order to make it possible to have the jubilee volume ready for the Bamberg conference.

After the essays came in, I found myself faced with another task that proved to be anything but easy. Reading the contributions, it became clear that there are at least as many forms of documentation on a global scale as there are notions of "English studies," and above all I had to make a decision between the form preferred by linguists and that normally used by literary scholars. If I choose the latter, this is only a matter of economising on copy editing, and I have to apologise to the contributing linguists if they find that their essays appear in an unaccustomed format.

Regarding the editing and copy-editing, I wish to thank Gordon Collier (final subediting and layout, and research on the List of Current Members), Marc Colavincenzo, Christine Buddensiek and Annette Obert–Sochor, as well as the students who supported them. Without their joint efforts, this jubilee volume would not be there in time to add what I hope is a jubilant note to IAUPE's celebrations.

Introduction: IAUPE Past and Present[1]

IAN KIRBY

THE INTERNATIONAL ASSOCIATION of University Professors of English, usually abbreviated to IAUPE, celebrated its Jubilee in the twelve months from the summer of 2000 to the summer of 2001; but the events that led to its foundation began somewhat earlier than 1951, the year from which its existence is officially dated. On his way back from the International Congress of Linguists at Paris in 1948, Professor R.W. Zandvoort of the University of Groningen wondered why linguists and others had their international congresses, while Anglicists did not. To remedy this state of affairs, he and the other editors of *English Studies*, together with certain other European and transatlantic professors of English, wrote to colleagues in British universities asking them to convene an international congress of English studies in a British university town.

In response, those who had signed the letter were invited to the annual conference of British professors of English at Edinburgh at Easter, 1949, to discuss the plan. Professor Zandvoort and Professor Simone d'Ardenne of Liège accepted this invitation, and set forth their ideas in detail. There was initially some reluctance among the British colleagues present to shoulder the burden: but when Professor C.L. Wrenn declared that he was willing to organise the first meeting at Oxford in 1950, the proposal was agreed.

This first conference duly took place at Magdalen College, Oxford, in the last week of August 1950; and it was apparently a great success, to judge from the recollections of those who were present. The records show that some 150 professors from all over the world attended, and that there were six sections: on the teaching of English in the universities, chaired by H.B. Charlton; on linguistic matters (Kemp Malone); on medieval literature (Karl Brunner); on Drama, in-

---

[1] Source references: John Lawlor, "In a Secretary Hand," *IAUPE Bulletin* (Summer 1996): 4–7; R.W. Zandvoort and Ian J. Kirby, "Thirty Years On," *IAUPE Bulletin* (Summer 1979): 1–19; and the archives of the Association.

cluding Shakespeare (F.P. Wilson); on sixteenth- and seventeenth-century literature (W.L. Renwick); and on eighteenth- and nineteenth-century literature (G.A. Bonnard) – apparently, so little interest had been expressed in contemporary literature that it was omitted! Three lectures, each scheduled to last fifty minutes, were given in each time slot, and were followed by over an hour of discussion introduced by a distinguished expert in the field. General meetings of the conference were addressed by Helen Darbishire, who spoke on Wordsworth, and Gilbert Murray, on Europe and the classical tradition. The academic programme was compressed into three very full days, which also included receptions offered by the University and the City of Oxford.

In the course of, or as a result of, this conference, a number of decisions were taken. The first was to accept a proposal made by Professor A.H. Koszul that the second conference should take place in Paris in August 1953. The second was that conferences should be scheduled every three years, alternately in an English-speaking and a non-English-speaking country. The third was that an International Association should be formed, and an International Consultative Committee elected to manage its affairs. The fourth was that the Association should be affiliated to the newly founded *Fédération internationale des langues et littératures modernes* (FILLM). The fifth was that a Newsletter should be produced; and this was the forerunner of the *Bulletin*, whose first issue appeared in 1956. The sixth was that the lectures given at the first conference should be published; and in fact they appeared in 1951 as the first issue of *English Studies Today*. The seventh, that a Constitution should be drawn up for the Association, was formally approved at the first Lausanne conference, in 1959. One of the provisions in this was that the prime mover in the organisation of each triennial conference should be elected President of the Association for the three years culminating in the conference. It will be seen that, in the main, the Association has remained remarkably faithful to the blueprint established for it by its founder-members.

The establishment of the Association was presided over by Professor Wrenn; and with his first report he published a list of 138 members, most of whom held chairs in Europe and North America, though the Indian subcontinent, Thailand, Nigeria, Egypt, South Africa, Japan, China, Australia, New Zealand, Ceylon, Singapore and Uganda were also represented. The founder-members thus fully reflect the international nature of IAUPE, which today has members from some fifty different countries.

The second conference took place in 1953 as scheduled, though not without some external problems, for this was the summer of the transport strike in Paris.

At one point it was uncertain whether the conference would go ahead, and quite a number of professors cancelled; but those who did come seem to have enjoyed themselves, partly, perhaps, because their Parisian hosts had laid in a stock of champagne which turned out to be more than adequate for those who came. Due seriousness was restored in 1956, when the Association met at Jesus College, Cambridge, under the aegis of E.M.W. Tillyard: the official programme contained a note that "professors are requested to be in College no later than 12 midnight"!

The fourth conference was held in Lausanne in 1959, under the presidency of Georges Bonnard, the then *grand patron* of English studies at the university there. At the general meeting, the Constitution in its earliest form was approved, and the first Secretary-General and Treasurer, Peter Butter of Glasgow, was elected. Since 1959, conferences have continued to alternate between the British Isles and Continental Europe, except for those held at UCLA in 1974 and Trent, Ontario, in 1992. Sometimes there has been a choice of venues, and the business meeting at the preceding conference has had to vote; sometimes there has been one offer only; on occasion, the Secretary-General for the time being has had to undertake major research in order to secure a conference venue. Most happily, all conferences to date have taken place more or less as planned, though there have on occasion been anxious moments: in 1971, the Istanbul Opera House, in which the Eighth Triennial Conference was to meet, burned to the ground only days before the opening, and the Association met instead in the Istanbul Hilton. A "baptism of fire," indeed, for the second Secretary-General and Treasurer, John Lawlor, who took over from Peter Butter in that year and, undaunted, graced that office until 1995.

IAUPE conferences have much in common with those of other associations, but there are some differences, too. For some time now, presidents have striven to attain the perfect balance between the three desiderata: that there shall be an academic programme which is thoroughly attractive to members both in quality and quantity; that there shall be time for professors to meet informally to discuss matters of academic and general interest; and that there shall be an opportunity to learn something of the culture and, yes, attractions of the conference venue. At the present time we are only too familiar with the short conference on a specific subject which lasts for two or three days, which has a choice of lectures each morning, afternoon and evening, and which we may easily leave having had only a brief moment during the coffee breaks and rushed meals to speak with colleagues, and having travelled only from the airport to the university and back again. In comparison, IAUPE conferences may well be either behind the times or ahead of them: for it is the hope of every President that members will remember the conference both for the excellence of the academic programme and also for the opportunity to do something other than the daily round of academic and administrative duties that is their normal lot. Twenty years ago, when soundings were taken among founder-members, this pattern of conference organisation was enthusiastically endorsed; it is perhaps time to see whether a new generation of professors is of the same mind.

At the business meeting at UCLA in 1974, members chose to accept the offer of Professor Jacek Fisiak that the next conference be held in Poznań; but the medievalists among them were equally delighted with the proposal made by Professor P.J. Mroczkowski that they should hold a post-conference meeting in Cracow. Thus was born the Medieval Symposium, which since 1977 has taken place either after or, more commonly, before the main conference and in a neighbouring university. It has usually attracted a modest attendance, though the delightful symposium organised by Professor Norman Blake at Sheffield in 1998 looked at one point like being far too "select" for comfort; and I was commissioned by the Executive Committee to write to all known medievalists a letter whose message might have been summarised in five words, "use it, or lose it!" Happily, our medievalists have decided, at least in principle, to use it, and Professor Hans Sauer hopes to welcome a somewhat larger gathering in Munich.

Certain questions about the Association and its policies have tended to recur in the course of the last half-century. One of these relates to Article 3 of our Constitution, which regulates admission to membership. Earlier, the policy was to admit to membership full professors of English in universities of international reputation, and other persons of distinction. Recently, this has been modified to place more emphasis on the individual as a scholar of distinction, rather than on the institution in which he or she teaches. It is too early to see what difference this will make to our membership; but there has already been one very pleasant development, in that several colleagues who have been welcomed into the Association as "other scholars of distinction" have subsequently been promoted to full professor by their universities.

Another aspect of the membership question, addressed recently by a specially chosen membership committee, relates to the relative smallness of the representation of certain parts of the world. For many years the countries with the largest number of members have been the USA and the UK, which is hardly surprising; these are followed (in the 1998 statistics) by Germany, then Canada, Japan, France and Switzerland. The next group consists of Norway, Sweden, Belgium and Spain; all other countries have fewer than ten members. South America is not represented at all; Africa, Asia (apart from Japan) and Australasia are thinly represented; so, in the main, is Eastern Europe. Members of the International Committee have been diligent in their attempts to improve this situation; and they hope that all members of the Association will second their endeavours.

From the first it was anticipated that a publication would be circulated regularly to members; and since 1956 the IAUPE *Bulletin* has been sent out two years in three – not, that is, in a conference year. It currently contains reports from correspondents in different parts of the world concerning the study of English, principally in universities, together with information about conferences likely to be of interest to members, such as those of FILLM. This informatory material has for some time been preceded by one or two articles on subjects considered by the editor to be of general interest to members.

It also seems to have been expected that conference papers would be published under the aegis of the Association; but this was never more than irregular. As mentioned, the first conference was celebrated by the first issue of *English Studies Today*, and some of the following conferences would also seem to have had their volumes, to judge from the fact that the fifth issue appeared after the eighth conference, at Istanbul in 1971. The rest, to date, is silence. However, the International Committee have been considering a proposal that it is time for the *Bulletin* to be transformed into a yearly learned journal which would more fully reflect the scholarly interests of the Association, while also retaining the traditional content of the *Bulletin*. As Andrew Breeze said in his first "Editorial Notes" in 1999, "IAUPE is changing and so is this *Bulletin*."

Is IAUPE indeed changing? And if so, for better or worse? I suspect that there may be almost as many answers to these questions as there are members (541, at the most recent count).

To begin with a few statistics: in the last ten years the membership has remained, numerically, fairly constant; it has not fallen below 500, nor has it risen substantially over 600. Gains have been keeping pace with losses, though it should be added that since the introduction of the database it has become easier to identify 'sleeping' members and alert them to their situation. More countries are represented in IAUPE now than ever before, although, as indicated earlier, most countries have only a very few members. So one of our priorities in the next few years must be to continue to act on the policy – at the forefront of discussions ancient and modern – to increase our membership, particularly in parts of the world which remain poorly represented, and particularly among younger professors and other distinguished scholars.

At a recent Business Meeting of FILLM, the representatives of the constituent associations of the Federation were invited to present their organisations, referring particularly to their individual strengths and weaknesses, and to the opportunities and threats currently facing them. My own presentation in regard to our Association touched largely on issues which have already been mentioned here; however, some aspects of these reflections may perhaps be worth recording on this occasion.

One problem shared by many of our fellow-members of FILLM is that of the venue of conferences. In the past, we have been extremely fortunate in always finding at least one member who has been willing to shoulder the burden of organising the triennial conference. This is clearly the ideal; for a Professor of English is far better equipped than a professional conference organiser to know what will please his fellow-members, and a university venue is likely to be much easier on the purse than one of the conference centres which are springing up all over the world. However, it is not at all certain that this happy state of affairs will continue well into the twenty-first century. Professorial duties, particularly in regard to administration, become more and more onerous, a fact regularly reflected in correspondents' reports in the *Bulletin*; and we all know eminent scholars who have refused promotion to chairs for this very reason. At the time of writing (October 2000) I have one offer for 2004, and none yet for subsequent conferences; FILLM currently has an offer for 2002, but none for 2005. The price of conferences is eternal willingness; whether it will continue to be forthcoming is another matter.

But there is at least one reason for optimism: the growing tendency for universities to establish their own conference centre, and the construction of state-of-the-art student accommodation such as that which many of us enjoyed at Durham in 1998. The policy of alternating between an English-speaking and a non-English-speaking country has meant that the heaviest charge of hospitality has fallen on universities in the British Isles, which have so far hosted seven of our seventeen conferences (Bamberg being the eighteenth). It is good for your Secretary-General (who may find himself having to try and persuade a doubtful colleague to undertake a task requiring the dedication of much of his spare time for three years) to be able to refer to the excellent on-site infrastructure which some British universities already have.

Another facet of this question relates to the geographical location of conferences. To date, IAUPE conferences have been held in Europe and North America. But we are an international association, and we have received, in the last twenty years, firm offers from Australia and Hong Kong. Why have these not been accepted? Because, it would appear, there was insufficient evidence that the conference would be well attended. In the same period, FILLM have held conferences in Africa and Asia. One may wonder whether our younger members will react as their predecessors did – next time there is an offer from outside the traditional regions.

I believe it can be said that, even if some have been less well attended than others, our conferences up to now have been successful if not highly successful, and are remembered with pleasure by all or most of those who were present. But it is not necessarily the case that elements which have made for successful conferences in the past will do so in the future. There are, in my view, two factors that should give us cause, if not for concern, then at least for reflection. The first is the proliferation of academic associations, and the consequent proliferation of conferences. In the last decade alone, two new associations have been founded which I have felt it imperative to join; in the summer of 2000 I participated in three conferences, of which two actively, and I would gladly have attended at least another three if time and money had permitted. The choice, of course, comes down to personal priorities. Our members have much more choice than in the past: and it would be very useful to know why about one-third of our members normally choose to attend IAUPE conferences, while about two-thirds do not.

One of the possible answers to this is suggested by the second factor on which we might reflect. One of the changes in the field of English studies is that (and I hope I shall not be misunderstood for putting it in this way!) today's professors tend to know more and more about less and less. Thirty years ago, the University of Lausanne tripled its English Department chairs because it was seen to be no longer possible for one professor to cover all aspects of English Language and Literature. Today, it is common in some countries for professors to hold chairs, not of (say) English Language, or English Literature, or Linguistics, or Medieval Studies, but of Semiotics, Victorian Literature, Sociolinguistics, or Chaucer: and a professor of Victorian Literature will not necessarily find it imperative to attend a lecture on Marvell, or a Chaucerian specialist one on *Beowulf*, even if given by Seamus Heaney.

What is IAUPE doing to meet the challenge of such developments? In the first place, we have already responded to the substantial increase in the number of colleagues whose principal interest is English linguistics by noticeably increasing the number of sections that might be expected to interest them. We are also trying to provide for those whose interests are in the "newer fields." In the last twenty years we have doubled the number of sections at a conference to cater for the greater degree of specialisation in our midst; it may well be that we shall have to go further in this direction. At the same time, we have to ensure that the traditional subjects continue to be well represented; and the database is now giving us invaluable information about the academic interests of our members. We can now help our presidents by listing at least the "top ten" fields of interest (led, currently, by Middle English), so that they may ensure that these are appropriately represented at the conference they organise.

But the academic content is not the only element that determines the success or otherwise of a conference. Twenty years ago, the *Bulletin* published a survey of the first thirty years of the Association. Included in it were comments made by founder-members. These included a reminiscence by Professor Erik Tengstrand (Uppsala) about the academic content of the first conference:

> I have now reread the published lectures, and I am again as impressed by their high quality as I was in 1950. The lectures on the British Dialect Survey were given at a crucial point in the history of that undertaking – one might say, in the history of English linguistics.

Not everyone was of the same mind: witness the opinion of Professor Clarence Tracy of Acadia, Canada:

> The papers, perhaps, have not always been as stimulating as I should have liked, but the leisurely pace of your conferences and the time given for reflection and discussion are a welcome change from the machine-gun-like pace of most conferences organized on this continent. I very much hope that that will continue to be the policy of this association.

If a similar survey were to be carried out among present-day members, it is to be hoped that the former view on academic content would prevail, and the latter on other matters!

Other comments related to particular memorabilia: the paddle-steamer excursion on Lake Geneva during which Professor Vivian de Sola Pinto recited "The Prisoner of Chillon," the final banquet of the Edinburgh conference in the Robert Adam library, the reception at the Guinness mansion near Dublin, the salt mine near Cracow which temporarily hosted the medievalists. However, the most typical view was best expressed by Professor A.R. Humphreys of Leicester:

> As I think back, my recollections are rather general than particular – I mean they concern the rewards of friendly meetings in interesting places and the sense of a very congenial international community it was good to be part of. I think if I had to select one feature of all which made the conferences valuable it has been the sense of the approachability, the companionable humanity of the world of the scholars of English.

This seems as good a point as any at which to end; but perhaps I may be permitted a personal note. Although I am still an "active" professor, and retirement is still some way away, I have been a member for more than thirty years; and I still have a vivid recollection of my first conference, at Dublin. The initial astonishment which greeted my appearance (I had recently celebrated my "thirtieth year to heaven") quickly gave way to the warmest of welcomes: then, as now, the Association was concerned with its attractiveness to younger professors. I hope that the newer professors among us will have the experience that Professor Humphreys described, and I can confirm.

What Rough Beast?

HAZARD ADAMS

I BELIEVE THAT THIS PAPER takes a direction different from that of most of the others in this volume, for I propose to concern myself not so much with old and new intellectual developments as with changes now going on and changes likely in the profession to which English professors belong – changes motivated by no means entirely intellectual developments. I do this because I believe that current changes, often quite externally motivated, will deeply affect what and how English scholars study, what and how they teach, and the relative importance of teaching and research to their professional lives. Yet what English scholars stand for and need to defend will, at the ethical level, not change very much, or at least should not. My subject remains that of innovation and continuity but with emphasis on the professional lives professors lead and will lead and how that will affect what they will have to think about. ("Have" in both senses, because the changes we are experiencing not only dictate new subject matter but also vastly increase the amount of it.) My project requires attention to the history of thinking about literature, though it will have to be brief and superficial. That will lead to discussion of the present situation of the scholar in the academy and in society and the smaller societies to which the scholar belongs, for the practice of literary study and its fate is tied to both, and that relationship is subject to change as well as to the forces of tradition. Discussion of this matter will not be nearly as brief.

What I shall be trying throughout to show, at least by implication, is the present and future importance of these matters to the English scholar's intellectual life. I add that I write from the perspective of and about the situation in the USA. When I write of English studies, I refer to the study of literature written in English, not a national literature, and not the language as such.

It has been widely acknowledged that English studies have fairly recently undergone significant (and, for many, painful) changes – so significant that phrases like "the culture wars" and "political correctness" have become common currency even outside of academe. As a symptom of the discontent that this has engendered, new scholarly organisations have appeared to challenge the Modern Language Association of America. One of the early functions of these groups seems to have been to provide opportunities for public fulmination against the influence of poststructuralist or postmodernist practices in literary scholarship (now principally known as "theory"). There is no need to review here the varieties of postmodernist thought and political movements that have been historically and sometimes ideologically intertwined with them. We have experienced post-modernism long enough to recognise in a series of abstract notions its character and the objects of its attack, among which are the unified subject, the transcendental signified, the motivated sign, all absolutes, metaphysics, humanism, and so on. It is well, however, to consider briefly the larger historical landscape from which this movement or, rather, congeries of movements emerged and to notice that they, including their generally deconstructive drive, are all at some level characterisable as political, either in motivation or in presumed result. It is no surprise that their heirs (sometimes oedipal) have been the so-called "New Historicism" and "culture studies." The claim raised in the 1960s that everything is political caused, at any rate, everything to seem political and, perhaps, everyone to want to be, though when everything becomes political the term itself dies of the disease of expansion. We have seen scholars take the opportunity this afforded to re-evaluate almost every famous writer and to discover as politically significant (for better or worse) writers forgotten or ignored by earlier generations with other interests (although it could be argued that there is really only one interest, the political, either badly or correctly pursued; thus a poem like Keats's "To Autumn" is read politically, a notion an earlier generation would have thought astonishing).

The speed with which all of this has occurred (and the speed with which things academic have generally been changing) has been breathtaking if one takes a reasonably long view, and we can expect the mills of academe to continue to grind ever more quickly and finely as there is more and more to grind and there are more grinders to do it. The reasons for this, in addition to the growth of the population and greater access to higher education, are various and perhaps obvious to some, but it is worth collecting them together, thinking about them, and considering their interrelations. They are changing, and will further change, the profession of English studies.

I shall discuss these matters under the following rubrics: I. a brief historical account of major phases in the history of literary thought (a term I now favour over "criticism" or "theory") in order to situate the present; II. consideration of the impact of the current technological revolution; III. consideration of the phenomenon of globalisation; and IV. a survey of the state of the university and the academic scholar under the preceding conditions, including the changed and changing character of the professoriate and its activities.

I An historical preface to what will follow

As a beginning, it is well to consider the historical conditions that strongly impinge on and frustrate the relations among the academic disciplines today. Anyone addressing what liberal scholarship and education ought to be must seriously consider the following: that we have passed through a "linguistic age"; that the distinctions between some academic disciplines, at least as represented by academic departments, have been blurred; that we have moved into an age of political moralism; and that the speed with which this has all happened and the uneasiness that the speed has engendered have been reflected in disputes over what books we should be studying and teaching. Disputes over the canon are byproducts of these developments.

1. *A linguistic phase*

Risking gross oversimplification, I am going to divide the history of Western thought into four ages or phases (the latter word may be better because the phases overlap): the ontological; the epistemological; the linguistic; and the politically moralistic. In the ontological phase, the principal question around which thoughtful discourse turned was the nature of Being. From before Plato all the way to the Renaissance, that question was paramount, whether the discourse was philosophical, theological, scientific, literary, or artistic. In Western literary thought, all through this long period the dominating term "mimesis" implied some truth the poet sought to imitate or represent. In the Renaissance, the question shifted and became an epistemological one, formulated in two great traditions, the empirical one of Bacon and Locke and the rationalistic one of Descartes. "How do we know?" was the question, and with it came eventually the notion of the modern self and the sort of subjectivity that eventually produced a radically new note in literature: the poem as an act of self-expression or self-study, or, as it has been called, the inner made outer. In most minds, the objective world was the province of scientific constitution; the subjective world was left to poetry and art. But not for long, because subjectivity itself became objectified in such movements as Freud's, and even in the area of literary art there were efforts at objectification such as Zola's. One witnesses the last gasp and death knell of the epistemological phase in the famous utterance of Walter Pater at the close of *The Renaissance*:

> Experience, already reduced to a group of impressions, is ringed round for each one of us by that thick wall of personality through which no real voice has ever pierced on its way to us, or from us to that which we can only conjecture to be without. Every one of those impressions is the impression of the individual in his isolation, each mind keeping as a solitary prisoner its own dream of a world.[1]

Already a new phase had begun, and it is no surprise that Pater's book had an air of nostalgia and loss about it. The new phase was one of the hegemony of language. Its first stirrings can be detected in Locke's remarks on language, followed by the work of the syncretic mythographers of the eighteenth century, the search for the origin of language and the hope that the discovery would unlock the mystery of Man. One sees the development of this movement from Rousseau through Herder to Humboldt, thence finally to the structuralist linguistics of Saussure, the opposed philosophies of Cassirer and Heidegger, Wittgenstein, the symbolic logicians, the analytic and ordinary-language philosophers, structuralism, and finally deconstruction. The question of knowledge, which was Descartes' question and still Kant's question, and even Husserl's question, had been replaced by what was regarded as a prior though not necessarily more important one. If all knowledge was mediated by symbols, did not the question of the nature of language have to precede the question of the nature of knowledge or the knowledge of nature? Gradually almost everything came to be seen on the model of linguistic structure. After Saussure's formulation of language as an autonomous system of signs, that which was signified by a sign came to be seen as but another signifier. Language rolled out in a differential chain of infinite length from which there was no escape into a nature apart from the symbols that structured it. Language was not principally a tool for knowing something prior to it, or a means of self-expression. It defined human beings. Rather than Man speaking language, language, as Heidegger remarked, spoke Man. "Wall-to-wall language," as Edward Said put it, deploring this prison-house view. Soon, as we know, everything was seen on this model: fashion (Barthes), mythology (Lévi–Strauss), the unconscious (Lacan), and so on. Banished was the old simple epistemological self or subject – caught up, transformed, and now but a construct of forces intertwined in these differential chains, which implied no origin, centre, or first principle.

---

[1] Walter Pater, *The Renaissance: Studies in Art and Poetry*, ed. Adam Phillips (Oxford: Oxford University Press, 1998) 151.

The linguistic model was amazingly revealing – and powerful; and its ubiquitousness influenced our sense of the intellectual disciplines. Thus my second point:

2. *Blurred genres*

I adopt the term from Clifford Geertz's *American Scholar* essay of 1980.[2] There he expanded the term "genre" from its literary meaning to make it refer to academic disciplines and other categories of research and thought. But the literariness of the term was present not by chance. Geertz argued that the traditional boundaries of the disciplines were being blurred. This is a fact that we have been observing ever since and everywhere in academic life. Some of the scientific departments and research groups flourishing today were unheard of even when Geertz wrote. Departments cross the division between natural sciences and social sciences, between social sciences and the humanities. Humanists now often give their principal allegiances to "centres" and interdepartmental committees, frequently theoretical in intent. These units are often themselves fledgling disciplines. At the same time, French professors still occasionally complain that professors of English have been teaching texts by French writers, philosophers and psychoanalysts. Old-line philosophers still occasionally deplore the appearance of philosophical texts in English or comparative literature classes or declare that certain philosophers like Jacques Derrida, who discusses philosophical texts as if they were literary texts, are not philosophers at all. But the trend has been otherwise. I picked up a book a few years ago entitled *A Poetics for Sociologists* and another about parallels between chaos theory in physics and contemporary literary theory.

The reasons for all this having happened are many and varied. The main one is the influence of forces from the phase of the hegemony of language, though there has been little acknowledgement of that fact at any level of the educational establishment. The old distinctions were being blurred, nevertheless. A simple example is what happened to the venerable opposition between prose fiction and history that Aristotle spent a significant paragraph on in *Poetics*. The work of Hayden White argued that any writer of history is governed by a master-trope, and this trope affects, maybe controls, the way he (all White's examples were works by men) produces his story. We came so far along this route that the term "literature" was itself blurred and in some camps was dispensed with entirely, since on this model and others like it all texts are literary texts: that is, sodden

[2] Clifford Geertz, "Blurred Genres," *American Scholar* 49.2 (Spring 1980): 165–79.

with tropes and narrative devices. Of course, when everything became literature it was just as easy to say that there was no literature, only writing. What began in structuralism as a system of differences produced a monolith. No longer did language point to an ontological or epistemological problem. Such problems were viewed as a product of language, and the term "language" soon became a ground for new intellectual communities, pacts and treaties.

Geertz, himself an anthropologist, unashamedly called things he studied (for example, cockfights) "texts," as if they were written. He then argued, "The properties connecting texts with one another, that put them, ontologically anyway, on the same level, are coming to seem as important in characterising them as those dividing them."[3] Geertz claimed that the value of the treatment of everything as a text was that it

> trains attention on precisely this phenomenon: on how the inscription of action is brought about, what its vehicles are and how they work, and on what the fixation of meaning from the flow of events – history from what happened, thought from thinking, culture from behavior – implies for sociological interpretation.[4]

Literary study seemed to have triumphed methodologically here, having invaded the social sciences. But in a profound sense literature seemed to have disappeared or become greatly impoverished, its study transformed into an activity with precisely the ends Geertz mentioned, in which questions of artistic value were rendered irrelevant or at best deferred.

Actually, this was the result of a process that began in the eighteenth century and has accelerated rapidly in recent times. Literary study, in addition to historical and philological scholarship, divided into two significantly different branches: I shall name them, for convenience, the moralistic and the aesthetic. As the linguistic phase waned, both tended to disappear into the prior problem of interpretation or hermeneutics – to the extent that one could seldom find anyone in a literature department who was interested in aesthetic evaluation (or the traditional kind of moralism, for that matter) or even called himself or herself a critic. Nearly everyone became a theorist. My anthologies *Critical Theory Since Plato* and *Critical Theory Since 1965* construed critical theory as literary theory: that is, the study of what literature has seemed to be, what it seems to be, how it is made, and what it does. The other definition of "critical theory" really belongs to social thought. It was formulated by the Frankfurt School, generally grounded in

---

[3] Geertz 166.

[4] Geertz 175–76.

Marxism. One of the ironies of recent intellectual history is that, as Marxism became almost universally discredited in practice, it reasserted itself in various quasi-forms at the end of the linguistic phase, partly as a result of the generation of the students of the 1960s gaining, with age, positions of power in the academy. The resurgence of materialism, now "cultural" materialism, and the suspicion of structuralism and some aspects of deconstruction as new forms of idealism was but one sign of another period of transition.

3. *Political moralism*

One of the reasons that the work of Michel Foucault became so fashionable, in addition to the power and scope of his writings, was that he went beneath or behind language, transforming the linguistic model of a system of differences into one of relations of power (all the time, for this reason, declaring he was *not* a structuralist). His notion of power made it somewhat ectoplasmic, but he did emphasise something the social theorists thought they understood, or at least wanted to understand better. Foucault was himself a figure within a transition from a period that concentrated on language as a model system to one that concentrated on power and therefore politics. It was perhaps in the phenomenon of the so-called "New Historicism" that, after Foucault, the matter of power became most prominent. Now all was no longer language; it was politics, and the paradigm was the pattern of power circulation. One aspect of this shift was a return to value-judgements with respect to texts (not "literature"), but judgements of historical and contemporary interest made entirely on political grounds, where the political grounds were themselves based on a series of secular moral imperatives ungrounded on now discredited "Truth." If the phase of epistemology signalled its demise in Pater's melancholy *reductio* to solipsism and the age of linguistics in the concept of "wall-to-wall language," the phase of political moralism has run the risk of reducing all issues to the questions: Who is to hold power, and: In whose interest?

One of the chief dangers to liberal education in this kind of phase is reduction, not to a common denominator (which would be dangerous enough because of the common denominator's tendency to trivialise), but to domination of a single question in all discourse, no matter how urgent that question seems to be. For a number of reasons, I am sceptical about a phase of political moralism having the power to persist in this crude form for very long in intellectual life. A modern poet remarked that people cannot stand too much reality; it is likely that people will not tolerate too much politics or, at least, a situation in which politics is the defining term and shape of everything from Washington, D.C., to every person's bedroom. In the classroom, politics can tend to take the form of the moralistic homily delivered by a stern, not to say single-minded or (less charitably) fanatical zealot. Another reason is that, being reductive, it misses or suppresses many things.

4. *Uneasiness and the canon*

One aspect of recent uneasiness has been quarrels over the so-called canon of great literary works. In the summer of 1988, I published an article on literary canons. I do not like to repeat myself on these occasions, though I am afraid I often do, and certainly not from an essay over twelve years old, but I shall nevertheless do so briefly here. I remarked then that literary canons are mostly the product of the invocation of power criteria but that the wholesale embrace of power criteria in canon-formation is dangerous and always has been because it tends to minimise healthy opposition and impoverish the potentiality of the canon as a means of intellectual liberation. Another point I made was that the literary canon has not been so static as many of its defenders and enemies would like to believe.

In periods of transition we become much more concerned about the notion of a canon. The recent uneasiness has been exacerbated by the acceleration of change. It took about 2,400 years for the phase of ontology to wind down, four hundred for the phase of epistemology, and about two hundred for the phase of language. The present age is likely to be much, much shorter; not so short as the fifteen minutes of fame Andy Warhol predicted for each one of us, but progressively shorter based on the model I have described. In any case, the uneasiness has some similarity to the radical literary and political discourse circa 1800 and an earlier time of debate about what should and should not be included in the Bible. Generally, of course, the pressure has been to bring works by women, minorities, and so-called Third-World writers into the canon.

Those of us in the USA who over the past decade have read such depressing journals as the *Chronicle of Higher Education* received outlandish reports of strife at Stanford and Harvard and read letters by people who climbed the barricades to defend the presence in the curriculum of books they had not opened since college or to attack books they may or may not have recently read. Canons have always changed; all things change faster now. There are more books to decide about and more parts of the world where writers are recording their thoughts and experiences in English. There are new matters of import unknown to past writers.

The real question should not have been whether the canon should change; it should have been how it changes, whether there will be a canon at all in the sense in which it was discussed, and the implications for literary education. If a canon does survive, we will have to assume that it is going to expand, and that somehow scholarship and curriculum must adjust to this fact. It will, however, be necessary to view sceptically wholesale attacks on canonisation that view the canon as reprehensibly representative of a bankrupt Western intellectual tradition that is declared to be phallogocentric, patriarchal, sexist, racist, perhaps vivisectionist, either for or against abortion, homophobic, or heterophobic, and generally against what is right – or left. After all, it is the Western tradition, including its capacity to change, its discovery of certain ideals of freedom, and its stumbling on the virtues of debate and dialectic that keeps reminding us that there is always a social agenda. Against some other traditions one might examine, this is a unique and fairly admirable accomplishment for 2,600 years of work.

II The new technology

The phase of political moralism comes, not surprisingly, in the midst of a cultural revolution profoundly transforming the way most people work and live. The revolution is technological or technologically driven more than it is political, though, of course, it creates political action and perhaps will create a new politics. As we all know, scholars have not been exempt from these effects. The production of books and articles is involved with computers from the first word composed to publication and distribution. Communication among scholars worldwide is common and nearly instantaneous. The availability of materials in electronic facsimile has grown rapidly. One can view all of Blake's designs with a click. Bibliographies and catalogues are increasingly available. Along with all of this comes a great amount of ephemera and trivia in the form of websites, unwanted e-mail, etc.

This revolution is inevitably affecting the kind of work being done in English studies. With the new technology there is a renewed interest in textual scholarship after decades during which that activity took third place to theoretical discourse and historical study. What used to take nearly a lifetime – a concordance, for example – can now be quickly accomplished. Textual scholarship is also flourishing because of the vast progressive increase in the number of books published in a variety of forms, providing a virtually endless supply of materials to edit. This phenomenon has occurred, along with feminism and the study of popular culture, at about the time that scholars were beginning to despair about what there was left to turn their attention to.

The revolution in book production has been what some call merely a first step toward the obsolescence of the book as we have known it and the advent of the electronic book, which, it is thought by many, will change reading habits. Actually these habits have already changed. Teachers of English have always struggled to develop in students the capacity to read, even when reading was one of the few domestic recreations. Now they face a body of students brought up on a barrage of visual and aural stimuli unknown to previous generations. These students are certainly as intelligent as those previous generations and probably better informed, but many lack experience in written expression and in reading relatively complex texts, mainly because they have less experience with them and their orientation is not toward them. Recently I taught a course in the history of literary theory and criticism to advanced undergraduates, a good number of whom were majoring in the new discipline of cinema studies. It became clear to me, after a puzzling couple of weeks, that these students thought differently from those I had been teaching and that they were fairly sophisticated visually and could "read" a film, but they were nearly helpless dealing with the written words of Plato, Aristotle, et al., or expressing their insights successfully. More and more students are likely to be in this state, confirming the view that "text" is no longer necessarily written or even verbal.

What will be the long-term effect on literary study? It is possible that it will become a small part of the curriculum, occupying a role like that of present-day classics departments. If this occurs, English professors will have been complicit in its academic decline. It is they who allowed and for the most part encouraged the division between the teaching of literature and that of expository writing, succumbing to the short-term utilitarianism of the university at large. No one has ever shown that the separation of the teaching of writing from the teaching of literary literacy produces the desired results, whatever they are thought to be. The division was an easy way to turn the chores of reading many papers over to exploited underlings and graduate students, and administrations found the savings attractive. Once the separation occurred, and on the heels of a shortage of jobs teaching literature (created in part by a glut of graduate students), there was spawned a group of specialists in so-called "rhetoric" with sketchy training in literature.

But let us assume that literary study will survive in some form. It is certain that there will be a greater emphasis on visuality and orality. The book, whether Gutenbergian or electronic, will be regarded as a composite of visual forms and words. This is, of course, not entirely new. In the nineteenth century many literary books were artistically illustrated, and, of course, there were the medieval manuscripts, now themselves works of art. Many of us identify the original illustrations to *Alice in Wonderland* and *Through the Looking Glass* as integral to the texts and are offended by later attempts to replace the engravings with new pictures. The Oz books of Frank L. Baum or those of Wanda Ga'g seem proper only if the original drawings are present. These are, of course, children's books, but the same might be said to apply to the novels of Dickens, Thackeray, and others. The study of design and verbal text will become fashionable, appealing to those who have grown up in the age of the electronic book. I think this trend will be seen to have begun in the late-twentieth century with scholarly work on Blake – by Frye, Mitchell, Wittreich, Viscomi, and others – the interest in Blake not being limited to the flower children of the 1960s, but now at least to those interested in composite art. This was not a bad beginning, because the relation of Blake's designs to his text is more than that of illustration, at least in its usual sense. We can expect the creation by poets and artists, often working together, of a great variety of such relationships. Generally, scholarly work in this area has been accomplished by literary scholars and not by art historians. This is not likely to change very rapidly, if at all; but literary scholars will have to become more sophisticated about design.

In the midst of all this, the storage of books as we know them will become even more of a problem than it already is, with no end in sight. The result will have to be electronic storage with, one might hope, everything at one's fingertips. But there will be so much of it that one might imagine a period of nostalgia for a manageable canon of great works and some criteria for their inclusion.

Almost certainly, the plethora of material will continue to blur the distinction between works of so-called popular culture and those of so-called high culture. There will be a twilight struggle between those who find only "culture studies" worthwhile and others who want to separate out "great art." The sheer amount of material to deal with will be more manageable under a high degree of abstraction, amenable to categorisation by political or other content, and this will continue to favour the cultural approach at the expense of aesthetic analysis. Nevertheless, aesthetic analysis will persist and even flourish under the impetus of composite books.

For literary study, the fundamental danger of the electronic advances (of which we have seen just the beginning) will be, as it has for so long been, the utilitarian drive of institutions; and now the vast amount of material will require ever more efficient ways to process it. What easier way than a judgement of immediate usefulness, whether political, psychological, or escapist? This has always been the bane of English professors, and they have had to create notions of long-term value not often convincing to their colleagues in engineering, medicine and business. The university as a whole finds it often easier to surrender to the utilitarian while yet uttering traditional phrases about the value of liberal education; but more of this a little later.

III Globalisation

We all know that as a result of technological developments the world has shrunk astonishingly and political change now occurs very rapidly. The rise of a new generation of Luddites, demonstrating in places as far apart as Geneva and Seattle, is but one symptom of this phenomenon with its attendant anxieties. On the profession of English these developments already have had an important influence, and the results will continue to be experienced. English literature in most parts of the world is no longer just the literature of England. It is an international literature. A student studying the English language in Taiwan is going to study and speak American English and read primarily, at least among the moderns, American writers or those whose English exists as the result of a dead British colonialism. But even beyond this, and perhaps to some extent because of it and the tremendous growth of what is available to read, the notion of a national literature, which will no doubt persist, will become less dominant and the notion of a world literature more forthcoming. Even for students of traditional English literature, beginning with *Beowulf*, it has always made sense to read translations of the fundamental literary influences – Hesiod, Homer, and the Bible – even though curricular requirements have tended to ignore these texts. The curriculum in the history of literary criticism and theory has, by contrast, not been tied very often to nationalism, it being almost impossible to treat the subject without Plato and Aristotle at its beginnings and a host of Europeans later on. It has also been held by some that critical and theoretical texts can be translated more accurately (whatever that means) than can poems, plays, and novels. This is a dubious proposition, however, and the notion of an international critical tradition is more likely the reason critical texts have been taught in translation without much complaint.

On the other hand, the Bible, being for many a holy book, has presented a terrible problem for teachers, who have had to avoid as much as possible discussion of the single most important literary influence in the West. It is doubtful that this situation will change where it would most count. Nevertheless, globalisation will offer the opportunity for some change with respect to the literary study of holy books. It will also make translated texts seem more legitimate while at the same time increasing attention to the whole problem and act of translation. With this should come greater recognition that translation is an activity acceptable for professional advancement, a legitimate form of literary scholarship. This will be especially true in the USA, the size and isolation of which from other languages (except Spanish) make the U.S. citizen not very good at foreign languages.

Globalisation will be a major factor contributing to the current breaking down of boundaries sustained by academic departments. I suspect that so-called "humanities centres" were originally formed as paranoid parallels to scientific research organisations on the principle that what is good for the goose is likely to be okay for the ugly duckling. Their main function seems to have become the fostering of activities that do not easily fit inside departmental boundaries. The rise of theory has played a major role here, but even as theory wanes as a fashion, globalisation will hasten the movement of the liveliest parts of literary study out of departments as we now know them. At the least, however, English departments will survive, there having to be some way of organising the bureaucratic university, universities being slow to change in any case. But English departments may continue to exist mainly as centres for language teaching, composition, and creative writing – unless these functions themselves are separately departmentalised.

Finally, it will be widely recognised in critical and theoretical practice that there are more literary traditions than just that founded in ancient Greece. The first stirrings of this have already occurred, with recent translations of classical Chinese critical texts. At the same time there has been an enormous interest among Chinese, Taiwanese, Japanese and Indian students in Western literary theories. It may well be that soon Eastern critical and theoretical texts will be assimilated into the canon of the history of criticism or theory as Westerners see it. The results of this will be puzzling and interesting enough to occupy Western comparatists and theorists for some time. The need for more translation of Eastern texts will quickly become more obvious, and there will be a shortage of people competent to do the job well or even at all.

IV The university and the scholar

Anyone with any sense and experience of universities in the USA knows that they are simply too large to be managed efficiently, let alone to control the educational process in any reasonable way. Since the Second World War and especially since the advent of the Cold War, they have been fuelled and enlarged by federal funding in the sciences; this has created an insatiable appetite for growth along with more and more scientific research, which in turn has generated more dollars for growth. Recently, with the collapse of the Cold War and consequent relaxation of federal interest in funding science in the name of national defence, business seems to have moved in to fill the gap, but with a different agenda. Business communities, usually high-tech, have appeared on the borders of campuses and in some cases even on university land in joint ventures with scientific faculties. This has been greeted with enthusiasm by state legislatures, who have always believed with Calvin Coolidge that the business of America is business, and have learned that if business supports university research, state taxes will not have to do so. Indeed, at my university the state provides only about 16 percent of the annual expenses and tuition only about 12 percent. Since institutions of higher education are often viewed with suspicion by the public – in part because of the behaviour of the arts faculty – all of this is convenient and perhaps necessary. But university administrators will have to be alert to possible adverse results. And faculty should not be loath to encourage vigilance.

Both the federal government and business have had a utilitarian influence on large campuses that has tended to marginalise the influence of the humanities, though a certain amount of "overhead" charged to the federal government found its way even into humanities departments and both the government and business have made connections between the university and society at large that were unknown to past generations. The trend with business is likely to continue and increase in intensity.

Here the humanistic scholar is in an odd situation. Most of the rest of this section is devoted to the situation of the humanistic scholar in the institution and in society at large, and it contains a good bit of comment on what the scholar will have to become if the humanities, clearly marginalised as a result of these developments, are to be an influential part of the university or even survive under these conditions.

Let me begin with the incursion of the term "research" into the life of humanistic scholars. It is in part a by-product of the influence of the federal government already mentioned, which, along with the enormous increase in the academic population, has dramatically changed the nature, conventions and mores of academia as a result of the domination of the sciences since the Second World War. "Scholar" is a term that has become almost solely the denotation of a good undergraduate. The developments from this have not by any means been all bad.

The huge overhead helped sustain some kind of balance; the National Endowment for the Humanities, a mixed blessing, I think, would never have been created if there had not already been a National Science Foundation (and if it had not been realised that the NEH would never be a big item of expense). The humanities follow upon and respond to the sciences in contemporary life, and this may be their proper role. It is certain to be their future role. How best to play it becomes the issue.

But to adopt, where possible, the language of scientific professionals has been a bad strategy. The term "research" tends to separate the activity it denotes from teaching. The term "scholar," with its implication of "student," tends not to. Well, in any case, the academic scholar, whether we call that person researcher or not, has relations with or belongs not just to society but to numerous societies. It is in these societies that the humanistic scholar is going to have to learn to move more successfully and be more visible. This presents an important difficulty, because the scholar is in certain ways properly apart by virtue of scholarly stance.

Something needs to be said here about a few of these societies, and, at the expense of sounding like the young Stephen Dedalus, I shall name some of them: the academic department, other academic units, the college and/or university, the local community, the state, the nation, and the world and humankind. In addition to these, and belonging to and overlapping them, are: the academic world; the community of scholars worldwide; and the various intellectual disciplines. There are also more abstract or amorphous notions of societies in the humanistic scholar's mind, such as the world of letters. They all call for their own allegiances. Finally, there is the society composed of students, to which the scholar–teacher both does and does not belong. Unfortunately, or perhaps fortunately if one believes that a degree of conflict prevents stultification, these different societies produce opposing views of and demands on the scholar. Though some scholars may wish to ignore the claims of one or another of these groups, they would do well to be aware of what is at stake if they do, and, for humanistic scholars, much will be increasingly at stake.

To an English professor in a large university, the society that most affects daily professional life has been the department. In a smaller college it may have been the college faculty organisation as a whole or some more inclusive division such as the humanities. English departments have not been identical with a discipline; they have been composed of many people representing many disciplines with different histories, conventions and fundamental assumptions. Sometimes their interests overlap; most of the time they do not.

Departments will persist, but more scholarly work will be done in organisations that cross the old boundaries. The tendency of some of these, of course, will be to become departments, keep changing focus, or die (some quite properly by intention, it would be hoped). What applies to departmental membership applies to these, which quickly form their own bureaucratic character under the impetus of the inertia of the university itself. Wise administrators will make possible the birth of these units and the easeful death of those that have no longer any sensible purpose.

In large universities, the college, the faculty governing body (if it may be called that) and its committees often seem remote or occasionally comical. As universities have grown, their structures have become more complex, with the result that long ago an administrative class grew up and continues to grow. Many faculty, rightly or wrongly, see it as foreign to them or even antithetical to their interests. There is no question that in these larger institutions it is difficult for the individual faculty member's voice or even the collective voice (if one can say there is one) of a department to be heard. If a department does not bring in the research dollars, it is even more difficult. Administrators, for their part, often, rightly or wrongly, perceive the faculty as isolated, unrealistic and intensely self-absorbed. Often they have good reason, for faculty are seldom intimately acquainted with administrative matters except when something suddenly impinges on their interests, at which point they enter the situation usually ignorant of its nuances, its history, and the larger internal political issues that contribute to its complexity. It has been said that administrators like solutions and faculty like problems. Few faculty in larger institutions involve themselves in its politics beyond their departments; most think participation a waste of time and interference with their real work, which is usually regarded as research. Yet many are willing to criticise, sometimes savagely, administrative actions. The situation of alleged powerlessness is exacerbated by such attitudes; power comes only with responsibility. In spite of their primary allegiance to their scholarship, faculty are likely to need to be more involved in the workings of the institution, slow and creaky as these workings may be; the institution cannot be a collegial intellectual enterprise if they do not. But few universities let it be known to young faculty that they are expected to participate actively in its politics, and not many encourage faculty to do so. Indeed, many administrators actively discourage participation by withholding responsibility from faculty or acting against faculty will without at least seeking consensus. Under such conditions it is no surprise that individuals become bored by what seems the sham of faculty governance and withdraw into sullen passive resistance. There is a thing called "university service" that is usually listed among criteria for promotion, but it rates third far below research and teaching; and almost nothing is said about it as a responsibility during recruitment of a prospective faculty member, except at certain smaller institutions, where the matter is regarded as quite important. It is unlikely that the situation just described will change very much without the development of a new form of collective responsibility.

The institution is rarely identified in the public mind with its faculty. Usually it is identified with the athletic teams, the campus, or the institution as a state budget item; or it is regarded as a monolithic force affecting traffic, parking, rentals and local zoning. When Dwight Eisenhower, as president of Columbia University, addressed the faculty as employees, an offended professor replied that the faculty *was* the university. But it is also true that in public institutions, at least, the faculty are employees of the state and therefore of the people. This is a fact that many faculty have forgotten or never understood. It will become more important not to forget in a society where the university is increasingly involved in a myriad of social relations. For English professors, who have been moving toward the margins of the institution, it will become a matter of survival to reassess their role vis-à-vis the public and, particularly, primary and secondary education.

The public sees English professors almost entirely as teachers of young adults, though this view lags behind the fact that people of all ages now attend college and more and more older people will. The public has little interest in literary scholarship, and often regards it as trivial. Since avoidance of teaching is a skill sharpened to a considerable art by a few scholars (or, rather, researchers), it will be well to remember that the public does not expect avoidance to be one of the arts professed. At the same time, faculty cannot be answerable to the public in a direct or passive way, for they ought to be exercising intellectual leadership in society. Answerability to the public, therefore, quite properly has its antithetical side, as does behaviour within the institution. With respect to both societies, the intellectual gadfly has always been a necessity and will continue to be, though under greater pressure from forces already mentioned. Whether in the future English professors will be allowed to be gadflies depends to a great extent on their finding ways to support literature and the arts in styles that the public can understand and respect. The most radical political critique has usually been tolerated with occasional grumbling by the academy and in the academy by the public if it is not carried on in adolescent ways, does not in itself suppress opposition, and is not taken into the classroom in a propagandistic way. Some may say that to take this view is in itself suppressive, for it domesticates and engulfs issues, trivialising any possible good effects. Although there is some truth to this, the reverse is generally true and certain styles harden resistance and generate needless opposition and suppression in return, to say nothing of occasional violence.

English professors have always taken a major role in criticising the academy and society. It has been in the humanities, appropriately, that substantial debate has occurred, but voices are heard only if they have platforms from which to speak, and English professors will have to struggle to build a platform under conditions of diminished power. They will need to establish grounds for new power by advocating and pursuing ways to articulate literary study from early childhood through college. The university is coming to understand this need, and the public will quickly understand it and respect the effort.

On the whole, university humanities faculties have not taken positive advantage of their positions in the larger academic society that includes primary and secondary education. Liaison, such as it has been and when it has existed at all, seems to have been limited to administrative levels, universities being inclined to create new offices for such matters instead of involving faculty directly; or it has been limited to a few faculty, usually connected with schools of education, which have often been part of the problem, not a solution. Humanities faculty could make a huge difference. They possess, in the public eye, despite all I have already said, the prestige of their disciplines, degrees and expertise; but this power is rarely harnessed in support of education as a whole. As a social force, humanities faculties will, out of necessity, I believe, have to pay more attention to their primary- and secondary-school colleagues. At present, few structures make possible such liaison, especially on the intellectual level, where it is most needed, and there are virtually no incentives for faculty to do anything to improve the situation. The larger academic society is fractured.

Recently I received a phone call from a local high-school English teacher asking me to come to her school to speak to the seniors there on the "humanities" in a programme called "humanities week." She had called the university's speaker's bureau and got no help. She admitted in our conversation that she and her colleagues did not really know what the humanities were. I was curious about how, since no one seemed to know what the humanities were, such a programme had occurred. It turns out that one of her administrators discovered in the state coffers funding for something called a humanities week in the schools, so he or she applied and got it. After all, it was money. The teacher was working in a high school that is among the top ten sending graduates to my institution and is rated one of the best in the state. Her seniors had never seen a college professor. I went, spoke, found everyone attentive, and may have done some good, or at least no harm. But no one in my institution would care that I went. I suspect that if the behaviour of university scholars does not voluntarily and systematically change with respect to this activity, society will force some ineffective bureaucratic form of liaison on universities. English professors should regard this matter as of prime importance and themselves find ways to foster a more intellectual, to say nothing of literate, attitude in primary and secondary teaching. It would be in their own interests to do so, and it might save literary study in the end.

Most professors of English have not been particularly aware of the fundamental relation between the university and the nation because that relation has apparently not impinged on their work to any great extent. They have perhaps read one of the many reports issued by acronymic organisations, the full names of which are hardly known at all. These reports, when they have treated the humanities, intone high-sounding phrases such as "knowing what it is to be human" and leave things pretty much as they were. Occasionally, noises meant to be inspiring and, not too long ago, noises more or less punitive issued from the Department of Education and from a director of the National Endowment for the Humanities who is now blessedly gone. The main virtue of these noises was to activate adrenalin, but generally things went on as they had. Task forces, blue ribbon panels, and commissions have come and gone. Organisations of various sorts have been established, and seminars and fellowships have been given. People in high places have written essays about preserving our heritage.

The situation has been quite different for scientists, and it is important for humanists to know this clearly, since it helps to explain the mores of their distant colleagues, into whose departments the bulk of funding flows. The influence of these mores appears in criteria for professional advancement university-wide. As I have already indicated, most large academic institutions have survived, as they are on the margin provided by overhead from government-supported scientific research, this and the immense cost of supporting the scientific enterprise having been the single greatest influence on the life of academic institutions. Young scientists have had little hope of advancement without the ability to attract a steady flow of government dollars. Indeed, this criterion for promotion has sometimes had priority over what a humanistic scholar is likely to think of as accomplishment. For the scientist, it has *been* an accomplishment. To the phrase "publish or perish" has been added "get grants or perish."

But in the present climate of technological boom, and with governmental resources waning, it is techno-business that is becoming the patron of university scientists, who may often rise to partnership. The influence of this change will, no doubt, have its dangers (as did governmental support). As I have already suggested, the spectre of utilitarian need is the greatest of these – at least from the perspective of the humanities. The saving grace, always belated, will be business's realisation (which has occurred cyclically in the past, with the university passively entering the spiral) that their hirees, despite their university degrees, are virtually illiterate, very narrow in imagination, and inept at communicating relatively simple information. Unfortunately the response to the mindless utilitarianism that turns this historical wheel is likely itself to be utilitarian and will work only for a short time unless professors of literature can convince people (often administrators) that the literary is the only practical way to the kind of literacy desired. Antithetical to the utilitarian drift, English professors will have to mount a stronger attack on the cyclicity I have mentioned. This means that they will have to resist aggressively trends toward making higher education into a bureaucracy producing, in the easiest and most economical way, phalanxes of whatever sorts of skilled workers some economic motive calls for. Such trends would not be quite so bad as they always have been if they did not bring about backlash and overproduction. There is nothing wrong with universities producing specialists, so long as they are effective ones who can think and communicate, preferably in more than one language, and have learned enough to function as thoughtful citizens of the world. Specialisation is a contemporary necessity. The degree of literacy needed cannot be treated as a skill as one usually thinks of skills. At least, it cannot be taught as if one were demonstrating how to take apart an automobile engine.

All scholars, of course, belong to the society of scholars itself, replete with its disciplinary subdivisions and official organisations. The English scholar's responsibilities are not so much to these societies as to scholarship itself. In the future these responsibilities will, of course, be exerted in new circumstances, but they will remain what they always should be: to address one's subject seriously, to respect the rules of evidence and rational thought, to seek awareness of and criticise one's own premisses. There will be temptations, some of which are familiar. One that has often been deplored is the tendency to popularise one's scholarship at the expense of its integrity. This is a danger, but the future will require the literary scholar to be more sensitive to the presence of the public and the need to defend the scholarly enterprise in ways that people will understand. Academic busy work in the form of uninteresting scholarship ought to be less tolerated, if only because the academy has not known how to dispose of such refuse any better than it knows what to do about nuclear waste. Almost every university has had a faculty committee fretting over the infinite expansion of the library stacks. On the other hand, technology may take care of that – in its own way – by making it possible to preserve in a small space absolutely everything written. That may be a prospect more frightening than one of libraries growing like polypuses.

Most scholars of literature believe they have a responsibility to the society of writers and artists, but it has been observed bitterly more than once that literary scholars must not like literature or they would not do to it what they often do. The observer is usually a novelist or poet writing from a different perspective, smarting from a bad review, or expressing writerly anxiety over what some scholar might turn up. It is true that the society of scholars does seem at times intent only on its own professionalism and not service to the arts that it studies. Indeed, in recent times there have been scholarly claims that literary theory stands at the same level as so-called creative work, though I know of no one other than some theorists who believe it. Throughout history there have been eloquent defences of and attacks on poetry, drama and prose fiction. The defenders well known to us have usually been poets. Scholars have edited and taught from these defences and have made occasional theoretical defences of the whole literary realm or of individual poets or works or schools. If literature is something to be studied, then it must have potential social value worth enunciating; this seems to have to be shown anew to every generation, which will be impatient with the defences of the past, now threatening to become cliché-ridden. New defenders will, no doubt, arise; but in an atmosphere in which the tendency of scholarship has been to become simply descriptive and, where not that, overtly politicised, the need for defence may not be recognised. Furthermore, the defenders will have to be more open than in the past to forms of verbal and composite expression that are strange and to new technologies that are bound to clamour for admission to "literature" and will establish their own turf if barred. Also, given the vast amount of material available to study, scholars will be even more seriously charged with determining what is worthwhile and what is not and why, and with championing writers of value who may have been overlooked.

The last society I shall mention, but by no means the least, is the society of students. Professors both belong and do not belong to this society. It is a commonplace to say that the scholar is always a student, but it should be the reverse as well. The student ought to be a scholar. To bring students into the society of scholarship for a time, where they can come to understand its values, responsibilities and (sometimes antithetical) social function, is of fundamental importance. To seek such an end in one's students involves a myriad of practical activities in addition to giving vent to the dramatic instinct in the classroom. One must be available as an intellectual source; one must try to make students feel engaged in enquiry. One must search for connections with other disciplines. More and more, students themselves are becoming involved in forms of scholarship, working in groups, critiquing each other's work by e-mail, and so on. Their impatience with lectures is not just simple childish rebellion or the result of a diminished attention-span. It involves the way they see the world and imagine the future. Probably as much as any change occurring, the formal relation of teacher to student is affecting the life of scholarship. The engagement of students in cooperative scholarly and creative ventures in the humanities is really just beginning, mainly as a result of technology that enables it in new and easier ways. The main danger will be the assignment of slavish activity helpful only to a professor's research. The connection to personal research works better in the sciences, but it is not likely to work nearly so well in the humanities.

I come now to take account of the usual oppositions that plague scholars and of which they frequently speak: scholarship (research) vs. teaching; careerism (professionalism) vs. purism (amateurism), specialisation vs. generalism. There are also sometimes opposed loyalties: to the profession/to the university; to one's subject/to one's students, the latter being responsible for the hollow claim "I don't teach [supply the subject], I teach students."

In his *Marriage of Heaven and Hell*, William Blake took note of oppositions he especially disliked and which in practice he regarded as dulling themselves and suppressing or "negating" each other, thus contributing to social stultification. He proposed active opposition to these oppositions. W.B. Yeats named a similar stance "antithetical." The oppositions I have just mentioned are pernicious when not opposed. There may be some difficulty for a young scientist in doing both research and teaching and making them complement and blend with each other. When for a humanist the two become separate, something is wrong either with the subject of scholarship or with the way the scholar sees the problem. It is indubitable that scholarship is a requisite of good teaching. Of course, scholarship in this sense does not have to result in publication, especially immediate publication, and much that results in publication is not scholarship. There is, however, considerable value in making scholarship an expressive art of some sort rather than simply a terminal act of reception. Publication in whatever form that may take in the future is one way of doing this. It will continue to be a way as part of the ongoing conversation of scholarship.

Humanistic scholars are by necessity slow learners. They have a lot to learn, seemingly an infinitude of texts, facts, thoughts and arguments. The problem for them is not the often alleged incompatibility of teaching and scholarship but an utter compatability corrupted into opposition by academic society's decision to make judgements about tenure on a career model driven by the rhythm of scientific achievement. No one I know, however, has suggested, except in jest, that the trial period for humanists be lengthened and the retirement age for scientists be made earlier. If humanistic scholars are going to survive with power and dignity, they themselves will have to rethink the grounds for advancement and insist on their imposition.

The careerist/purist opposition provides an uneasy refuge for scoundrels on either side or, rather, two categories in which to place those one wants to view with contempt. Faculty who actively participate in the larger society of scholars are often accused of blatant self-interest, while those who do not, or at least do so with restraint, are often accused of shirking scholarly responsibility or being out of touch. It is not necessary to copy either of these parodies. Scholars will best occupy a third, antithetical position in which they recognise the sometimes competing interests of activity in the larger world as well as the need constantly to evaluate the worth of such activities against the equally pressing need for rational distance. One can predict, in any case, that the day will continue to have only twenty-four hours.

As the production of scholarship becomes ever more rapid and overwhelming in size, the tendency in all fields is toward specialisation. As a result, it seems that the societies the scholar reaches decline in number; isolation and suspicion of uselessness threaten. I believe that society will more and more insist on demonstration that subjects professed are important and connect with societal concerns. It will ask what the point is of teaching them to undergraduates if they do not. For literary scholars this involves the careful reading of texts and then their relation with other texts, in order to address the role of literary texts in culture. Over the past century we have witnessed a cyclical movement that has privileged now the single text as an object, now the text as cultural phenomenon. But there has not been a lot of success in attempting to encompass both at any one time. This opposition is a negation like those mentioned above, and it seems to fall into an historical cycle in which one, then the other, dominates. If one studies the history of criticism in the past century, one discovers that one movement begins by opposing a suppression, gains power, dominates, and becomes repressive and decadent, as did the old literary history and then the New Criticism. From time to time, whole academic units have suffered internal disorders as a result. The danger is always present for every generation of scholars, each of which is inevitably trained in the dominant fashion of its time and risks carrying that fashion into obsolescence without recognising that the fashion was not itself Truth. The most important social role of the scholar will, therefore, continue to be to learn anew; to continue to regard oneself as a student.

The relation of the scholar to society is inevitably going to have what, begging your reverence, I shall call a public-relations aspect. This is not exactly new, but it will become more evident as greater demands are made. Traditionally, scholars have not been very good at or prone to public relations, nor have they needed to be. On the whole, public relations has been left to the development and university affairs officers, lobbyists, and the president, who sometimes wonders whether he is not the victim of a concerted effort by faculty to frustrate reasonable effort. The main obvious societal responsibility of faculty, as I have already suggested, ought to be and very well may become to foster effective cooperation with the society of teachers in secondary schools. Whether or not this will be the case, there is certainly a great deal that needs to be explained about what and why professors are doing what they do. This chore has generally been left to others, who do not do it, cannot do it, do it badly, or occasionally do it well but cannot concentrate their energies on it.

In the last analysis, the social roles of faculty need to be defined ethically, but not by some moral code. Rather, the scholar's ethical stance must be that of looking more deeply, more widely, and with a certain distance, so that culture and power come under constant scrutiny. This involves an activity that has had a recent beginning and will develop more fully: looking closely at the culture of scholarship and the university itself and its history, how it came to be what it is, and how it might become better. In this way, the best scholarship will be antithetical to itself, insofar as scholarship belongs to its own culture and has a way of endorsing its own limitations and failures.

When Yeats asked his famous question about the rough beast of the future (already emergent, incidentally, as the millennium turns), he was expressing cultural anxiety, but with a certain ecstatic anticipation. My rough beast, soon, as I think, to be born, has already brought about anxiety in its anticipation, as today most things do in greater degree. One thing I believe we know: this beast will not be a gentle one. English scholars had best be ready for a struggle.

Innovation and Continuity in English Studies

TODD K. BENDER

THE MOST IMPORTANT INNOVATION since the Second World War in English studies has been the introduction of computer technology and related systems, which greatly enhance both the opportunities and the challenges for coming generations of scholars. The response of English departments, libraries, universities and professional organisations like the Modern Language Association to the new technology so far has been sluggish, unimaginative and mainly ineffective. If the next generation of scholars does not respond more vigorously and intelligently in the coming millennium to the advent of computers and related systems, English departments, doctoral education in English, and our professional organisations as we now know them will be overwhelmed and discarded.

The impact of the electronic revolution on literature is such a vast topic that a short paper can only touch in a general way on a few of the most pressing issues, but a list of critical topics might include: (1) How can the next generation best preserve and transmit our literary heritage in an electronic age? What is the proper role of the literary scholar in the transition from storage of information on paper to electronic records? (2) How does the existence of an electronic file change our idea of a text? (3) How are ownership of and rights to intellectual property changed by the existence of computers? (4) How are financial control and the economy of printing and publishing shifting? (5) What is the impact of the new distribution of information on our traditional evaluation of scholarly publication? When once "publish or perish" seemed a reasonable way to verify professional competence, desktop publication and the World Wide Web now make unvetted publication available to all comers. (6) What future role do doctoral programmes and professional organisations have in validating and verifying scholarly work? (7) How does the computer enhance the reading environment and change our notions about the process by which the reader interacts with the author via an intermediate textual object? (8) As distance learning and study at remote sites becomes more common, what role does English have in the global distribution of knowledge? Is the audience for scholarly discourse about literature changing from university-aged students to adult, life-long learners as a result of unrestricted access via the Internet to dialogue and debate once confined within the walls of a classroom? (9) Is the English language itself subject to degradation and fragmentation through its electronic distribution, detached from its geocultural bases in the primarily anglophone world? Should teachers of English resist such evolution of the language? (10) What social changes follow from the distribution of English in a globally accessible, immediate, electronic vehicle? Finally, what deliberate action is it wise for an organisation like IAUPE to take today to respond to the new opportunities opening before us?

There is an advertisement currently running on television in the American Mid-West which urges buyers to choose a newfangled plastic milk container at the grocery store. A harried, middle-aged science teacher asks his middle-school students to bring from home an ordinary milk-jug for use in a class experiment. None of his students, perhaps all twelve or thirteen years of age, understands what he means by "milk-jug." He is so old-fashioned, behind the times, and "out of it" that a little girl finally asks him, "Mr Jones, were you really around before the Internet?" The message of the advertisement is that only the coming generation can cope with technical advance. Only young children keep up with new technical marvels. Only the young can programme the home video recorder, surf the Web masterfully, or (so far) snatch and burn a copyrighted rock song onto a blank compact disk for free, effortlessly, in the twinkling of an eye. In my university classes in English literature, I often feel like the unfortunate, old-fashioned Mr Jones, talking about milk-jugs to students who live in a jugless world.

I was myself a middle-school student, about twelve years old, when I first saw a television programme. I was a doctoral student at Stanford University in the early 1960s when I saw the first prototype of a Xerox copying machine – it was a sort of plastic pillow placed manually on each page and it produced damp, hot, very smudgy copies of a printed page. The same year I first "signed on" to use a computer. I happened to be enrolled in a seminar in Homeric Greek in which the professor was interested in phonetic patterns in Greek dactylic hexameter. Each student in the seminar was required very laboriously to translate by hand a few lines of the Greek text into a phonetic code. Then the phonetic code was again translated, using paper and pencil, into a string of numbers which was punched into Hollerith cards. A deck of these precious cards were then read into the Stanford University central computer, perhaps fifty to one hundred lines of the Greek text, and searched for recurring patterns of sound. One such computer run would tie up the entire computing capacity of Stanford University for over an hour and therefore could only be run overnight during the big machine's idle time. I am not aware of any substantial research discoveries produced by this exercise, but it represents my first exposure to computer applications in the humanities some forty years ago. Although I did not clearly understand it at the time, that early use of a computer signalled the beginning of very widespread changes in the study of literature.

Members of IAUPE must feel an obligation to preserve and pass on to future readers the archive of English literature. This basic archival function of our discipline in a computer age is more complicated than in the age of the scribe who copied Cotton Nero A 10, or the printer who first produced a Shakespeare quarto. We have an enormously larger body of material to sort and preserve today. Until our generation, the main vehicle for preserving documents was paper. Given the normal rate of oxidation of paper, we know that very few original artifacts created before the Second World War will be legible a hundred years in the future. Rather than editing and copying selected documents from one sheet of paper to another, the scholars of the future will almost certainly utilise electronic files to transmit and preserve the records of the past. We have the task of overseeing the transition from paper to electronic storage for our literary heritage.

Already today, almost every university library has some form of access to full-text electronic files of canonical works like the King James Bible or the plays of Shakespeare. A decade ago, students enrolling in a university course in Shakespeare were normally compelled to purchase a printed textbook containing the plays to be studied. At my university today, many students rely on reading those same plays for free, on-screen, perhaps downloading the textfile from a central source to the memory of their individual laptop computers to bring to class. This is just the beginning of a basic change in the archival function of our field of study.

Moreover, in the last forty years widespread uses of word-processing systems, e-mail and desktop publishing have generated primary literary documents which have never been written on paper at all. Will these early electronic records be lost to posterity, like Elizabethan prompt sheets used to wrap groceries? Not only do we have the responsibility for making a wise and systematic transition of traditional paper archives to electronic storage, we also have the task of preserving and passing on to future generations the electronic incunabula of the twentieth century. Consider the disaster of the "vinyl meltdown" in the music-recording industry when 78-rpm recordings were replaced by 33-rpm LPs and then by tapes and

CDs. What curse may scholars of the coming millennium direct at us for needlessly losing those priceless wax or vinyl disks of lyric poetry set to popular music and once on record in the years between the two world wars, but subsequently lost forever? How much more severe the curse will be if no record is in our archive of the early years of the electronic composition and distribution of the English language in cinema, radio, television and e-mail.

Organisations like IAUPE do not have the financial resources to create the literary archive of the future, but they do have the authority to guide policies shaping that archive. When material is sorted and classified, the raw data becomes sifted and transformed. For example, if the familiar letter had been regularly considered as a kind of writing on a par with, say, the lyric poem in our university courses over the last few centuries, what would now be the shape of our library holdings in epistolary documents? How might such a choice affect the balance or prominence of female versus male writers in our libraries? How would choices like these dictate what texts are preserved: for example, the proportion of preserved documents authored by the upper classes relative to those from the lower social stratum archived in our research libraries, or the proportion of preserved texts originating in metropolitan locations to those of frontier provenance? Priorities established by literary scholars determine the nature of the archive passed on to the future, especially at this juncture, as we move more and more towards large-scale electronic storage. IAUPE has a unique opportunity today to set the priorities, categories and technical specifications authoritatively recognised as necessary and worthy of the future archive of English language and literature.

If documents are stored in an electronic file, rather than copied on paper, the fundamental idea of what a text is becomes transformed. Initially, some forty years ago, literary scholars began to be aware that the new computer technology offered labour-saving ways to carry out traditional tasks such as making concordances, producing dictionary slips, collating several versions of a single text, setting type for a new printing, and so on. The idea that electronic data processing is merely a convenient new way to accomplish traditional bibliographic tasks is, however, extremely short-sighted. More importantly, the computer makes possible an enriched formulation of the architecture of the text itself.

Consider the case of editing a text that has survived in multiple, variant versions. "Stable transmission" of a text occurs when there is only one existing document originating with the author, followed by a series of increasingly corrupt copies by other hands. It has been a long-standing task for the literary scholar when confronted with the problem of stable textual transmission to seek the "author's final intention" by carefully comparing existing versions, determining the relation among the versions and eliminating errors introduced by copyists, in order to print as a final edited text a version that corresponds as nearly as possible to what the author most probably intended.

In the 1960s, Fredson Bowers, through the Center for Editions of American Authors, advocated with great energy that scholarly resources should be directed towards such a search for final authorial intention in American printed documents.[1] In this process, we might imagine a printed text as a two-dimensional array of information, like a checkerboard in which each square is occupied by a letter of the alphabet, a blank space, or a punctuation-mark. When two or more variant versions of a single text exist, the data might be visualised as a three-dimensional array, a stack of checkerboards, each representing a version of the text. The editor's task is to compare square one in line one in each layer of the stack to see if all versions agree, then square two, and so on. When a particular square deviates from others in the corresponding position in the stack, the editor must step in to judge why the deviation has occurred. Perhaps a careless printer introduced a spelling error when the second edition of the work, considered the second level of the data stack, was printed, thus corrupting the author's intention. The editor eliminates such errors and finally prints his own purified, edited text, which is another two-dimensional checkerboard approaching as nearly as possible what the author's "final intention" initially would have been.

At first, scholars were very hopeful that the laborious and error-prone process of manual collation to compare variant versions of a text could be alleviated by computer technology. Rather than assisting editors to find the author's final intention among variant texts, however, the effect of the new technology has been to show that the notion of a single final intention for a literary text is unsophisticated.

Determining the author's final intention depends on a stable transmission of textual information. Unfortunately, there are almost no cases of such stable transmission in modern printed texts. How can the editor proceed when the author's intention is legitimately equivocal, if the author himself is undecided or is of two minds? What if the author (for example, Wordsworth in *The Prelude*) writes a line when he is thirty years old and blots it out when he is fifty? What if the author ratifies one set of spellings and punctuation marks for an American readership and a different set for a British printing of his work? Does the editor

[1] See Fredson Bowers, *The Works of Stephen Crane* (Charlottesville: University of Virginia Press, 1970).

choose the artistically final or the chronologically final intention? What if spelling and punctuation, or even large matters of plot and ideology, are never firmly determined by the author alone, but produced by an ongoing process of negotiation between the author and his reading public? In such cases, is it not the very hesitation and doubt in the author's mind that is most interesting intellectually?

It is the point where the author hesitates in his negotiation with his audience that is often the very centre of critical interest. Yet if the scholarly editor makes a choice between two conflicting readings, selecting one as the final intention and another as a corruption, when the author himself was of two minds, does the editor not hide from the reader the most important bit of information in the data stack? Rather than suppressing variants and deciding on a single "intended" meaning, the editor's task would often appear to be to highlight the assumption that the author wavered or hesitated in what he intended. Is Bowers's conception of the editor's treatment of an unstable variant not a falsification of the data, a reduction of the complexity of the data stack, whenever the editor chooses one reading over another where the author was in doubt? If the text is seen as a representation of a series of unstable negotiations between author and reader, why does a scholarly editor feel compelled to print a single version, labelled as the authoritative scholarly edition?

Perhaps the editor feels pressure to select a single reading as dominant mainly because he, the editor, is obliged to present his final edited text as a two-dimensional array of information on the printed page as a product that can be sold to readers and students and justifies the editor's position as a qualified university teacher before tenure and promotion committees. The editor's product must be reduced to a printed page, a two-dimensional data structure with no "depth" in which to register variants. For this reason, most printed editions present the text as a two-dimensional code in positional notation, but also very awkwardly mount onto that printed text elaborate information about more or less plausible variants which are recorded in footnotes and/or appended tables.

Textual criticism of the 1960s as formulated in Bowers's "Preface" to the *Works of Stephen Crane* attempts two contradictory objectives: it presents a printed reading text in which all decisions have been made as to authorial intent and hesitation, so that the reader can rely on the "authority" of the words before him as if they were coming directly from the author's mind. At the same time, the editor is trying to build a structural model of the complex variables indicating instability in the process of creation and transmission of the text, indicating shifts and development in the author's thinking. The reading text must be a two-dimensional array, a printed page. In appended notes and other apparatus, the editor attaches to this printed medium information about variations and deviations from it which seem noteworthy.

It is because of the limitations of the two-dimensional printed page as a medium to present the editor's work that the full model of variation among versions cannot be captured in a printed edition. The editor's task often amounts to discarding "insignificant" variations among versions. What Bowers considered an exhaustive edition is a simplification of a set of data more accurately represented as a multi-dimensional array. The printed page is an inadequate medium to carry the full architecture of information involved in a series of versions of a literary text, but electronic data structures can provide more sophisticated representations of a text and its transmission.

The computer enhances the reading environment and changes our notions about the process by which the reader interacts with the author via an intermediate textual object. Experimental authors are already exploiting the formal possibilities of the new electronic medium by emphasising the negotiation or partnership between author and reader in constructing fictional texts which allow readers to dictate which direction to take among the forking paths that they are offered. Critical exploration since the First World War has stressed more and more the instability, ambiguity and linking of incompatible, contradictory value-systems at the core of many canonical works of literature.

The role of the future textual editor will be increasingly to model the instability of the interaction of author and reader, to construct a multi-dimensional array of electronic information so that the reader can extract from his computer provisional information shaped to his needs. Each reader can produce a reading text on the computer screen that conforms to what he wants at that instant: perhaps a text replicating the first printed edition, or the last revised edition, or the two superimposed for comparison, or perhaps those portions of the text that are created by a certain copy editor. The words of a text will not be confined to linear positional notation, but can as easily appear on screen arranged as a concordance showing the repetition of vocabulary in the text, or perhaps as a phonetic concordance showing the repetition of sound patterns in the text or, yet again, as sets of words occurring frequently in collocation.

A printed text is not the *same* as a poem or a novel, it merely *represents* the author's verbal structure in the shifting process of artistic creation and the counter-movement of disintegration through transmission. An electronic model and medium will provide in the future the possibility of much richer representation of literary texts.[2]

How are ownership of and rights to literary works currently in the public domain affected by the existence of computers? In American universities and colleges in the past, students customarily purchased at a local bookstore the texts set for examination by their teachers. So a student enrolled in a one-semester undergraduate course in the Victorian novel would probably buy six or seven Penguin or Norton paperback copies of novels by Dickens, the Brontës, George Eliot, Thackeray, and so on. This adds up to big business for the reprint publishing houses, the bookstores, and the scholars who establish the "authoritative" texts, prefaces and notes to such books. In recent years, however, students have been turning more and more to the Internet as a source for such texts, at little or no cost to themselves, although sometimes the accuracy of such computer files is questionable.

In the future the e-book will become very common. Rather than paying ten or twelve dollars for a paperbound copy of Joseph Conrad's *Heart of Darkness*, students can now easily get several different versions of the text from the Internet and, if they wish, print it out for the nonce inexpensively or store the file electronically in computer memory on a convenient laptop to carry to class. Moreover, these computer files are not just reading copies, but provide an enhanced reading environment. An electronic file provides analytic opportunities for the ambitious undergraduate to create searches for patterns of recurring imagery; to divide the text contrastively into the words of the inner narrator, Marlow, and the words of the nameless outer narrator; to distinguish the vocabulary of the fictive present-time level on the deck of the cruising yawl *Nellie* from the vocabulary involved in the fictive past-time level in Africa; the possibilities expand *ad infinitum*, bounded only by the limits of undergraduate ingenuity.

Since Conrad died over seventy-five years ago in 1924, the substance of his fiction is legally in the public domain. Traditionally, the cost of setting type and printing on paper has provided an alliance between scholarly editors and publishers to control, and profit from, readers' limited access to such public domain texts as form a literary canon. Today it is becoming quite common for university courses to set up websites for students listing course syllabus, discussion questions and assignments, often even interacting with student reading and writing via the Internet. It is likely that it will soon be customary for teachers to provide the

[2] See Todd K. Bender, "Computational Bibliography," *The Computer in Literary and Linguistic Studies*, ed. Alan Jones and R.F. Churchhouse (Cardiff: University of Wales Press, 1976) 329–38.

main texts they assign in computer files to be read by their students on screen. Or, more generally, college libraries will have full text archives of the more widely used texts which students can call up directly. But if a professor at, say, the University of Madison–Wisconsin can set up a website complete with the texts of canonical works, it is almost as easy for a private enthusiast to set up a competing website wherever a home computer glows. In such situations, how is the value and authority of the university, the classroom and the individual professor's position likely to become altered?

The authority of the professor or teacher depends on a broad network of conditions, but surely one important consideration bolstering the social power of the professor of literature is crude economics. Someone, the State or the individual student and family, has to pay dearly for access to the information, attitudes and opinions about canonical literary texts professed in a classroom under the direction of a single professor in charge. What if competing sources of information, perhaps so powerful as to shape public opinion itself, become easily available to all comers for free? How will the alliance of scholar, university and publisher change under these conditions?

Some fifty years ago, in the mid-twentieth century, almost all students entering an American college or university were required to enrol in a course in "Freshman English." Perhaps twenty-five percent of the cost of the first year of each student's bachelor's degree was devoted to this course of study. Although the actual pedagogical objectives and student work required in "Freshman English" varied enormously from campus to campus, the one constant among all such courses was that, in the economy of the university, nearly all students spent a quarter of their first year's scholarly "budget" for a "product" labelled "Freshman English" and the "income" from that course of study justified the existence of English departments, individual faculty salaries, and most of the cost of running the English Major and advanced degree courses.

At my university today, an interesting economic shift appears to be underway. At a high level of the university administration, a decision was taken about ten years ago that students who achieved a certain score in the nation-wide Advanced Placement Examination, administered by the College Board and Educational Testing Service, in English Language and Composition or in English Literature and Composition must be given credit by the university towards their Bachelor's programme. As a result, our state high schools have greatly expanded their classes directed at taking the "Advanced Placement English" examinations and the number of students successfully earning university credit by AP examination has increased accordingly. Partly for this reason, within the university enrolment in old-fashioned courses in "Freshman English" for entering students has dwindled, requiring a reformulation of subject-matter, and the budget of the Department of English has come under corresponding pressure.

What will happen if there is an explosion of the already existing Internet and distance-learning programmes to prepare American students for a national examination, like the AP English examinations, such that nearly all entering university students are exempt from basic English or Mathematics or Social Science courses now making up most of the budget for the entrance year at most American universities? In many ways, such a development would be good. It would provide a less costly, perhaps more effective, way to prepare students to enter directly into a high-level course of specialised study. On the other hand, it would surely erode the university and departmental budget seriously, greatly diminish the financial support available for teaching assistants and university teachers in the early stages of their careers, require a reformulation of the first year's course work in English, and shift control over the subject-matter of the study of literature away from the rather small group of university teachers who are now in charge of the university classrooms. How will organisations like IAUPE respond to these developments in the USA and worldwide?

How are the financial control and economy of printing and publishing shifting? Like many other university presses, the University Press of my institution is in financial trouble at the moment. Many such presses depend on the library sales of very expensive refereed journals and books for a major part of their income. All university presses focus on printing short-run, specialised scholarly studies which are unlikely to command a large readership. The cost of printing such books depends on guaranteed minimum library sales. In the past, such publications were very carefully evaluated by a team of readers before the press ventured the cost of setting type and printing the work. So careful was the scrutiny given to a book manuscript that promotion to a tenured position for a university professor in America frequently hinged on the successful publication of a first book by a university press.

The expense of setting type and publishing the book assured careful editorial assessment of a manuscript. Tens of thousands of dollars were at risk for every scholarly book produced by a university press. Today, computer-assisted desktop publication and direct online "publication" have reduced the cost of book and journal production and made it feasible for many presses to ask authors to bear the cost of supplying camera-ready copy. With reduced financial investment for each press riding on each individual title, publishing houses now find it advantageous to publish more titles so as to have as many chances as possible at a good yearly sale overall.

Low-risk, market-driven editorial choices naturally lead to topics that are "risky" or "unusual." University presses now seek to publish material which would have been unthinkable half a century ago. To some readers, the increase in titles on "scholarly" topics may appear to be a benign development, but to others it may seem to create a morass of undependable and opinionated propaganda. New topics gain easier admittance to publication today than was likely to have been the case in the economy of 1950. More and more, the slow process of journal publication on paper is being replaced by nearly instantaneous online journals. While more rapid dissemination of information is good, there is a trade-off in reliability.

What is the impact of the new distribution of information on our traditional evaluation of scholarly publication? "Publish or perish" was never a reasonable way to verify professional competence, but in the future universe of desktop publication and the World Wide Web, where unvetted "publication" is available to all comers, traditional measures of professional qualification will have to be reformulated altogether. Already we hear in tenure-committee meetings figures about the relative number of "hits" on Professor X's website compared to those on Professor Y's. Or, we hear of lists compiled by computer-tabulating how many references have been cited to works authored by Professor X as opposed to citations of Professor Y's publications in the footnotes and bibliographies of their colleagues' works.

What should be the role now of traditional graduate programmes and professional organisations in validating and verifying scholarly work? Is the typescript of a doctoral dissertation on the shelf worth more than, or less than, an active website on a popular topic?

As distance learning and study at remote sites becomes more common, what role does English have in the global distribution of knowledge? My university is now actively promoting long-distance learning. For example, we have an International Institute with regional subdivisions into centres for African, East Asian, European, Latin American and Iberian studies, and so on. Under their auspices it is possible to arrange for a joint seminar to be held in classrooms in Madison and virtually any place in the world via computer-linked digital cameras, monitor screens and microphones. Students and teachers at an American campus can engage easily, as classmates, in dialogue with their counterparts in Bamberg or Sydney. In some instances, such seminars have been arranged so that students are awarded credit towards appropriate degrees at their home institutions for work done, at least partly, under the direction of teachers at remote sites.

The impact of such long-distance learning on the field of English is at least twofold. First, it opens the study of English literature at the highest level to a much broader audience, particularly in the Third World or in geographical sites with restrictive political or economic circumstances which prevent students from visiting personally the great traditional centres of English study. Perhaps even more significant, however, is the fact that long-distance learning in every field of study, from medicine to economics and from law to the fine arts, must employ a common language for communication. English is the dominant language of cyberspace. But here the familiar science-fiction trope of the "possessor possessed" flourishes: it is not so much that the English language possesses the electronic world, as that the electronic world possesses the English language. As English develops into the global trade-language of long-distance learning and commerce, it loses its cultural roots in, say, Great Britain and degrades easily into jargon, dialect, or simplified code.

Not only is the English language subject to degradation and fragmentation through its electronic distribution, detached from its cultural base in the British Isles, but postcolonial diversity exerts another strong centripetal force on standard pronunciation, grammar, vocabulary, and the religious and cultural assumptions basic to the literature of England from the time of Shakespeare to that of Dickens. What are scholars of the future to make of the controversial claim that "Ebonics" or black English ought to be taught in some American schools, that "white" English is a language of oppression? No one can deny that people whose mother tongue was English have done some terrible deeds on the world stage: slavery, the subjugation of women, religious persecution, unequal distribution of wealth and power.

What social changes will follow from the ever-wider future distribution of English language and literature in an immediate, globally accessible vehicle? It is easy to understand that the colonised, the alienated and the persecuted users of English demand that this instrument of social injustice, as they see it, be dismantled and reshaped.

What action is it wise for an organisation like IAUPE to take in response to the new opportunities opening before us? It would perhaps be wise, from the outset, to divide English language and literature into three large domains for administrative and pedagogical purposes. First, there is the English language rooted culturally in the British Isles: in the religion, geography, ethnic variety, climate, history and traditions of England, Scotland, Wales and Ireland, from the time of the earliest inhabitants of those territories until perhaps the end of the Second World War.

Second, there is colonial/postcolonial English as it has developed in North America, India, Africa, Australia, and other places, where a new and different set of local conditions arises from the European invasion of the territory when the English language comes into contact with indigenous languages and cultures. Such colonial/postcolonial English mostly developed after the first settlement by Europeans in North America and reaches back in history only a few hundred years. In these situations, English has often been the language of domination, and perhaps it would be wise to include among the colonised the much earlier deeply rooted class and gender oppression evident in the traditional canon of British literature.

Third, there is a global English distributed mainly by electricity, which, beginning perhaps with recorded popular songs and the first talking movies, is only some seventy years old; this is the dominant language of radio, television, commerce and industry, e-mail and books, all computer files and cyberspace worldwide. Often verging on the incomprehensible to those trained in "proper" British English, this global English has been largely ignored by literary scholars and left, at best, to those interested in "communication arts." Yet it is global English that is most widely distributed and used today throughout the human community.

These three kinds of English require differing pedagogical objectives and methods in the coming years. The study of the language and literature of the British Isles requires a knowledge (but not necessarily a personal endorsement by student or teacher) of British culture, and of its main canonical or traditionally important authors and texts, mostly dead white males like Shakespeare, Milton and Dickens. One of its goals is to preserve and record historically "correct" or "standard" grammar, vocabulary and pronunciation. Most members of IAUPE were trained rigorously in this kind of English and see it undergoing a process of erosion in our universities today.

Colonial/postcolonial English may share some grammar, vocabulary or basic cultural values with English of the British Isles, but it is a different evolutionary step. In North America, Africa or Asia, the English language carried seeds of great promise for human justice, fair play, democracy and decency, along with the terrible reality of such conditions as slavery, economic and cultural exploitation, and imperial domination. Here English language and culture stand mainly in an antagonistic relation to indigenous people. The focus of scholarly interest here is mainly on how English is being refashioned into a variety of dialects carrying the aspirations of a great variety of non-British, non-dead, non-white, non-males. Perhaps colonial/postcolonial English resembles the fragmentation of Latin into the vernacular Romance languages. If so, the study of the English of the British Isles as opposed to the study of colonial/postcolonial English may in the future resemble the study of classical Latin versus the study of the origins of Romance literatures.

The phenomenon of global English is so recent that we can scarcely see the direction it is taking, though clearly it is of enormous importance for the future. Virtually no one inhabits the envelope of global English as a mother tongue. It is like a giant chat-room where strangers can meet safely only because they are not in real contact. Perhaps global English will become every human's second language, with one's deeper emotional and personal life conducted in widely differing parochial mother tongues while superficial business and commerce, and "virtual emotionality," can be negotiated in the global English of electronic space.

What actions might IAUPE take today to exploit the opportunities opening up before us? The canonical English language and literature of the British Isles was far more carefully and systematically studied in the last century than colonial/ postcolonial English or global English. It is essential that IAUPE transmit that knowledge without loss to future scholars. We have almost no economic resources and the task is enormous. We must start by taking small, practical steps: IAUPE should establish a website, with the first objective being to define a programme of study for students worldwide planning to enter university study of English language and literature. This first step must be harshly realistic regarding the hours of study available to an eighteen-year-old student in the real world. It would include perhaps three plays by Shakespeare, a novel by Dickens, selections from Milton and from the Romantic anthology, but not much more. The website should include full written text as well as the sound of standard pronunciation and other basic teaching apparatus. The chances are that such material already exists in excellent computer files scattered around our world universities. It is merely a question of an IAUPE committee discovering, selecting, standardising and endorsing such already established work.

Eventually, every school or home worldwide with a computer should be able to log on to the IAUPE website to find out the minimum endorsed course of study for entering university-level English studies. This website could also indicate a system of already existing examinations verifying the students' command of the recommended material. Probably such tests already exist and need only be scrutinised and approved by IAUPE. In North America, there are examining boards which will be delighted to underwrite the financial cost of any such authoritative endorsement.

Systematically from this first step, IAUPE could over decades create a standard for canonical British literature, expanding to cover more and more topics. From three plays by Shakespeare, the IAUPE endorsement might be extended to an advanced level of study for Shakespeare's complete works, if adequate computer archives can be found or developed. Seminars to study on such sites could be formed with students from two or more universities working in long-distance learning, in computer-linked classrooms, with several professors from widely differing areas directing the work of the students, who are no longer limited to a narrow age group or social background. In this way, the great accomplishments of the literary scholars of the past may be transmitted to future generations under the direction and guidance of a professional organisation.

With regard to colonial/postcolonial English, the task is more difficult. Here the focus of interest is how the alienated speaker transforms English from the language of oppression into a medium of expression for the aspirations of the erstwhile marginal. The same model of websites, archives and practical pedagogical tools as projected for the study of canonical British literature may be effective. Considering the harsh reality of the number of study hours available to a student preparing for entry into university study, what texts should IAUPE endorse and make available worldwide through its website in order to begin study of the colonial/postcolonial condition: Emerson, Gandhi, Cleaver? How do such writers transform the English language and literature?

Global English is so recent and as yet incompletely studied that the task facing future scholars is unclear. Yet it is obvious that some systematic archive needs to be established of the primary documents in English as it evolves in popular music, radio, television, cinema and cyberspace. Often this material is in oral form, rather than written. IAUPE needs to find and act to preserve these data for future analysis.

The endorsement of IAUPE, if carefully formulated and actively established, is something of great value. To establish, in a worldwide context, that X is a body of material which constitutes a solid background to begin university study of English, that Y is a test which will verify an acceptable level of competence, that Z is material which ought to be preserved in a research archive and studied in the future – all this will advance learning in the next century.

Theory, Post-Theory, and the Fate of the "Literary"

MURRAY KRIEGER†

PERHAPS IT WAS MILLENNIAL THINKING, a kind of hysteria produced by the approaching end of our millennium. As I look at recent tendencies in the humanities, ours seems to have become an "end"-moment, filled with eschatological pronouncements, as if in many areas we were to be concerned about "last things." This tendency first became especially apparent to us when, in 1992, Francis Fukuyama – prematurely, it turned out – pronounced "the end of history" in an exaggerated reaction to the dissolution of the Soviet Union and the Cold War that it helped create and oversaw.[1] His apocalyptic prediction, widely discussed, set off debates in many areas of discourse.

In our own area of debate, it seems that Fukuyama's "end of history" has also, if only implicitly and quite unintentionally, been extended to literary theory and to literature: in proclaiming an "end to theory" and an "end to literature," many are suggesting that we have been living in a post-theoretical – indeed, a post-literary – moment, thanks to a New-Historicist perspective and its consequence in cultural studies. There is a critical irony in the fact that it is in the interests of "history" – which, according to Fukuyama, has come to an end – that theory is now to be ended. Nevertheless, in what we used to call literary studies it is this new sort of historical reduction that would undo all previous history as we have known it, as it revises the previous readings of texts and characterisations of historical periods by insisting on beginning anew, on radically new grounds, unwriting our past in the effort to rewrite it. Having for several decades now been warned against the myth of origins, we may now be suffering from being subjected to a myth of endings.

But, it must be pointed out, just as it is only by means of historical analysis that Fukuyama could proclaim the end of history, so it is only by means of theoretical argument that many, in the shadow of historicism, can now proclaim that theory has come to an end, that we are now in a post-theoretical age. In distinction

[1] Francis Fukuyama, *The End of History and the Last Man* (New York: Free Press, 1992).

from history as a discipline, I am defining historicism, old- or new-style, as creating a theoretical model of interpretation that inflates sociohistorical contingency until it is seen as the exclusive shaper of our discourse – until it becomes what Aristotle would have deemed a "sufficient" as well as a "necessary" cause of all that happens in culture. Thus the transformation of history into historicism, despite the latter's distrust of the transhistorical claims of theory, elevates historical causality to theoretical status, carrying with it all of theory's hegemonic pretensions against which it complains. As in the age-old liar's paradox – the awareness that the claim "all men are liars" is self-denying since it, too, would have to be a lie – the anti-theoretical statement that all claims are historically contingent and thus relative is itself a universal claim contradicted by what it asserts. There is no privileged perch from which to make a universal claim, and to make such a claim – even an anti-theoretical claim – is to enter the realm of theory.

Despite this burden of self-contradiction, the reborn historicist industry gains much of its impetus because of its claim to replace the theory industry. By introducing the one universal of contingency, historicism argues that in its newer form it precludes the possibility of theory, thereby delegitimating theory as we have known it and ushering in what it sees as a post-theoretical period.

Let us give the argument that derives from the sole rule of historical contingency its full due. The assault on theory from the perspective of historicism, like the political position that follows from it, is always a tempting move by our deconstructive impulse. We are instinctively critical of our inclination to universalise our experience, to affirm the unity of being over the ever-changing variety of becoming, restricting being, of course, to what we, despite our limitations of time and place, find it to be. This narcissistic habit is as old as our urge to philosophy and imperialism alike. Trapped within what our own experience permits us to see, we retain the need – as old as Plato's in his war against the Sophists – to try and account for what we must believe is outside these limits, out there ready to be experienced by everyone. But the universalist pressure exerted upon us is opposed by what Bergson saw as the temporal flow of our experience, which is constantly differentiating itself, though the universalising wants to prevent us from seeing that differentness. The temporal consciousness leads to the historicist's, which constantly reminds us of the contingencies of our time and place – the differences of period, of ethnicity, of class, of social and economic and political constraints – and the limited perspective each of these imposes upon our capacity to see and to judge. Still, we persist in reifying the common elements we claim to find, treating them as universals that enable us to freeze the ever-changing flow of experience, the always differentiating histories of times and places, and then to congratulate ourselves for our philosophic perspicacity, our theoretical inclusiveness and conclusiveness. And our imperialist urge would impose our so-called discoveries on all times and places.

The notion of time and its changes is enemy to this desire of our intellect to contain and give structure to the varieties of historical experience and to the idiosyncrasies of our own position in history. In the past several decades we have been discovering anew that the intrusion of a precise and differentiating historical consciousness is itself a deconstructive act, because, in introducing change and difference, it gives the lie to our universalising ambition by relativising it: that is, by subjecting it to its place within our necessarily partial and contingent perspective. Historical difference thus makes our universal pretensions no more than creatures of our historically determined needs; it reduces theoretical grandeur, built on a single, time-defying, all-inclusive structure, to the culture-bound relativism of permanent revolution. In the realm of pure temporality it is as hard to clutch at a constant as it was way back in the realm of paradox ruled by Zeno. For, when it comes to our grasping at solid things, the realm of temporality is the realm of paradox.

To the extent that our theoretical ambition is undercut by the historical persistence of difference and the changes difference produces, we must see universal claims downgraded from the truths we attribute to nature to the deluding reifications projected by the partisan interests of historically conditioned institutions and their agents. So history replaces theory, as institutional sway replaces nature. We enter the domain of social constructs, from which we are never again to emerge into the light of any "discovered" universals. And the language of theory, for all its transhistorical ambition, is seen as responsive only to its self-serving assumptions rather than to the external data that it pretends disinterestedly to account for. It can be treated, then, as just another expression of an archive preserved by its moment in history; it is not permitted to step outside that archive even long enough to explain either its own moment in history or anything else. Where all is historically contained and controlled, there change will reign, an enemy to all universals but itself, excluding even the possibility of theory. Of course, this would have to claim that change, with its production of difference, is the only universal; and this is a self-denying claim, in that the dynamics of change cannot allow even that single universality, since that would acknowledge a sameness about change. After all, doctrines of change would then also be seen as social constructs arising in response to history's contingencies. Still, our time-bound condition seems to encourage us to affirm change, in all its ever-changingness, as the only timeless truth we would, though with some theoretical embarrassment, allow to stand.

I have been assuming an either/or relationship between theory and change, implying that to admit one is to exclude, even preclude, the other. But one could seek to bridge this disjunction by proposing a theory of change, such as a theory of progress or of cyclic repetition. Is there not always (shall I say: unavoidably?) a special temptation to absorb history's stray moments within one narrative form or another? I would put aside such proposals by pointing out that they are simply so many other theories, disguised versions of spatial thinking constructed out of closed, all-encompassing metaphors.

It is hardly new to observe that the scholar – because he or she has a theory, however implicit – resorts to his or her inevitable habit of converting history's accidents into pattern. Once it has happened, history does appear irreversible. But doesn't change deserve to be treated more radically, as a temporal particular that represents the errant moment in its momentous potential to disrupt the formation rules that govern all theories, theories of historical change as well as transhistorical theories?

Our words themselves are major perpetrators of our self-deceiving habit of reifying our experience, freezing its temporality into their own ontological space. Their very being militates in favour of theory and against a fluid experience. The substantives we use, with their deceiving implication that one word represents one thing, suggest constants beyond history's changes. Even as we may describe radical changes from one historical moment to another, we retain the generic noun and with it the sense that it is a common, essentially unchanging entity that is undergoing alterations, though untransforming ones. If we ask "What is it that changes?" then the language of the question itself persuades us to a single, constant "it," as we allow that nominal subject to trick us into essentialising it. As poststructuralists have reminded us, the generic term, representative of a static nominalism of language, often induces us into a false essentialism, so that we have, not the changing single entity (the "it") we think we are talking about, but only a constantly shifting field of differences that we carelessly mislabel as if it were one thing.

Still, the theoretical impulse in us persists and need not be altogether denied. Our discourse requires those very universals that may render that discourse untrustworthy because it blurs the facts of change. Nevertheless, we can, in our antinominalistic description, point to the fact that culture does function and establish its continuity by means of the verbal genres it holds onto despite the shiftings of time. Culture takes its generic nouns seriously, even literally; it allows those generic nouns, as its linguistic norm, to shape its development: from the inside, culture uses its myths to create its identity, thereby functioning to produce more culture. These are effects that the historian as well as the theorist must take account of, regardless of what the demythologiser within each of us persuades us is really going on outside the comforts of those productive, if deceiving, constructs.

But now, by way of considerations of language, we can move into the realm of literary history and literary theory, and nowhere is the conflict between continuity and revolution, between the designs of theory and the randomness of happenings, more evident. Viewed through the ambitions that give rise to it, literary theory exists to create a discursive unity that can accommodate history's variety, to synchronise the diachronic. Making transhistorical claims, literary theory seeks systematically to account for a broad variety of texts of many periods and literatures, flattening out the changes – even the apparent revolutions – that occur among them. Until recently, without self-questioning, literary theory had traditionally assumed that there is literature, and thus that there are peculiarly literary works; that consequently there is a legitimate discourse that creates a system to illuminate the performance of each of these works and – by extrapolation – of that body of works lumped together as what we had meant to create as our literary canon. Critical discourse and theoretical discourse about criticism were thus legitimised, and the criteria for our judging the relative value of this discourse rested upon those secure assumptions concerning the primacy, hence discursive privilege, of those literary texts to which such secondary critical discourse and tertiary theoretical discourse were ultimately to be beholden.

But these so-long-secure assumptions have been not only put in question but also utterly undermined in recent years. Instead of judging the face-value claims made by rival theoretical systems to account with consistency for the special kind of writing to which they were responsible, we are to see these claims only as they are contingent upon other-than-theoretical motives. There has been a shift in emphasis from questions about the inside of theory – what does it account for? what does it leave out? does it, in the relations among its terms and propositions, argue acceptably? – to questions apparently from the outside, which put in doubt the theoretical enterprise itself: what are the political pressures leading to the position taken? what is the relation between its so-called principles and the literary works it privileges? what non-theoretical subtext leads it to the critical judgements it asks us to make, presumably on disinterested grounds? in other words, what are its historical contingencies, however transhistorical it claims to be?

The historicist would thus unmask the theoretical project as a deceptive ploy in the service of historically identifiable forces. Theory, having been exposed by all that historical contingencies reveal, would prove to be a pseudo-discipline we can well dispense with. What we used to think of as "extraneous issues," as issues irrelevant to the theoretical project, now becomes central to our concern.

Is there any response to this reduction of theory's pretensions? No doubt theory is (and should be) always put in self-doubt by the data of the next text to come along, as well as by all the limitations of the viewer's perspective that are imposed by sociohistorical conditions, like those of class, gender and race or ethnicity. In spite of these qualms, we respond to the need to put our thinking together, projecting the human habit of seeking to generalise, even as we must be sceptical about the ties that thinking would enforce. So we have seen a healthy sequence of deconstructions, each of which grows into a new construct, each claiming dominance, though only to await its own deconstruction at the hands of its successor. This sequence is not necessarily progressive, but it is one way to see our culture shaped, moment by moment.

If we were to speak hypothetically rather than historically, we might conceive of a pre-theoretical stage of unmediated literary responses. Of course, this is only a heuristic notion: in every reading there is inevitably some theoretical predisposition, however primitive and unarticulated. What follows in literary culture is a series of articulated theories, each rising into prominence and then displaced by its successor. Each theory, perhaps in response to its favoured texts as well as its service to its historical moment, struggles to maintain its internal consistency in the face of other, less friendly texts that challenge its adequacy to such newer and unanticipated demands. But for a long time there had been this succession of theories, often in conflict, and the conviction that some sort of theoretical claims about literature, whatever their historical partiality and bias, are both possible and useful so long as they have to some extent been responsive to the characteristics and effects of literary texts.

As we have seen, both Old and New Historicism, like the political approaches that follow from the latter, are brashly universal from the start. They can hardly claim to be growing out of, or arising in response to, particular texts. They would see through all texts similarly, because for them the textual surface is not the primary object of interpretation. Critical theories may well have grown into a pride and imperialism that spread from the sort of text appropriate to a given theory to all texts, but those who would put an end to theory seek to subdue all texts similarly from the start. Their historicism may be the most universal, hence the most theoretical in its wilful blindness – an *a-priori* and thus uniform blindness – to what any new text would offer. Driven by a determinism, this historian–critic always presumes to know better than what the text explicitly suggests, and like Mynheer Peeperkorn in Thomas Mann's *Magic Mountain*, can claim to put every text in his or her pocket.

But have I given the New Historicism its full due in its attempt to evade the problems that literary commentary found with what now seems like the Old Historicism? How would we distinguish the two? With its prestructuralist assumptions, the Old Historicism assumed that, since history was seen to be a series of facts solidly out there, objective and verifiable, it was itself in no need of being interpreted. In other words, history was not problematical. On the other hand, literary texts were problematical and thus in need of being interpreted. We were to use the known to interpret that which is not yet fully known: we were to use history to interpret texts, to use history's "facts" to resolve problems of interpretation found in texts. It was a reaffirmation of the old distinction – as old as Aristotle – between history as real and texts as imaginative fictions. Such were the consequences of the naively positivistic conception by the Old Historicism of history as facts (actual happenings) rather than history as discourse.

Some decades back, with the advent of what we have been calling post-structuralism, history, like all other forms of discourse, was put into question. What if history was not merely a collection of external, "objective" facts? Was not history, after all, as a form of discourse, written as a narrative and as such already an interpretation of so-called facts? In other words, history itself came to be regarded as problematical, no less problematical than any other discourse, only perhaps more deceptively so, because it usually appears (pretends?) to be a factual report. History, then, is itself a text in need of interpretation and has no privileged relation to "reality" that would permit it to be used to interpret other, less "real" texts. So goes the poststructuralist argument about the textual character of history.[2]

So history is no longer, as it was for the Old Historicism, simply there, as a series of documents recording a fixed sequence of facts – of unquestionable knowledge – that, once established by the scholar, could be used to try to make sense of the more troublesome literary text. Poststructuralism and its historical

[2] The major theorist responsible for this turn was Hayden V. White, who, from his early work *Metahistory: The Historical Imagination in Nineteenth-Century Europe* (Baltimore, MD: Johns Hopkins University Press, 1974) to the later *Tropics of Discourse: Essays in Cultural Criticism* (Baltimore, MD: Johns Hopkins University Press, 1978), led the way for a rethinking of the narratological and tropological basis of history of discourse.

agent, the New Historicism, have taught us that we get those claimed facts out of books, books that are also interpretations and have their own narratological and tropological structures, have their own reasons for being written as they are, so that, whether we like it or not, they in turn stand in need of being interpreted. Indeed, the historical text may well take no less interpretation in the reading than does the literary.

This was the consequence of the one major claim of poststructuralism in all its varieties: that reading any sort of text should not lead us to dispute realities and unrealities in the world of facts. It is, instead, a matter of looking at the entire world of would-be knowledge as a world of language, a world of discourse or, better yet, of textuality. In the light of such a shift, the New Historicist discovers that the primary assumption made by the Old Historicists can no longer be made: we can no longer look at a given moment in the history of culture as if it were out there to be known directly, independently of language, as a collection of brute realities, so that we can simply apply those realities to literature in order to reduce the more resistant literary text to its place in its cultural moment.

Instead of this simpler assumption, we now are to assume that the reader must relate all sorts of texts to one another, like a juggler who has a number of balls all moving about in the air at the same time. One of them may be literature, another may be history or any text in any discipline within the "human sciences" or even in popular culture, and no one of them is, *a priori*, any more stable than any other. All texts are to be read similarly, as equally unstable bits of language requiring interpretation, with no one of them a fixed instrument to be used to unlock any other. So, once again, history as a series of texts can reveal no self-evident facts that allow it to be an interpretative agency for the uncertainties of the literary text. It follows also that literature should not be treated as a mode of discourse different from any other mode of discourse in so-called high or low culture, since all sorts of texts share a similar problematic of representation. Current methods of interpretation, consequently, tend to take what used to be techniques employed exclusively for reading literature and to impose them upon a variety of textual kinds, all now made similarly, if not equally, responsive to such readings.[o]

A commentator who seeks to be historical now must look at a variety of kinds of contemporaneous texts and relate them to one another by finding common elements among them – tropes, narrative structures: in short, Foucault's "discourse formations." The New Historicist, then, allows these texts from many domains to read one another, treating them all as parts of a single discursive moment in culture, as flowing into one another in what a founder of the New

Historicism, Stephen Greenblatt – in a metaphor borrowed from biology – calls a "circulatory system."[3]

Having canvassed the texts of a given cultural moment in order to discover a common discourse formation, New Historicists do not stop there in their historical concern. They eventually reach beyond discourse to uncover the sociopolitical forces that create the peculiarities of its formation at the moment in question. The particular discourse formation, seen displaying itself in its various textual manifestations throughout the culture, reveals common narratological and tropological structures that function rhetorically to prejudice judgement, elevating or at least protecting some elements in society by repressing others. In other words, it reveals certain hierarchies of power, of represser and repressed, within the social fabric of that moment, those hierarchies – of race, of class, of gender – that create its discourse. Who is wielding the power, and over whom? Who is being denied the power, and with what costs? How are the limits of discourse being defined and imposed? And whose interests are being served? It is not surprising that such questions lead historicism in a sharply political direction in response to pressures from marginal voices, long repressed, to alter the ruling discourse formation in order to impose their own, albeit no less repressively.

Within its historical moment, then, every ideology is seen as creating its language, and through that language speaking each variety of discourse, lying in wait under the text to capture the reader. New-Historicist theory, whether supporting cultural-materialist or neo-Marxist or feminist or minoritist or gay and lesbian critics, can alert us to the single subtext – driven by power – that each would find beneath all contemporary texts, and by means of that subtext warn us of the political mischief it would work upon the unwary reader. So New Historicists must finally be concerned about the actual power relations within a society, even though, as poststructuralists, they derive all their definitions of power from a reading of the way in which the varied texts of a given period, through mutual reflection, can be seen as controlling and speaking the language of the power they represent.

Since, as American critics have used it, the language-centred episteme they take from Foucault leads us beyond language to the *Realpolitik* of the sociohistorical context, the New Historicists' claim may in the end turn out to be not altogether unrelated to the claims of the Old Historicists, who were echoing the

---

[3] Among many other places in his work, see Stephen Greenblatt, "Capitalist Culture and the Circulatory System," *The Aims of Representation: Subject/Text/History*, ed. Murray Krieger (New York: Columbia University Press, 1987) 257–73.

earliest defences of an American literature as reflections of the newly emerging set of social relations that produced it. In this one sense, then, the New Historicism might be seen as at least an inheritor of the Old Historicism, if not an extension of it. In another sense, of course, its entire procedure means to be different, thanks to its theoretical need to merge historicism with the poststructuralist commitment to the special role of discourse.

We have watched theory struggling for survival against the resurrected dominion of historicism, whose all-reducing determinism threatens to undermine the universalising pretensions that have guided theory's rise to institutional power. This recently renewed dedication to the relativising hand of historical contingency would, of course, undermine the "literary" no less than theory does, so that both the literary and theory are now struggling to defend themselves against the claims of the New Historicism. Not only would theory lose its licence, but the literary text would be dissolved into the undifferentiated sweep of textuality by this historicism, just as it was by theory in its frequent overreaching moments. Of course, apologists for poetics would argue that the literary way of dealing with a text shows its resistance to the one, history, as freely as it does to the other, theory. So, whatever the mutually destructive rivalry recently generated between theory and history, it is a combat in which the literary can have little stake, since recent developments demonstrate that it cannot hope to be empowered by either, even as it resists both.

From the eighteenth century until now, we can observe a succession of oscillations between the dominance of theory at the expense of history and the dominance of history at the expense of theory. These have been oscillations between approaches built on spatial models to the exclusion of historical contingencies, and approaches built on temporal models to the exclusion of transhistorical universals. The philosophic urge to universalise our experiences sometimes has overpowered, and sometimes has been overpowered by, our awareness of contingency, of the temporal flow of our experience, which is constantly differentiating itself. Hence one kind of distrust, our distrust of the philosopher's claim that we can attain a standing from which we can transcend the time in which we – always a differentiated "we" – drift along, is matched by another, opposed sort of distrust, our Socratic distrust of the historicist who would doom us to a Heraclitean flux. Spatialising theorists have reified the common elements they presume to find, while historicising sceptics have worried about the constraints those theorists have had to impose on the always differentiated moments that they want to merge into that commonalty. And historicists have deconstructed the theorist's universal by subjecting it to the contingencies of the self-differentiating moment, but could do so, alas, only by universalising the dominion of the culturally relative. So, even in the extremes of historicism, we have seen that the temporal has been captured by the spatial, the historicist by the theorist within.

But I have pointed out that, in its recent form, the struggle between the rival institutions of theory and historicism, which I have suggested may well be viewed as just another struggle between rival theoretical institutions, seems to have proceeded with the undisputed understanding by both sides that the literary has no distinctive licence. In this agreement, the combatants reveal that they are participating in a single swing of a second succession of oscillations that we have undergone these past two centuries: that between moments in which the literary is the subject of a romantic idolatry because of the special visionary power it is granted, and moments in which the literary is taken as just one among many manifestations of a culture, without special entitlements. These days, both theorists and historicists often join in the second, sometimes even to the point of claiming that the category "literary" no longer has any authority or even, perhaps, any meaning, except insofar as it is the projection of an elitist's nostalgic wish. With a contempt reminiscent of Thomas Love Peacock's *Four Ages of Poetry* (1820), the protective attitude toward the literary is declared obsolete.

To propose that what is happening is only an oscillation in an extended series of oscillations is itself, of course, to take a long historical view. The historian might well unite with the theorist as joint ironists in asking, with Shakespeare, the double-edged question, "Whether revolution be the same." Embedded in the question is the ambiguity of the word "revolution," a single extension into substantive form of the two very different verbs, 'revolt' and 'revolve,' thereby suggesting at once utter disruption and bland continuity, both a breakthrough of the different and just more of the same. The opening of Sonnet 59, from which this line is taken, is, fittingly, "If there be nothing new, but that which is / Hath been before."[4]

This returns us to Fukuyama and his claim of a complete break with the past, with history as we have known it. The exhilaration surrounding any new conception that claims to transform for good all that had been thought is greatly dimin-

[4] Like all who have been concerned about the optimistic myth of progress on the one hand and the cynical acceptance of eternal return on the other, the speaker in the sonnet is asking whether the present truly represents an improvement over the past, "Whether we are mended, or where better they, / or whether revolution be the same." But, true to the Petrarchan convention that controls these poems, he concludes – though this is hardly supportive of my concerns here – by affirming the superiority of his beloved despite his sceptical awareness.

ished by the suggestion that we are only engaging in the repetition of a process that has gone before. Yet every revolutionary movement is encompassed by the rhetoric that would expunge, or at least radically revise, all that has preceded it through the centuries. Indulging the myth of progress as a narrative form that is more spatial than temporal, the self-proclaimed new movement announces with its advent the end of history, since all prior history is viewed as the history of error. Even when the appeal is to a historicity that proclaims no constancy except the constancy of change, it carries the implication that it has arrived at the final truth, so that theoretical history can at last have a stop.

But, of course, Fukuyama notwithstanding, history does not have a stop. Nor is it necessarily moving upward as it moves onward. Nor, if we are to believe historicist arguments, is history moving in accordance with any definable shape, lest it, too, be subject to a theoretics of space. Still, as we have seen, one cannot historicise away all theory except by using a historicist model that itself turns out, as we have seen, to be theoretical. So the attack by historicism on the possibility of theory – the denial of the very theoretical urge, as a self-deceiving, transhistorical, universalising impulse – is made from a self-indicting position once historicism itself proves to be just another theory. And, like any theory, at some point it tempts its propagator to essentialise, hence to thematise, it into an implicit metaphysic.

Although many have shown that the historicist's procedure is hardly exempt from being itself firmly grounded in theory, we seem not to have blunted the attempt, inspired to a large extent by historicism, to allow the notions of theory – and literature as well – to die with our millennium. We can see an analogue to the dismissal of theory in the dismissal of literature. But I argue that, after giving the historical argument its full due, after conceding that it (literature, like theory) is a product of its moment in culture – in effect, is largely made by history – one still may claim that the literary text can create for itself some freedom to make cultural history.

Until the past several decades, commentary had an unquestioning confidence in the separatist notion of the literary text as a privileged verbal structure, as if it had been out there as an inevitable category all the time. There was little awareness that "literature" itself, as a term and concept, came into Western thought as a late arrival on the scene and was itself a creature of historical conditions. But once it had been put into its historically contingent place as what we now call a "social construct," and having enjoyed that place, literature has now found itself blurred with all sorts of texts, thereby losing any claim to distinctness. But what shall we do without a notion of the literary so long as our reading habits continue to find in it the immediacies that alone, among the language arts, can resist, and even quietly dissent from, the ideological mediations of other sorts of texts?

The only theory that would tolerate this claim of the text's counter-ideological power is a theory that would undo both itself and the very theoretical urge, by acknowledging its own impotence before all that the text performs, all that it makes happen on its own.[5] Such a theory would empower the literary text to undermine the no longer altogether determining forces of history as well as the universalising claims of theory – even while that text is partly explained by both the historical forces and the theory whose universal claims it would also undermine. So it is only partly explained by them, and for the more modest theory the "partly" is not strong enough to account for, or to preclude, the text's performative power, a power that calls for the specially trained perceptions of the literary interpreter.

However, the New-Historicist version of theory that we have been watching emerge has been far less modest and self-effacing as it has pressed forward with its own imperialistic ambitions. In its present institutional role, that sort of theory would overwhelm the full performance potential of the individual literary text no less than historicism did when it took the form of the Old Historicism, which first prompted, by way of opposition, the rise of that early literary theory that authorised the New Critics to unleash the powers of the text.

The historicist theory, with its implicit determinism, imposes severe limits on a text whose emerging language system, wrapped in fictionality, would generate potential meanings beyond the *a-priori* predictions that can be made by any analysis of its sociopolitical moment in culture. The history of literature is the story of certain texts (and, happily, we have been broadly and even radically expanding their number in recent days) which remain teasingly out there, with a fullness in a part or the whole of them that challenges all we think we have known until we meet them; that keeps them beyond the confining reach of anything that either theory or history has allowed us to bring to them; that contradicts all efforts to level them into common discourse.

It is, then, hardly enough to replace theory as an institution with historical contingency as an institution because the latter also precludes the independently generative power of the text. The universal pretensions of theory are countermanded not only by historicist contingency, but – together with historical com-

[5] What I am saying here is similar to Hillis Miller's continual insistence, in his recent writings on the "performative" power of literature, that the text has the power to "make something happen." This is a strong way of seeing its force as primary, not relegating it to a mere reflection of a performative power lodged elsewhere, whether in theory or in history.

monplaces – also by the hold-out pressure of every resistant text. Theory must again be called upon to protect the literary text's resistance to ideology's repression, even though it is alien to its own universalising interests to do so. It is not easy. The literary text, as anti-ideological, is, in its anti-universal dedication, anti-institutional, so that a theory that would elevate the text (and the act of reading it) to the institutional level would have an anti-institutional safeguard – its commitment to resistance – built into it. As an institution, this sort of theory would be resisting its own institutional ideology in order to find a suppleness to match the suppleness of its endlessly restive subjects, the texts it is to account for. In other words, theory, by constantly putting its own universal pretensions in question, must resist enjoying the institutional status it has achieved; but it can do so only by bowing to the counter-theoretical pressure of the individual text. It must meet that text without seeking to overcome it. And in this self-denying mood it may discover its answer to historicism as well.

Such a theory bids that we hold it lightly, so that we can return to the text, reading as free agents, open to being surprised by a verbal sequence that we can endow with the seductions of a fictional containment which resists whatever we bring with us to capture – to contain – it with. And our reading habits have taught us that we can work upon more than what is called "literature" or, rather, can allow it to work on us its all-disarming magic. Where the freedom of a self-conscious fiction encourages the play of action, of characters, of trope, of language, it gives literature (or at least what we read as literature) a special – I dare say: privileged – place among the discourses, because it leads us to read momentary excursions into the literary by the other kinds of discourse, so that literature proper may function as a model for our reading the others, in part or whole, as literary. In this way, too, the study of the literary should resist any self-enclosure and can break beyond any discursive boundaries, though only while it continues to cherish the specialness of its own project.

So let us grant everything that should be granted to all situational contingencies; let us grant the partiality of our so-called judgements, results of prejudices that rationalise themselves as the "literary"; let us concede that the very category "literature," far from eternal, can be shown to be a creation of specific historical circumstances a few centuries ago. But still, must we not save what we can of the theoretical impulse and the literary texts toward which they are directed?

I am proposing the modest excursion into a theory that is always tentative, in that it leaves room for a reading which is open to a "surprise" found in the literary text – surprise to our theory and, even more, surprise to the deterministic suggestions of historicism. A reading, then, should be encouraged to explore and exploit the necessary role of "surprise," of the radically new text, or the unanticipated newness within any wrought text. Why else, I ask, should we bother to read, except for the possibility of being led outside ourselves and what we have been and known before this reading? Any reading that produces only self-reaffirmation is a reading that has failed. It is the openness to textual surprise that should challenge theory, and in doing so create a new dialectic with theory in its demand to be accounted for. But this is hardly the case with the theory I have associated with the New Historicism (which, despite its claims, is not a post-theory), because by predetermining its object of interpretation it makes itself invulnerable in advance. Its worth as an interpretative tool is diminished because it cannot make distinctions that are primarily influenced by the nature of what it is seeking to interpret. So it also represents the "end of interpretation," since it proceeds from a point beyond or before, but excluding, interpretation. If we judge theory by its distance from the object that it would accommodate, then, far from being an anti-theory or post-theory, this version of historical determinism is perhaps the most theoretical of all.

So long as readers of literary texts persist in seeking the surprising, neither literature nor our theoretical attempts to account for its special powers can be brought to an end by being reduced to the contingencies of history. I expect that there will be few if any millennial endings; and surely neither theory nor literature will be one of them, as I hope our descendants also will have found when yet another century, or even another millennium, comes to its end.

Why English Literature?

SERGIO PEROSA

I

FOR DECADES I HAVE INSISTED that I am a Professor of English, English and American Literature – not Studies. By name and vocation, our Department was of English Language and Literature: since 1997, it has split into a Department of English and Postcolonial Studies, and one of American Studies. The experience is fairly common, I believe, and it has good as well as bad implications and consequences. Let me emphasise at once that what I am going to discuss briefly is seen and reported from a "foreign" country and a faculty that is still called Faculty of Foreign Languages and Literatures, away from the "centre of empire," and that I must be at least partially autobiographical: this may be the reason why I have been asked to contribute.

In Italy, English literature came into its own, and emerged into our academic awareness, after the Second World War. It was welcomed with relish, and developed some peculiarities. When I decided to take up English as a major in college, it was because I knew nothing about it: one had French and German then, in my part of the country, practically no English; our best professor – and of a key subject, Germanic (or Teutonic) Philology – could speak eight to ten languages but knew very little English. I was a disappointment to all my previous teachers: being interested and fairly proficient in literature, one was expected to study the Classics; a second, less prestigious choice would have been Italian; French or German might do; but English.... Was not even Shakespeare described in our classical novel *I promessi sposi*, in the wake of Voltaire's opinion, as "a barbarian not devoid of talent"?

My choice, and that of our generation coming to cultural consciousness in the early 1950s, was a choice in favour of what was felt and proved to be a literature of empiricism and concreteness, of pragmatic thought and fairly immediate appeal, much less "classical" and *paludata* (an impossible word to translate;

"caparisoned," or something like *cothurnata* for tragedy) than our tradition was. In a sense, it was an anti-classical and anti-rhetorical choice: one could confront great writers there, dealing directly with down-to-earth, practical matters; no philosophical overdetermination, as in German literature, for instance, no deep involvement in neoclassical grandeur as in French; so much less influence of Greek and Latin authors and precepts.

Just out of the *liceo* (which taught mostly Latin and Greek), and emerging from the historical experience of Fascism, which had stressed our classical heritage, and classical rhetoric, *ad nauseam*, we could find notable relief from those shackles in English: the language itself (in spite of its impossible pronunciation) was so simple and linear in grammar and syntax, so paratactical as against German or Latin, so taut and practical against the demanding elegance of French. It fostered clarity and conciseness. The interest in, and the wide diffusion of, English literature, in the sense I just described, was so overwhelming in the academic and publishing world (one "read" mostly English in either), as to become a central feature of the 1950s and 1960s.

There had been an interest, of course, before. A forerunner and a scholar so influential in defining and spreading an awareness of English literature and English writers, and in laying the ground for their later blossoming, Mario Praz, had been active in the 1930s. But it was basically a single-handed contribution and endeavour. In line with his background and preparation, he had dealt *entre deux guerres* with English writers *within* the framework of Italian culture, often seeing and presenting them in terms of their "equivalent" Italian peers and predecessors, stressing the links (whenever possible, though with some exceptions) between Italian and English literature: Chaucer and the great Italian *trecentisti*, for instance, his difference from Dante, Elizabethan poetry and the Petrarchan tradition, the Metaphysical poets and the Italian *secentismo e marinismo*, etc.[1] When he edited and contributed to a complete Italian translation of Shakespeare, his idea was to use an approximation of seventeenth-century Italian, an equivalent of Giambattista Basile, and to keep obscurities where there were obscurities, clots where there were clots: no familiarisation was expected, Shakespeare was seen and presented less as a playwright than as a literary giant, and as a kind of *poeta ermetico* in his sonnets and other poems.

[1] See, for instance, Mario Praz, *Secentismo e marinismo in Inghilterra* (Florence: La Voce, 1925), *The Romantic Agony* (London: Oxford University Press, 1933), *Studi sul concettismo* (Milan: La Cultura, 1934) and *Machiavelli in Inghilterra e altri saggi* (Rome: Luminelli, 1942).

After the Second World War, when we were allowed a more direct approach, less influenced by Italian traditions and Italian eyes, we found suddenly and with glee that Chaucer was much more entertaining and less formidable (especially in his *Tales*), that one could laugh with him: with Dante you were always in a kind of hell, never forgetting its existence; his humour was always black humour (as for Ariosto, he was not prescribed, because he was too immoral, and too entertaining). Shakespeare proved a marvellous entertainer, too; in his comedies and general outlook, but also in his serious, tragic moods; he had a quality of down-to-earth directness, of "free" speech, touching so naturally on contemporary, felt issues. Above all, he was involved in the theatre, *playwriting* rather than being a *littérateur*, using a splendid form of diegesis unencumbered by classical models, tenets, rules. If I were to spot a steady trend and development in Italian studies of and approaches to Shakespeare from then on, it would be precisely a growing awareness of his role and greatness as a playwright, as a provider of scripts to be freely adapted, staged and, in the very process, transformed into a life experience.[2]

Italian Romanticism was Leopardi: gloomy, a thorough pessimist, harping on the curse of man and the decay of the world, on death-in-life. English Romanticism proved instead a revolutionary movement, full of iconoclastic and vital urges, an affirmation of life (in spite of its sombre moods and dejections), of the fullness of language and experience, of the power of imagination, with fewer lamentations in it than we were accustomed to. T.S. Eliot, to give a final example, allowed us to re-read Dante in a new, dramatic way, and to recognise in Eugenio Montale not so much the oft-quoted *male di vivere* as a recourse to the "objective correlative" as a principle of hard, disillusioned poetry.

English literature became, then, a form of liberation, an interest that fostered the discovery of life and ease in literature (in spite of the pompous Victorians, then much less read than they are now), rather than of literary principles, the study of which was removed from imposing tasks: I still remember, when I began teaching, the envy of my German colleague, who had to deal with Kant and Hegel most of the time. Along the same lines, and for the sake of completeness, a second dislocation took place – the growing interest in American literature as separate from English literature, a further step away from the *paludato* in the direction of immediacy, concreteness, contemporary issues, lived experience: hence the

[2] See, for instance, *Nel laboratorio di Shakespeare*, ed. Alessandro Serpieri (Parma: Pratiche Editrice, 1988) 4 vols.; the series of volumes edited by Mariangela Tempera, *Dal testo alla scena* (Bologna: CLUEB, 1982–), each volume devoted to one of the major plays; and, by a "philological" scholar, Giorgio Melchiori, *Shakespeare* (Bari: Laterza, 1994).

development of American Literature sections in our Departments of English and our curricula; a familiar story.

Given the classical premisses and background of so much Italian culture, this may be seen now as a typical *fuga in avanti* (a forward flight or escape), away from the burden of the past: American literature was even more concrete, direct, adventurous and down-to-earth, so much less "classical" (indeed, rejecting "classical" roots) than English literature itself had been or appeared to us.

A third aspect must be highlighted, also in view of what follows in my brief description. In Italy we had always entertained, and suffered from, a strong historical or historicist bias: literature seen not only in its historical momentum, but studied from an historicist point of view – sources, genres, a nation-building consciousness. In the 1950s and 1960s, moreover, an overwhelming urge towards social consciousness, political awareness, *engagement*, was shaping literary studies and the market: *neorealismo* was rampant in fiction and poetry, as well as in films. De Sanctis, with his *Storia della letteratura italiana*, was the presiding genius for the first aspect; Gramsci (of whom briefly hereafter), for the second.

English literature (in spite of the stance taken by its writers in the 1930s) was a way out of this prevailing atmosphere: it allowed a certain amount of freedom from such constraints, a spirit of open intellectual inquiry; it was less "political" than what came, for instance, from France in the wake of Sartre. To give just one example, Ezra Pound could be read and accepted as a good poet, despite his bad politics and the burning issues surrounding his behaviour.[3] As a corollary, or an enforcement, English and American "New Criticism" was finding its way into literary analysis (mostly through early Eliot and thanks to Wellek and Warren's *Theory of Literature*), and, for us then, it was a refreshing experience: literature could be studied as such, in its intricacies and complexities, in the texts themselves, not in its historical developments or through social and political lenses. I believe that to some extent, and in spite of obvious limitations, this was a fruitful and liberating experience in those years: it reconciled us with the practice of close reading, it familiarised us with issues of irony, paradox, and ambiguity that an excess of historicism and social awareness had forced us to neglect.

[3] When Alfredo Rizzardi translated Pound's *Pisan Cantos* as *Canti pisani* (Parma: Guanda, 1953), the wrapper specified that "good poetry" could be achieved with "wrong ideas"; predictably, a violent controversy ensued.

II

We are all too familiar with what happened next – the rupture and the break in the late 1960s and the 1970s. They were cultural, academic, and mainly political. The student revolts within the universities, and outside, very controversial confrontations in the world at large, took us by surprise, totally revolutionised our field and compelled new modes of critical pursuit.

There is no need to rehearse the story here, except, in my case, to notice two aspects. Vietnam was decisive in shattering the idyll with American literature and American culture: the USA was as class-torn, economically conditioned and politically at war as any other (at least European) country and culture. No more solace or liberation to be drawn from them – indeed, quite the reverse. A mood of contestation almost wrecked the academic subject, or in any case drew attention to other areas: social conflict, imperialism, the betrayal of equality, etc. "Canonical" American literature was thrown into the doldrums, wholly new issues were brought to the foreground: for a while, Italian publishers, till then so eager and active in promoting the dissemination of American creative writers of any kind, turned almost overnight to the publication of social and political essays; this was the first step in the oncoming removal of literature from the front line.

As for English literature, we might have thought we were relatively safe. Not so: I still remember the day when *my* break with the prevailing mood took place, my shock and disbelief on seeing one day, on one of the many posters or writings on the wall to which we were then accustomed, the ominous, unexpected declaration: *abbasso l'inglese, lingua borghese* (rhymed, as usual: down with English, a bourgeois language). Was it not the language we had chosen and cherished precisely because it was free from cant, direct, to the point, lucid – the kind of language that would prevent obnubilation and obfuscation, the conundrums and equivocations of political jargon, the rhetorical sweep that tends to cancel meaning? Was not English a culture that fostered and compelled clear issues and the assumption of responsibility for clear thought? And its being discarded as bourgeois ....

Not only the idyll, but the guidance, the safety from cant and rhetoric we had thought we had found in it, the balance between the past and the present, classical traditions and a more empirical, joyous approach to writing, were shattered. Everything had to be reconstructed from scratch, if we had energy enough. Reconstructed, that is, after the long deconstruction that followed in the wake. I thought that for a while we had missed or totally compromised our chance. For our purposes, it was not so much that the idea of relating to a crucial diversity in

English literature was lost, as that its very body was torn, broken and fragmented. We could cope without an idea of universality – and of the *uni*versity itself – but hardly with this.

It was the moment when one feared that English literature itself had vanished. On the positive side, a third, great rib of what was once its whole body was extracted from it. Commonwealth literature – later called Literature(s) of the English-Speaking Countries, eventually Postcolonial Literature – was separated from the main body and studied as such. This was all for the good. Writers whom we had ahistorically lumped together could now be read and interpreted in their national (colonial or postcolonial) roots: some *pour cause* (Canadian, African, Indian, Australian writers), others, I believe, with a degree of coercion that they would not have liked (those who before decolonisation carefully disguised or denied, as a matter of course, their origins: would Katherine Mansfield, for instance, or even Jean Rhys have liked the new classification?).

In spite of this, the further division was positive, as the separation of American Literature had been positive. New energies and a new cultural awareness were released in Italy, too, where the Centre for Emerging Literatures of the CNR (National Research Council), which had active groups in most major universities, sponsored and supported a series of research activities, sets of books and new magazines of the greatest impact (including the "America Africa Asia Australia" magazine, for instance, now in its twentieth issue).

What worries me, however, is the amount of that dismembering, the tendency to spread diversification so far that nothing is left to diversify from. Scottish and Irish writers, for instance, no matter when active, are made to be part of "colonial," postcolonial or national *cadres*, and in such a way that one wonders what would be left of English literature as such if these premisses were fully accepted. Few writers indeed: what would be left of Italian literature if Sicilian writers were to be separated from Venetian, Florentine from Milanese (after all, they wrote for the most part in "free," separate states before Italy was united)? How can we deal with Sterne, Goldsmith, Wilde, outside of the common context of English literature and English culture? Perhaps we should be rational, not necessarily bold, in changing the name to British literature, as we often do in contrasting it with its American counterpart. Postcolonial literatures are, of course, a different matter: but can one really consider W.B. Yeats as a colonial or postcolonial writer? And what has Kipling (or Macaulay, for that matter) to gain from an emphasis on his Indian roots? What about George Orwell in Burma, then, or Leonard Woolf in Sri Lanka?

At the risk of sounding "corny," one has to proceed on these grounds with a great deal of common sense, and much more than a pinch of salt. If pushed to extremes, such practices would prove disastrous for everybody involved – writers, in the first place. The other danger to avoid, and tendency to resist, is the levelling-down of English literature chronologically, as well as geographically, that we find in so may "new" literary histories. An overwhelming interest in twentieth-century literature, English and otherwise, has relegated the great writers of the past to a kind of almost shady background. A very valuable and impressive *Storia della civiltà letteraria inglese*, edited by Franco Marenco in 1996 – which superseded in the market and the universities Mario Praz's and David Daiches's previous histories of English literature (each a one-man effort) – is a case in point, *because of* its seriousness and importance. One full volume, out of three, is devoted to twentieth-century literature, while the first covers the ground from the Middle Ages to the end of the seventeenth century, and the second is devoted to the eighteenth and nineteenth centuries; Joyce is given 55 pages, T.S. Eliot 44, as against 35 given to Chaucer and 37 to Shakespeare.[4] It may be the vagaries of individual contributors, but the tendency is clear.

This is found in other recent literary histories as well, and it is at least partly a result of the growing interest in the "new" literatures, which are mostly a twentieth-century phenomenon and have influenced our shrinking of the English past, on cultural as well as political grounds. Each of us may be guilty of having played along with the trend, but it causes a distinct loss. While fully approving the widening of perspectives and scholarly pursuits, one should at least insist on a principle of reciprocity. Without begging the question: while fully agreeing with a multi-ethnic approach, one should wish or expect it to be multi-ethnic *in toto*, and not *solo*-ethnic: it should consider *our* ethos as well as *our* mythos, along with the rest. Our Western literary traditions, too, were a form of nation-building and ethnogenesis; they were certainly constructed as such in the nineteenth century, and, much as we may shy away from some of their implications (notably the imperialistic tendency), they should be studied, critically and with a new awareness, for what they are and what they meant for us. No part of literature should be studied at the expense of others. Reading and teaching in a global perspective, Great Britain can be no longer central; every place is central (including, then, Great Britain), and should be studied as such – if there is matter for study.

---

[4] *Storia della civiltà letteraria inglese*, ed. Franco Marenco (Turin: UTET, 1996), 4 vols. (the fourth volume is devoted to a "Dictionary of Authors" and a "Chronology").

III

As for the other, crucial contemporary "innovations," I must proceed selectively on a few major points. Deconstruction has reached such a point, it seems to me, that it has begun to deconstruct itself (as was to be expected: one can retort that critics do not really mean what they write in their texts – they really mean quite the opposite). The substitution of class, race and gender criteria for aesthetic or literary criteria is also ominous in its consequences, and not really viable in its application, despite well-meaning efforts.[5] The New Historicism has brought to light an incredible amount of useful *background* material, but at the risk of de-historicising its greatest asset – personal, individual authors, women and men.[6] I will consider these three main trends together, in order to provide some common answers to the danger they represent.

First, it seems to me that their farthest reaches – and there seems to be no end to them – have had an undeniable, pernicious effect: a split, a severe split, a widening gap, between the academics and the intellectuals, on one side, and the common, reading public, on the other. This may have been there from the beginning, certainly since Stendhal, Flaubert, the Pre-Raphaelites and the *fin-de-siècle* Decadents declared their secession from and against the philistine bourgeois and the institutions of learning: they were all *maudits*. But it was precisely the tradition of English literature to bridge that gap as much as possible, to work between the two sides. Mario Praz comes to mind, who wrote endlessly for daily papers and magazines; intellectuals like, say, Lionel Trilling or Philip Rahv, and numberless others of the previous generations, were active on either side, mediating between the academy and the world of literature at large.

Most of us since the 1950s kept a foothold in papers and magazines, as well as, in some cases, publishing houses: academic discoveries overflowed into the "market." It was only in a limited way an exercise of power; it was an exchange and a dissemination of views, which were constantly exposed to the test of a more general audience. I still believe – and this is the continuation I wish to reinstate – that we should, even in English studies, try to prove or to become "common readers." I do not know whether, or to what extent, with diversity and the multiversity on the one hand, and the spread of the Internet and the global market on

---

[5] The best example here is provided by the *Cambridge History of American Literature*, ed. Sacvan Bercovitch (Cambridge: Cambridge University Press, 1994–). Bibliography, some titles.

[6] I have no great quarrel with Stephen Greenblatt's major contributions – rather, with texts such as *Redrawing the Boundaries: The Transformation of English and American Literary Studies*, ed. Stephen Greenblatt and Giles Gunn (New York: Modern Language Association of America, 1992). The bibliography on this, and related matters, is boundless.

the other, this will still be possible; certainly some of us are asked to review "online," and I believe we should accept the challenge. After the split with the general audience, ways of communication should be reopened between academia and the rest of the world: the isolation of the former, as I perceive it, is just as bad as the drifting away from it of the latter.

Second: class, gender and race criteria are useful and should be applied in order to make us aware and appreciative of otherwise neglected or excluded authors. Race seems to me to be of greater relevance, and to harbour more possibilities, than the other two criteria. Black writers who were previously barred from the canon now find a suitable place in it, provided (one is compelled to repeat truisms) they are not simply read and studied as such, as providing a racial consciousness or *ethos* only, but are seen and studied in the wider context of other writers and issues, writers and issues of other races as well. This was the stance taken by Ralph Ellison, and should be honoured as such. Among other things, a principle which should not be renounced is that literature is by definition not reassuring, but disturbing; it does not contribute to our well-being and our self-assurance but, rather, the reverse – it questions and disconcerts our beliefs, in whatever area or race it exercises its function.

Gender criticism is fruitful in highlighting issues relating to women writers and readers; yet Virginia Woolf was recognised in any case as an outstanding writer even prior to the new consciousness, and so, though in a less spectacular way, was Kate Chopin. One criterion can work, after all, against the other: let us not forget that for a long time, especially in the 1940s and 1950s, Woolf was resented and neglected for being snobbish and elitist, highbrow and objectionable on class grounds. Few traces of these allegations are now perceivable, which is all to the good. This is one reason why I am less at ease with class, possibly because one had to suffer so much in those years from limited and constrictive forms of such criticism. Without wishing to sound flippant, finding Gramsci as a tutelary spirit of so much criticism of this kind today has to me a strong flavour of *déjà vu* (the fault may be mine).

The New Historicism is a more serious and challenging matter. Results seem tangible and important here, and lines of investigation very worth pursuing. It is the epigones, as usual, who mar the validity of their masters, by trivialising matters in disseminating a good deal of nonsense.

IV

All these tendencies or schools openly claim, or run the risk of fostering to various degrees, the death of the author (of the individual author) and, above all, of all forms of value-judgement, literary and otherwise. Here is our challenge for the future, here is where the destiny of our successors (if not our own destiny) will be decided.

Both ideas – the death of the author and the denial of value-judgements – go against all our everyday experiences with writers of any kind, race, gender, class, who are the providers of our food, the suppliers of our needs, without whom we would not exist professionally and otherwise. This is why I have insisted so much on the need to keep communication open with the world of letters, the market, the reading public at large. Any writer, working alone or in complicity with others to write his or her book (no matter what book), when encountered in panels, conferences, papers, on TV, in cafés or on the street, is invariably adamant that he or she is the sole author and proprietor of that book.

Proof lies in the fact that the writer rightly refuses, or considers suspect, every national or racial classification, any attempt to be grouped together with other writers, to be considered in a movement or trend (he or she may do so for very limited, practical purposes of self-promotion). Even a limited experience with, say, Canadian, Australian, Indian, Irish, British, black and women writers, confirms this point. Any writer of any standing, from whatever part of the globe – Sierra Leone, Nigeria, Zimbabwe – wants to be read and recognised, judged and esteemed, on the world stage, not in the village square (much as they may enjoy their neighbourhood). We should pay them this sign of recognition, this tribute to their individual efforts and qualities.

To put it in another way: it is not our time that "negotiates" their books; they negotiate their personal experience into their books, and all other considerations vanish into the background before this strongly asserted, hard-won awareness. If we were to listen more to writers – living and dead – and less to our theories, we would deflate the latter and not the writers themselves. Despite all necessary and unavoidable negations with his time and culture (which we do well to study), it was Shakespeare who wrote the plays – much as the conditions of English society and of his stage may have contributed to making them what they are, fluid and unstable, for sure, open to endless manipulations, but so overwhelmingly meaningful.

Here, with writers such as Shakespeare, or of any kind, some possible indications for the next millennium begin to loom large. We should go back to authors, I believe, stay with them as much as possible, not be afraid or suspicious of their existence. Despite, or even thanks to all that has happened to English literature and English studies, we should move fearlessly and unequivocally in what Dante, I think, called *ambages*, not by all means "new critical" ambiguities, but etymologically: *in ambas agi partes*.

It is precisely in the interplay of canonical, established, classic writers (and the great ones will keep reappearing in all contexts) with the new awareness of global diffusion, new geographical, gender-based and racial areas of inquiry, that the challenge lies, just as much as the authors of the second group, newer, not necessarily canonical writers, have everything to gain from daily confrontation, scholarly and academic, with those of the first group. Philology, which did so much to establish and make viable the first, can be a tool to be applied to the second for purposes of empowerment and clarification. I believe that medieval writers, Chaucer, Shakespeare and Milton, the Romantics,[7] have already profited and are profiting from this two-way traffic on our stage; it is to their advantage if African or Native American writers are made to perform, and are evaluated, on that same stage. How can one study V.S. Naipaul and Soyinka without projecting them from the first group of writers – the traditional ones, those they openly recognise as masters?

T.S. Eliot once wrote that the greatness of a writer is never determined by purely literary criteria, but whether one is a writer or not can be ascertained only by applying literary criteria.[8] Unless we do so, the appreciation of the writers I just mentioned by way of example will be diminished and discredited; they deserve consideration in the company they keep. We know we are now working in a global perspective, that Great Britain is no longer the centre of things (we learned

---

[7] I could cite here an imposing series of medieval texts being translated into Italian: William Langland, *Pietro l'aratore* (Cinisello Balsamo: San Paolo, 1994); Geoffrey Chaucer, *I racconti di Canterbury* (Milan: Leonardo, 1990) and *Opere* (Turin: Einaudi, 2000), 2 vols.; dozens of individual Anglo-Saxon and British texts (from *The Battle of Maldon* to Henryson, from *Sir Orfeo* to Laȝamon, from *Pearl* to Walter Map, and so on) in the bilingual series "Biblioteca medievale," at first published by Pratiche Editrice (Parma), then by Luini Editrice (Milan–Trento), and now in its seventy-eighth volume. *Sir Gawain and the Green Knight* is available in three translations. As for Shakespeare, two new, complete translations by various translators (with facing English text) were finished by 2000, *Teatro completo*, ed. Giorgio Melchiori (Milan: Mondadori, 1978–1991), 9 vols., and *Tutto Shakespeare*, ed. Nemi D'Agostino and Sergio Perosa (Milan: Garzanti, 1980–2000), 40 vols.; Agostino Lombardo is completing his translation of the tragedies (Milan: Feltrinelli) and histories (Rome: Newton Compton); individual titles are also available elsewhere in new translations.

[8] T.S. Eliot, "Religion and Literature," *Selected Essays* (London: Faber & Faber, 1958) 388: "The 'greatness' of literature cannot be determined solely by literary standards; though we must remember that whether it is literature or not can be determined only by literary standards."

that in Italy, for sure, and IAUPE, being by constitution international, knew that all the time, even when disguising it). We know that every place is now central, and we cannot proceed into the third millennium except along those lines, provided, I insist, we satisfy ourselves that there is something to work with and appreciate in those other centres, to practice with *in ambas partes*.

V

I have used the words "valuation" and "appreciation," and in my conclusion I must face the question that all practitioners in literature (let alone professors of English) must face, despite all vociferous disclaimers: the question of value-judgements. Anyone who has taught Shakespeare or *The Great Gatsby* (I yoke them together advisedly) in the classroom knows how easy it is (yes, easy) to show the reasons why both are so widely read and "canonical": there is a wealth of suggestions and possibilities – of possible applications to different times and places, of opposing views and allurements, of contrasting interpretations – to make them palatable to and debatable by almost any audience. There is, in old terms, a *structured complexity* in them, or (if preferable) a system of issues and options *en disponibilité*, that makes them puzzling and appealing to most; there is a "carry-over power" in them (I believe the term is James T. Farrell's) whereby, while centuries and decades change, they have holding power.

In more technical or academic terms, we must still ask what gives them holding power and makes them appealing. At a recent small conference on value-judgements in literature, well-organised by the Associazione Malatesta in Sant'Arcangelo di Romagna near Rimini, far from the seat and centre of empire, the issue was faced with commitment and common sense.[9] Two things emerged. Intellectuals – including professors of English – are still torn internally by a double allegiance to the principle of authority and the widening democratisation of culture. Who is to decide what to read and what to teach? The answer that forcefully emerged was, both: *in ambas agi partes*, in either conflict or convergence, but both.

Unless intellectuals – and professors of English – propose a certain hard-won, painstakingly achieved indication of authority, whereby students and readers are advised, induced, led (or, indeed, made to) read and study Chaucer and Shakespeare and the like, we have forgone our task and surrendered. Otherwise, what follows is something like Federico Fellini's short film *Orchestra*: one cannot per-

[9] The Proceedings of the conference are published in *Il giudizio di valore e il canone letterario*, ed. Loretta Innocenti (Rome: Bulzoni, 2000).

form unless someone is in charge. This is not being anti-democratic and elitist, but functional. If you are a soccer coach and a promising player can kick very well with his left foot, it is part of your task to teach him to play with his right foot as well. We should do no less with our students: making them read Samuel Johnson if they are naturally inclined to and conversant in feminism on their own; spurring them on to read André Brink if they are philologically inclined and dream of medieval texts only.... It will not create a balance, but provide a broader perspective in each case.

As for the charge of being anti-democratic or elitist, it has been observed that postmodernism and deconstruction are indeed much more elitist and compulsive in their non-admittance (not to say exclusion) of the wider public and the common reader, while political correctness can be just as constrictive and thwarting as earlier forms of cultural and ideological control. "The category of *politically correct* can be seen as a typical characteristic of [...a] tendency whereby a scientific community, no longer believing in traditional criteria of inner hierarchisation, replaces them with new ones that are derived from heteronymous fields and criteria, among which commercialism is bound to be prominent," as one conference contributor wrote.[10] Cultural studies do receive their qualifications from outside, rather than inside, the path of literature, and expose it to a preordained massification and to a blurring of boundaries.

Boundaries, no matter how you redraw them or break them down, reappear in different forms, and are re-erected every time you touch them: they can only be moved, or shaped differently. This cannot be done by mass culture, by class, race or gender concerns alone. It must be done (indeed, is done) by a process of choice in which the two principles – intellectual authority and new democratic perspectives – are at work (and, in deciding what is *literature*, we should keep at least some literary principles in the foreground).

Choice is a crucial word: it cannot be made either by a purely democratic "good for all" or by authoritarian dictum, but by a negotiation between the two. I may be culturally interested in Conan Doyle, but reading Shakespeare is a much greater, more involving, emotional, mental and active experience of engagement and disconcertment, passion and awe. The totality of our soul, mind, experience, is at play: why settle for less? Even on the purely intellectual level, writing allows for a greater value of discussion than any other form, even for social or political

---

[10] Franco Marenco, "Mike, il professore, e lo scrittore maledetto," *Il giudizio di valore e il canone letterario*, ed. Innocenti 27–44 (38).

purposes.[11] Innovation should not prevent us from insisting that literary and intellectual choices are very much part of our task, and we should not shy away from it: anyone who was ever involved in devising a syllabus knows it well – which brings me back to our need for action in, and not seclusion from, society, in touch with the wider audience, with the reading public and the media.

This was the second point to emerge from our conference. If you deal, however marginally, with daily papers or, say, publishers, you perceive immediately that the question of choice arises and must be faced at every point. There the real "negotiation" takes place. The paper will want readers for your article; the publisher, for the book you advised them to publish; the theatre will need spectators for the play you urged them to stage. Whether we like it or not, when devising one syllabus rather than another, editing one anthology rather than a different one, appearing on a panel discussion rather than staying at home, we are acting in the market. If this is a fact of life, our aesthetic choices had better be stronger than weaker, responsible rather than complaisant, obliging, loose. In this case, as a contributor who is a publisher's editor wisely maintained, using a *frase celebre*, making literary value-judgements is giving *surplus value* to all other considerations and values involved.[12]

This is what happens when I advise reading and/or staging a play by Shakespeare rather than a minor Elizabethan play – *Cambyses*, say, or *The Witch of Edmonton* (much as cultural scholars may find them equivalent for their purposes) – or when I advise the publication of Woolf's *To the Lighthouse*, rather than a contemporary novel: the first will sell, as well as read, better. It is my contention that literary studies, when pursued and implemented according to literary (and not other) criteria, can beat cultural studies or similarly fashionable forms of academic endeavour at their own game.

I believe, with Tomasi di Lampedusa, that one can dismantle a clock and reassemble it, but it is of no avail unless we are able to read the hour; with Baudelaire (*la morale du joujou*), that the value of a toy is proportional to its durability in the hands of the child bent on dismantling or destroying it while looking for its soul.[13] Should not we believe the same of literary works, and of our critical and scholarly work, well into the third millennium?

---

[11] Marenco 43.

[12] Ernesto Franco, "Il 'giudizio di plusvalore': Selezione e riproducibilità," *Il giudizio di valore e il canone letterario*, ed. Innocenti 89–99. See fn 8 above, for T.S. Eliot's related view.

[13] See Giuseppe Tomasi di Lampedusa, *Opere* (Milan: Mondatori, 1995) 1796, and Charles Baudelaire, "La Morale du joujou," *Oeuvres complètes*, ed. Le Dantec (Paris: Gallimard, 1950) vol. 2, 687.

Literature is still a feast of language, leading us into unknown territory, raising doubts and creating disconcertment in the face of dead-pan assurances, playing with invention and discovery. In order to make all this appreciable, one might go back to my opening explanation of the appeal English literature had for us when we first discovered it. Empiricism, common sense, the idea of the "common reader" – all seem to be viable applications that can save the study and, again, the appreciation of literature in the world.[14] Hard-line intellectuals and professors of English may find it hard to accept, dismissing it as "old-time" and objectionable: where is the empowerment, they will ask? Precisely here: this is what will save us as intellectuals, and English as a discipline, from the stifling embrace of theories and cultural dicta. It is a tradition in which we should continue.

---

[14] See Antoine Compagnon, *Le démon de la théorie. Littérature et sens commun* (Paris: Editions du Seuil, 1998) esp. section vii.

Communication:
A Counterbalance to Professional Specialisation

ROGER D. SELL

I

I SUPPOSE THAT MOST OF US still love the work we do as English scholars. Or, if "love" is a little too strong for some of us, perhaps we could at least say that we share a kind of curiosity or concern that is not self-interested. Certainly the professional service we provide is less directly utilitarian and marketable than that of, say, lawyers or doctors. Through our teaching and publications, we merely pass on our knowledge and understanding to other people. Obviously we would like to think that our efforts make the world a better place. But unless we happen to be cashing in on the EFL bonanza, most of us are not paid for directly applying our wisdom as a means to some specific end.

Yet, by the mid-twentieth century, to be an English scholar really was to belong to a profession, and one that involved particular kinds of role in colleges and universities. Scholarship as the pursuit of amateurs was increasingly a thing of the past. By the same token, academic life was becoming a promising site for ambition and the exercise of power. English scholars may be very poorly paid in comparison with business people, and have little say in how the world is run. But as with mountains, so with professional career ladders: some people are going to get a buzz from climbing.

The status of individual professionals is bound up with that of their profession as a whole. In the jargon of sociologists, professionalism is "an occupational strategy which is chiefly directed towards the achievement of upward collective social mobility and, once achieved, it is concerned with the maintenance of superior remuneration and status."[1] George Bernard Shaw was less long-winded. All

[1] Noel Parry and Jose Parry, *The Rise of the Medical Profession: A Study of Collective Social Mobility* (London: Croom Helm, 1976) 79.

professions, he said, are "conspiracies against the laity."[2] Throughout the ages, professionals have been satirised for snapping up pretty pickings, for living off other people's need, for amassing power into monopolistic systems of market control, and for using their mystifying or pompous jargon to reinforce their privilege and prestige.

English scholars will not want to be cynical about their own profession. Nor need they be, I think. Professionalisation has not only led to improved conditions of employment. It has also been inseparable from intensely focused research activity, formidably backed up with new editions of texts, bibliographies, journals, associations, networks and conferences. Many professional benefits are channelled through the major regional organisations such as the MLA and ESSE, bodies which promote an exhilarating *esprit de corps*, resulting in lots of very productive hustle and bustle. I dare say my own enthusiasm at the 1991 launch of ESSE was fairly typical in actually being rather altruistic. As head of a department, I welcomed what I could easily see would be an opportunity for younger colleagues to make contacts and get feedback on their work from a broad audience. And knowing, as I did, the conditions under which English scholars were working in countries behind what had been the Iron Curtain, I also saw ESSE as a way of channelling both spiritual and more practical support in that direction.

Professional consolidation does mean a great deal more than just badgering non-professionals into handing over fees, exclusive rights and royal charters. Nor is it as if professionals escape scrutiny. For one thing, any profession will have its own internal methods of self-regulation – various practices by which individual members are screened, certified, patronised, promoted and, if necessary, disciplined. So although being a professional may still occasionally carry an aura of gentility, it is actually no sinecure. A profession's "upward collective social mobility" is partly predicated on its individual members' behaviour and achievements within the profession's own arena. For another thing, as a collective the profession will have a very real concern for public relations. Its privilege and prestige will in the long run be unsustainable unless ordinary people recognise its professional legitimacy, which, at least nowadays, is very much a matter of learned credentials. The professional jargon really does have to be grounded in a body of specialist knowledge which is perceived as valuable.

All the same, a profession's internal self-regulation and the perceptions of the legitimating public can certainly get out of step. For instance, the profession's

---

[2] Shaw, *The Doctor's Dilemma, Getting Married, & The Shewing-up of Blanco Posnet* (London: Constable, 1921) xxii.

career structure may strike an outside observer as unnecessarily hierarchical. Even within the profession, individuals may wonder about this, for the spirit of collegial solidarity can actually be tempered with an element of competitive rivalry that is just as unrelenting as the profession's territorial vigilance within society at large, in which case climbing the ladder can indeed become too much of an end in itself. No less typically, the profession's cultivation of specialist knowledge, and therefore of jargon, can also come to seem excessive, perhaps with a host of sub- and sub-sub-specialisations whose refinements the general public does not immediately appreciate.

Such situations amount to nothing less than a crisis. If the profession is to prevail, it will have to convince the public that its professional practices are sensible, or make concessions to public criticism. Or, more likely still, it will have to do a bit of both. For English scholars, such a crisis would be especially delicate, precisely because the professional service they offer is not directly utilitarian in the first place.

Nor need a crisis be so very far away. Many English scholars I have spoken to say that competitiveness within the profession has become too fierce, and to the detriment of scholarly interchange. Some of the criticism focuses on the MLA, whose large conferences allow a lot of professional going-through-the-motions with, at worst, too many short presentations, rapidly delivered and little discussed except in terms of instant-reflex attack and defence. At such gatherings, some participants do clearly feel an obligation to shine, and to be seen to quell adversaries. Senior figures aspiring to the status of guru may just fly in and out for their own plenary lecture, sharing hardly a word of conversation, while many junior participants will be hoping to improve their prospects lower down, a goal they may realise by submitting themselves to the batteries of job interviews that run in parallel with the conference proper. So strong is the ethos of professional advancement here that young scholars actually sacrifice their Christmas holiday for it, and the time that Christmas might allow them with their families.

Of the great organisation which gives us, say, the MLA Bibliography, it would be simply irrelevant to complain that it discourages scholars from behaving like well-rounded human beings. Its first priority is professional consolidation. So, as a matter of fact, it does not give us its Bibliography. It cool-headedly sells it, for as high a price as it can get, to our university libraries, and the proceeds are ploughed back into further empire-building, from which all the profession's members in theory benefit.

But if a majority of English scholars were not well-rounded human beings, the profession would have a serious problem. Even if we shall nowadays hasten to add that well-rounded human beings are not cast in just some single mould, from the profession's point of view well-roundedness should include at least one *sine qua non*: an aptitude for the kind of communication that is needed if the specialisations of professional learning are to be legitimated.

In conversation, many English scholars now underline this point with a reference to the late-twentieth-century interest in structuralism and poststructuralism. At first it looked as if these developments might bring experts on different literary authors and periods together around a common theoretical concern, and this concern was itself said to be the result of a cross-fertilisation of literary thought with linguistic theory. But, today, a fairly widespread assessment seems to be that Theory (as it came to be written) soon ended up as one of the most prohibitively jargon-ridden enclaves of all.

As for publishing in the field of English studies more generally, many colleagues comment on a very marked limitation of activity to three main categories: specialist books genuinely intended for specialists; specialist work merely published in order to avoid perishing, and hardly read by anyone at all; and coursebooks, which talk down to students, who within new-liberal economies are in any case just customers. Publications directed to the interests of the general educated reader have become more unusual.

If professionalism is beginning to cut off the branch on which it will always have to sit, research assessment exercises are hardly going to bring scholars to their senses. Very properly, the powers-that-be have wanted to ensure that the profession is not using public monies against the public interest. But a conspiracy against the laity is actually condoned by the very criteria of assessment. In one case I know of, the head of a literature department – not English literature, as it happens, but it could easily have been – was criticised by the peer reviewers because her own most recent publication was, in effect, too readable: a book about adultery, both in real life and as a motif in the literature of several different countries. In her own part of the world, this stimulated a great deal of public discussion, and doubtless opened up literary texts to many new readers. But, by professionalist and assessment standards alike, it was not nearly specialist enough.

II

But if, socially speaking, the professionalisation of English studies was the biggest twentieth-century innovation, then the most important continuity with the past was the amateur scholar's keenness for genuine and shared enquiry. This, I am suggesting, is still with us today, even though it can take different forms in different academic cultures. In Finland, the clearest example is the institution of the public doctoral defence. In a long and well-mannered conversation, a doctoral candidate and an external examiner will compare notes about whatever it is they are experts on, and at the same time will explain and, yes, legitimate their interests to a wider circle.

For English studies internationally, the most notable embodiment of this same spirit must surely be IAUPE. To outsiders, however, IAUPE's distinctive character is not always clear. At the bureau meetings of UNESCO's *Fédération Internationale des Langues et Littératures Modernes* (FILLM), IAUPE is sometimes the butt of friendly jibes, along the lines of "Well, if people want to belong to an elitist club, ..." Even some professors of English are sarcastic at IAUPE's expense, sometimes acerbically so. Shortly before my own first IAUPE conference, the one in Lausanne in 1989, I heard from two colleagues, one with a Swiss background, the other with a British, that they would not be participating. IAUPE, they said, was not their pint of beer. It was too genteel, too Oxbridge, too Ivy League, with too few women, and too many old buffers.

True, of the eighteen associations currently affiliated with FILLM, IAUPE is the only one for which membership is restricted to professors or scholars of equivalent competence, the seventeen others being open to scholars on any rung of the career ladder. But if IAUPE does represent an elite, then it is a meritocratic one. Citizens of all free societies can reasonably aspire to membership, under conditions of equal opportunity and with no fear of exclusion except by scholarly criteria. If it were otherwise, IAUPE would not actually have been eligible for affiliation under the terms of FILLM's own constitution.

True, IAUPE gatherings do attract a fair number of emeriti. But they are not old buffers. Relieved from the cares of office, their intellect is usually very sprightly. As for the charge of racist, class and gender prejudice, this may have been warranted in the past, but is nowadays just a travesty. At Durham in 1998, there was a plenary discussion of how best to guarantee that the association really does draw in accomplished scholars from many different backgrounds.

What the sarcasm quite overlooks is that a membership made up of scholars who have already clambered to the top of the ladder entails a huge communicational bonus, in that they can only experience each other as equals. Simply taking high standards of scholarly excellence for granted, they feel little need to shine or to be seen to quell adversaries, and can afford to remain sufficiently unegotistical to be really interested in what other members are thinking and doing. Far from having to leave their families at home during the Christmas holiday, moreover, many participants in IAUPE conferences take family members with them, for what can itself be a delightful holiday in summery weather and pleasant surroundings. It is precisely through such suspensions of the normal pressures of career and everyday work that IAUPE is able to foster a kind of epicurean disinterestedness. I do not mean that participants in a IAUPE conference completely forget their involvement in real worlds of action and ideology. The point is, rather, that, if their involvement happened to come up for discussion, they would probably be very honest about it, and very happy to consider anybody else's involvement as well. This is the dispassionateness which human beings can rise to in moments of contentment, when they are under no obligation to do this or that or really anything at all, and when they feel totally unthreatened, seeing their companions as peers whose intelligence and human decency are above suspicion, and whose attitudes and opinions a simplistic Manichaeism of "right-thinking" and "wrong-headed" could never pigeonhole. A IAUPE conference, with its rhythm of the two or three carefully probing scholarly sessions in the morning, followed for the remainder of the day by excursions, entertainments and general conviviality in the society of colleagues and accompanying persons, is a leisurely banquet of the mind and senses, than which nothing is more likely to encourage new ideas and frank discussions free of animus. Especially if members can carry something of this same ethos back to their own departments, and into other scholarly fora as well, the counterbalance to professional competitiveness and specialisation will be very real.

When we are caught up in such a spirit of genuine, shared enquiry, how, in fact, shall we tend to place some particular professional specialisation in relation to all the others? Well, the two most common types of answer to the question "What is English studies?" have been the purist and the eclectic. The extreme purist answer, which makes a very strong weapon in profession-internal power disputes, is that English is a single subject of study which, at most, can be mapped out into different areas, of which some will in any case be more central than others, and one the most central of all. Sometimes this most central area is also said to be the most ancient. Sometimes it is said to be some new area which makes an older central area seem less important. And what is regarded as old and new partly depends on the particular local tradition within which the contest is taking place, and on the particular phase of that tradition's history. The extreme eclectic answer, by contrast, which is a bit difficult to explain to the holders of purse-strings or to a tidy-minded student, is that English has ended up by historical accident as a conglomeration of three fundamentally different subjects of study, language, literature, and culture, each of which is itself approached in many different ways. According to this view, there is no common denominator except that all discussion in English departments is somehow or other related to the English language – or languages!

But there is also a *tertium quid* kind of answer, for which the editors of the present volume have already opted in their invitation to contributors. In suggesting that we write something about our own specialisations and interests, they refer to these as our "sub-disciplines." The beauty of this compromise is that it suggests a unity, but a unity made up of parts that are not hierarchically arranged – a kind of loosely coherent plurality, in other words, which will encourage scholars both to do their own thing and to talk to each other.

If our professional competitiveness gets out of hand, it affects not only the profession's personnel but the types of knowledge and insight they stand for, too. This means that, at any given time, any given specialisation will be perceived as either winning or losing. The spirit of genuine, shared enquiry, by contrast, is not the slightest bit interested in league tables, and is hospitable to specialisations of every kind, quite regardless of whether they are very ancient and rare, currently very popular, or very new and strange. Everything is open to a free and fair discussion, in which scholar X and scholar Y do not concentrate on establishing one of them as right and one as wrong, because they are much too keen to discuss phenomenon Z as seen from their different angles. Each wants to try on the other's perceptions and interpretations for size, as it were, as the most likely way to discover some shortcomings or further consequences of their own approach to date. What they both realise is that after a genuine dialogue the world never looks quite the same.

But if the counterbalance to professionalism is to remain effective, such open-minded conversations may need to be positively facilitated. One important task for IAUPE, it seems to me, would be to encourage exactly those kinds of scholarly venture that an excessive professionalism leaves to one side: the book or the journal or the research project which seeks to relate a specialisation to something other than itself – most obviously to other specialisations within English studies, but also, perhaps, to other things as well. By definition, this is the type of undertaking which would bring English scholars themselves into communication, and which would also reach out to interested non-specialists who, in a sense, can never bring themselves into being unless we write for them. At the same time,

IAUPE would be recognising something which no merely regional organisation can ever emphasise quite so clearly: that English studies come, and must inevitably come, in many shapes and forms. This in turn would be a way to help the profession distance itself from the bitterness of some earlier disputes.

So how, in practice, might such constructive moves begin? Would it be helpful, for example, to enter into them with the explicit goal of eventually fusing all the various specialisations into some new and single subject which truly could go under the name of English? – a discipline with no subdisciplines, as it were. No, clearly not. This would be quite contrary to the spirit of genuine, shared enquiry. Free discussion really must be free, with no holds barred.

On the other hand, there are certainly perspectives within which it is possible to view a number of different specialisations simultaneously. Two examples with which many English departments are already familiar are feminist approaches and area studies (American, Canadian, British ...). Both of these have very much increased the range of interests shared among a variety of experts on language, literature and culture. In this, they can be seen as giving substance to a model of English studies as a loosely coherent unity of unranked parts. At the same time, they are also very helpful to non-specialists who have the intellectual curiosity to wonder about larger bearings. Feminist approaches and area studies have already begun to draw English scholars into what amounts to professional legitimation by genuine communication.

Perhaps IAUPE could be on the alert for new perspectives of this same sort. In this case, one of the most promising candidates, it seems to me, would be human communication itself. With this in mind, I have already begun to describe IAUPE's own amateuristic spirit of shared enquiry as communication of a very specific kind. I have also hinted that under the pressure of extreme professionalism communication can turn out very differently, and may even become a kind of pseudo-communication. As a next step, I can perhaps make a few general ideas about communication more explicit.[3]

---

[3] For a fuller account, see Roger D. Sell, *Literature as Communication: The Foundations of Mediating Criticism* (Pragmatics and Beyond, New Series 78; Amsterdam: John Benjamins, 2000), and "A Historical but Non-Determinist Pragmatics of Literary Communication," *Journal of Historical Pragmatics* 2 (2001): 1–32.

III

As a first premise I will take a very traditional one, which in the twentieth century received a new lease on life from work in the field of philosophical hermeneutics. As emphasised by Hans–Georg Gadamer, a situation in which communication is genuinely taking place is triangular. Two parties communicate about some third entity, as when IAUPE member X and IAUPE member Y discuss phenomenon Z from their different points of view.

The basic situation can still be thought of in this way even when the two parties are the two halves of one and the same self-communing individual, as when we talk to ourselves or write a diary, and even when the third entity also includes one or both of the communicating parties, who in that case speak of "me" or "you" or "us." Equally well, the third entity can be somebody or something quite unconnected with the communicants themselves, and can actually involve an element of hypotheticality or even outright fiction. This is the case with many jokes about celebrities, and with most of the texts we label as literary.

Regardless of the precise way in which the communicational triangle happens to be realised, genuine communication can be seen as a form of interpersonal activity, which may bring about a change in the status quo. Changes in the status quo begin as a change in the communicants' perceptions and evaluations of the real, hypothetical or fictional entity under discussion. Communication is a semiotic process by which people try, at least ideally speaking, to negotiate a balanced and even shared view of that entity. In doing so, they inevitably open themselves to the possibility of mental re-adjustments, whose scope can range from the merely very minimal to the absolutely all-embracing. This means that communication is, in point of fact, inseparable from the processes of human growth and individuation. The otherness of some of the people with whom we communicate will turn out to be a significant otherness for us. Directly or indirectly, what happens may eventually even contribute to changes in an entire communal world, and may also lead to any number of different courses of action.

But even if Professor X finally influences Professor Y a good deal more than Professor Y influences Professor X, the prerequisite for genuine communication is an acceptance by both parties of interactional parity: a mutual respect which recognises that influence could just as easily have flowed the other way, or could have been perfectly reciprocal. This is a factor which descriptions of communication in terms of the binarisms sender/receiver, speaker/hearer, writer/ reader or narrator/narratee can underestimate. They all too easily prioritise the binarisms' first terms as agentive, thereby associating the second terms with a kind of passivity after the event. By emphasising, by contrast, the triangulation of the two communicants with a third, negotiated entity, we also recognise that, if communication is really to take place at all, then receivers, hearers, readers or narratees are at least as important as senders, speakers, writers or narrators. Granted, they may not actually say or write anything. There may not even be a feedback channel for them. But the ways of responding are by no means restricted to an explicit use of language. And, vice versa, the sender, speaker, writer or narrator need not be physically present or even alive. Instead, such agents' words may be preserved in some form of legible or audible record. Even at its strongest, the role of initiating participants can never be more decisive for how the communication actually turns out than the role of those who respond. So, as at a IAUPE conference, conditions promoting a sense of human equality will always be invaluable as a safeguard of communicational standards.

Even under optimal conditions, the role of both initiating and responding can admittedly be performed with either greater or lesser success. The plain fact is that words can be taken in a very different way by one party from that intended by another. To the extent that such discrepancies are not wilful, they derive from differences of evaluation and contextual understanding. A use of words emanating from one particular conjuncture of sociocultural history and circumstance, when processed by somebody representing some different conjuncture, may offer a considerable challenge. It may well presuppose linguistic knowledge, more general knowledge, plus various kinds of attitudinal overtones which, at the second conjuncture, cannot be taken for granted. On the contrary, many other items of knowledge, and some very different evaluative and attitudinal stances, may be far more readily accessible there. When Professors X and Y meet each other at a IAUPE conference, this may well be a convergence from opposite sides of the planet. Although they both have a professional interest in English, the difference between them will be more than a matter of their scholarly specialisations. Their normal everyday worlds may be very different as well, and this may easily affect the nature of their interest in English.

Even two communicants whose everyday worlds seem at first glance to be one and the same do not come to an act of communication with exactly the same knowledge and attitudes. The current context of responding is always different from the context of initiating, quite regardless of whether the separating distance be one of whole centuries or wide oceans, or of only the very slightest shades of collocated awareness. Helen Gardner and John Carey both had a British background and were both trained at Oxford, where they both became leading experts on seventeenth-century English literature, and where Carey actually succeeded Gardner to the Merton Chair. But this does not stop him from approaching John Donne from a rather different starting point. Whereas Gardner finds it so "difficult to imagine ... [Donne] wishing to assume the love-sickness of Lesbian Sappho" that she questioned his authorship of "Sappho and Philaenis," even though it appeared in the first edition of his poems and in several good manuscripts, Carey finds it "only too easy" to imagine that the story of a homosexual relationship was just what Donne needed in order to convey the idea of a union of lovers so complete that "the two identities, being identical, sink into one."[1] The inevitable disparity between the preconceptions of communicants even as close as Gardner and Carey has real consequences for any interchange between them. It can actually be thought of as part of the reason they might have for communicating in the first place.

But although such facts of macro- and micro-positionality crucially affect the way people interact with each other, human nature and behaviour are not entirely determined by them. If they were, communication would never get off the ground at all. If communication between people with their differing positionalities is to stand any chance of satisfying both parties, the human imagination has to be sufficiently autonomous to project itself into modes of being and doing that are different from the ones valorised within its most immediate milieu. This is not to say that imaginative empathy will necessarily turn into sympathy. Nor can a permanent change of outlook ever be simply foisted upon people. On the contrary, the empathising sentiment so necessary to their grasp of an unfamiliar manner of thought, behaviour or feeling may well be closely accompanied by a degree of critical self-distancing. Even so, they really are possessed of a certain heuristic flexibility of mind. Mental flexibility is intimately bound up with that stance of mutual respect which is the one great communicational imperative. Freely ranging empathetic imagination is a potential which the most competitive and jargon-ridden kind of professional specialisation tends to restrict, whereas a IAUPE conference can truly bring it into play.

The power of empathy is a vital aspect of a larger human autonomy. Men and women are nothing if not social beings, but are actually social individuals. Not only are they capable of empathising with sociocultural formations different from their own, they are also endowed with qualities of temperament which may be very different from the personality types most clearly scripted within their own society, and they actually enjoy some freedom of choice. In influencing the way

[1] John Carey, *John Donne: Life, Mind and Art* (1981; London: Faber & Faber, 1990) 257.

Professor Y thinks, Professor X need not be completely unmotivated and directionless. Nor need the motivation and direction stem from some force that is beyond Professor X's own awareness and control. Professor Y's change of mind is something that Professor X can want and try to bring about. And Professor Y can just as keenly want, and try to bring about, a change of mind in Professor X. Their entertaining such hopes is in no way incompatible with either their feelings of mutual respect or their overriding interest in phenomenon Z, the third entity which they are negotiating.

Here I must qualify the more extreme forms of structuralist and poststructuralist theory, for these tended to view human beings as, in one way or another, wholly determined. To this extent, theory belied its claim to foundations in Saussurean linguistics. The seminal distortion was that of Claude Lévi–Strauss, for the purposes of his own variant of cultural anthropology. What he claimed to have shown was myths "think[ing] themselves out in the men and without men's knowledge."[2] But for Saussure, whereas language (*langue*) was not actually a function of the speaker but a product that is passively assimilated by the individual, "speech [*parole*], on the contrary, is an individual act. It is wilful and intellectual."[3] Or, as Raymond Tallis has more recently put it, no matter whether the structured system be that of language, the psyche, society or culture, human beings operate the system, and are not to be conflated with it. Without reinstating the sovereign independence of the human subject as seen in traditional liberal humanism, Tallis nevertheless asserts

> the centrality of individual consciousness, of undeceived deliberateness, in the daily life of human beings. We are not absolutely transparent to ourselves but we are not utterly opaque either; we are not totally self-present in all our actions but nor are we absent from them; we are not complete masters of our fates, shaping our lives according to our utterly unique and original wishes, but neither are we the empty playthings of historical, political, social, semiological or instinctual forces.[4]

In genuine communication, the relation between the social and the individual aspects of the self is crucial. Language users have to use the linguistic and generic resources that are available within the particular culture, and have no choice but to appeal to the structures of knowledge and evaluation that are available, too.

---

[2] Lévi–Strauss, "Overture to *Le cru et le cuit*," *Structuralism*, ed. Jacques Ehrmann (1964; Garden City, NY: Doubleday/Anchor, 1970) 31–55, esp. 46.

[3] Ferdinand de Saussure, *Course in General Linguistics* (1916; London: Collins/Fontana, 1974) 14.

[4] Raymond Tallis, *Enemies of Hope: A Critique of Contemporary Pessimism, Irrationalism, Anti-Humanism and Counter-Enlightenment* (Basingstoke: Macmillan, 1997) 228.

Otherwise, like professionals who resort to excessive jargon, they will not establish enough common ground with other people. But if common ground is the only thing they offer, they will not be communicating either, or at least not in the dynamic sense I have in mind. They would merely be leaving society as they found it, just like scholars when they publish only in order to avoid perishing. What happens in genuine communication is that communicators adapt to society in the hope that society will adapt to them. Here we can speak of a co-adaptation, then, and all successful rhetoric is co-adaptive in just this sense. As Aristotle long ago pointed out, persuasive orators try to meet their audience half-way. Professors X and Y will make as many concessions to each other as they honestly can.

But for any particular instance of communication, rhetoric is clearly specific to the particular circumstances obtaining when communication is initiated. If the communication's text is processed by people operating under circumstances very different from those originally catered to, the rhetoric will not work in anything like the same way, unless the new respondents make an effort of imaginative empathy with the respondents originally anticipated. In point of fact, this is an effort they are obliged to make, both out of a desire to know what was originally intended and also out of respect for other human beings and out of self-interest, too, in case the otherness should turn out to be significant for them. But even then, the rhetoric's effect can never be quite the same, since the new recipients will also inevitably and by human right bring to the text their own knowledge and system of values as well. Paradoxically, what was originally the social and what was originally the individual can, under the new circumstances, swap places. What was conventional within one cultural milieu can seem very strange and suggestive within some other milieu, while what seemed strange and suggestive in the first milieu may in the other milieu seem less remarkable. Beyond its original circumstances, in other words, the initiator of a communication has no control over how it will be received *in toto*. If Professor X were to publish the arguments by which he finally persuaded Professor Y, half a century further on they may no longer be quite so convincing. By that time, Professor X's point of view may have become so widespread that Professor Y's point of view now seems more interesting by its very unfamiliarity. The concessions which Professor X's rhetoric made to Professor Y may even undermine Professor X's own position. This is the communicational explanation of how ideas, or values, or approaches which become unfashionable can later be rehabilitated in some new form.

One further complexity is that the context of the third, negotiated entity will often, in the nature of things, be different from the contexts of both initation and response. In that case it will be represented as such, and the difference will be part of what is negotiated. Like the context of response, moreover, the communication-internal context can actually proliferate. With communications in narrative form, this is especially obvious; the internal context changes as the story itself moves along. But in the case of drama, internal context and its proliferation can have an even greater salience because dramatic "showing" tends to play down both the writer's context of initiation and the audience or reader's context of response. So, except when a playwright through dialogue renders different worldviews on stage, drama tends to imply that there is only a single way of assessing the events presented, and sometimes that this is an assessment arising out of the communication-internal context itself, which *ipso facto* must therefore correspond to the initiator's own judgements. Especially in this last case, the apparently self-withdrawing "showing" of dramatic presentation is actually more coercive than even the most intrusive of "tellings." To a greater or lesser extent, the text of a "telling" has to represent or imply differentiated personae and sociohistorical contexts for both the initiator and the respondent.

This suggests another way to describe the difference between a paper at a IAUPE conference and a lecture that is more fiercely professionalist and specialised. The former will be closer to a telling, the latter to a dramatic showing. It is all a question of whether or not the possibility of different viewpoints is recognised or suppressed. An ambitious professional whose lecture suppresses it is less likely to be praised for signs of thoughtfulness than for strong commitment or a charismatic performance.[5] The warmest appreciation of all might come from a theatre critic.

IV

Communication is a big topic, which is already being professionalised as an academic subject in its own right. But perhaps I have at least said enough to make two complementary features of one of the possible approaches fairly clear: a strong emphasis on the complexities and consequences of sociohistorical situa-

---

[5] The same contrast can also be described as a contrast between a rhetorical tradition that stems from continental Europe and one that is Anglo-Saxon. See Maria Isaksson–Wikberg, *Negotiated and Committed Argumentation: A Cross-Cultural Study of American and Finland–Swedish Student Writing* (Åbo: Åbo Akademi University Press, 1999). Here, though, I have not wanted to emphasise this dimension. The professionalisation of English studies is not an exclusively British and American phenomenon, even if it has been much influenced by Anglo-American rhetoric, just as European scholarly discourse up until the Second World War, and before the most recent phase of professionalisation, was strongly influenced by the Germanic tradition.

tionality; and an equally strong emphasis on the human being's imaginative, intellectual and moral capacity for communicating in spite of this, and even in such a way as to bring about both personal and social change.

Described in these terms, then, what kind of a perspective does communication offer on the research into language, literature and culture that happens to be carried out within English studies? How can it bring the different kinds of specialists into conversation, and help non-specialists to get a sense of their bearings?

By drawing attention to the situational disparity between initiators and respondents, a communicative perspective could speed up a development that I think would be very timely in English studies generally. What is needed, it seems to me, is precisely a rejection of something we might call the unitary-context assumption: the deep-rooted and usually quite unconscious assumption that a context, even at the outset of communication, can be identical for the initiator and the respondent, and sometimes for the entity under negotiation, too. Even in pragmatics, the branch of linguistics most directly concerned with the relation between language use and context of use, one tradition has tended not only to adopt this unitary-context assumption, but to define context in the narrowest possible way, in terms of the most immediate circumstances of use, together with the co-text (the text which directly precedes and follows a particular expression under examination). In the scholarly search for tight pragmatic rules, the number of variables has simply been restricted here, resulting in a behaviouristic kind of methodology which never really asks what communicants might actually mean or want to do, even less how this might tie up with social and ideological differences between them. In literary scholarship, meanwhile, New-Critical formalism tended to dehistoricise both writers and readers altogether, as did some later deconstructive criticism, while evaluative critics, both earlier and much more recent, have hardly done much better. All too often, they have simply judged the there-and-then by the standards of the here-and-now, allowing the likely judgement on the here-and-now by the there-and-then to pass quite without comment. To which the reaction of historical purists has been just as inappropriate, since they have merely gone to the opposite extreme. According to them, the significance of an instance of language use or cultural production is to be defined by, and restricted to, the exact circumstances under which it took place, so that communication between different positionalities is impossible and/or undesirable, and the current reader of an old or alien author is not entitled to a personal judgement. As for cultural studies, finally, a society's culture is still sometimes thought of as a kind of indivisible essence, with no sense of otherness on either a diachronic scale, between different periods of the same tradition, or synchronically, between what is now a whole range of positionalities within polycultural postmodernity.

And what about a communicative perspective which so strongly emphasises ethics – the role of imaginative empathy and mutual respect, the human being's relative freedom of choice, the connections between communication, human individuation and social change? The great benefit of this, it seems to me, might be to coordinate a re-humanisation of English studies that would be no less fundamental. The behaviouristic and synchronic methodology of structuralist linguistics resulted in a wealth of important information about the way a language hangs together as a formal system, but did not at all concern itself with the way languages are used in historical processes of interaction. And when, in the late-twentieth century, use and context did come into the picture, there was sometimes – for example, in critical discourse analysis – an implication that context was all-powerfully determining. In literary studies, similarly, aestheticist formalism gave way to a whole range of approaches which, pretty much in the spirit of Lévi–Strauss, saw human beings as the merely passive channels of anthropomorphised abstractions such as history, culture, society or language.[6] Nor was cultural studies far behind: when the difference between one subcultural grouping and another did get recognised, this was often regarded as an "all-the-way-down" barrier to any genuinely inter-subcultural communication.[7] Any particular grouping was seen as locked into an unabating antagonism with other groupings, involving a paranoid "rhetoric of blame"[8] to which the only alternative was a kind of token political correctness – a mere papering-over of inevitable cracks. What all these varieties of English studies have tended to overlook is that human beings do not always take the line of least resistance. Although men and women certainly are social beings, as individuals they also have the imaginative, intellectual and moral capability to resist and even improve their own immediate social milieu, not least by way of communication with some world that is "other."

Not that the human race will ever arrive at some sublime consensus. On the contrary, Heraclitus was surely right in thinking that "life, and liveliness, within the soul and within society,"[9] consists in perpetual conflicts between rival impulses and ideals, and that harmony and consensus come only with death, when human faces no longer express conflicts but are immobile, composed, and at rest.

---

[6] See Roger D. Sell, "*Henry V* and the Strength and Weakness of Words: Shakespearian Philology, Historicist Criticism, Communicative Pragmatics," *Neuphilologische Mitteilungen* 100 (1999): 535–63.

[7] Cf. J. Hillis Miller, "The University of Dissensus," *Oxford Literary Review* 17 (1995): 121–43.

[8] Edward W. Said, *Culture and Imperialism* (London: Random House/Vintage, 1993) 96.

[9] Stuart Hampshire, *Innocence and Experience* (1989; Harmondsworth: Penguin, 1992) 189.

Difference and conflict are probably inevitable, and can be the stimulus to huge creative energies.

Yet Habermas does also have a point, when he speaks of the desirability, and possibility, of living together in a disagreement that is reasonable.[10] In many spheres of human activity, reasonable disagreement is already an ancient and everyday reality, its only precondition being genuine communication. In fact, a perspective on English studies which at one and the same time strongly emphasises the facts of positionality and the human capacity for dealing with them will also suggest how both intra- and inter-cultural communication can be positively assisted by people who take upon themselves the role of mediator. By exploring the linguistics of mediation, by developing a literary criticism which can mediate between authors and readers representing differing positionalities, and by establishing a similar orientation within a wider cultural critique as well, the various types of English scholars could do much to legitimate their profession for a general public which is increasingly self-conscious about communicational problems and possibilities.

This is probably the closest English scholars will ever come to presenting their professional services as directly utilitarian. At the same time, they would doubtless be learning new ways to mediate between their own professionalism and their amateurism. There, for them at least, is one of the conflicts within which, as far as I can see, "life, and liveliness," will still have to be sustained.

---

[10] Jürgen Habermas, "Struggles for Recognition in the Democratic Constitutional State," *Multiculturalism: Examining the Politics of Recognition*, ed. Amy Gutman (Princeton, NJ: Princeton University Press, 1994) 107–48.

Does the Canon Have a Future in English Studies?

ULRICH BROICH

WHEN I STUDIED ENGLISH at the University of Bonn in the 1950s, every student was given a reading list which was called a "*Lektürekanon*" and which we were supposed to have read by the end of our course of studies. This list contained more works than even the hardest-working student was able to read during his time at the university, and yet it was taken more or less seriously because we knew that only part of the oral examination would be devoted to our individual reading list. Therefore most students tried, in between other obligations, to read as many works of the canon as possible. At that time everybody took the canon for granted.

All this has changed in the course of the last thirty years. In what follows I shall first recapitulate the developments and arguments which caused a crisis in the canon. I shall then try to assess the present situation, and finally to answer the question whether, from the present point of view, the canon has a chance of surviving, or, rather, whether anything like a canon ought to have a future in English studies.

I

The canons that existed in many English departments of the 1950s were based on a narrow conception of literature. In the decades following, a wider conception of literature prevailed and at the same time new groups of texts attracted increasing interest, in teaching as well as research. Among these groups were children's literature, travel writing, biographies, literature of ethnic minorities written in English, newspapers and political speeches, and genres like detective or science fiction which had hardly been regarded as "literature" before that time. But also "texts" of an entirely different kind assumed greater importance in English studies: on the one hand, "texts" from other media – cinema and TV – became objects of study; on the other, theoretical texts were becoming so important that they almost formed a canon of their own. In fact, what happened in English studies was an "explosion" of texts.

A number of reasons can be given for this development. There was not only an increasing number of writers in English who produced an increasing number of books, but also a rapidly growing number of English departments at universities all over the world with a growing number of scholars, many of whom turned their backs on what they thought to be "over-researched" areas of English studies and who were looking for "fresh woods and pastures new." But the real driving force behind this development was the fact that many university teachers of English questioned the criteria on which the traditional canon was based, and this caused an attack on the canon and on continuity in English studies which was probably unprecedented. Strangely enough, these "canon wars" or what Theo D'haen has called the "twentieth-century battle of the books"[1] have hardly been reflected in the rather peaceful agenda of the conferences of IAUPE.

As in so many other fields, the USA took the lead in these developments. In the 1960s there had been a growing consciousness in the USA that minorities were discriminated against and excluded from power on account of race, class and gender, and that power in society and politics was still mainly held by white males. Very soon it was realised that the traditional literary canon was part of this power structure, that it privileged White Anglo-Saxon Protestant authors, who were polemically called WASPs, and that it more or less excluded women, the lower classes and the ethnic minorities of the country. There were energetic attempts at redefining American national identity, and among the consequences of these attempts was either the demand for abolishing a canon which was said to be representative only of the male, white and upper-class tradition in American literature or the demand to open up the canon and make it representative of the growing plurality of American society. It was because of this plurality that the canon wars were much more intense in the USA than in other countries and that their prime concern was the change of the canon of classic American, not so much of British, texts.

Very soon, however, the scope of these attacks was extended and directed against the whole of what Harold Bloom was later to call the "Western Canon." When in 1971 Louis Kampf, in his presidential address to the MLA Conference,[2]

---

[1] Theo D'haen, "Working the American Canon: Reflections of a European Canon-Watcher," *Rewriting the Dream: Reflections on the Changing American Literary Canon*, ed. W.M. Verhoeven (Amsterdam and Atlanta, GA: Rodopi, 1992) 233–44 (235).

[2] Louis Kampf, " ' It's Alright, Ma (I'm Only Bleeding)': Literature and Language in the Academy," *PMLA* 87 (1972): 377–83.

demanded that the humanities contribute to a radical change in contemporary society, this demand included an attack on the whole of the Western canon.[3] Another symbolic event was, in 1988, the conflict about the "core list" of fifteen classic texts[4] in the course on "Western Civilization" which had been required reading at the until then rather traditional Stanford University. The Stanford Black Student Union lodged a complaint against this course because it was based on texts from which they felt excluded, and the battle-cry "Hey hey ho ho, Western Civ has got to go" soon resounded through the Stanford campus and all over the country, and was echoed even in Europe.[5]

But it was not only the students who called the canon into question. An enormous number of scholars intervened in this controversy, among others Leslie Fiedler and Houston Baker in *English Literature: Opening Up the Canon*,[6] Sacvan Bercovitch in "America as Canon and Context"[7] and Barbara Herrnstein Smith in *Contingencies of Value*.[8] Of course, there were also some books which defended the traditional canon, such as Allan Bloom's *The Closing of the American Mind* and E.D. Hirsch's *Cultural Literacy*,[9] but it was obvious that the majority of the teachers of English studies who took part in the canon wars were in favour of either dismantling or radically revising the canon.

---

[3] Kampf 1972.

[4] The following were the required texts in the Stanford course on Western Culture before it was abandoned: *Hebrew Bible*; Genesis; Homer, major selections from *Iliad* or *Odyssey* or both; At least one Greek tragedy; Plato, *Republic*, major portions of Books I–VII; *New Testament*, selections including a gospel; Augustine, *Confessions*, I–IX; Dante, *Inferno*; More, *Utopia*; Machiavelli, *The Prince*; Luther, *Christian Liberty*; Galileo, *The Starry Messenger* and *The Assayer*; Voltaire, *Candide*; Marx and Engels, *The Communist Manifesto*; Darwin, selections; Freud, *Outline of Psychoanalysis* and *Civilization and its Discontents*. Reported by Herbert Lindenberger, "The Western Culture Debate at Stanford University," *Comparative Criticism* 11 [1989] 225–34 (225). Of course, this is not a canon for English studies.

[5] Lindenberger 227; Christoph Bode, "Singing the Canon: Warum Mehrstimmigkeit eine gute Sache ist," *Kanon und Theorie*, ed. Maria Moog-Grünewald (Heidelberg: Carl Winter, 1997) 65–77 (74); Michael Böhler, "' Cross the Border – Close the Gap!': Die Dekanonisierung der Elitekultur in der Postmoderne und die Rekanonisierung des Amerika-Mythos; Zur Kanondiskussion in den USA," *Kanon Macht Kultur: Theoretische, historische und soziale Aspekte ästhetischer Kanonbildungen*, ed. Renate von Heydebrand (Stuttgart and Weimar: J.B. Metzler, 1998) 483–503 (488).

[6] Leslie A. Fiedler and Houston A. Baker, Jr., ed. *English Literature: Opening up the Canon* (Baltimore, MD: Johns Hopkins University Press, 1981).

[7] Sacvan Bercovitch, "America as Canon and Context: Literary History in a Time of Dissensus," *American Literature* 58 (1986) 99–107.

[8] Barbara Herrnstein Smith, *Contingencies of Value: Alternative Perspectives for Critical Theory* (Cambridge, MA: Harvard University Press, 1988).

[9] Allan Bloom, *The Closing of the American Mind: How Higher Education Has Failed Democracy and Impoverished the Souls of Today's Students* (New York: Simon & Schuster, 1987); E.D. Hirsch, Jr., *Cultural Literacy: What Every American Needs to Know* (Boston, MA: Houghton Mifflin, 1987).

The intensity of these conflicts may seem strange to many Europeans, and some of the arguments of the more radical decanonisers may even give a European observer the shivers. At the same time, Europeans ought perhaps also to envy a country in which a "battle of the books" can still be fought with such intensity and in which literature matters so much that not only academics but also journalists, politicians and ordinary readers could quarrel about literature, even though the opposing sides held quite different views about the definition of the literature that matters. The canon wars soon affected the major European countries as well, but here they were not fought with the same degree of violence, perhaps because the societies of these countries had not yet become as multicultural as the USA, perhaps because in Europe such controversies are usually not fought from such fundamentalist positions.

In the UK, neo-historicists, feminists and cultural materialists devoted their energies not so much to decanonisation as to an anticanonical interpretation of canonical texts, such as in the contributions to John Drakakis's *Alternative Shakespeares*. There was something like a "canon war" *en miniature* when, in 1992, several hundred university teachers of English, among them Catherine Belsey and Alan Sinfield, protested against a curriculum which made Shakespeare compulsory in secondary schools. The most important challenge to the traditional form of English studies and to its privileging of texts on account of their aesthetic value, however, came from the cultural-studies movement. This movement very often ignored texts from the past and turned to contemporary texts far from the traditional concept of literature: texts from pop culture, the new media, advertisements, comics, the tabloids and many other fields of contemporary mass culture. In many British universities, however, British cultural studies did not swallow or replace English studies in the traditional sense; both came to exist side by side. In some cases, there was the unspoken implication in this coexistence that "high literature" did not form part of contemporary culture or, rather, that it was no longer of importance when one wanted to study British culture. On the other hand, the development of British cultural studies into a discipline in its own right made it possible for English studies with its privileging of "high literature" and of classic works to continue to exist.

In Germany, the situation was again different. When, after 1968, students and younger scholars fought against traditional German studies and demanded their politicisation, some of them used slogans like "the death of literature" or "abolish

German studies."[10] A side-effect of these demands was, of course, a critique of the canon and the demand to do away with it. But while discussion continued in the USA and the UK, it seems to have died down in German studies in Germany quite early.[11]

In English studies in Germany the debate was even less intense, and there was certainly nothing like a "canon war." One reason may be that, because English is taught as a foreign language, the problematical nature of the canon in English studies does not touch on German identity and the national heritage. Only once, in 1987, did the *Anglistentag*, the annual conference of the German Association of University Teachers of English, make the problem of the canon the subject of a plenary panel discussion. This discussion was by no means very controversial, and some speakers even called the problem marginal and not important enough for a plenary session of the annual conference.[12]

Nevertheless, the canon discussion in the Anglo-Saxon countries also left its imprint on English departments in Germany. In the 1960s, as I have indicated, most departments had a reading list for students which was supposed to be compulsory, even if it was often not called a "canon" but "recommended reading." In the 1970s, however, such lists were often officially or tacitly withdrawn, ignored, forgotten or deprived of any consequence for the way English literature was studied. In many cases it was not so much the ideological opponents of a canon who were responsible for this development but, rather, liberal-minded university teachers of English who felt that a canon was an unacceptable restriction of a student's freedom to decide what to read,[13] and who also expected a liberating effect on their own work from the abandonment of the canon.

II

It is difficult to say whether this situation changed materially during the 1990s. At first sight, however, there are numerous symptoms that may be read as a tendency towards a return to a canon.

---

[10] Walter Erhart, "Kanonisierungsbedarf und Kanonisierung in der deutschen Literaturwissenschaft (1945–1995)," *Kanon Macht Kultur*, ed. von Heydebrand 97–121 (108).

[11] Erhart 112–13, 116.

[12] Ursula Kimpel, "Forumsdiskussion 'Kriterien der Kanonbildung': Protokoll der Diskussion," *Kriterien der Kanonbildung: Anglistentag 1987 Tübingen*, ed. Hans–Werner Ludwig (Forum des Anglistentags Verband Deutscher Anglisten 2; Giessen: Hoffmann, 1988) 44–47 (44).

[13] Ulrich Broich, "Anglistische Lektüreempfehlungen in der Bundesrepublik: Entwicklungstendenzen und Forderungen," *Kriterien der Kanonbildung*, ed. Ludwig 22–32.

The most spectacular of these symptoms was the publication in 1994 of Harold Bloom's widely read *The Western Canon.* Of course, there had been books defending the canon even earlier, like those by Allan Bloom and E.D. Hirsch. But Bloom's book was unique in two respects. On the one hand, it was an overall attack on all those who, in Bloom's view, wanted to deconstruct the Western canon: feminists, cultural materialists, multiculturalists, representatives of cultural studies and others. On the other, it was an attack characterised by its aggressive tone and by its rejection of any compromise. Bloom called all those in favour of decanonisation the "School of Resentment";[14] according to him, the result of their work was that "mere anarchy [was] in the process of being unleashed."[15] He selected the works that he regarded as parts of the Western canon exclusively by means of aesthetic criteria, and he uncompromisingly refused to include any texts that had recently gained increased interest for other reasons, such as works by authors from minorities which so far had been excluded from the canon.[16] Although he included Jane Austen, Emily Dickinson, George Eliot and Virginia Woolf, the majority of his "books of the ages," from Dante, Chaucer and Shakespeare to Proust, Joyce and Beckett, are works written by men, all of them white and most of them European. With its radical position and its polemical tone, Bloom's book was a provocation, and a heated controversy pro and contra Bloom followed which showed that in the USA the canon wars are by no means over. Quite recently Bloom intervened again in these wars with his book *How to Read and Why.*[17]

In Europe, a different development seems to have taken place in the 1990s, the reason for which, according to Bloom, being the fact that the "multicultural virus" which infected American universities is much less virulent in Europe.[18] However that may be, in Europe it was the publishing houses, among others, that made a great effort at recanonisation during the 1990s. This was attempted through the publication of new series of texts by "classic" authors (or by intensified advertising of existing series), by the publication of new histories of English

---

[14] Harold Bloom, *The Western Canon: The Books and School of the Ages* (1994; London: Macmillan, 1995) 23.

[15] Bloom, *The Western Canon* 1.

[16] Bloom included the following authors from world literature in his "Western Canon": Shakespeare, Dante, Chaucer, Cervantes, Montaigne, Molière, Milton, Dr Johnson, Goethe, Jane Austen, Walt Whitman, Wordsworth, Emily Dickinson, Dickens, George Eliot, Tolstoy, Ibsen, Freud, Proust, Joyce, Virginia Woolf, Kafka, Borges, Neruda, Pessoa, Samuel Beckett.

[17] Harold Bloom, *How to Read and Why* (New York: Scribner, 2000).

[18] Harold Bloom, "Der Kulturkrieger," interview with Harold Bloom conducted by Willi Winkler, *Süddeutsche Zeitung* (5–6 August 2000): 16.

literature and, even more characteristically, of lists of recommended books. Of course, there are commercial motives behind these efforts. Decanonisation means that there are far more books with a much smaller circulation, so a publisher will be happy about all English departments that agree on a number of "set books" which each of their students has to read. At the same time, some publishers feel that sections of the general public – not so much the university teachers of English – have a new desire for cultural orientation and thus also for recanonisation.

One work representative of this tendency is Andrew Sanders's *Short Oxford History of English Literature* (1994),[19] which is mainly confined to a discussion of the authors and texts in the traditional canon. The same applies to Michael Alexander's *A History of English Literature* (2000), which openly "concerns itself with what has living literary merit, whether contemporary or medieval."[20]

Even more characteristic of what might be understood as a return to the canon are four books published in Germany in 1994 and 1995. In 1994, Reclam published recommendations for reading under the title *Die Leseliste: Kommentierte Empfehlungen*, and in the same year Erich Schmidt followed the new trend with two such lists: Wulf Segebrecht's *Was sollen Germanisten lesen?* and Frank Baasner's and Peter Kuon's *Was sollen Romanisten lesen?*[21] Of greater interest for university teachers of English is, of course, the third book of this kind published by Erich Schmidt: *Was sollen Anglisten und Amerikanisten lesen?* (1995) by Christa Jansohn, Dieter Mehl and Hans Bungert. I shall therefore look at the last of these books a bit more closely.

Although the title – "What should students of English read?" – seems to indicate that this is another book advocating return to a canon, the three authors go out of their way to negate the normative claim of the title. In their preface they stress that their reading list is by no means a canon and that it is so long that nobody could expect to work right through it.[22] Indeed, this list is three times as long as that published by the same publisher for books written in the Romance languages, and Dieter Mehl's list of twentieth-century texts from the British Isles is

---

[19] Andrew Sanders, *The Short Oxford History of English Literature* (Oxford: Clarendon Press, 1994).

[20] Michael Alexander, *A History of English Literature* (Houndmills and London: Macmillan, 2000) 3.

[21] Sabine Griese, Hubert Kerscher, Albert Meier and Claudia Stockinger, *Die Leseliste: Kommentierte Empfehlungen* (Stuttgart: Reclam, 1994); Wulf Segebrecht, *Was sollen Germanisten lesen?* (Berlin: Erich Schmidt, 1994); Frank Baasner and Peter Kuon, *Was sollen Romanisten lesen?* (Berlin: Erich Schmidt, 1994).

[22] Christa Jansohn, Dieter Mehl and Hans Bungert, *Was sollen Anglisten und Amerikanisten lesen?* (Berlin: Erich Schmidt, 1995) 9.

almost a *Who's Who* in twentieth-century English literature. The whole book contains more texts than even a university professor of English is likely to read or can hope to read. The book thus reduces its own claim – to provide students with an orientation – to absurdity. By including virtually all texts from the traditional canon and incorporating numerous others as well, Mehl does precisely what Harold Bloom criticises in the following words: "Expanding the Canon [...] tends to drive out the better writers";[23] thus what at first glance looks like, and what may have been intended by the publisher as, a return to the canon is in fact nothing of the kind.[24]

If we want to know more about the texts which are likely to be taught to students of English, we may draw some conclusions from recent anthologies with high circulations. The *Arnold Anthology of British and Irish Literature in English*,[25] which was first published in 1997, has included more fictional and nonfictional prose and more works by women and minority writers than earlier anthologies. This brings the anthology to 1,578 pages, but on the whole it emphasises the classic authors who belonged to the canon before it was called into question. The *Norton Anthology of English Literature*, however, the sixth edition of which was published in 1993, shows, in an even more obvious form, the same tendency that characterises Dieter Mehl's reading list for students of English – to retain authors who had long been canonical and to add whatever has become of interest lately. In two volumes far exceeding 5,000 pages in all, it assembles an overwhelming number of texts and extracts from texts and thus offers a great deal to a knowledgeable teacher of English to choose from, but will intimidate, discourage and disorient most students. Anthologies of American literature from the 1990s go even further than those of English literature. The fourth edition of the two-volume *Norton Anthology of American Literature*[26] from 1993–94 presents to the reader, apart from texts by classic American authors, a great number of texts from American Indians, African–Americans, Hispanics etc. in more than 5,400 pages. The most extreme example of a collection that attempts to avoid excluding minorities is the *Heath Anthology of American Literature*,[27] which in its second

[23] Bloom, *The Western Canon* 540.

[24] Ulrich Broich, review of Jansohn, Mehl and Bungert, *Was sollen Anglisten und Amerikanisten lesen?*, *Anglia* 114 (1996): 565–70.

[25] Robert Clark and Thomas Healy, ed. *The Arnold Anthology of British and Irish Literature in English* (London: Arnold, 1997).

[26] Nina Baym et al., ed. *The Norton Anthology of American Literature*, 2 vols. (New York and London: W.W. Norton, 4th ed. 1994).

[27] Paul Lauter, ed., et al. *The Heath Anthology of American Literature*, 2 vols. (Lexington, MA: D.C. Heath, 2nd ed. 1994).

edition of 1994 tops all other anthologies with a length of more than 6,000 pages in two volumes, and in which the classic authors are all but marginalised. This anthology is certainly the most "politically correct" of them all, and willingly pays the price of abandoning wholesale any attempt to tell the student what, according to the editors, the most memorable writing in America really is.

Though it is easy to analyse the trends in the 1990s in published reading lists, anthologies or literary histories, it is much more difficult to find out what texts are actually taught in English departments in different countries. I do not think that many departments introduced new reading lists for all students – or reactivated "dormant" reading lists – during the last decade. But there may be a certain number of departments in which there is a growing consensus among teachers that a considerable proportion of undergraduate courses ought to be based on core authors rather than on marginal ones.

Nevertheless, two examples which give a different impression may be not untypical of the present situation. In the English Department of the University of Munich there is a recommended-reading list for all students, but few know of its existence and even fewer take it seriously, and it has no consequences at all for their course of studies. As well as this, there is a reading list for students in their first and second years on which the intermediate exam is based. But this list comprises twenty-one groups of texts, from which an undergraduate must choose three or – if he or she studies English as a minor subject – two groups. From these groups, a minimum number of texts has to be selected, but some texts can be replaced by others of the student's own choice. This gives the individual student a certain amount of guidance and a greater degree of freedom, but the result is that, among the students sitting the intermediate exam, there may be very few who have all read the same texts. Hans–Jürgen Diller has called this situation "canon formation on the second floor,"[28] but the question is whether in this case we can justifiably speak of canon formation at all. There is no such guidance as far as the final exam in Munich is concerned: here students are expected to have read at least thirty long texts, but it is possible to leave university with a degree in English without ever having read or studied Shakespeare or lyric poetry.

The other example comes from Stanford University. After the compulsory course on Western Civilisation had to be abandoned after massive protests, a new first-year course was introduced called "Culture, Ideas, Values" (C.I.V.). The teachers were still supposed to teach basic texts from the history of mankind in

[28] Hans–Jürgen Diller, "Selbstkritisches Nachwort," *Kriterien der Kanonbildung*, ed. Ludwig 48–55 (53–54).

this course, but now they were free to assemble their own selection. The teacher's freedom was restricted only by the demand to fulfil certain quotas: there had to be not only texts from antiquity and from the Middle Ages, but also by women, minority authors and "persons of color."[29] Heated discussion ensued in the press and on TV.

To sum up: at the turn of the century, the canon wars do not seem to be over in the USA but seem to have faded out in English studies in Europe. And yet the situation for students of English seems to be similar in English departments on both continents: the old canon appears to be dead, attempts at recanonisation have been half-hearted or unsuccessful, and for the student there is a combination of freedom – and disorientation.

In one respect, however, the canon wars effected an increase in knowledge and orientation as well. Particularly in the 1990s, some of the discussion of canonicity was no longer concentrated on the pros and cons of a canon but on questions of how canons were formed and structured, how they underwent change, and how they were an expression of power relations and the class structure in a given society. The impressive volume *Kanon Macht Kultur* edited by Renate von Heydebrand in 1998 shows what interesting results can be expected from this field of research. In books of this kind, canon research has become a rewarding new field of literary studies in which analysis is more important than polemic, just as part of feminism has moved from the struggle against discrimination towards the more analytical approach of gender studies.

III

What conclusions can be drawn from the developments of the last few decades? One may well ask if recent attempts to return to something like a canon will become stronger in the future, or if the canon has had its day. Literary critics, however, have always been bad prophets, so it may be wiser to ask whether the canon, or a canon, ought to have a future.

Before I try to answer this question from my own point of view, it is necessary (somewhat belatedly, I admit) to differentiate among the senses of the word "canon." Whereas in the present essay "canon" has mostly been used in the singular, von Heydebrand makes a highly systematic distinction between a considerable number of different meanings of the term.[30] For my purpose here, it is not

[29] Lindenberger 232; Böhler 488.

[30] Renate von Heydebrand, "Kanon Macht Kultur: Versuch einer Zusammenfassung," *Kanon Macht Kultur*, ed. von Heydebrand 612–25 (612–16).

necessary to recapitulate the different types of canon she proposes. But when asking whether a canon is desirable in the future, it ought to be made clear whether we are referring to a generally accepted list of core texts for research, for teaching English studies at the university, or for the general reading public.

Research certainly ought not to be restricted to a canon. On the contrary, it is in the nature of research to discover not only ever-new questions and approaches but also ever-new texts. Therefore, Diller justifiably speaks of the "'anti-canonical' nature of research in English studies."[31] To give an example: when Anne Mellor demanded that research on Romanticism ought not to be confined to the six canonical lyric poets, who all happen to be male, and when she published her findings on other Romantic writers, many of whom were writers of fiction and most of whom were women, she was endeavouring to correct the traditional view of Romanticism in some respects and to contribute to a partly new view of the period.[32]

But even though the core authors and texts in English studies may seem "over-researched" to some, it will not do to abandon research on them. The classics have to be reinterpreted to every new generation of readers and thus kept alive in the cultural memory of all those interested in literature, and it is certainly one of the major tasks of university teachers of English to do so and to "promote" them among educated readers.

Moreover, Ulrich Suerbaum has rightly pointed out that the "density" of research and the quality and quantity of open questions and research opportunities are much greater in core areas than in marginal or new areas of research.[33] This may well explain why many of the current publications on Shakespeare are more complex and more rewarding than, for example, some of the writing on authors of popular literature who had been neglected by earlier scholars. The masses of books published by what has been called "the self-perpetuating Shakespeare industry" thus have a positive aspect as well.

There is, moreover, another negative consequence if research in English studies moves too far away from authors and texts well known to most members of the academic community. If the major conferences, like IAUPE, that attempt to cover the whole field of English studies were to offer mainly presentations on little-known or marginal authors there would be a marked decline of interest

---

31 Diller 54.

32 Anne K. Mellor, *Romanticism and Gender* (London & New York: Routledge, 1993).

33 Ulrich Suerbaum, "Schwierige Ermittlung: Die Suche nach gattungsgerechten Programmen zur Untersuchung von Kriminalliteratur," *Unterhaltungsliteratur. Ziele und Methoden der Erforschung*, ed. Dieter Petzold and Eberhard Späth (Erlangen: Universitätsbund Erlangen–Nürnberg, 1980) 7–17 (10).

among scholars in attending these conferences. What is more, there would be little or no interest in such conferences on the part of the general public, newspapers or sponsors. This probably explains why, in Germany, no national newspapers carry reports on the annual conferences of the German Association of University Teachers of English but regularly report on the annual Shakespeare conferences, and why books on Greek and Latin literature meet with greater interest among educated readers than books on English literature.

I shall now turn to the question of whether a canon in the teaching of English studies is desirable – which is the proper subject of this essay. So long as Humboldt's ideal of the unity of research and teaching is maintained, the situation in the teaching of English literature cannot be completely separated from that of research. As was stated above, the number of genres, authors and texts which have recently become the object of academic research has increased immensely. Consequently, university teachers will want to include on their courses the texts on which they are carrying out research. If, however, the interests of many academics in the field are respected without restriction, this will lead to the kind of inflated reading lists published by Dieter Mehl,[34] or to even more inflated anthologies like the Norton and the Heath.

When we compare such gargantuan lists or anthologies with the reading capacity of students of our time, we encounter a paradox. On the one hand, it seems, at least in Germany, as if students of English read far less than they did forty years ago. On the other, they are confronted with anthologies which become more voluminous with every edition and with teachers who, for various reasons, often refuse to give them guidance by means of a realistic list of prescribed or at least strongly recommended texts. I know of a number of cases in which students have demanded such guidance from their teachers, but they have often met with reluctance or even the inability of the faculty to agree on a reading list or canon. In one case, a colleague told me, the faculty had given the students the list they had desired, but "with gritted teeth."[35]

I do not think that students ought to be left in this state of disorientation, wherever it still exists. When every teacher teaches, and every student reads, different texts from an ever-increasing number of possible texts, there will be none that are familiar to all students. No physicist or chemist or even historian would accept a situation in which every student in his discipline learned entirely different things. Although the university teacher must to some extent be free to teach,

---

[34] Jansohn, Mehl and Bungert, *Was sollen Anglisten und Amerikanisten lesen?*

[35] Broich, "Anglistische Lektüreempfehlungen" 26.

and the student to read, texts of his or her own choice, there must be a number of core authors or texts, a canon – and we should not shrink from this as though it were a four-letter word – which is agreed upon and which is taken seriously. It is only in this manner that the centrifugal tendencies that are so strong in our discipline today can be balanced by centripetal ones, in order that some continuity can be maintained in a period of rapid change. One could also say, with Ulrich Schulz–Buschhaus, that after a period of a "canon of expansion" the time has come for a "canon of restriction."[36]

On which criteria ought such a core canon to be based? Some colleagues are convinced that a canon should include exclusively works of high literature and that the criteria on which such a canon is based ought to be solely aesthetic. These criteria, however, are not easy to define. Is complexity or ambiguity a criterion of aesthetic value (as the New Critics believed)? Is it formal innovation? Or is it "strangeness" (the central criterion of Harold Bloom's book on the Western canon)? Apart from the fact that the criteria for aesthetic evaluation are controversial, aesthetic evaluation itself is something highly subjective or, rather (as Barbara Hermstein Smith puts it), contingent. This also applies to the criterion of the effect of a "classic" on the reader. Joyce's *Ulysses* may serve as an example of the subjectivity of both these criteria: many readers are convinced that *Ulysses* is the greatest twentieth-century novel in the English language, whereas many of our students fail to appreciate its aesthetic achievement and do not manage to get beyond the first few pages or chapters. The aesthetic criteria ought thus to be supplemented by standards that are less subjective. I think that one such criterion ought to be the importance of a text for the cultural memory of a nation or culture. The consequence of this, however, would be twofold. On the one hand, a list of required reading would not only include literary texts in the narrower sense but also texts like John Locke's *Two Treatises on Government*, Wollstonecraft's *Vindication of the Rights of Women* and John Stuart Mill's "On the Subjection of Women," which are important parts of the British cultural memory. On the other hand, a case could be made for including Harriet Beecher Stowe's *Uncle Tom's Cabin* in a canon of texts from American literature or a Sherlock Holmes story by Conan Doyle in a canon of texts from English literature, despite their probably inferior aesthetic value, because these texts have become part of the cultural memory of the American or British nation. But even this criterion will not make

[36] Ulrich Schulz–Buschhaus, "Kanon der Restriktion und Kanon der Expansion: Zu Tendenzen der literarischen Kanonbildung im 19. und 20. Jahrhundert," *Kanon und Theorie*, ed. Moog–Grünewald 227–44 passim.

decisions in individual cases easy. One could make a convincing case for the most important works of Anglo-Saxon literature as important parts of the English cultural tradition. The Oxford colleges, however, recently came to a different conclusion when they decided that an undergraduate in English studies should no longer be required to study Anglo-Saxon texts.

Another problem is caused by the fact that in many universities there are courses of "Eng. Lit." and British cultural studies side by side. It goes without saying that the lists of required reading for both courses ought not to be identical. Locke, Wollstonecraft and Mill have a greater claim to be included in a reading list for British cultural studies, provided it is accepted that cultural studies should not include contemporary culture only but also texts from the past which still form part of our cultural memory, yet a student of Eng. Lit. ought to be expected to handle texts of this kind as well. By the same token, a canon for cultural studies ought to include classic literary texts as well, because literature is one of the most important fields of culture, which makes the teaching of British culture in which "high literature" is excluded very reductive. The reading lists for Eng. Lit. and British cultural studies, though they should not be identical, ought thus to overlap.

I am not going to sketch such a canon or canons but, rather, shall suggest some further guidelines which ought to be considered by those who put together lists of required or recommended reading for students in English departments.

1. A canon should not be inflated to such an extent as to reduce itself to absurdity. It should be restrictive and realistic and should leave time and space for the individual interests of students and teachers.
2. In many cases, a canon should name authors rather than individual texts – Shakespeare rather than *Hamlet*, or Jane Austen rather than *Emma*.
3. The more the canon approaches contemporary literature, the more options it should give.
4. It is absurd for a department to have a list of required reading without providing accompanying teaching and student assessment. There could, for instance, be survey lectures or reading courses which conclude with a written test, and in the final examination, as well as questions on the special subjects selected by individual students, there should be questions concerning texts from the core canon.
5. A canon ought to be open to revision at all times. Some of the texts to be found in reading lists of the 1950s have now disappeared; texts that are in

fashion among students and teachers nowadays may be considered negligible by later generations.

6. There should be no quotas guaranteeing the inclusion of texts on thematic grounds.

IV

To conclude. When I suggest that those departments of English which in the past shirked the task of orienting and guiding their students by providing lists of required reading ought to do so in the future, I am well aware that this demand makes sense only so long as there is a consensus among the general public of educated readers about a body of great literary works of the past and about the necessity to keep them alive as part of our cultural memory. Despite the fact that our culture is becoming increasingly multicultural and less literature-oriented, I am certain that this consensus still more or less exists. One could even say that the increasing speed of change has gone hand in hand with a growing need to keep our cultural memory alive. This consensus relates not only to great works of literature but also to those of architecture, painting and music. Decanonisation, at least in Europe, has been a concern not so much of the general public but of teachers in our own discipline. It is precisely for this reason that hopes for a canon with a future do not seem to be unfounded.

Representing the Oppressed

LAURENCE LERNER

WHAT WE TEACH, AND HOW WE TEACH IT, results from three converging pressures: our own interests, the policy of the institution, and the wishes of our students. During the 1970s, our students (or at least the most articulate among them) wanted to talk about oppression (many still do). During the 1980s, sophisticated critics wanted to talk about representation: its methods, its difficulties, even its impossibility. This essay emerges from reflections on these pressures, and so can at least claim the merit of treating the concerns of our time.

First, who are the oppressed? In general terms the answer seems obvious, but it will vary according to the criterion of oppression: race, class or gender. Racial oppression is not important to students of earlier English literature, for the obvious reason that English society has on the whole been racially uniform. This has not prevented a vivid awareness of the Jews as a racially contrasting group: The *Prioress's Tale*, and Barabbas, Shylock, Fagin and Svengali, form part of the long history of anti-semitism – the first three written at a time when there were very few Jews in England. Black Africans and Afro-Americans are today far more numerous than Jews, and the question of their oppression has now become important to the literary student for two main reasons: the study of American literature (race being a far more important issue in American society than in British – at least until recently), and the worldwide spread of English studies, so that there are now thousands of Indian and African students who start from a natural concern with the way in which they are represented: Conrad, Kipling, Forster and postcolonial writing inevitably become topics of special interest to them.

Gender is certainly the most important of the three criteria to us, for the obvious reason that we are all directly involved with it. It was possible for those in the worlds of Richardson and Jane Austen to have very limited contact with the poor and virtually none with blacks, but contact with the other sex is inescapable: we all have parents, most have spouses or siblings or children, and a literary work which does not show us both sexes is a rarity – and when we find one, as in some tales of heroism or adventure, the nature of masculinity will probably be its central theme. Gender is inescapable.

In this essay I propose to discuss the third form of oppression, that of the have-nots by the haves, or employees by employers, or the poor by the rich, for three good reasons: that it is better to treat one thing as fully as possible than three things more cursorily; that this one is now rather less fashionable than the other two; and that it is a strong personal interest of mine. To this one might add a further reason, that it concerns the oppression of the many by the few. This may seem obvious, but it is worth mention. Racial oppression, in Britain and America, is the oppression of the few by the many: joined with the oppression of homosexuals, it has given rise to the term "minority" to designate an oppressed group. We ought to remind ourselves how extraordinary this is. The history of humanity is the story of a privileged few and the subjected many: a society in which the many oppress the few is in some sense a great leap forward – though not, of course, for the oppressed minority. Whether one is worse off suffering the specific discrimination imposed on one's minority, or suffering the immemorial lot of the poor and the many as Conrad famously described it – "they were born, they suffered and they died" – is a comparison most of us are fortunate enough not to be able to make.

Next, who does the oppressing? The obvious answer is, the powerful: kings and emperors, popes and archbishops, generals and bankers and robber barons. One thing is obvious about such a list: that it does not include many poets and novelists. The powerful do not do their own representing.

> The glories of our blood and state
> Are shadows, not substantial things,
> There is no armour against fate,
> Death lays his icy hand on Kings.
> Sceptre and Crown
> Must tumble down
> And in the dust be equal made
> With the poor crooked scythe and spade.
>
> Some men with swords may reap the field,
> And plant fresh laurels where they kill.
> But their strong nerves at last must yield,
> They tame but one another still;
> Early or late,
> They stoop to fate,
> And must give up the murmuring breath,
> When they, pale captives, creep to death.

The Garlands wither on your brow,
  Then boast no more your mighty deeds,
Upon Death's purple altar now
See where the Victor–victim bleeds,
    Your heads must come,
    To the cold Tomb;
Only the actions of the just
Smell sweet, and blossom in their dust.[1]

This classic statement of one of the great poetic commonplaces of our tradition reminds the powerful of their vulnerability, to provide comfort to the oppressed. The second stanza does this with some vigour, and even disrespect: "some men" is no way for a seventeenth-century subject to speak of his prince, or even of a military commander. The irony in "reap," too, is a social reversal. Kings are mocked because that is the only kind of reaping they can do. This establishes the "poor crooked scythe and spade" as the poem's norm: those who use them will not, after all, be so poor when they can watch their oppressors "creep to death" and learn what it is like to be humiliated.

But, for all its fierceness, the poem is not really subversive: by assuring the agricultural labourer that Death the Leveller will render him equal with kings, you are removing the levelling to the next world. Since all will be put right when we are laid in the dust, there is no need to do anything about it now, and no peasant is intended to read this poem and say "Why wait for Death?" James Shirley himself, and most of his readers (who were not, of course, peasants), may have thought that this great commonplace would bring comfort to the poor, and perhaps it often did: but that does not prevent it from functioning as ideological reinforcement of the status quo. That is the way such reinforcement works.

And who was James Shirley? A parson and schoolmaster who converted to Roman Catholicism and wrote dozens of plays, he did not wear a crown or wield a sceptre, and did not reap the field with swords (nor reap real fields with a scythe either). He had no power, but this does not prevent his poem from speaking for those who did. It is important to the powerful that there should be an ideology of the status quo, but they do not devise it themselves: they delegate the task to those whom Coleridge called the clerisy and whom we call the intellectuals. It is a commonplace of radical theorising that the small number of those who exercise real power are supported by a larger number of apologists who explain that the way power is exercised rests upon a moral order, and it is also of course a com-

[1] James Shirley, Dirge from "Ajax & Ulysses," *Dramatic Works & Poems*, vol. 6 (1659; New York: Russell & Russell, 1966) 397.

monplace of Marxist or Foucauldian criticism to point out the way poems and pictures, sermons, stories and many apparently objective forms of representation serve such an ideological function. This is the way we have all learned to read the implicit politics of poetic commonplaces: but such a political reading must not be oversimplified. Most rulers are not hypocrites, and want to be assured that by continuing to exercise power they are doing good – helping their subjects, averting social chaos, even saving their own souls. To provide this assurance, the clerisy needs to sound genuine – that is, they must mean what they say, offering independent-sounding apologies, not the whitewashing of a tyrant. The only convincing way to sound independent is to be independent, which means that a ruler's apologists will always be in a position to turn against him: professors may join demonstrations, bishops may tell prime ministers that they are waging an unjust war, playwrights may support the status quo in deeply ambivalent ways.

Whether a preacher or a journalist has turned to biting the hand that feeds him is usually obvious; whether a literary work is subversive is much harder to be sure about. Here is an instance:

> L'on voit certains animaux farouches, des mâles et des femelles, répandus par la campagne, noirs, livides et tout brulés du soleil, attachés à la terre qu'ils fouillent et qu'ils remuent avec une opiniâtreté invincible; ils ont comme une voix articulée et quand ils se lèvent sur leurs pieds, ils montrent une face humaine, et en effet ils sont des hommes; ils se retirent la nuit dans des tanières où ils vivent de pain noir, d'eau et de racines; ils épargnent aux autres hommes la peine de semer, de labourer et de recueillir pour vivre, et méritent ainsi de ne pas manquer de ce pain qu'ils ont semé.[2]
>
> (Certain wild animals, both male and female, can be seen all over the countryside, black, livid and quite sunburnt, attached to the land which they dig and stir about with unconquerable obstinacy. It's as though they make articulate sounds, and when they stand up they show a human face – and they are, in fact, men. At night they retire to their hovels, where they live on black bread, water and roots. They free other men from the task of sowing, ploughing and reaping in order to live, and so they deserve to have some of the bread they sow.)

Is this written with contempt, amused curiosity, or fierce compassion – or a mixture of all three? Was it read by La Bruyère's contemporaries with the same feeling with which he wrote it – and if not, which is the authentic historical reading? And when we read it, in our democratic age, are we being unhistorical if we replace amusement with sympathy, contempt with indignation? If we get the meaning right, even to appreciating the rhetorical strategy of the second sentence as it moves gradually towards tossing us the fact that these are human beings – if

[2] La Bruyère, "Les Caractères" XI.128, *Oeuvres complètes* (1689; Paris: Pléade, 4th. ed. 1951) 333.

we do all this but experience it with a quite different emotion from contemporaries, are we misreading? Is the reader's emotion part of the meaning, or does it exist alongside meaning, changing as society changes?

What I want now to try and do is to use a particular situation to explore the different ways in which the poor have been represented, and I have chosen child labour in industrial England. The early days of the industrial revolution produced a large urban working class living in conditions of unprecedented squalor and poverty. Whether they were worse housed and worse fed than their parents and grandparents who lived in rural squalor is a question that economic historians have not been able to decide; what was certainly unprecedented was that urban slums were virtually enclosed ghettoes constructed so that the well-off need never enter them. "The members of the money aristocracy," claimed Engels, "can take the shortest road through the middle of all the labouring districts to their places of business, without ever seeing that they are in the midst of the grimy misery that lurks to the right and the left."[3] Very few members of the clerisy penetrated these slums, and those who did were appalled – by the filth, the smells, and the realisation that fellow human beings lived in such conditions. Thomas Carlyle may not have done much penetrating himself, but at least he thought that urban squalor was an issue which should be placed on the political agenda:

> The condition of the great body of people in a country is the condition of the country itself. Yet read Hansard's Debates or the Morning Papers, if you have nothing to do! The old grand question, whether A is to be in office or B [...] – all manner of questions and subjects except simply this, the alpha and omega of all! Surely Honourable Members ought to speak of the Condition-of-England question too.[4]

Enough novelists read this plea, and with enough agreement, for a minor subgenre of the realistic novel to arise in the 1840s and 1850s, which is sometimes called the Condition-of-England novel. The very respectable Elizabeth Gaskell, wife of a Unitarian clergyman, wrote her first novel about working-class people in Manchester, and did not scruple to take her readers into the slums, which they would certainly never have penetrated for themselves, and show them the filth, the overcrowding, even the smells: "Women from their doors tossed household slops of every description into the gutter; they ran into the next pool, which overflowed

[3] Friedrich Engels, *The Condition of the Working-Class in England in 1844* (1845; London: George Allen & Unwin, 1952) 46.

[4] Thomas Carlyle, "Chartism," *Critical & Miscellaneous Essays* (1839; London: Chapman & Hall, 1903) vol. 3 112.

and stagnated."[5] Here is an extract from what is probably the earliest of these novels, published only one year after Carlyle's pamphlet, so perhaps conceived independently of his influence:

> The party entered the building, whence – as all know who have done the like – every sight, every sound, every scent that kind nature has fitted to the organ of her children, so as to render the mere unfettered use of them a delight, are banished for ever and for ever. The ceaseless whirring of a million hissing wheels, seizes on the tortured ear [...] The scents that reek around, from oil, tainted water, and human filth [...] render the act of breathing a process of difficulty, disgust and pain. All this is terrible. But [...] who can think of villainous smells, or heed the suffering of the ear-racking sounds, while they look upon hundreds of helpless children, divested of every trace of health, of joyousness, and even of youth! Assuredly there is no exaggeration in this; for except only in their diminutive size, these suffering infants have no trace of it. Lean and distorted limbs – sallow and sunken cheeks – dim hollow eyes, that speak unrest and most unnatural carefulness, give to each tiny, trembling, unelastic form a look of hideous premature old age.[6]

Why is child labour so shocking to us? We believe childhood should be a separated and protected time, in which human beings can take advantage of their delayed sexual maturing in order to learn. Attending school is an essential part of our modern conception of childhood. I used sometimes to ask my students, when they were studying nineteenth-century literature and society, to make the case in favour of child labour as it might have been made in the 1830s: learning to put the clock back is, after all, one purpose of historical study. If they were perceptive, they would realise that before universal education the arguments would have to be different; if very perceptive – and historically minded – they might think up some of the arguments of Cooke Taylor, a staunch defender of capitalism and apologist for child labour, which he described as "a national blessing, and absolutely necessary for the support of the manifold fiscal burdens which have been placed upon the industry of this country."[7] That has a familiar ring nowadays: reforms are considered unwise because of the cost to industry – abolishing child labour then, the minimum wage now. Though we are not likely to accept Cooke Taylor's arguments today, we need to respect the fact that he had first-hand knowledge:

> The house-accommodation of the operatives in large towns are necessarily very limited: if the children were excluded from factories and workshops, it is not very clear what would become of them. At home they could not remain even if they were disposed to do so; there is no legal provision for compelling them to attend

[5] Elizabeth Gaskell, *Mary Barton* (1848; London: Smith, Elder, 1906) 65.

[6] Frances Trollope, *The Life & Adventures of Michael Armstrong, The Factory Boy* (1840; London: Frank Cass, 1968) 79.

[7] W. Cooke Taylor, *Factories & the Factory System* (1844).

> schools – their only resource would be the streets, with all its perils and temptations. If juvenile labour were itself an evil, which we emphatically deny, it would still be preferable as the choice of evils, for juvenile vagrancy and juvenile delinquency are infinitely worse.[8]

Schooling or its absence, which for us would probably be the first issue to be considered when deciding how children should spend their time, is mentioned only in passing by Cooke Taylor (and does not loom large in Frances Trollope's account either). The provision of schools by the factory, and arrangements for the children to attend them, was set up by the Factories Act of 1833, but was widely neglected in practice; it is not easy to say whether a working-class child's opportunity to attend school was better or worse if he worked in a factory.

Comparing Frances Trollope with Cooke Taylor (they were writing at much the same time), we are likely to feel ourselves on her side; but the reader who has any literary sensibility will also be struck by the contrast in tone. Her indignation is so intense that it invades every descriptive detail. Pleasant smells are not just absent, they are "banished for ever and ever," unpleasant smells are "villainous," the children are "suffering infants." "There is no exaggeration in this," she assures us, but "exaggeration" is an ambiguous term, with both a referential and a stylistic meaning. I have no hesitation in accepting her facts, but the manner of writing is exaggerated in the extreme: it is a crude didactic gesture.

Does this, then, mean that the more sober Cooke Taylor is a more reliable guide? The contrast between the fierce moralising of the indignant female and the patient refutations of the well-informed male is a familiar one, and one soon learns that such contrast in style may not be a reliable guide to who is right: bias can appear through selection of evidence as easily as through emotional colouring. Even the best-informed economic historian might hesitate to pronounce that either of them is completely right or wrong; my more limited aim is to compare their strategies of representation, and I suggest that Mrs Trollope's obvious bias does not necessarily mean that the calmer and more apparently objective Cooke Taylor is the more reliable guide. Can we go further, and find something that is genuinely objective?

Report of Mr Philip's Spinning-mill at Dysart,
Fifeshire. 17 May 1833

> Ann Berry, fifteen years old. She has been at this mill for six years. The long hours work tires her much, and makes her sleepy, and sleep in the mill 'many a time'. Her legs sometimes swell. Sometimes, when the frames go ill, she throws

[8] W. Cooke Taylor.

> herself down quite fatigued, when the work is done, and falls asleep before having her supper. She never has been at school since she came here. When she first came the overseer used to strike her, but never now. There have been a good many accidents; she cannot say how many; at least half a dozen since she came here. She gets ten-pence per day. She would prefer shorter hours and less wages to ten-pence a day, which she now gets. No school at this work, nor is there any medical attendant. She is very much choked with dust, which makes her hoarse and breathe uneasily. She was never at any other factory.[9]

Surely this girl is telling the truth. The extract comes from the 1833 Report of the Select Committee of the House of Commons that took evidence from the factory workers of Lancashire and Yorkshire: we would need to be very biased, or very deeply infected by the hermeneutics of suspicion, to suggest that Ann Berry, along with the dozens of other operatives whose evidence appears in the Report, who did not know one another, and could hardly have had the opportunity to conspire together, are misleading us. But to the literary student, such a passage has another interest besides the question of its objective truth and its bits of useful evidence, like the fact that she got ten pence a day. We value it because we can hear the voice of someone who would otherwise be forgotten: not so much for its objectivity as for its authenticity. Ann Berry had no literary talent, no way with words: why are these crude sentences so moving today?

The struggle to be articulate can itself be deeply moving, whether we hear it in the voice of the poet himself – "I see by glimpses now; when age comes on May scarcely see at all," wrote Wordsworth in one of the most powerful passages in *The Prelude* – or in the voice of a dramatic character – Macduff saying "I cannot but remember such things were, / That were most precious to me." Obviously I am not suggesting that Ann Berry was a mute inglorious Wordsworth: his struggle to be articulate produced a great and complex poem, but that poem contained traces of the struggle towards articulateness, and for that too we value it, as we value not only the expression of Macduff's grief, but our awareness of his difficulty in finding words for it. In the case of Ann Berry, the effect depends on the patient, skilful questioning of the interviewer: what we see is how he enables her to say what she could not otherwise say. The words are hers, he is a necessary midwife, and the result is authenticity plus a vivid sense of how she could not have conveyed it by herself.

[9] Report of the Select Committee of the House of Commons on Child Labour in Factories (Michael Thomas Sadler, Chairman) (1833).

My next example must, perforce, be rather longer. A young man, accompanied by his schoolteacher, is on his way to visit his sister at the house where she lodges, and has an unexpected encounter:

> The boy knocked at a door, and the door promptly opened with a spring and a click. A parlour door within a small entry stood open, and disclosed a child – a dwarf – a girl – a something – sitting on a little low old-fashioned arm-chair, which had a kind of little working bench before it.
>
> 'I can't get up,' said the child, 'because my back's bad, and my legs are queer. But I'm the person of the house. […] Take a seat.' [...]
>
> They complied in silence, and the little figure went on with its work of gumming or gluing together with a camel's-hair brush certain pieces of cardboard and thin wood, previously cut into various shapes [...] The dexterity of her nimble fingers was remarkable, and, as she brought two thin edges accurately together by giving them a little bite, she would glance at the visitors out of the corners of her grey eyes with a look that out-sharpened all her other sharpness.
>
> 'You can't tell me the name of my trade, I'll be bound,' she said, after taking several of these observations [...] 'I'm a doll's dressmaker.'
>
> 'I hope it's a good business?'
>
> The person of the house shrugged her shoulders and shook her head. 'No. Poorly paid. And I'm often so pressed for time! I had a doll married, last week, and was obliged to work all night. And it's not good for me, on account of my back being so bad and my legs so queer.'
>
> They looked at the little creature with a wonder that did not diminish, and the schoolmaster said: 'I am sorry your fine ladies are so inconsiderate.'
>
> 'It's the way with them,' said the person of the house, shrugging her shoulders again. 'And they take no care of their clothes, and they never keep to the same fashions a month. I work for a doll with three daughters. Bless you, she's enough to ruin her husband!' [...]
>
> 'Are you alone all day? […] Don't any of the neighbouring children —?'
>
> 'Ah, lud!' cried the person of the house, with a little scream, as if the word had pricked her. 'Don't talk of children. I can't bear children [...] Always running about and screeching, always playing and fighting, always skip-skip-skipping on the pavement and chalking it for their games! Oh, I know their tricks and their manners!'[10]

Another form of child labour, this. First, because this child is self-employed, and so, as well as the slavery of long hours, she knows the difficulty of running a business; and second, because it is not immediately clear how much of a child she is. We learn, as the novel goes on, that her real name is Fanny Cleaver, but she is known as Jenny Wren; that she is thirteen, perhaps fourteen – no older, after all, than Little Nell, that very archetype of the sentimentalised child. But great pains are taken, both by Jenny and her creator, to throw her childhood into uncertainty:

---

[10] Charles Dickens, *Our Mutual Friend* (1864–65; Oxford: Oxford UP, 1987) Book II 222–24.

she refers to herself as "the person of the house," she treats her drunken father as if he were her child, she keeps others in order as if she were the adult, speaking fiercely to them. She is, in fact, one of Dickens's fascinating portraits of liminality, placed on the boundary between child and adult. This of course makes the last paragraph particularly fascinating. "I can't bear children [...] Always running about and screeching" has the ring of the irritated old maid, but the fact that it comes from a thirteen-year-old cripple turns it on its head: it becomes a cry of longing, an account of the true childhood Jenny cannot admit that she longs for.

The sick or dying child is a standard item of Victorian pathos, which the reader (depending largely on when he lives) may find moving or embarrassing. Jenny Wren is aware of the pathos of her situation, but she distorts it: her handicap is not the occasion for tears, but for a mechanical formula ("my back's bad and my legs are queer") which she repeats over and over as if she were one of her own dolls. The inconsiderateness of her customers, projected onto the dolls, becomes absurd as the customers are seen as toys. Dolls into people, people into dolls: the mechanical and the living merge into each other.

Is this oblique, quirky, teasing form of writing a way of representing the poor? Is this our finest example, or have we moved from socially responsible representation to comic self-indulgence? The question, of course, is unanswerable. If like responsible historicists we wish to study the past through its literary representation, Dickens is both a worse and a better example than Frances Trollope or even Elizabeth Gaskell. He often spoke of his own novels as if they were responsible social criticism; he would quote from them when making speeches to, for instance, the Metropolitan Sanitary Association, as if his reforming and his creative activities were a seamless web – but they were not. They are a distorting lens, and he had no more right than Frances Trollope to claim "there is no exaggeration in this." But whereas her writing has the exaggeration of the indignant rhetorician, who does no harm to the factual content of her account but deprives it of any deep literary interest, he gives us the distortions of a quirky genius, not interested in representative facts but in creating an unforgettable world that, since it does not aim for the truths of a Royal Commission or a Select Committee, does not mislead.

The factories were bad enough; but the mines were worse. We know about working conditions in the mines from the Report of the Royal Commission on Child Employment in Mines of 1842, one of the great series of grimly factual, unforgettable blue books (unforgettable because so grimly factual) that do such credit to the early-nineteenth-century public servants who wrote them. We cannot repeat the comparison with the Condition-of-England novels because the novelists, as it happens, did not turn their attention to the mines. In England we had to wait almost a century until a miner's son became a celebrated writer, but then we are amply rewarded. *Sons and Lovers* contains what may well be the most authentic and moving scenes of working-class family life in our literature. It also enables us to ask about how a novelist is to represent poverty, and to ask this I want to compare it with another great novel of mining life, Emile Zola's *Germinal*.

The comparison suggests at least one striking contrast. Is poverty seen in terms of deprivation, as a contrast to the life of the rich, who can do and consume so much that the poor have no access to? Or is it seen as a set of interactions in a family who love, hate, feel, think and behave with the complexity that is inseparable from being human? The more political and programmatic the novelist's vision, the more he is likely to offer the first, and *Germinal* is certainly a more consciously radical novel than *Sons and Lovers*. It sets the life of the mining families in deliberate contrast to the elegant dinners in the house of Monsieur Hennebeau, the mine manager. Maheu and his family have none of the comforts, pleasures and opportunities that the Hennebeau have (and fail to enjoy). The Maheu live on the bread line, and the mother has an unremitting struggle against debt: when for any reason the family income drops (as it does from time to time, at first through the petty tyranny of the engineer who seizes every shortcoming, real or imaginary, as an opportunity to dock wages; then, more drastically, through the strike which is the main action of the novel), they have to cut down their already minimal consumption. The result is a frightening monotony, corresponding to the monotony of their constant struggle to survive. There is a raw power in Zola's depiction of poverty, but it is achieved at a literary price, as we immediately see if we contrast the Maheu with the far more complex family life of the Morels, which is also aware of deprivation but does not allow it to dominate the representation of experience. To read *Germinal* is a distressing experience for the comfortable bourgeois reader, and I am reluctant to say anything that seems to dismiss this; but what makes for literary power also makes for simplification. Zola's politicisation shows poverty as an extreme situation; *Sons and Lovers* is less harrowing, less shocking, but a richer reading experience.

Not that generalisation is necessarily impoverishing to a novel, as we can see if we turn to *Women in Love*. This is a more rewarding comparison for *Germinal*, because it too shows the interaction between rich and poor, and tries to offer a general picture of the mining industry. Zola shows how easily the small capitalist, as soon as there is industrial unrest, is ground between the violence of labour and the power of large capital: the locally owned mine of Jean–Bart is the ultimate loser in the troubles. Lawrence's exploration, concentrated in a single remarkable chapter, "The Industrial Magnate," is an account of how Gerald Crich modernised the mines, sweeping aside the sentimental, inefficient system of his father in order to apply his vision of "the pure instrumentality of mankind," and of how the miners, after an initial resistance, came to accept the change in a way that showed how part of their humanity had died. Lawrence's terminology in telling us this is sometimes vague and old-fashioned ("their hearts died within them, but their souls were satisfied"); but his idea is strikingly similar to the Marxist concept of alienation ("the worker is alienated from his species being"), though Lawrence had certainly not read the Economic and Philosophic Manuscripts. Both Marx and Lawrence drop into abstractions that sound remote from experience and are strikingly similar to each other: "Estranged labour turns man's species being, both nature and his spiritual species property, into a being alien to him [...] It estranges from man his own body." – "It was [...] the substitution of the mechanical principle for the organic, the destruction of the organic purpose [...] The first and finest state of chaos." The huge difference between the two texts, of course, is that, as we read on in *Women in Love*, the abstractions become meaningful, as we see them illustrated in terms of human experience. If we did not greet that with relief, we would not be literary students.

By the time we reach Zola and Lawrence, the reticences of the earlier nineteenth century are over; both novelists allow themselves what Henry James rather coyly called "the larger latitude." So, in comparing *Women in Love* with *Germinal*, I want to turn not to capitalist organisation but to how they treated class differences in sexual behaviour. First, M. Hennebeau:

> M. Hennebeau, qui justement rentrait à cette heure, monté sur sa jument, prêtait l'oreille à ces bruits perdus [...] N'étaient-ce pas là ses rencontres habituelles, des filles culbutées au fond de chaque fosse, des gueux se bourrant de la seule joie qui ne coutaient rien? Et ces imbéciles se plaignaient de la vie, lorsqu'ils avaient à pleines ventrées, cet unique bonheur de s'aimer! Volontiers, il aurait crevé, de faim comme eux, s'il avaient pu recommencer l'existence avec une femme qui se serait donnée à lui sur les cailloux, de tous ses reins et de tout son coeur. Son malheur était sans consolation, il enviait ces misérables. La tête basse, il rentrait, au pas ralenti de son cheval, désespéré par ces longs bruits, perdus au fond de la campagne noire, où il n'entendait que des baisers.[11]

> (M. Hennebeau, on his way home, mounted on his mare, listened to the sounds. Every evening he came across it, boys and girls taking their pleasure behind walls,

[11] Emile Zola, *Germinal* (1885; Paris: Pocket, 1990) Book IV 298.

> young women tumbling into every ditch, these paupers stuffing themselves with the only pleasure that costs nothing. And these imbeciles grumbled about their life when they could have their bellyful of love, that unique pleasure. He would gladly have starved like them if he could only start life over with a woman who'd give herself to him, body and soul, lying on the pebbles. His misery was inconsolable, he envied these wretches. Head bowed, he returned home, his horse walking slowly, plunged into despair by the prolonged noises lost in the distance on the dark fields, where he heard nothing but kissing.)

Thirty years later, a rather younger mine manager was present at much the same scene, but this time he was accompanied. The scene this time is described by the woman:

> And she knew that under this dark and lonely bridge the young colliers stood in the darkness with their sweethearts, in rainy weather. And so she wanted to stand under the bridge with her sweetheart, and be kissed under the bridge in the invisible darkness. Her steps dragged as she drew near.
>
> So, under the bridge, they came to a standstill, and he lifted her upon his breast. His body vibrated taut and powerful as he closed upon her and crushed her upon his breast. Ah, it was terrible and perfect. Under this bridge, the colliers pressed their lovers to their breast. And now, under the bridge, the master of them all pressed her to himself! And how much more powerful and terrible was his embrace, than theirs, how much more concentrated and supreme his love was, than theirs, in the same sort! [...]
>
> So, the colliers' lovers would stand with their backs to the walls, holding their sweethearts and kissing them as she was being kissed. – Ah, but would their kisses be fine and powerful as the kisses of the firm-mouthed master? Even the keen, short-cut moustache – the colliers would not have that.[12]

So Gerald Crich has what poor M. Hennebeau so longed for, a woman willing to give herself to him, body and soul, lying on the pebbles. In both these episodes, we have stumbled on a moment when the miners are seen through the eyes of an outsider, and the differences between the two points of view are subtle but fascinating. M. Hennebeau, the helpless cuckold, is a pathetic, almost ridiculous figure, but we are not here being invited to think that his perception of the miners is wrong: they are indeed lying in every ditch, stuffing themselves with the one pleasure that costs nothing (the same wording was used to describe the sex between Maheu and his wife – though considering the number of children they have to feed, it is hardly true that it costs nothing). The melodramatic envy of M. Hennebeau does perceive accurately, but it is related, too, to the melodramatic imagination that pervades this powerful, simplifying novel.

---

[12] D.H. Lawrence, *Women in Love* (1921; Cambridge University Press, 1987) 330.

In *Women in Love* there is even less detachment from the speaker. When a Lawrence character feels that "his body vibrated taut and powerful as he closed upon her, and crushed her upon his breast. Ah it was terrible and perfect," she is not being treated ironically: this is the intensity of sexual passion that quivers in the final part of *The Rainbow* and which made Lawrence so loved and (sometimes) so hated a novelist. But the account does not stop there: Gudrun's sexual intensity is immediately placed in a social context. Gerald, "the master of them all," is with a queer kind of perversity behaving like his own employees (such a streak of perversity is central to his character: it made him a brilliant manager, and ultimately a failure as a human being); Gudrun realises this, and for her it enhances his attraction: she likes the fact that she can tell herself that he is not really like one of the miners. And then she illustrates the point from facial hair: the "keen short-cut moustache," which adds a tang to the kiss as mustard does to meat, is seen as a sign of class. The detail is precise and observant, with an economy seldom found in Zola: but it also hovers on the comic in an inadvertent way that Zola hardly ever does. The miners, we presume, all have droopy moustaches.

In both novels, the soldiers are called out to put down a strike. This is always a complex situation socially and politically, since the soldiers are from much the same social background as the miners whom they are being asked to shoot. Zola makes this point explicitly in the case of the young Breton sentry whom Etienne tries to fraternise with, and who is eventually stabbed by Maheu's delinquent son Jeanlin simply because he felt like killing him, and whose body is then so effectively hidden that the army decides he has deserted. There seem to be two equally futile possibilities for the helpless conscript: change sides or be killed. Without even a name, this young sentry sums up the helplessness of the individual soldier.

A soldier, one would think, is hardly a natural symbol of the oppressed, because of his ambivalent status: but here is one soldier who is quite unambiguously a helpless victim:

> They throw in Drummer Hodge, to rest
>   Uncoffined – just as found:
> His landmark is a kopje-crest
>   That breaks the veldt around;
> And foreign constellations west
>   Each night above his mound.
>
> Young Hodge the Drummer never knew –
>   Fresh from his Wessex home –
> The meaning of the broad Karroo,
>   The Bush, the dusty loam,

And why uprose to nightly view
Strange stars amid the gloam.

Yet portion of that unknown plain
Will Hodge forever be;
His homely Northern breast and brain
Grown to some Southern tree,
And strange-eyed constellations reign
His stars eternally.[13]

This anonymous soldier (for "Hodge," of course, is simply the generic nickname for a farm labourer), killed and buried hugger-mugger on the other side of the world, "never knew" the meaning of something. Of what? This crucial detail lies at the heart of the poem. Sent out, like so many common soldiers, to fight in a foreign land, what did he know of the causes and issues of the Boer War? The cannon-fodder are unaware of why wars are fought: there is but to do or die – ingloriously.

That is a political reading, but the poem seems to point to another way of understanding the meaning of the broad Karroo. Though Hodge did not understand it, he has become a part of it. He is a portion of that unknown plain as Adonais is a portion of the loveliness which once he made more lovely, or as Housman's young man who hated the cold "has made of earth and sea / His overcoat for ever / And wears the turning globe." This is the familiar Romantic theme of being absorbed into Nature, accompanied by the awe which means so much to poets in this Wordsworthian tradition, who "did but half-remember human words / In converse with the mountains moors and fens."[14]

Fifty years ago, I am sure, this is the reading that would have occurred to most readers; today, many will want to give the more political meaning to what Hodge never knew, and are likely to accuse the more Romantic readers of occluding the politics. The Boer War was, after all, fought for hard-headed economic reasons, not to teach pantheistic wonderment to untravelled yokels.

How is such a disagreement to be settled? Here again we have seen a change. If authorial intention is our criterion, we must surely plump for the Wordsworthian reading, since it fits with so much else in Hardy: Giles Winterborne's understanding of natural processes, Tess's magical mornings at Talbothays, the

13 Thomas Hardy, "Drummer Hodge," *Collected Poems* (1899; London: Macmillan, 1968) 83.

14 Percy Bysshe Shelley, "Adonais," *Collected Poems* (1821; London: Oxford University Press, 1905) 441 (st. 43); A.E. Housman, "Last Poems, XX," *Collected Poems* (1922; Harmondsworth: Penguin Books, 1956) 126; J.M. Synge, "Prelude," *Plays, Poems & Prose* (1908; London: Everyman's Library, 1941) 232.

awesome, brooding power of Egdon Heath – varied in emotional colouring, but all concerned with the "meaning" of the rustic setting, its power to evoke awe at the presence of nature.

But we live in the age of reader-response criticism, in which the meaning of a literary work is determined not merely by authorial intention but also by the reading community, a community that tends to read more politically than its parents did. Even our perception of authorial intention – culled, as I have just been doing, from the author's other works – will depend on our choice of other works. Casting an eye onto the facing page of the *Collected Poems*, we find "At the War Office London," another poem about the Boer War, which contains no element of Romantic awe but has one memorable, biting line about "the hourly posted sheets of scheduled slaughter." Is this not a more appropriate context for "Drummer Hodge"?

I conclude with as much uncertainty as I have attributed to the poem. To abandon what I have called the Wordsworthian reading would break my heart: it would seem a rejection of what made me a poetry-lover in the first place. But to abandon the possibility of a more political reading would also seem to betray something. In terms of the signifiers, we have only one poem; but in terms of the signified, ought we to say that we are dealing with two different poems, or two ways of reading the same poem?

One last soldier, from an earlier and very different radical writer:

London

I wander thro' each charter'd street,
Near where the charter'd Thames does flow,
And mark in every face I meet
Marks of weakness, marks of woe.

In every cry of every Man,
In every Infant's cry of fear,
In every voice, in every ban,
The mind-forg'd manacles I hear.

How the Chimney-sweeper's cry
Every black'ning Church appalls;
And the hapless soldier's sigh
Runs in blood down Palace walls.

But most through midnight streets I hear
How the youthful harlot's curse

> Blasts the new born Infant's tear,
> And blights with plagues the Marriage hearse.[15]

This poem combines directness of passion with verbal subtlety in a way one would hardly have thought possible. Zola's brief sketch of the Breton conscript works with an economy that could make the whole novel seem long-winded; yet Blake's two lines about the soldier seem written with a profounder kind of economy, and somehow to say everything that Zola says. Is the "hapless soldier" a deserter being shot or (perhaps the subtler reading) a reluctant trooper quelling a riot? This is one of the poem's many ambiguities – beginning with "charter'd," whose repetition insists that we read in anger, yet at the same time draws attention to the shift in meaning. A charter is a stuffy old document that grants privileges and restrictions, and is also a document offering freedom, so that the very first line invites contrasting readings: London is a place where everything is regulated, even the river; or, London is liberated by a charter which was granted to every street – even the river, and therefore means nothing. Both indignant.

There is no resounding conclusion to this essay – rather, an admission that the very title I chose – representing the oppressed – seems to imply radicalism, and so I have left aside the question of what it would be to write a great conservative novel about the poor. (By a delicious irony, one of the great conservative political novels in English is actually called *Felix Holt the Radical.*) To explore this, we could start from Engels's famous preference of Balzac to Zola, on the grounds that the novelist's insights are more important than his opinions. That would, of course, require another essay.

Two observations may perhaps take the place of a rousing conclusion. First, the claim that we can read with political awareness while also being aware of the oversimplifications of politics; and second, that putting Zola's novel next to these two poems makes one realise the enormous economy and compression of poetry that can make us, in certain moods, think of all novels as long-winded. To say nothing of all literary discussions.

---

[15] William Blake, "London," *Songs of Experience: Poetry & Prose* (1794; London: Nonesuch Library, 1961) 75.

Nursery Rhymes and History: Poetry as Induction

JEAN–JACQUES LECERCLE

I Karl Marx

I SUFFER FROM GRECIAN URN SYNDROME. I want my brides of quietness left unravished. I want beauty, which is truth, left unadulterated, immune to the ravages of time. I want to be able to deal with the question of the relationship between poetry and history with one short answer: links there are none. In short, I am in the grip of a nostalgic and outdated idea of art, which can be formulated in two theses. 1) Art endures, it is unaffected by change, by the corruption of history – art is not subject to history and, conversely, does not reflect it. 2) Poetry is the very emblem of art in that sense.[1]

There is an immediate problem with this position. By using words like "outdated" or "nostalgic" to describe it, I have reintroduced time and change; in other words, history. The ideology of the non-historicity of art is itself steeped in history, which casts doubts on the non-historicity of its content. I am afraid that, contrary to my inclination, I must historicise the Grecian Urn, which I shall do by taking two names or symptoms, in the old sense of "symptomal reading": the Greeks, and John Keats.

My spontaneous belief in the non-historicity of poetry, in the capacity of art to endure, finds an unexpected supporter in Karl Marx. The eternal charm of Greek art and the eternal significance of Greek culture – a typical nineteenth-century theme, what we might call the Dover Beach syndrome, that eternal note of sadness which Sophocles heard long ago, and which still moves us to poetic musings – are the subject of a page in Marx's 1857 *Contribution to the Critique of Political Economy*, that archetypal Marxist text, which opens with the famous preface on which historical materialism, at its most didactic and reductive, was largely

[1] This is the text of a plenary lecture delivered at the "Poetry and History" conference in 1996 at the University of Stirling.

erected. It is all the more surprising, and invigorating, to discover, hidden away in a neglected corner of the text, a page full of apparently un-Marxist views on Greek art.

This page occurs at the very end of an "introduction," left unfinished and suppressed by Marx, but usually published as an addendum to the main text. It occurs at the end of the fourth section, which is a mere sketch, where Marx at last embarks on the question of the superstructure – not merely the relations of production, but also the forms of consciousness induced by such relations. In this hodgepodge, where one recognises the usual desultory treatment of the superstructure by the later Marx (at the end, if there is time, and there is never time), eight questions "not to be forgotten" are asked. Number six deals with art, with the uneven relations between the development of material and of artistic production: the notion of "progress" is too abstract, which means that the two developments are not parallel, and that the development in each field is non-linear.

The page I am interested in[2] is the sketch of an answer to the sixth question. Here is a brief summary. The first paragraph suggests that the best art (Homer or Shakespeare) occurs in primitive conditions. It occurs before the material or the artistic conditions for it to appear are satisfied. In other words, the best art anticipates the development of society, and the development of art itself (I leave you to ponder on the baffling question of how art can be an anticipation of itself). The non-historicity of art – primitive art is still a source of inspiration to us – is a surface effect of a complex historical or temporal trope, the trope of *anticipation*. The surface non-historicity and deeper historicity of art result from this non-coincidence with, and anticipation of, the present state of society and of artistic development. The greatness of great art lies in its intimation, or intuition, of things to come.

The second paragraph inverts the relation, by considering ancient art from the point of view of contemporary society. What is the *Odyssey*, Marx asks, at the time of the printing press? What is Vulcan compared to a steel magnate, Jupiter compared to the lightning conductor, and Hermes compared to the Credit Bank? Behind the apparent vulgarity of this debunking, there is the beginning of an analysis of the social conditions for the appearance of Greek art; and of the formative, should I say "esemplastic," power of mythology, which solves in imagination the problems that material conditions leave unsolved. Greek art emerges out of Greek mythology, itself linked to the state of Greek society: here the tem-

[2] Reference is to the French edition, Marx, *Contribution à la critique de l'économie politique* (Paris: Editions sociales, 1957) 173–75 (174).

poral or historical trope at work is *correspondence*. And since those social conditions are irretrievably past, Greek art, which anticipates future developments, is also *passé*, outmoded because it must somehow coincide with its material conditions of production. Here, the father of all Marxists is recognisably himself.

The third paragraph, however, very briefly suggests a third temporal trope, delay or, rather, *survival*. For Greek art, in Grecian Urn fashion, is still very much alive long after its historical conditions have vanished. This, which is less recognisably a Marxian thesis (although the question of the partial survival of defunct modes of production has always preoccupied Marx), is presented both as a fact and as a difficulty, which compensates for the reductive determinism of the previous paragraph. But this third trope is in fact the logical consequence of the first two – what we have is, in fact, three Heideggerian temporal *ek-stases*: like the *Dasein*, art is characterised by its tension towards the future, by its capacity to anticipate. And it is this power of anticipation, of temporal dislocation or discrepancy, that accounts for its capacity to survive. The argument can already be found in the preface to Hegel's *Phenomenology of Mind*, where this dual power of anticipation and survival is ascribed to language: it is language that can make a falsehood endure, by phrasing it, but that can also anticipate truth, by stating what is now false but will later become true.

So far, we have a dialectic of temporal *ek-stases* (anticipation, coincidence, survival, or: future, present and past) that is not strikingly original. The last paragraph, however, seeks an entirely different, and un-Marxian, way out of the difficulty of the survival of art, by abandoning the three temporal tropes for an wholly different trope: *antimetabole*. The reason for the survival of Greek art, Marx says, is that the childhood of art is the art of childhood: in other words, that we enjoy our own childhood again in contemplating the childhood of mankind, that ontogeny recapitulates phylogeny – another typically nineteenth-century theme. But it does seem that the father of all Marxists has read Wordsworth: there are intimations of immortality in the childhood of art or of mankind. We all experience nostalgia for the past, and this nostalgia is all the more pleasurable and memorable as it is desperate or pointless: those social conditions, that art, can never return, like our personal past; hence their charm. This is, in fact, no etymological nostalgia, since there is no *nostos*, no return, for us to long for. But long we do, a perverse longing for the impossibility of return, a kind of *anostolagnia*, if you pardon the awful coinage, through a kind of Freudian denial in which not the object, but the very impossibility of its existence, is the source of desire. Despite appearances, the *antimetabole* is in fact a garbled temporal trope, for which I borrow the linguistic concept of the perfect: a double temporal relation that recognises the pastness of the past but envisages it from the vantage point of the present.

There is, however, a clear division within my four tropes. The first three (anticipation, coincidence and survival) allow us to develop a dialectic of the historicity of art, in a rather more complex movement than linear progress and parallelism between superstructure and base. The fourth trope, *antimetabole*, or the perfect, shifts to the point of view of reception (how the past is seen from the point of view of the present) and provides a formulation of the ideology of the non-historicity of art. It constructs the perfection of art – what Marx calls the "eternal charm" of Greek art – by ascribing to art the structure of the linguistic perfect, of the fixation of the past in the present. The temporal duality of the perfect organises and fixes, as varnish fixes paint, the three temporal *ek-stases* that constitute art in its historicity. We understand how the Grecian-Urn syndrome is produced and why it is so effective.

In the rest of this essay, I shall attempt to show how the dialectic of the historicity and non-historicity of art, or poetry, works, not in the abstract language of philosophy, but by reading literary texts. And since Marx's first concern was the childhood of art, mine will be the art of childhood: in other words, English nursery rhymes. Intuitively, it seems that my four temporal tropes must indeed be at work there. Nursery rhymes are both eternally charming (they seem to escape history by having no apparent link with it, except the antiquity of their unfathomable, timeless origins), and yet to be steeped in history, in that they can be shown to anticipate, to coincide with and to survive historical conjunctures. And one can give a more dynamic version of this relation of inversion or mirror-image: history works on poetry by "inducing" it (hence my title), but, conversely, poetry works on history by fixing it in an eternal present: that is, by corrupting, dismembering and remembering it in order to survive. We shall try to see how poetic sense is made of history, and how historical sense is constructed in, or out of, poetry.

II Elsie Marley

Elsie Marley is grown so fine,
She won't get up to feed the swine
But lives in bed till eight or nine,
Lazy Elsie Marley.[3]

At first sight, there is no obvious link to history in this timeless jingle. Elsie can be any child, a fellow traveller to Shock-Headed Peter or Cicely: that is, the object

[3] Iona and Peter Opie, *The Oxford Dictionary of Nursery Rhymes* (Oxford: Clarendon Press, 1951) 159.

of a cautionary tale in the manner parodied by Hilaire Belloc. The only link to history is that the cautionary tale is a now outmoded Victorian genre, which reached its climax, and its end, in Belloc's pastiche. Nowadays, pedagogic correctness might object to the terrorist directness of such an attack.

The rhyme, however, must also be historicised in another way. It is a reflection of a past which, if not bucolic, is at least agricultural: hardly any children nowadays have to get up to feed the swine and, on the whole, eight or nine o'clock seems to be a reasonable time for leaving one's bed. So we shall not be surprised when we discover in the Opies' *Dictionary of Nursery Rhymes* that the rhyme has, in fact, a precise historical source. Alice Marley (1715–1768) kept a pub near Chester-le-Street and enjoyed a wide reputation, celebrated in countless songs, from one of which this is a garbled extract. The Opies coyly add that her reputation was not owing mainly to the quality of her ale, and refer the reader to another nursery rhyme, the story of Little Blue Betty, who also "sold ale to gentlemen" but had a sad tendency to "hop upstairs to make her bed." It would appear that the object of the cautionary tale, far from being an innocent child, was a North Country Fanny Hill, which places the poem on a similar footing to Hardy's "The Ruined Maid." I cannot resist the pleasure of quoting its beginning:

> O' Melia, my dear this does everything crown!
> Who could have supposed I should meet you in Town?
> And whence such fair garments, such prosperity? –
> 'O didn't you know I'd been ruined?' said she.[4]

It would appear that the eternal charm of utter childishness has a precise historical source – is made up of sedimented, and dehistoricised, history. The corruption of the text is not merely philological, a gradual blurring of the original meaning of the poem, but also semantic in the widest sense, as the poem abandons its original genre and historical conjuncture, to make sense anew in another genre and another conjuncture. If I generalise this to the whole corpus of nursery rhymes, as indeed I may, even if "Elsie Marley" is an exception in that its historical origin can be traced in its minutest detail, I realise that the free play of boisterous meaninglessness that characterises nursery rhymes conceals the work of historical sedimentation and corruption and requires an archaeological enquiry. The blandness, innocuousness, meaninglessness of nursery rhymes, which account for their conservation, and for their conservatism (they cling, or appear to cling, to good old values), are in fact the surface effect of the historical work of corruption, so that nursery rhymes conform to the four Marxian tropes indicated

[4] Thomas Hardy, *The Complete Poems*, ed. James Gibson (1976; London: Macmillan, 1981) 158.

above and have the dual temporal structure of the perfect: a timeless present built upon a sedimented and repressed past that returns at the first opportunity. The art of childhood does refer, if not always to the childhood of art (although it does just that in myth), at least to the past state of the art: that is, to the temporal dialectic of anticipation, coincidence and survival.

Hence, although nursery rhymes appear, and perhaps even claim, to be outside the scope of history, the following two theses can be defended: 1) There is history in nursery rhymes, in a vestigial state, it is true, but susceptible to recovery or discovery. 2) There is a history of nursery rhymes: the whole genre, and not merely each individual rhyme, is steeped in historical conjunctures. The second thesis is of peculiar interest to me, as it immediately divides into two, and neatly illustrates my tropic account. On the side of *antimetabole*, there is a mythical history of nursery rhymes, which is coincident with – indeed, constitutive of – the appearance of the genre: the genre appears in the middle of the nineteenth century, together with a long and venerable history, constructed in the retroactive mode of the always-already. According to this mythical account, nursery rhymes are the archives of the national past, among the most ancient monuments of our Anglo-Saxon ancestors. Their origin is lost in the darkness of first beginnings, so that, ontogeny recapitulating phylogeny, each child as she recites her favourite rhymes symbolically reappropriates, in her language, the past of her culture, her race. That such mythology must be historicised is obvious: most nineteenth-century and early-twentieth-century British folklorists who develop such ideas express a nationalist belief in the Nordic origin of the rhymes, which is a way of laying a claim to the Nordic origins of the race. Humpty Dumpty is the British version of the Danish Lille Trille or the German Humpelken Pumpelken.

In contrast to the mythical account, on the side of my three other historical tropes there is a real (or at least less mythical) his*ory of nursery rhymes. We can describe the actual process of their constitution as a genre through the two collections made by James Orchard Halliwell, which appeared in 1842 and 1849.[5] He is not only the inventor of the genre, he is also the leading exponent of the myth. As a well-known philologist and Shakespearean scholar, he established the corpus of the rhymes by applying the latest techniques of philological enquiry (or, at least, he appeared to do so: the Opies suggest that he invented a few of the rhymes he claimed to have collected from ancient manuscripts). But this relationship was used to bolster up an ideological construction in which the historicity of the genre

[5] J.O. Halliwell, *The Nursery Rhymes of England* (1842; London: The Bodley Head, 1970), and *Popular Rhymes and Nursery Tales of England* (1849; London: The Bodley Head, 1970).

is denied through the trope of the perfect: a typical sentence from his introductory essay to the second collection, "Nursery Antiquities," would be: "Many of the metrical nonsense-riddles of the nursery are of considerable antiquity." The invention of a genre within a determinate historical and ideological conjuncture is dehistoricised through a myth of origins.

I can now go back to my first thesis, and show that individual rhymes deal with history according to my first three tropes. Nursery rhymes do correspond to, or reflect, contemporary history, as is clear in the case of "Elsie Marley," even if the bawdy or comic song loses its asperities in constant repetition and only reaches the nursery in a heavily censored and innocuous form. They also demonstrate a capacity to survive, a characteristic that provides a justification for the construction of the myth. The survival of "Elsie Marley" is yet modest, but we may follow the Opies' detective work on "London Bridge is falling down":[6] they trace its origin, step by logical step, back to a Florentine game played around 1328, and even further back to the horrendous – and, one hopes, largely mythical – practice of walling in a child to protect a newly erected bridge, which gives sinister resonance to the well-known line "Set a man to watch all night." Lastly, they can also be said to anticipate. The Queen of Hearts and her tarts first appeared in 1782, as part of a burlesque poem about the four suits of cards. The lines were used by Canning in his satire of poetic criticism and by Lamb in 1805 as a basis for one of his children's books. But there is, I believe, a non-trivial sense in which the rhyme was, always-already, destined for *Alice in Wonderland* as its proper context (and Carroll's tale, as we know, is built around a number of rhymes, poems and songs, which it allows to unfold into their final form like so many Leibnizian monads). The rhyme anticipates not only its proper context, but also the development of the genre it illustrates into an art form – a feat that is achieved with the *Alice* books. Marx's view was not so bizarre, perhaps, when he said that primitive art anticipated itself.

Such are the complex notions that animate Halliwell's collections, and are denied by the mythical work of *antimetabole*, which dehistoricises the poetry of childhood by treating it as the eternal childhood of poetry. The *antimetabole*, with its chiastic inversion, turns the other three temporal tropes upside down, separates survival from correspondence and anticipation, and erects it, under the name of eternity, into the sole temporal mode of poetry. Against this work of mythification, we must describe the actual work of corruption, which is the true temporal mode of nursery rhymes. Here history acts on poetry, and poetry works on his-

[6] Opie 270–76.

tory: the genre of nursery rhymes is a corruption machine – a re-writing machine – which operates through a) distortion (the meaning of real origins, of the original historical conjuncture, is lost in "Elsie Marley"); b) extraction (the original text is separated from its historical context, but also from its co-text, by being cut, and sometimes more or less re-written to suit new contexts); c) censorship (this is obvious: the Victorian nursery is a heaven of peace protected from the aggressions of the real world); and d) absorption (nursery rhymes have a capacity to absorb all other poetic genres by re-writing them: this is the case even for "Higglety, pigglety pop! / The dog has eaten the mop,"[7] a jingle created by the American Samuel Goodrich, alias Peter Parley, an active hater of nursery rhymes, who was trying to ridicule the genre and ended up contributing to its corpus; and the rhymes are also plastic enough to absorb all new historical contexts, as occurred in 1941 with "London Bridge" and the Blitz). This work of historical corruption, with its loss and re-creation of meaning, is not peculiar to nursery rhymes, even if it is peculiarly obvious in them: remember the militant Luddite in E.P. Thompson's *The Making of the English Working Class*, whose slogan was not "Long live the Revolution" but "Long live the Levelution," because his culture still remembered the levellers.[8]

III W.H. Auden

So far, the work of history on poetry has appeared to be spontaneous and arbitrary: there is no determinism in the work of corruption, only chance. Alice Marley had no more right to immortality than countless numbers of her colleagues. History being a process without a subject, corruption is applied by an invisible hand. What happens, however, when the hand becomes visible, when the work of corruption becomes the centre of attention, when it is reflexively applied to nursery rhymes themselves? This is the moment when poetry takes her revenge, when, by re-writing nursery rhymes (a traditional game, already played by Lamb and Coleridge), poetry applies to history the same kind of Freudian work that history has applied to it. This occurs with W.H. Auden's poem "Nursery Rhyme,"[9] which I would like to read not merely as a pastiche of a genre, but as an historical intervention by a poet with a political past (the poem was written by Auden not in his *engagés* 1930s, but in the 1940s). The term "historical intervention" denotes a) a

---

[7] Opie 208.

[8] E.P. Thompson, *The Making of the English Working Class* (1963; Harmondsworth: Penguin, 1968) 753.

[9] W.H. Auden, "Nursery Rhyme," *Collected Shorter Poems, 1927–1957*, ed. Edward Mendelsohn (London: Faber & Faber, 1969) 219–20.

deliberate use of poetry to act upon history in the widest sense, by acting upon language (it was Lenin who wrote a pamphlet on the capacity of the right slogan to move the masses into action) and b) the return of a corrupted, mythified or denied history to destabilise the genre of nursery rhymes. The reading of the poem can be summarised in a pastiche of Adorno's famous maxim: "it is no longer possible to write poetry after the Second World War."

In a superficial way, the poem does correspond to its title. All the paraphernalia of nursery rhymes and children's bedtime stories are present: woolly bears and toffee are the stuff that kiddies' dreams are made of. It is not merely a question of cuddly toys and food, the daily preoccupations of the child – the marvellous that her imagination is supposed to feed upon is also there: talking frogs and coaches possibly nostalgic for their pristine pumpkin status. The diction, the images belong to the poetry of childhood and so do the syntax and prosody:

> Their learned kings bent down to chat with frogs;
> This was until the battle of the Bogs.
> *The key that opens is the key that rusts.*
>
> Their cheerful kings made toffee on their stoves
> This was until the Rotting of the Loaves
> *The robins vanish when the ravens come.*
>
> That was before the coaches reached the bogs;
> Now woolly bears pursue their spotted dogs.
> *A witch can make an ogre out of mud...*[10]

The use of generic articles appeals to established convention and shared knowledge (whose learned kings are those? Why, "theirs," of course); the gnomic form of the sentences, much enhanced by the fact that sentences strictly correspond to lines, turns the poem into a collection of seeming proverbs (which, of course, lack the main characteristic of proverbs: that they are proverbial: i.e. common knowledge); the regularity of meter and rhyme, the presence of a burden, strongly remind us of the regularity and repetitive patterns of nursery rhymes and other children's poems. All the appearances, therefore, are present in a rather insistent fashion.

That these are mere appearances, however, is equally obvious. One element disrupts and contradicts all the others: the atmosphere is not right, it is too gloomy to be truly puerile. Witness the last stanza:

---

[10] Auden 219.

> The blinded bears have rooted up the groves;
> Our poisoned milk boils over on our stoves
> *The key that opens is the key that rusts.*[11]

One is reminded of those tragic absurdist readings of *Alice in Wonderland*: but what is a curiosity where Carroll is concerned becomes a necessity here. In spite of the chiastic structure of the stanzas, there is a semantic progression in the poem towards dereliction and death. A simple lexical study would note the abundance of words denoting disappearance and despair, and their increased presence as the text unfolds. An analysis of the stanzas will focus on the strong and ubiquitous contrast between a happy "before" and a miserable "after," while the gradual invasion of the text by the present tense (which is both the natural tense of the proverbial burden and the contrastive mark of the horrible "now") parallels the invasion of this wonderland by bodily corruption. Those nursery animals that become lethal or poisonous and die off break a cardinal rule of children's poetry – that disease and death cannot be mentioned, or, if they are, that it should be with such ironic distance that they cannot be felt as actual threats.

A first interpretation of this gloom would be to treat it as an embodiment of the work of corruption, both linguistic and historical, that produces nursery rhymes. All bearings have been lost, the specificity of original events is veiled under the genericness of false proverbs, and the poem very cleverly pastiches the facile grandiloquence of certain types of children's poems (cautionary tales or falsely prophetic religious texts) by withdrawing any recognisable meaning from its portentous lines. But there is, I think, more to it than such vague *mise en abyme*. By letting history return in a chaotic and garbled way, the poem seems to intervene on or in history.

First we must note a number, even a network, of corrupt allusions to history as taught in schoolbooks. Those "learned kings" that "chat with frogs" belong to the world of medieval romance; when they make "toffee on their stoves" they are a variation on Alfred and the cakes; and there is no need to tell you of which event in Irish history the "Battle of the Bogs" reminds us, or to which Biblical scene the "Rotting of the Loaves" alludes. This is no mere indulging in mythical history for school primers, this amounts to exposing the myth by mocking it – for here mythical history proliferates and even obtrudes. In turn, this exposition, which threatens the apparent non-historicity of nursery rhymes, re-historicises the poem: this is no longer the confident atmosphere of Victorian childhood, of toys in the nursery, tales told by nurse and croquet on the lawn, this is the deep despair of

[11] Auden 220.

another historical conjuncture, one which destroys the irrepressible optimism of Victorian child literature. There is no "*vert paradis des amours enfantines*" after Auschwitz, and the poem explores this new structure of feeling even as it exposes the outdated one. Whether such pessimism is a new historical myth – whether there is, for that matter, history that is "actual" rather than "mythic" – is another problem. But Auden's poem broaches the following problem: the false proverbs, false because coined by the poet and not by common sense, deny the communal construction of meaning through common phrases and maxims (clichés, formulas, etc.) that is precisely called common sense. Both nursery rhymes and proverbs play a part in that construction: in the world of Auden's War, such linguistic linking, a modern form of *religio*, is no longer possible.

The global meaning of the poem, therefore, is to be found in the shift from the pleasure of unmeaning nonsense, whose function it is to bolster up common sense, to the horror of the contemporary construction of sense and the impossibility of a sense that could be said to be common (for a prose version of this, see Patrick Hamilton's novel *The Slaves of Solitude*). The non-historicity of Victorian nursery rhymes is meaningful, expressing a belief in progress and the meaning of history (this is why Karl Marx is so keen on *antimetabole*, which expresses and structures such meaning, at the cost of constructing a myth); the historicity of Auden's poem, its reflection of and intervention in the context of the War, is meaningless (sense is no longer common, history no longer has a meaning). The poem, in fact – here lies the gist of what I have called its "intervention" – subverts both the *antimetabole* (the art of childhood is no longer celebrated as the childhood of art: this spurious nursery rhyme is full of elderly, wizened, dying characters) and the other three temporal tropes. Or, rather, one temporal *ek-stasis*, the present and not the future, expression without anticipation, dominates and even cancels the other two. The black epiphany of the present has corrupted the past and blocks all hope of a future. There is no survival, no anticipation: the present in its horror has devoured all.

IV Rudyard Kipling and John Keats

I would like to illustrate the complex relationships I have tried to sketch not only between history and poetry (poetry is presented as non-historical; it is worked upon, in the Freudian sense, by history, and it intervenes in and on history), but also between history and myth (*antimetabole* erects a myth on and against the three historical tropes of anticipation, coincidence and survival), by using a parable. Or, rather, by reading a short story by Kipling, "Wireless," as a parable.

"Wireless" is included in the collection *Traffics and Discoveries*.[12] It is difficult to do justice to this extraordinary story – I duly apologise for the summary that follows. The scene takes place in a chemist's shop, in a small seaside town in the South of England. The narrator has come to watch the chemist's nephew operate an early Marconi wireless set and try to make contact with the neighbouring town of Poole. It is a difficult and lengthy process, which will be successful only after the end of the story. Meanwhile, the narrator's attention is focused on the chemist's assistant, a young man obviously suffering from tuberculosis, whom the narrator tries to invigorate by concocting a drink for him out of a number of the chemist's drugs. The drink has a strong and unexpected effect on the assistant, who goes into a kind of trance, and begins to speak – in fact, to spout lines of poetry in which the spellbound narrator recognises Keats's "Eve of St Agnes." The main body of the story deals with those unconscious attempts, first clumsy and inelegant, then more and more precise, to re-create what is obviously not merely the correct but also the right line. Towards the end of the story, the assistant wakes up from his trance as he is painfully working his way towards three lines from the "Ode to a Nightingale," said by the narrator to be among the best ten in the English language. To the narrator's eager question, he answers that he has never heard of John Keats ("I haven't much time to read poetry [...] Is he a popular writer?") and, when told he was a colleague, he promises to "dip into him" ("What did he write about?"). On the very last page of the story, we learn that the nephew has not managed to make contact with Poole yet, but has picked up signals from the open sea, where two dreadnoughts are trying to communicate with defective wireless sets that transmit, but fail to receive, messages ("Can make nothing out of your signals" – "Signals unintelligible" – "Disheartening – most disheartening"). In the very last paragraphs, clear signals come at last from Poole but the narrator refuses to stay and listen, and goes to bed.

It is easy to see how the story can be taken as a parable: it seems to embody our two main concepts rather neatly. We may take Keats as the emblem of poetry (of the eternal charm and non-historical endurance of art) and the Marconi set as the emblem of history, of the technological progress which is the motor of history (with its three types of anticipation, survival and correspondence: the dreadnoughts are the very symbol of the conjuncture, the latest technological marvels; they hark back to the venerable history of the British navy; and they point, in anticipation, towards a glorious future – the story was written in 1899, the dread-

[12] Rudyard Kipling, "Wireless," *Traffics and Discoveries*, ed. Hermione Lee (1904; Harmondsworth: Penguin, 1987) 181–91.

noughts went into action, and glory, in 1914). The link between the two concepts, and the two plots, is explicitly made by the narrator through the concept of induction. A Marconi set works by way of an induced current that enables a coherer, like a steam valve, to activate a printing circuit. But a "Keats set," in other words: the human mind, also works by way of causal sequence "as inevitable as induction." At first flabbergasted by what he hears, the narrator, an admirer of Marconi and contemporary of Sherlock Holmes, therefore a man with a scientific cast of mind, offers two hypotheses:

> "If he has read Keats, it's the chloric ether. If he hasn't, it's the identical bacillus, or Hertzian wave of tuberculosis, plus Fanny Brand and the professional status which, in conjunction with the main-stream of subconscious thought common to all mankind, has thrown up temporarily and induced Keats."

Fanny Brand is the name of the assistant's redheaded girlfriend, which of course reminds us of Keats's own Fanny Browne. And it is, as we saw, the narrator's madder hypothesis that proves to be true, since the assistant is genuinely ignorant of Keats.

But what is the meaning of this parable of induction? It appears to say that mechanical induction, and therefore the induction of history, for which it is a metaphor, is a failure. Technological progress produces flawed and uncertain wonders: the coherer fails to induce communication, and incoherence prevails. On the other hand, spiritual, trance-like induction, and therefore the induction of poetry, for which it is a metaphor, succeeds.

Moreover, this poetic success seems to be brought about by a form of *antimetabole*: beyond the crude materialist reduction of the same bacillus and the same professional environment producing the same effects (you have to be an apothecary to write about nightingales), there is the eternal nature of the human psyche, that subconscious substratum common to all mankind in all circumstances. What succeeds is indeed the induction of love: like passions produce like poems, the assistant becomes Keats under the influence of the tender pash, as Bertie Wooster calls it, and it is only natural that he should reinvent "The Eve of St Agnes," where Madeline on the fated night seeks to induce the image of her lover, with resounding success. But it is also the secondary induction of poetry, as the Hertzian waves of love induce the current of poetic language.

As you have guessed, there is an element of tongue-in-cheek on Kipling's part in all this, mixed with a modicum of fantastic seriousness: he makes sure the assistant falters on the "Ode to a Nightingale," thus preserving a space for genius. But the end of the story does reaffirm the superiority of poetic over historical induction: communication with Poole does occur, but the narrator is no longer interested.

I would like, however, to move beyond this rather trite conclusion. One way of doing this is to realise that the story stages and contrasts several pragmatic situations. Thus, we may be able to go beyond the impression that *antimetabole*, which states the eternity of human nature, triumphs over the three temporal tropes of history.

The first situation is the normal, commonsensical, situation of communication, as represented by the normal workings of the Marconi set: an addresser and an addressee exchange a message. What historical progress does to this situation is to enlarge its possibilities: instant oral transmission no longer requires physical presence and close proximity. But this commonsensical situation never occurs in the story, only after the end. It is not so much impossible as uninteresting, hence its failure: history is trivial, poetry is exciting. The second pragmatic situation is induced by the actual workings of the Marconi set within the story: the two dreadnoughts transmit but fail to receive, as a result of which no communication is possible. The nephew who receives but does not transmit the dreadnought's protestations is a kind of listening Tom, who wonders at the mysteries of transmission and is awed at their failure. Common sense, the language of the community that makes historical sense, is a failure: all it induces is a useless form of stammering, as the dreadnoughts unknowingly repeat each other's words. The third pragmatic situation involves the human mind as transmitter. Here, communication does work, although it is again heard by a listening Tom, the narrator, rather than by the real addressee, Fanny Brand, for whom the poetico-erotic outpourings of the assistant are destined (again, "The Eve of St Agnes" is an apt choice, as it is one of the most sensual of Keats's poems, and contains a literal scene of peeping-Tommery). The reason why communication works here is that, behind the apparent dialogue between the assistant and the girl of his dreams, there is the eternal poetic dialogue between Keats and his reader, in this case the narrator.

In Kipling's story, therefore, the tropic links between text and history appear to fail. Technological communication is not established, because history is speechless. History cannot speak, for lack not of a listener or witness, but of an addressee: it can only speak *à la cantonade*, like the dreadnoughts: that is, to no one. *Antimetabole*, on the other hand, the eternally perduring analogy between the art of childhood and the childhood of art, seems to work: the nature of the human mind does not change, and the poet, beyond the grave, beyond the centuries, always finds an addressee. The bride of quietness may remain eternally unravished – she turns out to be eternally garrulous.

I wonder, however, if we cannot go a little further. I wonder whether history, which fails to address anyone through the mode of progress (that is, through correspondence with the contemporary conditions of production and anticipation of developments to come), does not address us through poetry via another historical trope, which lies beneath the mythic trope of *antimetabole*: namely, repetition. Here, the father of all Marxists will be recognised again by his children. He had, as we know, a concept of historical repetition as farce: the original force of the historical event is lost in its reappearance in another conjuncture, and *Napoléon le petit*, the inglorious nephew whose military campaigns almost always ended in disaster, is but the farcical shadow of his uncle, the military genius. Yet, farcical as it may appear, historical repetition is also a necessity: we make sense of the new conjuncture by equating it with an older one, as we metaphorise the little-known in terms of the better-known. This is what happens with the "Keats set," which works not so much by way of *antimetabole* as by way of *repetition*: poetic repetition institutes a common language, in which like experiences, in materially similar but temporally distinct circumstances, can be described in the same terms. The assistant's attempts to re-invent Keats, no less heroic for being unconscious, are not farcical, even if they are treated with gentle irony by Kipling. And a certain history – another history, not the technological history of Marconi sets and dreadnoughts – speaks through them: the history of daily life with its structures of feeling; a textual history, a tradition in which the medieval legend of St Agnes is revived first in early-nineteenth-century London, then in the South of England at the end of the century; a history of the mind in which poetic possession, the granting of aesthetic epiphany, is forever repeated in different periods and different contexts (the assistant is both the ancient Pythia and the modern medium – remember this is the period of spiritualism, of Conan Doyle and Madame Blavatsky, even if the narrator never suggests the spirit of Keats is speaking through the assistant). The three historical tropes of anticipation, coincidence and survival work within the framework of what has turned out to be the true fourth historical trope, the central trope not of *antimetabole* but of repetition. This is why, if history works on poetry through corruption, it also needs poetry to find a voice. Poetry without history is deaf, but history without poetry is dumb.

The Changing Landscape: Some Dates in Romantic Period English Studies, 1951 to 2001

J.R. WATSON

IN 1951, WHEN IAUPE WAS FOUNDED, I was in the Sixth Form at school, studying English, French and History. The English syllabus, I remember, included two Shakespeare plays, Chaucer's *The Knight's Tale* (I had done the Prologue to *The Canterbury Tales* before), and a miscellany of other books, including Milton's *Areopagitica* and Congreve's *The Way of the World.* As a preparation for an Oxford examination, I was given I.A. Richards's *Principles of Literary Criticism* to read: I think it must have been the only book available with any kind of theoretical content, certainly the only one which my English master had ever heard of. I found it absolutely baffling.

Meanwhile, I muddled along through the texts, uncertain of what I was looking for: we must have discussed them, but I cannot now remember how. I know that at the time, having visited the Lake District for the first time a year or so earlier, I was totally enraptured by Wordsworth: I can only guess, with hindsight, that this was because in his work I found my own inarticulate response to the landscape given speech, in a most sublime and memorable form. But the only guide to Wordsworth's poetry that I had was Matthew Arnold's essay. The other books that I remember reading at the time were David Cecil's *Early Victorian Novelists* and Quiller–Couch's *Studies in Literature*; neither was much help. I was a traveller without a map, certain of one thing only – that somewhere in this treasure-house of literature were riches, and that I was searching for them with a passion that even now fills me with a certain amazement.

I was, I think, rather badly taught at school (no one showed me T.S. Eliot's essays, for example, which I might have found helpful); but C.S. Lewis, who interviewed me at Magdalen, must have seen something in my hesitant stumblings after truth, because I was offered a place to read English. By the time I had finished my National Service in the army, however, he had gone to Cambridge, which may have been a blessing: I am not sure that I could have stood up to his forceful tutorial method. Criticism in Oxford was primarily philological (with plenty of Anglo-Saxon and Middle English), often explicatory, occasionally historical: in essays, students went through a text with care, bit by bit, pointing out features *en route*. I cannot remember ever being asked (or thinking to ask) why I was doing it this way. Nor did we question the content of the Oxford degree: brought up at home and at school, and then in the army, to habits of strict obedience, we did not question the absurdity of a syllabus that ended in 1830: we just got on with it.

I begin with this biographical excursus because the history of IAUPE, and its role in English studies, needs to be seen in the context of a subject that has changed out of all recognition. Founded in 1951, IAUPE rebuilt relationships between countries and re-established lines of communication that had been broken by the Second World War. We need to remember, when we think of the early members, that in 1951 communications were slow and often difficult. Usually, messages went by letter, for using the telephone for international calls was rare. Most travel to America or Canada, or to Australia and New Zealand, was by ship, and in Europe it was by train. The days of quick and convenient journeys to a conference were far away in the future. So were computers, faxes, and e-mail. So were the great multitude of English professors in every country in the world. In 1951, in Great Britain, there must have been, at most, about thirty professors of English, solemnly writing letters (usually in long-hand) to one another; now there must be something in the region of four or five hundred, dashing off e-mails without a second thought.

Those who met in 1951 were the great men and women of their profession, the eminent ones, signalling to one another from the lofty mountain-tops that they had climbed. Membership was (and still is) by election; it was a mark of distinction. Today, this is no longer understood: when I was trying to organise the Durham conference, I wrote (on the recommendation of a member) to one professor, who was not a member, and whom I did not know. She replied, politely but tartly, that she did not wish to be associated with an organisation that denied admittance to junior members of the profession. We live in egalitarian times, in which the exclusion of anyone from anything is seen as undesirable; certainly the idea of singling out individuals as distinguished is disappearing (my second university, Glasgow, has recently decided to abolish the prizes, often of some antiquity, which used to be given for class work or for special essays).

IAUPE conferences have benefited enormously from quicker travel and more professors. At the same time, the subject has expanded out of all recognition and become very different from the one which I studied, in my naive and uninformed way, at Oxford. What began as a journey through a work, picking out things to be noted, has become much more disciplined and organised. In former days, it was sufficient to be a good critic, to be able to read a text, and then to write about it with more sensitivity than others. A good critic noticed things that others did not. A really good critic, such as F.R. Leavis or Northrop Frye, took the things he had noted and made them into a critical principle, such as Leavis's sense of the line of wit in English poetry, or Frye's ascent and descent. And literature was, for many critics, related to "life." No one stopped to ask questions about what "life" was, and whether it was the same for people living in Africa and Europe, or America and India; or whether it was the same for a man and a woman; or whether it was the same for a poor man and a rich one, or for a middle-class woman in America and another in Japan. There was a kind of general sense of shared humanity, which literature was thought to refer to, and writers were often judged in relation to their supposed relevance to that humanity.

Part of the difficulty of English studies during the last fifty years has been the constant reappraisal of what is meant by such a concept as "humanity." It has involved an ideological and global struggle, with the initiatives taken principally by those who have stood for equality of human living conditions and equality of respect, and who have sought to combat oppression in all its forms – physical, cultural and ideological. Equality has not been achieved, of course, nor oppression banished: but we have changed our ways of thinking about it, and in so doing have changed our ways of understanding literature. We have also come to realise how much of our critical effort is conditioned by our ways of thinking about the world: that, as Hans–Georg Gadamer has pointed out, our judgements are conditioned by our pre-judgements – "The understanding and the interpretation of texts is not merely a concern of science, but is obviously part of the total human experience of the world."[1]

I am not suggesting, of course, that the 1951 members of IAUPE were part of an oppressive global system. They were some of the most enlightened, scholarly, and well-intentioned people of their time. I am just remembering that the world was a very different place in 1951, and that anyone communicating at that time would have been a part of it. For whenever a lecture is given, or a chapter is written, something is included and something is left out.

---

[1] Gadamer, *Truth and Method*, trans. G. Barden and W.G. Doepel (1960; London: Sheed & Ward, 1975) Introduction, xi.

In considering how things have changed, especially with reference to the Romantic period (which is the one that I know best), I have chosen four dates. The first is 1951, the IAUPE foundation year. In that year appeared a volume of essays entitled *Wordsworth Centenary Studies*, edited by Gilbert Dunklin, which consisted of lectures that had been given at Cornell and Princeton in 1950 by some of the great and good of English Literature.[2] It is a strange, unquiet, restless book, with praise for Wordsworth but also full of gloom about his work; and somehow the gloom and disparagement are as memorable as the praise, in spite of John Crowe Ransom's radiant affirmation that Wordsworth was "one of the giants."[3] Douglas Bush stated roundly that Wordsworth was "not an active force in our time";[4] and Lionel Trilling began his lecture by suggesting that "if Wordsworth were not kept in mind by the universities, he would scarcely be remembered at all." Wordsworth, in his view, was "not attractive and not an intellectual possibility":

> He was once the great, the speaking poet for all who read English. He spoke both to the ordinary reader and to the literary man. But now the literary man outside the university will scarcely think of referring to Wordsworth as an important event of modern literature; and to the ordinary reader he is likely to exist as the very type of the poet whom life has passed by, presumably for the very good reason that he passed life by.[5]

This was no ordinary critic writing these words: this was Lionel Trilling, one of the great figures of mid-twentieth-century criticism, the champion of the liberal imagination, author of a masterly study of Matthew Arnold.[6] Indeed, Trilling's diagnosis in the final sentence echoes Arnold, who quipped (too easily and facilely, in 1849) that "Wordsworth's eyes avert their ken / From half of human fate."[7]

Trilling and Bush were judging Wordsworth as a poet who did not seem to "speak to" their time. Trilling's response to this is even more interesting as evidence of the way in which academics thought in 1950: if Wordsworth was no

---

[2] Gilbert T. Dunklin, ed. *Wordsworth Centenary Studies* (Princeton, NJ: Princeton University Press, 1951).

[3] Ransom, "William Wordsworth: Notes Toward an Understanding of Poetry," *Wordsworth Centenary Studies*, ed. Gilbert T. Dunklin (Princeton, NJ: Princeton University Press, 1951) 91–113 (91).

[4] Bush, "Wordsworth: A Minority Report," *Wordsworth Centenary Studies*, ed. Dunklin 3–22 (20).

[5] Trilling, "Wordsworth and the Iron Time," *Wordsworth Centenary Studies*, ed. Dunklin 131–52 (131).

[6] Trilling, *Matthew Arnold* (1939; London: Unwin University Books, 1949).

[7] Arnold, "Stanzas in Memory of the Author of 'Obermann'," *The Poems*, ed. Kenneth Allott (London: Longman, 1965) 132, ll. 53–54.

longer important, Trilling argued – well, that was what universities were for. Universities were under pressure "to prove our usefulness," but "in preserving and finding interesting a spirit that the world at this moment thinks dead and done with, we do something to fulfil one of the essential functions of the university in our society."[8]

What is extraordinary about this is first of all the authority with which Trilling and the others made their pronouncements, and secondly the lack of evidence for what they were saying. This was just how it seemed to be to them; and they were the great men of the profession.

We may picture the professors of 1951, some of them no doubt fired by this kind of agenda, their *raison d'être* being to keep alive that which was in danger of disappearing. This is a perverse but very honourable tradition. At its best, it was a kind of *professores contra mundum*; at its less attractive, it led, as in France, to the proliferation of huge and meticulous theses on writers who had been neglected for centuries. But both were part of a high culture, opposed to materialism, cynicism, and crude or coarse thinking and living. Literature provided understanding of the self and others, reflected upon the making of a good and bad society, and held up for our inspection the great conceptions of the human mind. To study it was to "hold high converse with the mighty dead."

That line, from James Thomson's *Winter*, is a reminder, if one were needed, of the burden that English studies carries today as a substitute for Latin and Greek. These languages survive in some schools and in some universities but, for the most part, courses in English supply what they once provided, a shared body of knowledge with its own treatment of myth, history, society and science. These are open to all: no longer are they the preserve of the few with the required qualifications in difficult languages. The situation is suddenly, I suggest, strangely parallel to what happened at the Reformation, when the Bible became available in the vernacular. Up to that point, the teaching of the church had been through the authority of the priest who knew his Latin: now the Bible was in full view, could be read by all who could read in their own language, and listened to by everyone. The result was a century and a half of chaos: sectarian strife, individual hermeneutics, intellectual squabbles, pamphleteering, wars of religion. English studies seems to me to have become like that, only more properly and healthily: so many people have access to it, and it has become so important as a cultural communication that it is argued over by rival schools of critical thought, and by rival theories of education too. Who, for example, were the "mighty dead" that Thomson loved

[8] Dunklin 152.

to read in the winter? Dead, white, European, male. Why read them? Why not read living authors? Women writers? Postcolonial writers?

The answers are obvious: of course we should read them, without forgetting the others; and IAUPE conferences have responded quickly and precisely to these new demands, as well as defending the right to study the authors that Thomson knew and loved. Indeed, one of the most interesting developments in IAUPE has been the growth of new sections since 1951, corresponding to the way in which the subject itself has grown. "Revising the canon," which was something of a radical idea when Marilyn Butler commended it in her inaugural lecture at Cambridge in 1987, is now a commonplace of educational and critical practice.[9] But another consequence of the "post-Reformation syndrome" which I have invoked as a parallel with today's world of English study is the growth of rival critical schools, the sectaries of today's critical world. We can choose to follow the leaders of one or the other – myth criticism, semiotics and structuralism, Marxist criticism, feminist criticism, deconstruction, historicism, cultural materialism. This produces controversy, and sometimes narrow-mindedness: but one similarity between the present-day critics and the seventeenth-century pamphleteers is that they both make us ask questions about what we are doing and where we are.

We should remind ourselves, also, that criticism depends upon scholarship. Textual scholarship, in particular, has made great advances in the last fifty years. The most important of these advances have been in the discovery of new materials and the establishing of accurate texts. Drafts are available to everyone in editions such as the Cornell Wordsworth, which have used photocopies of the original manuscripts alongside the reading versions; and poets such as Blake and Byron have benefited greatly from the textual foundations of David Erdman and Jerome J. McGann. A spectacular example of a "new" text is found in the six-volume Oxford edition of John Clare, the grandeur of which would surely have astonished the poet himself: it is fascinating to see (in the unpunctuated poems before the Knight transcripts of the late years) how differently the poems read now from the versions given to the world by J.W. and Anne Tibble in 1935. Those two splendid and well-intentioned pioneers regularised Clare's sentences, gave his poems full stops and semi-colons, and produced poems which said what they thought he was trying to say. Now we prefer an unpunctuated original: the words have more freedom, can combine and re-combine, become multiple and polysemic artefacts. We think that we are "closer," somehow, to what Clare wrote

9 Marilyn Butler, "Revising the Canon," *Times Literary Supplement* (4 December 1987): 1349, 1359–60.

if we go back to his original manuscripts, confusing though they often are (the order of his "Child Harold" will never be incontrovertibly settled, unless a new and authoritative manuscript turns up). This leads in turn to a new orthodoxy, which is to prefer, as if it were somehow self-evident, the earlier version of a poem to the later. The argument has raged over Wordsworth's *The Prelude*, and over *Frankenstein*; and most remarkably, perhaps, in the principles of a major critical edition such as the Edinburgh Edition of the Waverley Novels, which (in the words of the General Introduction to one volume) "produces fresher, less formal and less pedantic novels than we have known." Fresher and less formal they may be, and less pedantic too: but the formality and the pedantry were added by Scott himself for the "Magnum Opus" edition that appeared between 1829 and 1833. There are times when the pedantry adds to the effect: Scott's essay on the Dalrymple family, for example, adds richness and authenticity to the wildness and passion of *The Bride of Lammermoor*.

These are matters of editorial practice and principle which will continue to be argued about. What is incontrovertible is the work that has been done on some very important source materials. The finest examples in Romantic-period scholarship are probably the editing of the Coleridge notebooks by Kathleen Coburn, Donald H. Reiman's work on various Shelley projects, and G.E. Bentley, Jr.'s, *William Blake's Writings* and *Blake Books*; but there have been revised editions of the letters of Wordsworth, Lamb, Byron, Keats, Austen, and many more. At the same time, the period becomes more intricate with every new discovery: revising the canon has led to the recovery of forgotten authors, often women: their contribution helps towards an understanding of the period in more complex ways. In the same way, Scott and Wordsworth look different because we can set James Hogg beside them, fresh in the new finery of the Stirling/South Carolina edition. In the light of these advances, I am glad that the IAUPE conference at Durham had a section on "Texts and Editing."

Criticism has moved less certainly than textual scholarship, generally advanced by single-author monographs which have changed our way of thinking about the writers in question. Geoffrey Hartman's *Wordsworth's Poetry, 1787–1814*, for example, published in 1964, was very influential in banishing the idea that Wordsworth was somehow no longer a meaningful poet for our time. Simply by taking Wordsworth seriously, and discovering patterns of meaning in his work, Hartman made the groans of the 1951 essayists seem antiquated and irrelevant. Earl Wasserman did the same for Shelley, quietly ignoring Leavis's criticism of Shelley as a poet who was "essential lyrical," who had a "weak grasp upon the actual."[10] David Erdman's *Blake: Prophet Against Empire* was perhaps even more influential, a forerunner of the new historical criticism which contextualises a poet in his or her time. Marilyn Butler's *Jane Austen and the War of Ideas* similarly inaugurated a new era of Austen scholarship. M.H. Abrams's two great books, *The Mirror and the Lamp* (1953) and *Natural Supernaturalism* (1971), were massive guides to the ways in which the Romantic poets thought and felt, especially in relation to the eighteenth-century tradition, while Harold Bloom's *The Anxiety of Influence* (1973) saw them as wrestling with their forbears in creative acts of misreading that destroyed their predecessors in a Freudian struggle with the father figure. More recently, Jerome J. McGann has questioned the Romantic poets' presentation of themselves, and has also drawn attention to the neglect of women poets of the period.

In that these women poets are a part of the dense historical context of Romantic period writing, I am sure this is justified, though in terms of the visionary company (Harold Bloom's phrase) of Romantic poets I am not so persuaded. I mention this because the Romantic period has become one of those battlegrounds for criticism in which we struggle to see the poetry clearly through the smoke of critical variance. The poetry has always been susceptible to the poststructuralist sense of indeterminacy and polysemic utterance: its discourse is marked by shifts of meaning, open endings, complex and indeterminate signifiers. The systems of signs provide endless opportunities for critics to establish self-referential texts which end in mid-air, or with a question-mark. Authors, at one time the centre of much interest, have become author functions. The texts are full of concealed meanings. Lovers of puns and wordplay find them in Shelley's conjunction of the River Arve and the word "raves" in "Mont Blanc"; long ago William Empson pointed out the many meanings of the word "sense" in Wordsworth's verse. In opposition to these critical techniques, the new historical critics search for the ways in which social, economic and political assumptions condition the production of the text, and I think it is true to say that much of the best current work in the period is based, in some form or another, on these critical premisses.

In chronicling some of these changes (and to return to the matter of literature and what Gadamer called the experience of the world), I turn now to my second date, which is 1970. This was a year (more strictly, one might speak of years, from 1968 to 1970) in which the relationship between the teaching of literature and the world of human affairs became strangely interesting. During the 1960s, Blake had been a figure who had seemed to be wholly admirable: fearless, in

[10] F.R. Leavis, *Revaluation* (1936; London: Chatto & Windus, 1949) 206, 208.

opposition to the establishment of his time, radical, energetic, one who believed that "the tigers of wrath are wiser than the horses of instruction." His work was very popular with undergraduates, and with certain faculty members, either because they were genuinely in sympathy with his ideological standpoint or because they were glad to be part of a popular wave. That all ended in 1968. In that year, there was widespread student unrest (following earlier episodes in 1964 and 1965 in the USA) in North America, partly because of the Vietnam war, but also because students wanted more of a say in their own affairs. The problems of the University of California at Berkeley and of Columbia University transferred themselves across the Atlantic to the London School of Economics and, most spectacularly, to Paris. What were referred to by French academics (in 1970, with furtive looks round) as "*les événements*" led to a general strike and the end of the government.

Les événements sent shock-waves through the educational systems of the Western world. In the study of Romantic-period writers, they are revealingly recorded in the fall 1970 number of *Studies in Romanticism*, in which one can hear, quite distinctly, the sound of academic back-pedalling and door-slamming. Harold Bloom, with a reference to "our current rabblement," quoted E.R. Dodds (quoting T.H. Huxley): "A man's worst difficulties begin when he is able to do as he likes."[11] He added: "Romantic poetry, in its long history, has been saved from those worst difficulties by its sense of its own tradition, by the liberating burden of poetic influence." The phrase "liberating burden" would not have appealed to Blake. Nor would Geoffrey Hartman's "we have too wide a stake in the world to be messianic"[12] have had much to say to Daniel Cohn–Bendit, the revolutionary student leader. Karl Kroeber, again speaking of Blake, added, "It might be salutary if our library-bound critics who are so thrilled by his radical spirituality more frequently met the purveyors of apocalyptic visions in the open street." He continued: "In my view it is for the worse rather than for better that apocalypse is so popular today [...] the central Romantic mode is undogmatic, even anti-apocalyptic in the Blakean sense."[13]

This seems to me to be rather desperately seeking to deny the power of Romantic vision and trying to shape Romantic-period criticism to current needs, sometimes in highly intellectualised language designed to give the new position

---

11 Bloom, "First and Last Romantics," *Studies in Romanticism* 9.4 (1970): 225–32 (231).

12 Hartman, "Reflections on the Romanticism in France," *Studies in Romanticism* 9.4: 233–48 (235).

13 Kroeber, "The Relevance and Irrelevance of Romanticism," *Studies in Romanticism* 9.4: 297–306 (298).

some kind of intellectual eminence. Morse Peckham, introducing the set of essays, drew attention to the importance of Hegel's *Phenomenology*:

> Kroeber is very Hegelian in his feeling that at the present time the popularity of the apocalyptic is dangerous and that what is needed is real Romanticism, "the participation in the phenomenal processes," not a transcendent, apocalyptic construct imposed without correction upon phenomenal processes.

I take this to be a complicated way of saying that we ought to be more rooted in some kind of "real world," and that this world is somehow related to "real Romanticism." What "real Romanticism" was for Professor Peckham seems to be what he (and some others) thought it ought to be in 1970: "To regard Blake as a paradigm for understanding the Romantics and Romanticism is, I believe, to make a profound mistake."[14]

We need to remember that these distinguished critics were writing in an age which had seen a veritable *trahison des clercs*: but thirty years later, one reads their work with a kind of astonishment. They were learned men (no women in this number), capable of writing with sophistication about Hegel or Rousseau: but they assume a criticism in which the critic brings to literature a great deal of contemporary cultural and political baggage. Hang on to the traditional, and watch out for the apocalyptic, for you never know where it might lead: students, armed with "the tigers of wrath are wiser than the horses of instruction," were formidable challengers, opening the possibilities of unrest or even anarchy.[15] Against this the eminent critics attempted to wrench the perception of Romantic-period literature to suit their own concerns: we are invited to contemplate "real Romanticism," without questioning what that might be. Kroeber's phrase about "library-bound critics" is intended to set up some people as armchair revolutionaries, in a way which also suggests that we should not question those who (like himself and Peckham) are out there fighting in the pages of *Studies in Romanticism*.

Questioning (Matthew Arnold's "we are all seekers still") is necessary; and criticism, if it is responsible and aware, is forever asking questions of itself and of its subject. This brings me to my third date, which is 1984, halfway (almost) between the present and that *Studies in Romanticism* number of 1970. The occasion was Maynard Mack's Presidential Lecture to the Modern Humanities Research Association in London. Mack, under whose benign chairmanship I gave my first paper at a conference of IAUPE (at Lausanne in 1989), took as his starting point

---

[14] Peckham, "On Romanticism: Introduction," *Studies in Romanticism* 9.4: 217–24 (220).

[15] In our own time, Pink Floyd sang "We don't want no education / We don't want no thought control."

the Orwellian year 1984. It was the year in which Orwell set his futuristic vision of a society without proper language, a society of Big Brother and of Newspeak. The lecture (it can be found in the *Modern Language Review*, October 1984) was entitled, with typical but unnecessary modesty, "Alexander Pope: Reflections of an Amateur Biographer" (Mack's fine biography appeared in 1985). Pope, said Mack, "saw clearly and communicated vividly what most of our leaders today seem incapable of understanding: that human achievement is fragile, the human hold on civilization precarious." Just as the 1970 critics argued against a background of the cultural crisis in universities, so Mack argued from the depths of the Cold War: "Everyone remembers the stars going out one by one at the end of the *Dunciad* as the lights went out over Europe in August 1914, and again in September 1939, and again, – this time for ever – when?" And Pope, who wrote in the *Dunciad* III of the eclipse of the sun of learning, knew, said Mack, "that the gravest threat to civilization was never the barbarian without but the greater barbarian within."[16] He was worried, in other words, not just about the Cold War, but about the state of intellectual life – and especially literary criticism.

Mack gave an example of anti-eighteenth-century writing, dating from 1946 (mercifully, he does not name the author) – "it is when the Romantics [...] come in sight that the lights begin to go up." These words, Mack said, and rightly, "tell us something about how not to conduct literary criticism." Throughout the lecture he was asking questions, examining different accounts of Pope's life, probing all the time for truth and accuracy, demonstrating prejudice and bias. At the end of the lecture, however, he turned his attention to what he saw as other threats, "in this Orwellian *Magnus Annus*":

> A writer's text, we are told from one quarter, is inevitably self-reflexive, can have no commerce with reality, is words, words, words, about words. 'Nonsense! There is a text', interrupts a voice from another quarter, 'but it is the one I make up as I go along, for which, please note, I am worthier of your admiration than the author.' 'All texts are equal, however', pipes up a third: '*Paris Match*, *Gone with the Wind*, and *Oedipus the King*: they are all indistinguishably *écriture*.'[17]

Mack, a great biographer, was clearly spelling out his allegiance. His caricature of structuralist and poststructuralist critics, of Barthes and the "writerly" text, was forceful because it was one-sided: it was as if he was invoking the spirit of Pope and the ghost of George Orwell to confront them. But if we have learned anything

---

[16] Mack, "Alexander Pope: Reflections of an Amateur Biographer," *Modern Language Review* 79.4 (1984): xxiii–xxxv (xxxiv).

[17] Mack xxxv.

during the last fifty years of IAUPE, it is surely that the study of literature cannot be the monopoly of any one critical mode, and that schools of criticism, whatever we may think about them, challenge our assumptions. We may want to be sceptical about extremists, but we should also be wary of the cultural expectations that were brought to bear on literature in 1950, or 1970, or 1984.

Whether we side with Mack or not, what I think has happened since that time is that criticism has been attempting to see itself more clearly: to discipline itself in line with the discipline of textual presentation that I referred to earlier. It has asked questions about what literary criticism is doing, about the ways in which our world is constructed, and about the kinds of literature that we should be studying in different parts of the world. What has happened between 1951 and 2001 is nothing short of a revolution. The years of IAUPE have marked the overthrow of subjective, unchallenged (and unchallenging) opinions which passed for criticism, and their replacement by an attempt (for all these things are incomplete) to try and understand literature more accurately, with more knowledge and understanding, and with less prejudice. We try to perceive what the text hides as well as reveals, how the writer relates to the world in which he or she wrote, determined by class and race and culture, and in turn, how we as critics relate to that world. The best of all criticism united the warring factions: lessons of deconstruction have been applied by the new historical critics to both the literary texts and the world in which they were written.

We have seen, in 1951, some airy dismissals of Wordsworth; in 1970, some anxious summoning of non-Blakean literature to alter the perception of Romanticism and thus of the world of 1968; in 1984, anxiety about the precarious nature of critical freedom and individual morality. My final date is 1998, the year in which Frank Kermode followed in Mack's footsteps as President of the MHRA. In his Presidential Address, Kermode was in a somewhat similar frame of mind to that of Mack fourteen years before. The lights were going out, in English studies as elsewhere in education:

> it is held that because students now arrive with much less prior instruction than formerly they ought not to be confronted with unfamiliar and therefore difficult works [...] Literature must be democratized, there should be no exclusions short of complete illiteracy [...] pulp fiction, sitcoms, comic books, are regarded as just as worth study, and far closer to the needs of the moment, as Shakespeare or Goethe.[18]

[18] Frank Kermode, "The Discipline of Literature," *Modern Language Review* 93.4 (1998): xxxi–xli (xxxiii).

Kermode was further exercised about the state of professional literary criticism, warning of the danger of becoming too enclosed within its own world, of speaking only to those in its immediate circle, to those who were familiar with the language and the habits of thought of a particular critical mode:

> What is even more curious is the way in which many of the instructors write about literature. Far from seeking simplicity and ordinary language, such as might be accessible to these underprivileged students, they have become extraordinarily recondite. Theirs is a dialogue clearly not meant for the instruction of the innocent; it is addressed to cliques and readable only by professionals.[19]

Kermode singled out the misuse of cultural materialism as a particular example: "What a poem fails to say is the true critical subject. What is the relation between the Peterloo massacre and the Ode to a Nightingale, a contemporary poem? Concealment, of course."[20] His irony was not misplaced – and yet, and yet: at least these critics are making us defend ourselves, even at the expense of appearing to be conservative in matters of critical practice. If critics condemn Romantic poets such as Keats and Wordsworth for not writing about something, or not addressing agendas which they should have addressed, what do we say to them?

Kermode's warning is significant, because it relates to the theme that has been underlying the whole of this essay – the relationship of literature to the world around it, both at the time it was written and now. As Walter Benjamin put it: "Every image of the past that is not recognized by the present as one of its own concerns threatens to disappear irretrievably."[21] So the "now" is important, and it is our duty to maintain it in such a state that it can be receptive to the richness of the past. This is what Lionel Trilling thought that universities were for; this is what Maynard Mack was pleading for in his spell-binding lecture (I heard it, and it was a marvellous experience). We might say that it is one of the things that IAUPE is for. But we would also, I think, want to stress that IAUPE is also for the purpose of enquiring into what we do, and why.

It is also an international association, one that has a world agenda and not one that is set by a few countries: when we think of "the present" in Benjamin's statement, we have to remember that the greatest changes that have occurred since 1951 are the end of the Cold War in 1989 and the destruction of the symbolic Berlin wall, together with the granting of independence to many countries which were ruled by colonial powers. IAUPE is one of those places where we under-

---

19 Kermode xxxiii.

20 Kermode xli.

21 Walter Benjamin, *Illuminations: Essays and Reflections*, ed. Hannah Arendt, trans. Harry Zohn (London: Jonathan Cape, 1970) 257.

stand differences of culture and the need to respect those differences. It is here that I think that the greatest changes will come in the new century: they will concern the relationship of the subject to cultures and problems of many different countries in many different circumstances, problems of class, and tribalism, and religion, and of the ever-increasing demands on natural resources.

No one could have foreseen the immense changes between 1951 and the beginning of the twenty-first century, and no one can confidently predict what will happen to English studies in the next fifty years. My guess is that the "canon" will continue to expand and become more flexible, and that "English" as a subject will become less stable as it becomes more international. This may point us to one of the Association's functions in the twenty-first century: to be a body which can challenge the other forces of globalization, with their domination of world markets, their ownership of newspapers and television stations, their control of advertising, and their ability to alter the decisions of democratically elected governments. Constructions of our human and institutional reality that depend on stereotypes of race, colour and creed need to be set against individual needs, local situations, and cultural understanding.

Mack was right in seeing Orwellian dangers in 1984: it may be that in the twenty-first century those dangers need to be addressed even more urgently, because they are nearer than we think. If IAUPE can play a part in helping to identify and address such questions, it will have earned an honoured place in the history of academic life; and the study of language and literature will continue to be alive and important.

Cultural Diversity and the Problem of Aesthetics

EMORY ELLIOTT

SINCE THE LATE-1960S, social, political and technological changes throughout the world have accelerated the cultural diversity and synergism of many nations as people and forms of cultural expression have increasingly crossed or have been crossed by altered national borders. Just as movies and popular music from the USA are distributed, broadcast and available for sale in hundreds of countries, so have millions of people migrated and immigrated to the USA. While economic hardships, social tensions, and political conflict have often accompanied these population changes, the cultural production of the new immigrants often mediates the social pressures of change as people bring with them foods, styles of dress, religious practices, forms of art and expression, and perspectives on all aspects of human experience that daily transform the cultural fabric of their communities and of the USA. Although such hybrid cultures express and often allay social tensions, there are also many sources of conflict present in the clash of cultural forms, especially between generations within the immigrant communities and between those communities and their new neighbours. Still, it is almost a journalistic commonplace now to say that such forms of popular culture function as catalysts for social cohesion. Recent studies have documented the cultural blending and hybridity that have characterised the cultural expression of the Americas and have presented a more complex picture of the relation between society and cultural forms.[1]

When one person makes an aesthetic judgement about another in declaring that person to be physically or spiritually beautiful or, more important to our work here, in decreeing the other's cultural expression and artistic productions to possess superior qualities, the aesthetic functions as a positive bridge across the

[1] A longer version of this essay will appear as an "Introduction" to Emory Elliott, ed. *Cultural Diversity and Aesthetics: New Challenges for Literature and the Arts* (New York: Oxford University Press, forthcoming December 2001), and will contain a full bibliography and more extensive notes. For an overview of recent work on cultural hybridity, see Cathy N. Davidson and Michael Moon, ed. *Nation, Race, and Gender: From Oroonoko to Anita Hill* (Durham, NC: Duke University Press, 1995).

gap of difference. At the same time, however, when the person making such a judgement is in a dominant position politically, legally or economically over the other and renders aesthetic judgements that demean and subordinate the other by pronouncing the person or his or her cultural production to be inferior, beneath consideration, or objectionable, the aesthetic may operate as a tool of divisiveness, enmity and oppression. The critic who assumes that there are universal standards of beauty – that "we all recognize a beautiful face or a great poem when we see one" – will be likely to erase or subordinate an array of human differences and forms of creative expression as being inferior to a select few. Those who do not recognise themselves or their works of art in the features of the putative universal ideal will either feel diminished and inferior or systematically excluded and marginalised. Thus, the aesthetic is always in danger of being exploited in the service of individual prejudice or of nationalism, racism, sexism and classism. This has been true for several millennia and remains the case today; one just has to think of some of the ways in which recent global migration and the expanding ethnic diversity in the USA are affecting cultural productions and necessitating reassessment of the nature and role of aesthetics in our contemporary society.

During the last three decades, a revolution of theory within the academic disciplines in the humanities and the arts has transformed the subject matter and methods of study of all forms of cultural expression. A new philosophical scepticism has questioned the epistemological foundations of judgement, arguing that all critical standards in the arts are constructed from within certain limited ideological positions. Of course, because practice does not always follow consistently from theory, many of the same critics who have challenged the foundations have also continued to make critical judgements in keeping with their own standards of taste, although their evaluations have tended to sound more tentative. What has been fairly consistent is that scholars and critics who had, in the 1960s, begun to challenge the established canons of art and literature for political reasons recognised the usefulness of theories of deconstruction in providing epistemological grounds for demonstrating how matters of class, gender and ethnicity have always played crucial if subtle roles in decisions about artistic merit and aesthetics. Such recognition led some critics and scholars to discredit the systems of evaluation themselves, arguing that ideological, economic and nationalist prejudices underlie and inform critical distinctions such as those between major and minor writers, sophisticated and naive art, and serious and complex works as opposed to superficial and obvious ones.

This reassessment of traditional critical standards for literature and the arts encouraged critics and scholars to work towards the formation of new and far more historically informed and politically self-aware standards for judging works of cultural production. As a result of this critical shift, assumptions on which critical evaluations of cultural forms had been previously based have been called into question and, in many cases, discredited. Paradigms of analysis that had structured the subject matters of the disciplines – such as the distinctions between high forms of artistic expression and low or popular forms – have been challenged and, in the view of many, rejected for being based on relative, political and philosophically insupportable distinctions.

Within the context of this period of theoretical reformulation, the growing awareness of the cultural diversity of the USA, both in the present and throughout its history, generated a remarkable expansion in the lists of texts and artifacts counted as worthy of study. On the part of artists, scholars and teachers, a growing awareness of the cultural diversity of the USA and a corresponding alteration of social consciousness about matters of gender equity and sexual preference began to open up the possibilities for more serious attention to cultural productions by women and gay and lesbian artists. Thus, for there to be fair opportunities for works of art and acts of cultural expression that had previously been rejected by the application of such narrow aesthetic standards, many of the prior aesthetic criteria needed to be re-examined and certainly the traditional hierarchies of merit needed to be challenged.

The recognition that works of art are inevitably political in some way and that those engaged in political action nearly always employ forms of expression which are to some degree artistic has inspired new research under the banner of "cultural studies" and has disturbed many traditionalists who still hold to the ideal of "art for art's sake." With such remarkable historical and theoretical developments occurring simultaneously, it is not surprising that many inside and outside these disciplines have experienced a sense of disorientation and confusion; many are troubled about the current state of the academic fields and the value-systems and standards, as well as the proper material and major research projects on which they were formulated. At the same time, even those most committed to relativity of values, to the point of rejecting the terms "art" and "literature" as class-bound and elitist, have recognised the impossibility of avoiding judgements. Thus, while academic self-critique and sceptical analysis have shaken the foundations of taste and judgement, critics and teachers are still called upon daily to make selections and judgements from among an abundant array of texts and artifacts.[2]

Whereas, in the marketplace, people are purchasing music, books, films and other cultural forms on the basis of their own individual tastes, those critics and academics entrusted by society with the responsibility for deciding what is worth preserving and disseminating through college and university courses, libraries, museums, film and other archives have resisted making judgements. But judge they must when pressed by the leaders of institutions such as art museums and libraries to provide guidance and direction. Publishing houses, the entertainment industries, even cooking schools and ministries of tourism, seek the advice and judgement of those who are the valued experts. Indeed, cultural-studies scholars, anthropologists, art historians and social historians address institutions besides the academy, often taking museum and archival methods or the study of the practices of contemporary communities as their research focus. It is time to end the divisive "culture war" debates that have raged for over a decade. Now is the moment to reassess the relationships between minority cultures and the dominant culture and the ways in which social and political upheaval and personal struggle often generate acts of cultural production and transmission through which human experiences of transformation are expressed.

Of course, despite the theoretical problematic, judgement is inevitable when selecting some texts and artifacts rather than others for transmission in one way or the other – library, archival and museum preservation, scholarly and critical analysis in classrooms, publications, or display materials. The challenges now facing scholars in the disciplines of the arts, humanities and social sciences require careful consideration. We must ask ourselves how best to consolidate the breathtaking advances in theory and interpretative method that inform our disciplines with the wealth of new knowledge and cultural materials that make up our subject matters today and compete for our judgements. Breakthrough research and extraordinary leaps in theory and knowledge are necessarily chaotic and disturbing. Once the wealth of new data is before us, however, it may be possible to formulate new terminologies, categories, and processes of assessment and to restructure the disciplines along new directions that are in accord with current theories. Such reconstitution of the disciplines will need to be accomplished in ways that will enable students, researchers and informed citizens to find ways for

---

[2] On the theory of political constructivism and on the problems of values and judgements, see Martha Woodmansee, *The Author, Art, and the Market: Rereading the History of Aesthetics* (New York: Columbia University Press, 1994).

expressing the significance of a wide array of creative expressions and forms of cultural production.

These challenges to the humanities involve nothing short of the construction of entirely new principles for evaluating cultural productions within a context of the fullest possible understanding of the social, political and economic conditions in which they are produced. They involve, as well, the creation of new terminologies and explanations for how and why elements of creative production affect us as they do. To do this, we need not only to study the histories of the arts in various parts of the world but also to examine more fully the new technologies, knowledge and human interactions around the globe that are opening new channels of communications, responses and understandings of human expression and creativity. Beyond these issues involving the evaluation and categorisation of artistic productions and close analysis of texts, we also need to consider more fully the roles of institutions of transmission – libraries, museums, publishing houses, the entertainment industry, and others, as well as the university and the public and private K-12 school system – in the preservation and dissemination of culture in a multicultural society. Such a research programme must include the contributions of anthropologists, economists, sociologists and others who might be more interested in modes of transmission than in textual analysis or production. Indeed, in terms of methodology and new knowledge, the major contribution that cultural studies has made to more hermeneutically oriented disciplines like English has been to bring literary interpretation to such issues as the processes of cultural exchange and the affective and economic relations that structure the transmission of cultural productions.

For the present moment and for the purpose of the current discussion, issues of ethnic and racial difference are central in rethinking art and culture in the USA. At the same time, it should be recognised that a wide range of discussions of subjects related to aesthetics and culture are being carried on with little reference to multiculturalism. For example, many scholars and artists over the last three decades have concentrated on the ways in which many issues of gender and sexual preference affect matters of aesthetics and the critical evaluation of art. This is an enormous subject that sometimes shares common ground with similar issues of ethnic identity, but also reveals important gender divisions within ethnic groups. Meanwhile, other critics are passionately engaged in writing articles and books on the aesthetics of the poetry of Ovid, Dante, Li Po and other long-established authors of the traditional Western and Eastern canons. In academic journals and in the public media, scholars of linguistics and politics are analysing the rhetorical language and physical appeal of political candidates, while each day hundreds of reviewers produce aesthetic judgements on performances of operas, plays, television performers, rock bands, hip-hop word artists, and every type of human performance that elicits aesthetic judgement. It is not as though the ethnic diversity of the USA has suddenly resurrected a long-dormant conversation about art and aesthetics. Aesthetic issues are always with us, and, within various personal and social contexts, matters of beauty and taste function significantly in all dimensions of our lives.

Terry Eagleton's *The Ideology of the Aesthetic* provides a useful starting point for considering the issues. Indeed, many feel that the recent theoretical revolution has made the term "aesthetic" and the cluster of ideas it contains outmoded and irrelevant. For those who believe that art itself is an elitist concept which serves only to sustain false hierarchies of expression, aesthetics is a divisive notion that does more harm than good. As long as people review and evaluate cultural expression and make choices about what to preserve, study and recommend, however, they will seek to define standards of judgement and thereby fall back into aesthetics. The issue, then, is not whether we can rid ourselves of the disciplines that address the desire for beauty and art; rather, it must be how to redefine the parameters of "art" and formulate new questions for evaluating cultural expression in ways that are fair and just to all.

While Eagleton is optimistic in his affirmation of the aesthetic, he also is careful to underscore the risks of returning to it, for the aesthetic can always be used by every brand of extremist ideologue:

> The left turn: smash truth, cognition and morality, which are all just ideology, and live luxuriantly in the free, groundless play of your creative powers. The right turn … forget about theoretical analysis, cling to the sensuously particular, view society as a self-grounding organism, all of whose parts miraculously interpenetrate without conflict and require no rational justification.[3]

When the right embraces the aesthetic, Eagleton observes, there often develops an alliance between those intellectuals who privilege the aesthetic and the most rigid cynics concentrated in "the upper echelons of fascist organisations" (369); both groups share contempt for the utilitarian and an arrogant motivation to control and discipline.

Recently, in the USA, it has usually been the right, rather than the left, that has found aesthetic politics most attractive, and when it does so, the right usually embraces a notion of the transcendence of art that tends to ignore and erase

[3] Eagleton 368.

history. Such conservative uses of aesthetics also foster notions of timeless and universal appeal that ignore cultural and historical difference and seek to impose the "universal" taste and values of a cultural elite upon the rest of society. There often emerges an alliance between a conservative politics that privileges the powerful and wealthy few in politics and society and a conservative aesthetic that recognises only a select pantheon of important writers and artists. However, there are exceptions to this general principle: many academic critics claim to hold positions that result in their being progressive in politics and egalitarian in economics while holding conservative positions on matters of the arts and culture. For example, Daniel Bell asserts: "I am a socialist in economics, a liberal in politics, and a conservative in culture."[4] There will always be heated debates on the conscious and unconscious motives of those who claim to want equality and justice for all while also insisting that reason, taste and learning support their view that there are only a few meritorious writers and artists.

At the same time, the continuing culture wars in the USA provide ample evidence of the continuing alliances between conservative political leaders and those intellectuals and academics who cling to aesthetic values that lead them to celebrate a mainly white, male Euro-American canon of artists and writers. Many of the conservative arguments have been characterised by their hyper-canonisation of the "world classics" and by their insidious *ad hominem* attacks on what they assert to be the lack of knowledge and intelligence of their opponents. There is also a strong tendency in the arguments from the right to universalise beauty and art and to judge objects and artifacts on the basis of how they measure against the ideal. Of course, what is posited as universal and essential is nothing more than the classical Western canons of art and literature that were primarily constructed by white male anthologists, literary editors and genteel intellectuals over the past two centuries. Such emotionally charged issues in which conflicts of identity and culture are inscribed do tend to produce extremism of the right and left and silence among those who seek to negotiate the unstable middle ground.

An example of an argument from the right that has had broad appeal appeared in a 1999 review, in the *New York Review of Books*, entitled "The Decline and Fall of Literature." In his call for a return to New-Critical standards of evaluation and for the literary canon of the glory years of criticism in the 1950s, Andrew Delbanco effectively tapped into the current panic that many traditional scholars feel about the erosion of the profession of literary and art criticism. Using several

---

[4] Bell, "Foreword" to *The Cultural Contradictions of Capitalism* (New York: Basic Books, 1976) iv.

recent books on the embattled state of the profession,[5] Delbanco writes a jeremiad chastising scholars for their failure of belief, their rush to self-destruction, and their abandonment of their divine mission to preach the word of great literature.[6]

Lacing his attack with religious terms and metaphors, Delbanco blames the current decline on a backsliding generation of scholars who have fallen victim to heresies from abroad and to their own fleshly desire for fame and profit. He laments the passing of the patriarchs, the "respected practitioners," of English studies who "enjoyed their greatest prestige in the secular academy when they held most closely to the tradition of scriptural exegesis from which they derived." They were "primarily undergraduate teachers," he says, and "under their spell, the classroom became like a Quaker meeting" (36). Delbanco calls for

> a full scale revival [which] will only come when English professors recommit themselves to slaking the human craving for contact with works of art that somehow register one's own longings and yet exceed what one has been able to articulate by and for oneself. This is among the indispensable experiences of the fulfilled life, and the English department will survive […] only if it continues to coax and prod students toward it. (38)

While Delbanco writes of literature as expressing transcendent universal human longings, he says very little, and certainly nothing positive, about the impact that the increasing ethnic diversity of our society has had upon responsible teacher–critics, prompting them to consider the connections between the books they teach and the lived experience of the non-white Americans in their classes. Indeed, Delbanco views the opening up of the literary canon as one of its biggest problems. The "English Department," he says, "has paid overdue attention to minority writers," and he cites a study by the historian Lynn Hunt where it is stated that the English Department "along with the humanities in general has failed to attract many minority students." This extraordinary dismissal of unnamed writers who happen to be members of ethnic "minority" groups and college students who happen not to join English departments is quite shocking. Which of these undesirable writers are to be eliminated and why? Why should we assume that the reason more minority students do not enrol in English Departments should have any relation to the number of minority writers being taught in their courses? Is Delbanco suggesting perhaps that, if a Department has a small number of students of Irish, Jewish or Italian descent, it should cut back the number of writers from those

[5] Cf. Carl Woodring, *Literature: An Embattled Profession* (New York: Columbia University Press, 1999), one of the books discussed by Delbanco.

[6] Delbanco, "The Decline and Fall of Literature," *New York Review of Books* (4 November 1999): 32–38 (33). Further page references are in the main text.

groups taught in the courses? Here is an instance in which a scholar perceives politics and aesthetics to be at odds and his responsibility as being to mount a defence against those who threaten the integrity of art. Ironically, Delbanco never engages the subject of aesthetics and literary merit but merely implies that "artistic merit" and "minority writers" are mutually exclusive terms. This review, which presumes to guard some threatened artistic treasures, demonstrates why it is necessary that matters of aesthetic achievement be openly debated and that value judgements be articulated. When such claims are left unchallenged, the real debate on artistic merit is elided by familiar presumptions – that T.S. Eliot, say, belongs in the canon because his greatness is long-established while Langston Hughes is intruding on sacred territory for political reasons. And so on.

Among the many books of the last several years on the subject of making aesthetic judgements and teaching literature in contemporary society, a few, such as Mark Bauerlein's *The Pragmatic Mind* and Robert Scholes's *The Rise and Fall of English*, have favoured a more pragmatic approach over nostalgia and lament.[7] These works stress the need for clarity, reason, self-awareness and demystification, and both stress the practical consequences of the choices before us. For example, Scholes does not dismiss theory in constructing a solution but tries to employ it. He engages these issues of professional doubt and belief and constructs an argument for what should constitute the discipline of English today. In his chapter entitled "no dog would go on living like this," he states his thesis this way:

> If there is no appeal to realities or principles beyond what we may happen to believe at any given time, then we have no arguments either in favor of changing things for the better or for resisting a slide back into superstition and dogma. And we live in a world where we are threatened by superstition and dogma at every turn. On very pragmatic grounds, then, I would want to argue in favor of what Rorty calls a realistic position, as opposed to a pragmatic one, because it is 'good' for us to believe. Quite specifically, it is good for us to believe that our beliefs are grounded in something firmer than belief itself. We need the love of truth, neither because we can attain ultimate truth, nor yet because it will 'make us free' – but [because] we need a sense of a shared enterprise, to which we may contribute something. As educators, we need the sense that we are presenting to students and colleagues ideas, methods, and information that are neither false nor useless. (53–54)

Certainly many teachers and scholars are motivated by these ideals of shared intellectual goals, by a common search for truth, and by the desire to enhance the lives of students and thus improve society in general through reading, writing and

---

[7] Mark Bauerlein, *The Pragmatic Mind: Exploration in the Psychology of Belief* (Durham, NC: Duke University Press, 1997); Robert Scholes, *The Rise and Fall of English: Reconstructing English as a Discipline* (New Haven, CT: Yale University Press, 1999).

teaching. Yet many practitioners in the field of arts and literature are sceptical toward Scholes's plea for belief and truth. With the rise of science and the decline of religion among major segments of our society, we have witnessed a shift in our academic institutions. The growing importance of technology and applied sciences has placed greater value on research that yields immediate quantifiable results, and such emphasis has resulted in a diminished appreciation of contributions from fields involving the analysis and interpretation of human actions, feelings and ideas, such as literary and cultural studies. Academic leaders who accept such a revision of intellectual priorities are inclined to perceive rhetoric and composition as the most important subjects in the humanities because they appear to fulfil a practical need to train students for the marketplace.

Such external pressures have combined with internal ones, especially the scepticism and massive psychological depression that came upon many professors of literature in the 1970s and 1980s. Scholes quotes Derrida's 1992 address at Columbia University, in which he expressed his perception of the demoralised condition of humanities professors: "We feel bad about ourselves. Who would dare say otherwise? And those who feel good about themselves are perhaps hiding something, from others and from themselves" (39). Derrida went on to argue that the reason we feel bad is that we live within a paralysing contradiction between the realities of our institutional contexts and the values that drew us to our calling, such as a love of language, imagination and creativity; the desire to share our passion for reading and analysing works of art and literature; the satisfaction of vigorous, committed and constructive intellectual debate over ideas and subjects that have mattered to humanity in the past and matter still today. Derrida considered the following points:

> And who are we in the university where apparently we are? What do we represent? Whom do we represent? Are we responsible? If there is a university responsibility, it at least begins with the moment when a need to hear these questions, to take them upon oneself, is imposed. This imperative for responding is the initial form and minimal requirement of responsibility. (44)

The immediate and pressing problem that confronts teachers and scholars in the arts and humanities remains one of presenting the knowledge required to be a university-educated person to the generation of students in today's classrooms. To approach this set of tasks as a profession, we must objectively reassess the issues of canon formation, the evaluation of works of art and literature, and the presentation of interpretations that have meaning and value for our current students. For these reasons, we must take serious notice what a scholar of the stature of Hazel Carby says in her essay "The Multicultural Wars":

> As a black intellectual, I am both intrigued and horrified by the contradictory nature of the black presence in North American universities. We are, as students, as teachers, and as cultural producers, simultaneously visibly present in, and starkly absent from, university life.[8]

Regarding even the reconstructed literary canon in which writers of colour are included in American literature courses, Carby observes:

> From the vantage point of the academy, it is obvious that the publishing explosion of fiction of black women has been a major influence in the development of the multicultural curriculum, and I have tried to point to the ways in which the texts of black women and men sit uneasily in a discourse that seems to act as a substitute for the political activity of desegregation. (197)

She goes on to point out that the white suburbs in which such black texts are popular and the colleges in which they are taught are usually separated from urban centres by apartheid-like structures, so that those who read these texts and those whose lives are written about "lack the opportunity to grow up in any equitable way with each other" (197). Carby's observations and those of many others whose essays fill some of the recent volumes of work on multicultural America have so far had little effect on changing those structures.

Frequently, students of African, Asian, or Hispanic descent who enrol in college literature courses that include texts by writers from ethnic minorities are disappointed with the ways in which those texts are presented. They may find minority writers approached with condescension, or at best, with no recognition on the teacher's part that the cultural differences that have informed the aesthetic qualities of those works might require knowledge and training that the instructor does not possess. Too often, teachers cover mainly the biographical, historical and political context and evade discussion of the formal qualities that they normally would have considered in the case of established white writers. Some teachers focus only on the political and personal experiences depicted in the works and are so culturally insensitive as to ask the minority students in the class to tell others how they do or do not identify with the characters, as though they were "native informants" from a marginal society. Students recognise this variant of approach, reading it as a lack of interest in the work itself or as an indication that the teacher

[8] Hazel V. Carby, "The Multicultural Wars," in *Black Popular Culture: A Project by Michelle Wallace*, ed. Gina Dent (Dia Center for the Arts Discussions in Contemporary Culture 8; Seattle, WA: Bay Press, 1992) 196.

does not respect authors and texts as being serious art worthy of literary explication.

Ten years ago, this problem was less conspicuous than it is now. Until very recently, there was so much excitement on the part of faculty and students who were becoming newly acquainted with the writings of a wider range of American authors that the necessary contextual information for reading their works was considerable and often did not leave time for close analysis of the writing as art. But a shift has occurred, and we are beginning to see the emergence of tools for analysis of the literature itself. For example, works on the Black Atlantic by Paul Gilroy, Joseph Roach, Joan Dayan and others have explored the ways in which African religious and aesthetic traditions circulated through the Caribbean and cities such as New Orleans, and a wealth of research on black culture and the African diaspora has examined the blending of African and European forms and expressions over the last three centuries. There is now also a substantial body of criticism on the Black Aesthetic, so that teachers of literature today should be well-equipped to discuss the artistic merits of texts by African–American artists with reference to both African and European aesthetics.[9]

Now that courses and anthologies include many writers previously excluded for reasons of race, ethnicity and gender, and we have begun taking up questions of artistic forms and methods again, we need to develop the tools that will help us to understand what those writers are doing as artists so that we can teach their works more effectively. Rejecting these texts as artistic failures or as having merely political value is not a fitting intellectual response to the major intellectual, demographic and educational challenges we face.

While it might seem attractive to some to resurrect the formalist principles of the 1950s, such a move would surely be counter-productive, for those terms and systems of analysis remain historically bound to their cultural time period. This is not to assert that all art works and critical standards are entirely relative, but it is also not to say that they are universal and transcendental, either. We need only look at representations of human beauty over the centuries and across cultures to see that notions of beauty vary depending on time and place. For our time, our place, we need to formulate new terms and definitions and perhaps also a new system of analysis for describing the characteristics of art and literature as they

---

[9] Paul Gilroy, *The Black Atlantic: Modernity and Double Consciousness* (Cambridge, MA: Harvard University Press, 1993); Joseph Roach, *Cities of the Dead: Circum-Atlantic Performance* (New York: Columbia University Press, 1996); and Joan Dayan, *Haiti, History, and the Gods* (Berkeley: University of California Press, 1995).

relate to the feelings and intellectual pleasures they invoke in the particular diversity of the people we are today.

Indeed, as frequently happens, some artists are already ahead of us in this endeavour. Toni Morrison suggests that the "classic white American authors," even those who were conspicuously racist in their personal lives, need to be studied by readers possessing a new set of critical tools with which to reveal the Africanist presence previously hidden in many of these texts.[10] By so doing, we not only discover how closely intertwined the lives of black and white Americans have been on this continent since the sixteenth century, but how images of Africans and of African cultural elements have been integral in the formation of Euro-American history and U.S. national identity and the literature that represents them. The implications of Morrison's insights for American studies and for rethinking a literary aesthetic are far-reaching, suggesting that we need to devote as much time and attention to the histories, cultures, languages and artistic value-systems of the African peoples as we have been doing for hundreds of years to the cultural contributions of the European peoples. It is not enough simply to recognise, as many critics have now, that Africanness is often present in white-authored U.S. texts even when disguised under various representations of otherness. We must examine more deeply the ways that structure, form, verbal rhythms and American English have been permeated and reconstituted by cultural elements from our African heritage.

Just as students of twentieth-century music of the "highest" forms can no longer approach their subject without a sound knowledge of blues and jazz, we must be able to bring to the texts we teach a higher degree of informedness about African cultures and African–American history and expression in order to understand the patterns of language construction that inform those texts. As Sterling Stuckey's important historical investigations into the sources of Melville's *Benito Cereno* have shown,[11] a critic who does not bring to that work some knowledge of Ashanti funerary customs and other cultural traditions will fail to understand important nuances of Babo's masquerade. Indeed, such critics will fall into some of the less obvious traps Melville set to catch racist readers. And, of course, how could we begin to make sense of many elements of Morrison's own novels without delving into African–American history and the African religious and spiritual traditions which so fully inform these texts? In her

[10] Toni Morrison, *Playing in the Dark: Whiteness and the Literary Imagination* (Cambridge, MA: Harvard University Press, 1992).

[11] Sterling Stuckey, *Going Through the Storm: The Influence of African American Art in History* (New York: Oxford University Press, 1994).

famous essay "Unspeakable Things Unspoken,"[12] Morrison has given us a signpost for directing our attention both to Europe and to Africa when we study her works by showing how her opening sentences function, somewhat in the way of Shakespearean prologues, to alert readers to certain themes and major events that will later be elaborated. In that essay, she demonstrates how aspects of her literary aesthetic came down to her from the classics of the European past as well as from the forms of expression and storytelling she learned from her African heritage. Her argument is a useful demonstration of the way in which a process of inclusive 'both/and' thinking plays a key role in our analysis of her art, as opposed to the Manichaean 'either/or' logic that, as Abdul JanMohamed has notably argued, is at the core of much of the racialisation found in cultural critiques.

Morrison's arguments extend more broadly, of course, to the other previously marginalised and undervalued cultural influences on U.S. writing such as those from Latin America, Asia and the Pacific-Rim countries. If lasting changes in the canon are to occur, resulting in greater cultural inclusiveness, we must be able to train all graduate students of "American" literature in the cultures and aesthetic traditions of the peoples of the world whose influence on U.S. culture and literature is an undeniable fact. Indeed, no serious criticism of the latter can take place any longer without the possession of extensive knowledge of the wide variety of recently recognised cultural influences on the USA.

Of course, works by authors who descended from non-Western and non-Anglo-European heritages present new challenges for teachers and scholars trained in the New-Critical or historical schools in the USA, for the unfamiliar aesthetic systems that are inscribed in texts and artifacts are from African, Asian and Latin-American or Hispanic cultures. In a process akin to teaching texts in translation without knowing them in their original language, teachers have been attempting to reveal to students the complexities of works by Asian–American, Chicano and African–American authors whose works are steeped in the artistic traditions of their cultures. The only way to approach this challenge is the way that scholars of medieval European and Renaissance literature have traditionally approached their subjects. By educating ourselves more fully and energetically in the languages and cultures of those parts of the world whose aesthetic contributions are now understood to be part of the culture of the USA, we will be much more competent to demonstrate to our students why texts by writers of

[12] Toni Morrison, "Unspeakable Things Unspoken: The Afro-American Presence in American Literature," *Michigan Quarterly Review* 28 (Winter 1989): 1–34.

African, Asian and Hispanic descent are as rich and aesthetically pleasing as they are. Scholarly competence in the rich and diverse literature of the USA requires larger, not downsized, literature programmes.

Along with the continued emphasis on political and theoretical developments in the fields of literature and the arts, there have also been indications over the last few years of a return to an interest in aesthetics. Eagleton's *The Ideology of the Aesthetic* makes a good beginning in the attempt to mediate between those who argue that aesthetics is somehow independent of political ideologies and those who hold that aesthetics is merely a component of a bourgeois ideology to be purged from the arts and humanities in the current process of reconstituting those fields. Eagleton enables reconsideration of the demystification of aesthetics as ideology by rehistoricising this contemporary confrontation within the philosophical debates of the last two centuries that have produced the current intellectual gridlock.

From a rather different angle of enquiry, a number of philosophers, psychologists, and theorists and critics of the arts have been developing new strategies to investigate the cognitive issues involved in the responses of the mind to what we call art and literature. In *Emotion and the Arts*, a collection edited by Mette Hjort and Sue Laver, scholars in various fields from several countries present germinal work on issues of agency and "some of the ways in which an agent's beliefs, intentions, desires, and attitudes are constitutive of his or her emotional engagements with art."[13] These authors contribute to the broader examination of the role of the emotions and aesthetics that characterises the work of Martha Nussbaum, Michael Taussig, David Novitz and Elaine Scarry.[14]

Because of the increasingly diverse student bodies at American universities and colleges, those of us who teach language, arts and humanities are especially well positioned to begin the formidable work of constructing a system or systems of aesthetics consistent with current theories and cultural conditions. The new fields, terminologies, methodologies and aesthetic principles that emerge from this work and others like it will better enable scholars, teachers and students to assess and organise the cultural expressions of past and present and to describe

---

[13] Mette Hjort and Sue Laver, ed. *Emotion and the Arts* (New York: Oxford University Press, 1997).

[14] See the various arguments set out in Martha Nussbaum, *Poetic Justice: The Literary Imagination and Public Life* (Boston, MA: Beacon Press, 1995); Michael Taussig, *Mimesis and Alterity: A Particular History of the Senses* (London and New York: Routledge, 1993); David Novitz, *The Boundaries of Art* (Philadelphia, PA: Temple University Press, 1992); Elaine Scarry, *Dreaming by the Book* (New York: Farrar, Straus & Giroux, 1999) and *On Beauty and Being Just* (Princeton, NJ: Princeton University Press, 1999).

and judge the cultural productions of the postnational, richly diverse community of cross-cultural global societies that many expect to constitute the world of the twenty-first century.

Counterpoints: Nationalism, Colonialism, Multiculturalism, and Spirit

Ihab Hassan

> It is necessary to uproot oneself. Cut down the tree and make a cross and carry it forever after.[1]

I

The perspective of this essay is personal, a record of passages and crossings – not left, not right – of lived and meditated experience. Call it autobiography, a way to enter the subject, a way to question theory, ideology, the pride of mind. But autobiography deceives. And in a bullying age, it often serves as self-empowerment: "I was there, I suffered, *hear me!*"

The autobiographical passages counterpointing this essay insinuate, I hope, a different query: "I was born in Egypt, I have crossed, so what?" I regard my birth in Cairo as fortuitous, an accident, not a destiny. It is an accident, of course, full of resonances, gravid with memories. But do these suffice to sustain the pathos of exile, mummeries of alienation, horrors of revanchism and irredentism?

True, I have lucked out. Unlike Bosnian or Palestinian, Haitian or Vietnamese, Cuban or Ulsterman, fortune has granted me a place. This is humbling. But destiny dispenses with gratitude as it does with cant. It needs only lives.

II

Autobiography simulates the past in the present. It feigns recollection. But it can not escape the pressures of its moment, the prejudices of its author. Why not admit, then, these pressures, these prejudices, from the start?

I confess a certain antipathy toward the intellectual tone, not the moral ideals, of current postcolonial and multicultural studies. Exceptions, of course, abound:

[1] Simone Weil, *Waiting for God*, trans. Emma Craufurd (1950; trans. 1951; New York: Harper & Row, 1973) 7.

for instance, some essays in Barbara Johnson's collection *Freedom and Interpretation*, or in Tom O'Regan's *Critical Multiculturalism*. Still, the tone, in America at least, repels thought. Consider a gross instance. The Nigerian Nobelist Wole Soyinka reports that after a lecture in New York, on African history and literature, a young, black American woman stood up angrily to ask him: "What about the role of the Jews in enslaving Africans? Why did you leave that out?" Soyinka replied that he had done much research, and had found evidence of English and Dutch, French and Arab forts, used in the slave trade, but no evidence of Jewish forts. The woman shot back: "Facts don't matter." Before outraged, no, outrageous desire, what can avail? Auschwitz did not happen, nor Hiroshima, nor Gulag, nor the Middle Passage with its ten or twenty million slave victims.

"Facts don't matter"? They matter enough when they serve grievance. In any case, I live in another climate of assumptions, another ambience of discourse. I share other dispositions. First among these I count a pragmatic distaste for "strong" explanations, purporting to call the turbulence of history to order. (Have we something to learn here from chaos and complexity theories?) Such explanations often disregard error, misprision, sheer contingency in understanding other peoples, other times and places, and they often are self-serving. I count, too, a growing allergy to politics, always the same gauche politics in academe, politics as the ultimate horizon to which all our ideas, passions, words must tend. Is not culture, is not morality itself, the expression of our resistance to power, raw politics? Like others, I have wearied also of the "culture of complaint" (Robert Hughes), the "routinized production of righteous indignation" (Henry Louis Gates, Jr.). It is one thing to write as Frantz Fanon did in *On National Culture*, drawing deeply on the experience of colonial humiliation; it is quite another to rant by rote. Nor do I believe that everything is "socially produced"; such a view blurs the infinite variations within biosocial space, within the same family even. Nor do I subscribe to the so-called "materialist" view of existence; in the language animal, "mind" and "matter" interact enigmatically. "What is matter?" William James asked. "Never mind. What is mind? No matter." Nor do I concede in every case "cultural relativism" – what about slavery, torture, suttee, cannibalism, female mutilation, castration to make singers or guard harems...? Above all, a loner, I reject "identity politics," forced filiations of an exclusive sort – that is why I came to America in the first place. No doubt, the mackerel, starling and warrior ant adheres each to its kind with primal ferocity. But in human beings, solidarity by blood, tribe, nation, class, gender, colour, caste? Is this the final fruit of five billion years of evolution?

Here we need to ponder George Steiner when he overstates: "The polis is that structure designed to execute Socrates. Nationalism has 'the necessary murder' and warfare as its direct sequel." We need to ponder him when he avers that no community, "no nation, no city, is not worth leaving on grounds of injustice, corruption, philistinism."[2] For behind these statements also lies Bergson's persuasive argument, in *The Two Sources of Morality and Religion*, that the morality of "aspiration" merits a larger role in human affairs than the morality of "pressure" or obligation. Granted, the two moralities join: "That which is aspiration tends to materialize by assuming the form of strict obligation," Bergson remarks. "That which is strict obligation tends to expand and to broaden out by absorbing aspiration. Pressure and aspiration agree to meet for this purpose in that region of the mind where concepts are formed."[3]

That region of the mind, alas, has not taken charge of our geopolitics. Instead, the "mass-soul in ourselves" seems to rule; it "foams," Elias Canetti says in *Auto-da-Fé*, like "a huge, wild, full-blooded, warm animal in all of us, very deep, far deeper than the maternal" – a theme he elaborates majestically in *Crowds and Power*.[4]

III

Valéry considered every theory a fragment of autobiography. In the present instance, autobiography has led us only to a fragment of theory: "the mass-soul in ourselves" as agent in history. Nationalism, colonialism, multiculturalism, I would here submit, draw their immane energy from the adhesive instinct, "the warm animal in all of us." That is only the beginning, the beginning and perhaps even the end – alpha and omega – but still not the middle. I mean history, how the "mass-soul" assumes all the forms we know, how, it specifically inhabits the various "isms" of the age.

Let me address nationalism, therefore, before turning to its autobiographical expressions, nationalism as synechdoche of certain geopolitical forces shaping our lives. A single word, nationalism is yet myriad, myriad and sometimes muck,

[2] Nathan A. Scott, Jr., and Ronald A. Sharp, ed. *Reading George Steiner* (Baltimore, MD: Johns Hopkins University Press, 1994) 227.

[3] Henri Bergson, *The Two Sources of Morality and Religion*, trans. T.E. Hulme (1932; trans. 1935; Garden City, NY: Doubleday, 1954) 256.

[4] Elias Canetti, *Auto-da-Fé*, trans. C.V. Wedgwood (1935; trans. 1946; New York: Seabury Press, 1979) 411; and *Crowds and Power*, trans. Carol Stewart (1960; trans. 1962; New York: Seabury Press, 1978).

as Donald Barthelme says about "the nation-state – which is itself the creation of that muck of mucks, human consciousness."[5]

Muck may be right: the origins of nationalism recede into prehistory, into fogs and bogs and hominid instincts, back to a sociobiological imperative, pitting Us implacably, invariably, against Them. The Pharaohs of Egypt and Satraps of Persia, the Myrmidons of Thessaly and Zealots of Massada, knew the power of those instincts. So, of course, did the people of Han or Yamato. For nationalism, in my sense, precedes nations, and ethnic or bonding passions can make and unmake empires. Barbarians – fierce in their tribal, not civic, sentiments – toppled proud Rome. Mongol hordes felled the Middle Kingdom from its high complacency. We know what ethnic nationalism has wreaked on the Soviet behemoth. Some wonder: can old Uncle Sam survive the fury of separatism?

In the broadest sense, nationalism may rest on biological, ethnic, religious, cultural, linguistic, political, or geographic premisses. These have never coincided in recorded history, though modern nations, notably Japan, may boast of their insular "purity" – call it "homogeneity," for tact – or indulge in "ethnic cleansing." Indeed, as we shall see, nationalism creates, then thrives on, a myth of unity. Yet nationalism itself remains a plural phenomenon, no less various than the group behaviour of humankind.

Interestingly, modern state nationalism began to wane in industrial societies after the Great War, except in defeated nations like Germany, and in others playing catch-up like Russia and Japan. Nationalism of a particularly fiery temper, however, began to wax elsewhere: in former colonies (of both the First and Second Worlds), in developing nations, in suppressed ethnic or religious communities of various sorts. Thus liberal democracy, still favoured by rich industrial societies, now confronts nationalist conflagrations around the earth.

The anguish fanning these fires is real. It is the anguish of social injustice, recollected outrage, persistent deprivation, technological change, shifting values, collapsing empires, desperate human migrations. Yet anguish and violence do not guarantee liberation. Racism, reaction, xenophobia, the lethal "narcissism of minor differences," as Michael Ignatieff calls it in *Blood and Belonging*, ride the hot winds of planetary change, even if they can find no final sustenance in the scorched earth they waste. Thus anti-semitism may still burn in Germany or Poland, with scarcely any Jews around, and ethnic or religious hatreds may flash wherever human beings feel dislocated, deprived, confused. Indeed, the more a society fails, the more it seems to find current solace and future redemption in na-

[5] Donald Barthelme, *City Life* (New York: Bantam Books, 1971) 179.

tionalism. But for how long can the promise last, without bread, lies, or iron curtains?

Beyond the "mass soul," nationalism, we can agree, is complex, compound, the word finally misleading. But so are its sub-manifestations: terrorism, tribalism, separatism, fundamentalism, multiculturalism. What have the sentiments of the Zapatistas in Mexico's Chiapas, the Moslem fundamentalists in Egypt, the Azerbaijani in Kazhak or Armenians in the Caucasus, the Afro-Americans, Hispanics or Native Americans in the USA, the Basque, Palestinian, Tamil or IRA terrorists, the neo-Nazis of eastern Germany or extreme Rightists of Japan, the Zulus of South Africa and Lapps of Sweden, the Fijians, Okinawans, or... – the list is endless – what, I repeat, do their sentiments share, beyond hope and rage?

And is nationalism always rightist, as some believe, or can it also be leftist, centrist, or indeed nearly apolitical? What are its gradations, internal conflicts, hidden tergiversations? What obligation, for instance, does a Harvard-educated Iranian woman, wearing the *chador*, feel foremost: toward her occidental ideals, her family, her gender, her religion, or her country? And would a Somali rather starve than see a U.S. Marine strutting around his village? In other words, what is the hierarchy of loyalties, values, and commitments within a society, let alone in the gallimaufry of the world?

The times, always out of joint, require from us now a cunning commensurate with the patchwork fantasies – not just hope and rage – of a technological age. Such fantasies can be retrospective; once empowered, they invent "traditions," as Eric Hobsbawm has shown.[6] But nationalist fantasies can be prospective too – "The Thousand Year Reich" – or prospective and retrospective at the same time, as in some Islamic movements, which recover the Middle Ages to instaure the Millennium of the Faithful. Indeed, how can one know to which group, to which nation one is supposed to belong, except by fantasy or fiat? Colour of skin? There are so many shades. Circumcision? In Arabs and Jews. The long slender fingers that a Serbian woman believes distinguish "true Serbs" from Bosnian and Croats? We do not all carry calipers in our pockets. A language? Some, like myself, speak all languages with a foreign accent. A community of suffering? Perhaps, but what of those who have suffered little or who can transcend their pain?

Still, the arbitrariness of belonging, the contingency of nomination, will not deter the nationalist sentiment, potentially exclusive, however temporarily liberating. I do not underestimate the power of that sentiment, not in myself, not in

---

[6] Eric Hobsbawm and Terence Ranger, ed. *The Invention of Tradition* (Cambridge: Cambridge University Press, 1992).

others. Nor are all those sentiments baneful; some may be quixotic, others enabling, even glory-sped. On some days, though I count myself unhyphenated American, I take a certain pride in the ragged, invincible cavalry of desert Arabs who swept across the world on the edge of their scimitars and inexorable faith. On other days, I recall the cruel splendour of Rameses II and Thutmose III. Such distant pride becomes tenuous, though, weary with time. And why did the British invade Egypt instead of the Egyptians invading Britain in the first place?

IV

The question returns me contrapuntally to autobiography, scenes recorded variously in *Out of Egypt*, passages and crossings in my life.[7]

I was born in a country belatedly feudal and still colonial in my youth. Once Mameluks skewered "insolent" fellahs on great, iron spikes. A century after, in the bougainvillea-draped villas of La Compagnie Universelle du Canal Maritime de Suez, foreigners plundered the wealth of Egypt and flouted its laws. My childhood, I came slowly to realise, lay in an imperceptible force field: colonialism.

As child and boy, though, I had no aversion to the French or English language; Arabic was the only subject I failed in school. True, the phrase *El Ingileez* would sometimes catch my ear, carrying some hint of menace or obloquy. True also, before my birth, the British had detained my father three days for some unacknowledged political act; that single feat provided my family with its myth of heroic resistance for years. But the sting of colonialism remains often invisible; its ravages lie within. The British rumoured themselves civilised colonials, and so they were, compared to the Spanish or Portuguese. Subtle, distant and discreet, the British divided to conquer, and acted ruthlessly in whatever touched their needs. How else could they have ruled Egypt for seventy-five years?

Like every schoolboy, I grew up with fantasies of liberating Egypt, which remained for Nasser's Free Officers Movement to accomplish in 1954, with a little help from history. But, like most schoolboys too, I had never directly experienced the "oppression" of the British. Once, during the war, when the Afrika Korps threatened Alexandria, I saw a red-nosed "Tommy," taunted beyond endurance by two students, knock one of them down. That, and a few tanks rumbling on the way somewhere, was all I saw of British power in Egypt. Even their large barracks at Kasr El Nil, displaced now by the Nile Hilton, might have blended easily into Cairo's cluttered landscape except for the high-flying Union Jack. Urchins on

[7] Ihab Hassan, *Out of Egypt: Scenes and Arguments of an Autobiography* (Carbondale, IL: Southern Illinois University Press, 1986).

the street would sometimes look up and, seeing a British soldier lean casually across his window bar, make some wildly funny face or obscene gesture which the man above invariably ignored.

The British, I repeat, divided to conquer: in this, the squabbling political parties of Egypt seemed eager to oblige. Ultimately, Britain ruled through a decadent royal house, a corrupt Egyptian bureaucracy, and a landed oligarchy, inept, venal and vain. After the revolution of 1952, after the confiscation of royal properties in 1953, schools and hospitals rose rapidly everywhere, more in that year, Sadat claimed, than in the preceding twenty. Still, I wonder: had Britain brought illiteracy and disease to Egypt in the first place? Did it impose poverty on the fellah for millennia? Who makes imperialism possible? And how healthy, free, or affluent are Egyptians four decades after their liberation?

Like some invisible worm, the colonial experience feeds on all those seeking redress for old wrongs and lacks. Self-hatred, self-doubt, twist in their bowels, and envy curls there with false pride. "*Baladi, baladi*," Egyptians cried to dismiss someone uncouth or vulgar, forgetting that the word means countrified or native. But Egyptians also feigned scorn for Europeans whom they strove to emulate. Was European skin a little fairer? "Allah, what difference can it possibly make? My cousin is fair." Was European literacy, or power, or technology, preeminent? "*Ma'lesh*, never mind. Those *frangi* perform no ablutions and eat pork. How foul!" Thus the tacit principle of the colonial complex: to extol only such differences as serve oneself, other differences to depreciate or ignore. Thus, too, the colonial complex both constitutes and institutes its necessary bad faith: necessary for resistance, self-respect, sheer survival, yet shady, shifty, abject nonetheless.

Long ago, in Cairo, beggars sometimes addressed me as *khawaga* (foreigner), presumably because my appearance diverged from their idea of an Egyptian. And what idea could that have been? The French and British, after all, had invaded Egypt only after Hyksos, Lydians, Medes, Greeks, Romans, Arabs, Mameluks, Turks and Albanians had cleared the way for them. As for myself, out of pride or pain, pain at seeing the legacy of colonialism maim so many, I resolved early never to give it a place in myself.

V

We all know the horrors of colonialism, though I suspect few of us have ever crawled in atonement on a jungle floor. It is enough to read a casebook on *Heart of Darkness* to recognise the abominations of Belgium in the Congo. It is enough to read Robert Hughes's shattering work, *The Fatal Shore*, to realise the ultimate degradations of Anglo-Celtic convicts in Australia. (Nota bene: the first gulags in history were perpetrated by an enlightened colonial power against its own English and Irish poor; white on white, you might say.) Colonialism, in any colour, is blight.

Where's the surprise? I have never regarded Europe with untrammeled esteem, nor regarded Europeans as paragons of the human race. Cultured, creative, even genial, they are murderous still. Think for a moment about their "civilised" nations: within living memory alone, they have filled trenches with the blood of a generation while the century was young, decimated Spain, bred the unsurpassed malignancies of Fascism, Nazism, Communism, gassed, bombed and tortured their way through Ethiopia and Algeria, and continue their "ethnic cleansing" to this very day. Can Asia or America – despite its mushroom terrors – begin to match this record? I understand well Fanon when he cries: "Leave this Europe where they are never done talking of Man, yet murder men everywhere they find them, at the corner of every one of their own streets, in all the corners of the globe."[8]

Yes, colonialism is blight; yes, Fanon here, if not always, is right. And yes, Camus has a point when he mordantly remarks on the disease of Europe, which is to believe in nothing while claiming to know everything. But let us be lucid. After decolonisation, what? In Africa, Bokhasa, Idi Amin, the Somali lords of death, the genocides of Rwanda; Ghaddafi and Saddam among the Arabs, Khomeini alive still in a version of Islam; Pol Pot in Cambodia; in China, the Cultural Revolution, the Gang of Four, Tiananmen Square; religious wars in India, Bangladesh, Pakistan; the Shining Path in Peru and revolutions perpetual in Latin America. And for the rest? Poverty, illiteracy, famine, torture, plagues, tyrants, sects, castes and tribes all running amuck. Are all these merely the inheritance of colonialism? Are all these cancers, ravaging the world south of the Tropic of Cancer, simply a metropolitan disease?

I find something abject, ignominious, in the eagerness of so many people nowadays to claim the status of victims. In the case of colonialism, I find continual self-exculpations craven. These narratives of self-absolution debase the colonised even more than the coloniser. Ironically, just as the discourse of "orientalists" once embalmed natives in derogatory images, so does a certain emancipatory discourse embalm them in images more disparaging still. I recognise myself in

[8] Frantz Fanon, *The Wretched of the Earth*, trans. Constance Farrington, preface by Jean–Paul Sartre (1961; trans. 1965; New York: Grove Press, 1968) 311.

none of these images. If this is what psychoanalysts call "resistance" on my part, it has not proven acutely disabling.

But the issues, again, are not wholly personal. They concern ideological discourse, concern its nuances: that is, the form truth takes in a pragmatic (non-transcendental) age. They concern, more pointedly, some Third-World writers who sometimes betray a kind of self-colonisation, a surrender to idioms generated in Paris, London, Frankfurt, Moscow and New Haven. Invoking all the idols of the hour, such writers hope to turn the metropolitan idiom against itself. This impulse may or not may avail. It reminds us, at any rate, that the critiques of Western hegemony most often derive from Western thought itself.

We can ignore such prevarications; they may be intrinsic to the project of self-liberation itself. But what of the penchant for hyperbole, self-excited exaggeration? It is not confined to America. In the last decades, for instance, some Australian academics seem intent on deprecating Anglo-Celtic lineages, as an expression of tolerance for newer immigrants, and in expiation of the massacres of Aborigines in the past. This intention leads to statements, in a textbook called *Constructing Culture* (what else?), dismissing the last two centuries of colonial rule as a "brief, nasty interlude." Does Aboriginal dignity or restitution really require such condescending claptrap?

In America, of course, many critics consider the voyages – I dare not say discoveries – of Columbus as unmitigated disaster. And so they were for certain populations of the Americas. But unmitigated, really? Many revision American history, from Plymouth to Port Huron – I have in mind the radical Port Huron Statement of 1962 – in the light of elisions and suppressions in former narratives. And indeed, elisions and suppressions abound in conventional American histories. Yet, in exposing a portion of that history, should we not guard against propounding counter-myths? How easy it is for liberal critics who claim the "end of American literature" to find themselves companions in absurdity to conservatives who claim the "end of history"?

Serious criticism comes naturally to serious writers in every epoch. Consider Herman Melville. Even young, he showed in all his white-man wanderings a critical attitude toward imperialism. In *Typee* (1846), for instance, he shadowed his Marquesan exoticism with ambivalences. The narrative questions Church and State, Nature and Civilisation, Cannibals and Christians, questions its own motives and veracity. The anti-heroic voice already carries darker resonances. Sometimes the voice angrily cries against the "fatal embrace" of the imperialist, against his destructiveness toward himself, thus proving "the white civilised man as the most ferocious animal on the face of the earth." Sometimes the voice cries against "the fickle passions which sway the bosom of a savage" – no academic tenure for that author![9] Nearly always, the voice probes, qualifies, hesitates between the ambiguities of its own subject, the ironies of its own echo. Melville, writers as diverse as C.L.R. James and Martin Green have noted, ended by offering us a de-energising myth of empire, a myth of metaphysical shades and political nuance. We call it self-criticism.

VI

Self-criticism? This recalls me to autobiography again. Egypt was not addicted to it, nor to cultural introspection. But that is not why, on a burning August afternoon in 1946, I boarded a Liberty Ship called the *Abraham Lincoln* in Port Said, bound for New York. That is not why, gliding past the great bronze statue of Ferdinand de Lesseps, who rose from the barnacled jetty above breaker and spume, one hand pointing imperiously east, I could only think: "I did it! I am leaving Egypt!" That is not why I never returned to my native land.

Why, then, was I so eager to cross? Once again, I must decline powerful explanations. (How, in any case, explain a preference for the fluency of water over the clotting blood?) Let me offer instead shards of recollection: images, as I now see it, of boyish aspiration, openings on a larger life. Or are they only fictions of self-re-creation?

School days were not happy. The government schools, primary and secondary, I attended proved intellectually demanding, socially bruising, physically dismal. Once inside the lead-hued gates, privileged and unprivileged children alike abandoned all hope. They jostled, relying on their wits, fists, and unbreakable skulls – a quick sharp blow with the head to the enemy's nosebridge – to absolve themselves of cowardice, effeminacy, class. Though I belonged to no racial or religious minority in Egypt, I was tormented more than if I had been a freak. Perhaps I was: an only child, tutored first at home, I was shy, solitary, a little perverse. I liked to go against the grain. And I liked literature, especially English and American literature.

Most pupils perceived only the ludicrous quirks of their teachers. One, dubbed "The Klaxon," kept tapping his hip pocket during class to check on his wallet; another, called "The Clutch," reached for his crotch and glared to stress a point in the lesson; a third, nicknamed "The Bullet," fired chalk pieces with the accuracy

[9] Melville, *Typee: A Peep at Polynesian Life* (1846; Harmondsworth: Penguin Books, 1972) 63–64, 123, 180.

of a high-powered rifle at nodding or chattering boys. Other teachers, however, evoke images of richer hue.

I recall Mr Miller, who taught us the King's English, and conveyed a certain hurt radiance even to the rowdiest spirit. His pale, pinched face and distant, sunken eyes rendered all the horrors of W.W. Jacobs's "The Monkey's Paw," and his flashes of mock braggadocio infused in *King Solomon's Mines*, *The White Company*, *Montezuma's Daughter*, *The Coral Island*, *Kidnapped*, and *The Prisoner of Zenda* a delightful irony without impairing their romance. He had a taste for things Gothic, a gentle way of shaming obscenity into silence. He may also have inspired me to work for the first prize I ever won at school: a handsome combination desk calendar and writing pad, inscribed, "For Excellence in English."

Mr Miller had reached the dreamer in us, awakened in some a long desire to travel. "There is no frigate like a book / To take us lands away," as Emily Dickinson knew, and I found in the attic of our dilapidated country estate many galleons and frigates. In some unfurnished rooms, I found books piled there on books and across buckling shelves; magazines rose in teetering columns from the floor; and the scent of thick, musty paper greeted my nose in closed, high-ceilinged rooms, a call to faraway times and places.

Pell-mell, I found French novels, classical Arabic poetry, English detective stories, German technical manuals, medical books in sundry languages. I found old wrinkled maps of the earth, glimmering celestial charts, inscrutable surveying deeds, spectral anatomy drawings, still lifes in ornate, gilded frames, and sepia photographs of mustachioed men and crinolined women, some with *yashmak* (veils), whose names I never came to know. Rows upon yellow rows of the *National Geographic* magazine took me around the world in an hour; and huge folios of the *London Illustrated Gazette* unfolded before me the Great War, Ypres, Châlons, Amiens, Verdun, the Marne, mud and blood filling trenches of battles that rumbled still in my family's talk.

Strange country pleasures these, that enchant though they may also swathe a boy in unreality. Unreality? No, I believe these were my first encounters with other people – call it multiculturalism as romance. I could not resist these invitations to voyage, and promised myself secretly, desperately, to leave some day on an endless journey, and see all the sights and strangers in the world.

A few years later, the strangers came, Yanks. Like many Egyptian students, more frantic than informed in their idealism, I saw Rommel in 1942 as a liberator. Surely, we thought, the enemy of our enemy must be a friend. Yet when the

Allies defeated the Desert Fox at El Alamein, the same students, changing allegiance, found in Americans, if not liberators, new models for their aspiration. We consumed Coca Cola, devoured the *Reader's Digest*, affected Ray Ban aviator glasses, and gawked at all those gangling, loping, gum-chewing, foot-propping GIs who began to appear in Cairo, their drawl so different from any sound we had ever heard. Hollywood seemed almost within reach. But the Yanks, some of them, also brought books, fragments of the American Dream. America began to seem then, in F. Scott Fitzgerald's phrase, "a willingness of the heart." Half a century later, I would wonder if it had become a tyranny of resentments, an imperium of degradations.

The day came: the Egyptian Government sent me on a generous Mission Fellowship to study in America for a PhD in electrical engineering, and return to help build the Aswan High Dam. I studied for a PhD in English, instead, and stayed. I have never felt exile.

VII

My sense of multiculturalism certainly emerges from the labyrinths of a personal past. But multiculturalism, now international in scope, also engages the geopolitical realities of our moment. That is why I began by addressing nationalism and colonialism. Nationalism insists on the identity, cohesion, often exclusiveness, and finally force of a group. It can lead to imperialism, since, as Nietzsche knew, the will to power is a will not only to be but also to be more. When empires break or recede, however, when superpowers crumble, the colonies, the tribes, the sects, find their freedom again. But this is a most equivocal freedom. The axis of violence is no longer vertical only (oppressor and oppressed) but residually vertical (colonisation by other means) and also horizontal, as all the fragments collide. Think of Africa, Asia, Europe, the Middle East. These collisions, these ethnic confrontations, less military than cultural, religious and economic, breed multiculturalism in its postmodern guise. Thus the legacy of European or Ottoman imperialism can haunt multiculturalism across oceans; thus separatism in far places cracks windows next door.

Multiculturalism may be the child of decolonisation from within (African–Americans) or from without (African–Nigerians), but revolutions have been known to eat their children. Put more equably, it is a "complex fate" – the phrase, interestingly enough, is Henry James's about Americans in the last century – to live multiculturally and still maintain personal, moral and intellectual poise, all the more so when personhood, personality, even a personal name, are all challenged in favour of some human abstract called "gender," "class," "race," or most frequently "cultural identity."

Paradoxically, I have said, multiculturalism can tend to separatism. As Georg Simmel perceived long ago: "Groups, and especially minorities, which live in conflict [...] often reject approaches or tolerance from the other side. The closed nature of their opposition, without which they cannot fight on, would be blurred."[10] Thus, seeking wider recognition, the group enforces its isolation, very much like artistic vanguards that thrive only on shock, agonism, antagonism, even as they yearn, deeper still, for acceptance.

The situation of the individual from an impoverished migrant group is no less paradoxical, no less complex. The more "developing" his or her country of origin, the more he will tend to bristle in his "developed," adopted land. Where hunger and deprivation menace existence, the economic motive will, of course, prevail; beyond that point, dignity, self-esteem, the need for transcendence – yes, immaterial motives all – will capture the affective life. Thus the immigrant cries: "I may come from a backward country, but I have my culture, I have my honour. Don't look down on me!" Yet he or she knows in the bone that the very fact of their displacement implies a judgement on his origins. Thus self-worth struggles with self-contempt, and the guilt of desertion wrestles with pride in both his abandoned and acquired land. How more admirable and rare to look at the world with level gaze, eschewing the colonial complex, with all its insidious feelings of inferiority and superiority, resentment and defiance.

Intellectuals in exile or self-exile may experience these ambiguities even more keenly. They live in the West, earn generous Western wages, marry Western women or men, carry Western passports, speak, read, write Western languages, and, as we have seen, assume Western critical values by which they criticise the West. What identity can they claim? What authority? What mediating role? The complexity remains even when the intellectual is, like Agnes Heller, a European. Born in Hungary, she emigrated first to Australia, then America, and now reflects on the concept of home at the end of the century. What can substitute for "the binding sense" in exiles, in migrants, in nomads, in intellectual errants, she wonders? "They are searching for an identity to replace the home, but this can ultimately lead to an obsession with gender, racial and ethnic differences," she remarks.[11]

---

[10] Quoted in Eric Hobsbawm, *Nations and Nationalism since 1780* (Cambridge: Cambridge University Press, 1990) 175.

[11] Lecture at the Ashworth Center for Social Theory, University of Melbourne, reported by Carolyn Jones, "Philosopher of Nomadic Necessity," *The Australian* (10 August 1994).

Is multiculturalism, then, simply an ideological substitute for roots, for homes? The answer cannot be single; for multiculturalism reflects all the geopolitical havocs of our time and reflects as well the need to surmount, transcend them. Still, one may enquire: how far can multiculturalism go without rending societies, devouring its host, the earth? Can the limits of tolerance, in Britain or Germany, in Canada or Australia, in the USA particularly – with its enormous African, Asian, Hispanic populations, with its drugs, guns, poverty, plagues, illiteracy, its fantasmic violence and broken families – can the limits of tolerance stretch to permit a genuine multiculturalism, with commitments to margin and centre at the same time, if not quite *E Pluribus Unum*? Or do we face, nearby as in far places, the "blood-dimmed tide"?

Again, the alternatives here may not be quite so stark. Certainly, societies have been multicultural from the dawn of history. But this does not mean they have been multiculturalist. Certainly, multiculturalism pervades the experience of our daily lives, nearly everywhere in the world. But this does not mean that it coincides with the claims that ideologues make for it, left and right. Nor is multiculturalism itself uniform: it takes different forms in Australia, America, Singapore, Lebanon. Nor is the "West" any less various than "Africa" or "Asia," though the internal diversity of the West hardly precludes shared values and interests that may justify its name, and so may feed the oppugnancy toward it in the "southern tier."

These are but small nuances in a field that begs for, and begs, nuances. Someday, we may hope for an aesthetics of multiculturalism to match its ethics and politics. Why not read, for instance, read tactfully, works like Sally Morgan's *My Place* and David Malouf's *12 Edmonstone Street*, about Australian multiculturalism, instead of textbooks like *Constructing Culture*? Someday, history and morality may coincide, not simply converge, as so many theorists of the subject seem constantly to presume. And someday, a society may emerge, wholly innocent of dominant and subordinate cultures, and immaculate of power relations. Meanwhile, we might hope, with Sara Suleri, for a multiculturalism that knows how to locate its holes and lacunae, and to undo temporarily the distinction, say, between mosque and temple. Such a multiculturalism would also know how to reach beyond itself. That way tough pluralism lies, the pluralism of William James at his best, the pluralism of Isaiah Berlin or Henry Louis Gates, Jr., when he revisions Berlin.

VIII

For the last time, I turn to autobiography, from which we can never wholly depart. Valéry we have encountered; Emerson saw temperament as "the iron wire" on which our opinions are strung; Wittgenstein gave the idea a further postmodern turn. "It is sometimes said that a man's philosophy is a matter of temperament, and there is something in this," he wrote. "A preference for certain similes could be called a matter of temperament and it underlies far more disagreements than you might think."[12] My own metaphors, I admit, tend to motion, an independent stance.

Multiculturalism simulates diversity, multeity, but its primal instinct, in most cases, is rootedness – the power of the term resides in "-culturalism," the care and cultivation of roots. I find my diversity elsewhere, and prefer other similes: wind, water, fire, errancy, dispossession. In *The Need for Roots*, Simone Weil argued that money (fluidity) and the state (totality) have uprooted us all. Multiculturalism, then, may embody not only the "mass-soul" in us but also our revenge on money and on the state, ubiquitous agents of our time. Still, I like other tropes: literature itself. Harold Bloom remarks: "Literature is not merely language; it is also the will to figuration, the motive for metaphor that Nietzsche once defined as the desire to be different, the desire to be elsewhere."[13] That will to figuration, that desire for empathic difference, difference not from other groups but within one's own group, may serve as breakthrough for a new kind of multiculturalism, a sensation of one's own being as sensuous and sharp as water traced on Helen Keller's palm.

As an immigrant, an Egyptian of mixed Arab, Turkic, Albanian – and what else? – extraction, I have never experienced prejudice in America, nor would I have recognised it necessarily had it come my way. Once, when I had completed my doctorate at the University of Pennsylvania, I went to see the chairman of the English Department about an instructorship. He leaned back in his chair and said benignly: "We have given you scholarships and we have given you fellowships, but an instructorship is another matter. There are still non-standard elements in your spoken English." Those "non-standard elements" persist in my speech, but they have not crucially affected my academic life in America.

---

[12] Ludwig Wittgenstein, *Culture and Value*, ed. Georg Henrik von Wright, trans. Peter Winch (Chicago: University of Chicago Press, 1980) 20.

[13] Harold Bloom, *The Western Canon: The Books and School of the Ages* (New York: Harcourt, Brace, 1994) 12.

Men and women have flocked to Australia, Canada, America, fleeing or seeking, driven by the most diverse motives. But psychological exiles stand apart, their case shadier, thicker with complicity and silent intrigue. Who are these beings, full of dark conceits, rushing to meet the future while part of them still stumbles about, like a blind speleologist, in caverns of the past? What urgency speaks through their self-banishment?

All leaving is loss, every departure a small death – yes, journeys secretly know their end. Yet self-exile may also conceal, in counterpoint, a deeper exigency. It is not an exigency that multiculturalism can meet. Yet few, very few, can, like Simone Weil, so deeply intimate with affliction, uproot themselves and carry their tree perpetually as a cross.

"Strands in the Labels" Innovation and Continuity in English Studies: A View From Singapore

EDWIN THUMBOO

I

IN RELATIVELY HOMOGENEOUS, independent nations, what maintains continuity, and drives change – the key words defining the general theme of this volume – hinges on people, time and place, a sequence with its own prioritising logic. The first is intellectual source and creative agency; the second and third, primary locations. Time is least complicated when framing an approach: we decide how far back, or forward, to go; when to pause, or digress. Place is geography and promise, until shaped by people into environment, then nation, as they evolve a substantial, common identity. Major programmes are mounted to meet the needs of individual and society. Over time, these grow into a network of beliefs, values, aesthetics, likes and dislikes, a sense of the permissible, and so on, and policies of progress that convert them into structures, institutions and organisations. This network and its interlinked, defining parts reflect the deep spirit and substance of the principles, moral codes, and social, political, educational, artistic and other expectations and practices. They are the manifest and latent content of a people, time and place. They are "cultural universals."[1] They embody core ideas, which are the blueprint for action. Their mobilising power represents a first-order activity. Mutually reinforcing, these universals constitute and support "reality,"

[1] Melville J. Herskovits, *Cultural Anthropology* (1955; New Delhi: Oxford & IBH Publishing Co., second Indian reprint, 1974) 117. There are other universals in addition to those mentioned, each with head and subheads relating to a range of second and third order activities exemplified respectively by, say, making, then implementing, legislation. Furthermore, powerfully complementary, permanent national interests are deeply embedded in these universals. They frame policy, format strategy, and drive action. Though their authority varies at different times, universals are necessities, their health crucial to survival. For the world today soon reveals its extensive Darwinian harshness: progress or perish.

which is that picture a person, his larger community and ethnic group have of themselves, their society, their nation.

These universals create an over-arching, putative national ideology and national identity. Moreover, people, time and place, in that order, define the unity-sequence of an independent nation, the sequence of *satu bangsa, satu ugama, satu negara*, established and affirmed by their internal dynamics. Energies supporting unity and identity far outweigh factors causing division. To be less disruptive, dissent is kept civil by a climate of manageable debate, a process of consensus to cope with disagreement and confrontation. In such a precinct, individuals, communities and social classes close ranks, in times of major crisis, especially when they contend with the outside "other." All these service and strengthen a singularity whose intellectual–moral–aesthetic agencies monitor external influence, and internal change, through second- and third-order institutions and activities. Permanent interests are permanent guardians. A pervasive, powerfully operative spirit, a robust identity-agenda, primes their sense of self as, say, English, French, Chinese or Japanese.

That cultural universals are found in every nation is patent enough. But not so the enormous variations in the actual elements making up their substance, their full environment.[2] The sets of facts are dissimilar; they configure differently. Unless they are grasped and taken seriously, the risk of partiality, of inaccuracy, from overview down to particular judgements, explanations and annotations, undermines even the most enlightened of critics.[3] That grasp is indispensable if we are to understand and evaluate another literature. That is one of the tasks which English studies should seriously set for itself, with thought and forethought. When we cross into another literature, in another language, we get comparative, and therefore sensitive to difference. Even then, the tendency to appropriate, and to think the analytical understandings developed and honed by studying our language and literature safely apply, exists. But this linguistic check is not there

[2] Edwin Thumboo, "Self-Images: Contexts for Transformations," *Management of Success*, ed. Kernial Singh Sandhu and Paul Wheatley (Singapore: Institute of Southeast Asian Studies, 1989) 749–68.

[3] See, for instance, Edward Said's introduction to his excellent edition of Rudyard Kipling's *Kim* (Harmondsworth: Penguin Books, 1989) where he quotes from the Lama's moment of epiphany, and says that "There is some mumbo-jumbo in this of course, but it shouldn't all be dismissed" (19). On what basis is the judgement made? And Mt. Kailas, which the Lama mentions with the Middle Way and the Four Holy Places, is glossed in the Notes as "the Himalayan peaks" (342). Kailas, the earthly manifestation of Mt. Meru the heavenly abode of the Gods, bridges the two worlds, and is holy to both Hindus and Buddhists, especially the Tibetan. It is the throne of Shiva and the home of Demchog (Chakrasamvara). Apart from demonstrating Kipling's grasp of his material, the rich, powerful religious associations Kailas commands enrich his narrative.

when dealing with the new literatures in English, because they are in English. If familiarity does not breed contempt, it does something that is possibly worse: it breeds the assumption that you have the "know" and the "how." That kind of check is not always there when examining Nigerian, coloured South African, Indian or Filipino literatures in English. They are in English, after all; or so it seems. It is not fully the case that where the language goes the full criticism gallops along. In each the language is given a local habitation and a name. Memorable instances include Raja Rao's *Kanthapura* (1938) – containing a foreword now much adopted as a manifesto for creative departures and arrivals – Amos Tutuola's *The Palm-Wine Drinkard* (1952) and Gabriel Okara's *The Voice* (1964).

These are reminders that no nation is alone. Neighbouring people, in their time, their place, each have their unity, their interests. But they are in contact. The diffusion of culture meant the diffusion of the second- and third-order substance, of which respective examples are easily absorbed ideas and practices, and items of material culture. On the other hand, first-order, architectonic occurrences are rare. The spread of Islam in the Middle East, then across North Africa and into Spain, that so fundamentally altered culture universals, starting from religion, is perhaps the best known. An example of the possible effect on an individual would be the great Mauryan emperor–conqueror Ashoka, who renounced war after conversion to Buddhism.

Generally, differences between neighbouring nations were largely matters of degree, not kind. When any of the Four Horsemen rode, they shook foundations other than the broad ones of culture. In contrast, the contact generated by post-medieval colonialism was far more corrosive. Great distances were involved. They leapt over the familiar, and encountered cultures with universals quite different from theirs. Moreover, as colonialism bit deep, the unity-sequence of the colonised was reversed, an altogether drastic fracture. Time was the new dispensation; place mattered as a source of raw materials; people, having been subdued, were subordinate. Restoring this unity-sequence was the hope of nationalism, and the primary aim of newly independent states and nations.

The history of that contact in the colonies, from the time such studies were introduced as a colonial undertaking to the changes consequent upon national independence, as peoples responded to contextualising local political, educational, literary and other forces, have not received the attention they need, let alone the attention they deserve.

And that is not all. First, while the non-Anglo-Saxon parts of the British Empire, from Aden to Zanzibar, with India, the East and West Indies, Ghana, Nigeria and others in between, shared the tensions and the depredations of colonialism, their different histories, and the unique content, packaging and emphases of their cultural universals, made each of their experience, *in situ*, unique. Colonial fundamentals remained consistent as they evolved. But their prosecution took forms tailored to best exploit each dominion, colony, protectorate and dependency, according to its cultural universals, natural resources, and strategic location, all in the metropolitan interest. Secondly, there was, and is, in the ex-colonies – some a considerable distance from their colonial past – an over-arching, essentialising vision, generated by the desire to be free, to be politically, economically, psychologically and culturally independent. It is these, and their processes especially, that ask to be seen steadily, and seen whole, if we are properly to understand and judge each of the new literatures in English.

Studying these literatures involves dealing with difference and, therefore, two sides, comprising ex-colonial masters and ex-colonial subjects, who were, moreover, connected exclusively by a period of unequal history. While connections remain after independence, chiefly through a language, similarities in certain institutions in law and education, and membership in organisations like the London-based Commonwealth of Nations, difference counts increasingly as national cultural universals revive and strengthen.

A fruitful approach is to note how English spread. It took two basic but radically contrasting forms, *settlement* (migration) and *colonisation.* While the full context of cause and effect for each of them draws in issues ranging from freedom of religious worship to strategic advantage over other rival European powers, the concern here is English studies. Apart from a common debt to English literature in their early life, the literatures in English that each gave rise to have contrasting origins and settings. The former was marked by the combination of people and language. Relatively full cultural universals were thus transplanted. The latter by officials and language. Comparatively limited, and selective, cultural universals took root.

Settlements were direct inheritors of all things English, including one of the world's greatest literatures. It had accumulated since Geoffrey Chaucer, starting with his *Boke of the Duchesse* and the better-known *Canterbury Tale*. It includes William Shakespeare and his contemporaries. Interestingly enough, Samuel Daniel, one of them, had this to say in "Musophilus"(1599):

> And who in time knows whither we may vent
> The treasure of our tongue, to what strange shores
> This gaine of our best glorie shal be sent,

> T'inrich vnknowing Nations with our stores?
> What worlds in th'yet vnformed Occident
> May come refin'd with th'accents that are ours?
> Or who can tell for what great worke in hand
> The greatness of our style is now ordain'd?
> What powres it shall bring in, what spirits comand,
> What thoughts let out, what humours keep restrain
> What mischiefe it may powerfully withstand,
> And what faire ends may thereby be attain'd.[4]

When the Pilgrim Fathers landed in America in 1620 they carried English cultural universals, Daniel's "our stores." It was the first long-distance English literary expansion. It was the beginning of the Anglo-Saxon diaspora that took the English cultural universals to America – "great in English wealth, English thought, and Englishmen"[5] – at least up to the Declaration of Independence in 1776. Then came Canada, Australia, New Zealand and South Africa. Subsets of them formed as these settlements acquired their own character, tradition and authority, the American to such an extent that its contemporary cultural universals, and spin-offs, are the most influential. But major continuities and links remain, held in place by a broadly shared inheritance, linked by powerful sentiments, language and strategic interests, the most recent instance of which is the common position America and Britain took on Iraq and Yugoslavia.[6]

Similar sentiments and links do not mark British colonisation in the nineteenth and early-twentieth centuries, and its aftermath. Nor do we expect any, because that took officials and language to the colonies, not people who intended to settle.[7] Compared to settlements, the numbers were small. Consequently, except for those dealing with rule and power, British cultural universals were not transplanted, at least not vigorously enough to dominate across the board, or to survive *in toto* after colonialism. They formed a thin but strictly enforced upper crust, centred in the Club, the *maidan*, the barrack-room, images of which are in Rud-

---

[4] Samuel Daniel, *Poems and A Defence of Ryme*, ed. A.C. Sprague (1966; Chicago and London: University of Chicago Press, 1972) 96.

[5] Jim Hicks, "Rebellion and Global War," *The Horizon History of the British Empire*, ed. Stephen W. Sears (New York: Heritage, 1973) 78.

[6] *The Sunday Times* (Singapore; 5 November 2000) carried the following report:

> One of Britain's most disgraceful acts of colonial bullying has been condemned with a (British) High Court ruling that the eviction of 2000 Indian Ocean islanders, 30 years ago, was unlawful.
>
> Britain forced the islanders, known as Ilois, from their homes in the idyllic Chagos Archipelago, east of Africa, to allow the USA to build a huge air and naval base on the biggest island, Diego Garcia. (22)

[7] The exceptions are Kenya, Rhodesia and South Africa, where significant numbers settled.

yard Kipling's *Kim* and E.M. Forster's *A Passage to India*. Unlike the French, who assimilated talented colonial subjects – Léopold Sédar Senghor comes to mind – the British did not create a colonial elite after their own image.[8]

Settlement literatures differ fundamentally in origin, affiliation, substance and character from the new literatures in English. The former had substantial continuity with England. In contrast, the new literatures, being ex-colonial, and in English, had a measure of initial continuity with Britain, but one soon modified by radical differences in assumptions, role and operative paradigms.

Continuity and change in English literature was evolutionary; in settlement literature more rapid and varied through acts of growing self-definition, as in American literature – although the Revolution of 1778 did not seriously alter America's cultural intimacy with Britain for at least a hundred years. In terms of lines of descent and growth, change in the new literatures was tempestuous, and far more complex in terms of contexts and circumstances. The writers inhabited two cultures. Although the first generation were – with few exceptions – students of English literature, they had deep roots in their own cultural universals, as Tamils, Ijaw, Gikuyu, Cantonese, Samoans, South Africans – Coloureds, Africans and English-speaking whites – Malays, Maoris, Filipinos, the occasional Thai, and so on. Moreover, many wrote of and out of interruptions of life before, during and immediately after colonialism; and of the freedom that promised national resurgence. We are talking about quite different writing contexts, each with unique factors of production. The "other" has an expressive face. Consequently, the processes enabling talk of continuity and change can neither reflect the radical experiences nor characterise the range of environments producing new literatures. Nor are they meant to. Those environments – built around people, time and place – have had their continuity disrupted to such an extent that change, following independence, is more revolutionary than evolutionary. The two crucial events – separated by anything from fifty to three hundred years – are the arrival/insertion and the departure/expulsion of colonialism. The first was often violent, in any case disruptive; the second generally less so, with exceptions such as the Mau Mau national reassertion and other instances of conflict, such as the communist uprising in Malaya, which was not always fully linked to colonialism. As interrelated processes, continuity and change in homogeneous, independent nations are less dramatic; and if dramatic, like the Puritan or French Revolutions, less sus-

[8] Instead, an English-educated middle class emerged which, in time, produced the first nationalists. As a group educated in English, they provided a bridge linking the major ethnic/linguistic sectors, compacting them into a single colonial geography.

tained. Those who oppose each other, however bitterly, are still largely subject to the same national cultural universals. In contrast, when colonialism is imposed on a country/nation, or when colonies are created by cutting across pre-existing boundaries that have kept peace and ensured stability, as in the Cameroons,[9] or there is a significant imported population, as in Fiji, conflicts are more extensive, and sustained. The dangers of politics and economics turning bitterly racial are there. But this is to anticipate.

II

Various colonial systems developed.[10] Cultivated by the British, indirect rule was perhaps the most efficient. Based on maintaining control through indigenous institutions and structures, it saved on manpower, and left the colonised leadership the trappings of authority. As masters, they arranged or re-arranged the economy, and matters in other key areas, but left culture by and large alone. The 1874 Treaty of Pangkor (an island south of Penang, and just off the coast of Perak, West Malaysia), formalised indirect rule. Useful native institutions were kept. And it made sense to apply lessons learnt in one part of empire to another.[11]

Whatever their precolonial status, the colonised lost control of their destiny when their military power collapsed. "People" is replaced by "colonialist," re-inscribing the sequence as "colonialist – place – time," then "people." The old sequence no longer exercises any prioritising power. "People-centred" becomes "colonial-centred." Other changes follow. In the imperial/colonial design, place is

---

[9] Here a people and their geography are separated into British and French Cameroon which, when they reunited, needed a bilingual literary journal, a fact indicating the complexity of postcolonial problems/challenges.

[10] Perhaps the most wide-ranging exposé is a mid-nineteenth-century one about the Dutch in the East Indies. See Multatuli (pseudonym of Eduard Douwes Dekker), *Max Havelaar, or The Coffee Auctions of the Dutch Trading Company* (London: Heinemann, 1967). It was originally published in Dutch in 1860 as *Max Havelaar of De koffyveilingen der Nederlandsche Handelmaatschappy.*

[11] According to V.G. Kiernan, when a revolt broke out in 1962 against Aden's feudal rulers, "bombing raids were made on the tribesmen, while 'food control' measures that winter meant burning of crops and driving thousands out of their villages in the hills – a *modus operandi* derived from north-west frontier policing, and by remoter ancestry from the conquest of Ireland"; *European Empires from Conquest to Collapse, 1815–1960* (Bungay: Collins/Fontana, 1982) 211. Systematic "food control" to deprive the enemy of rations was refined by the British during the "Emergency" in Malaya when the Communists organised a "revolt" in 1948 which lasted for more than a decade. The mention of Ireland is of particular interest. We tend to assume that Spain and Portugal were the first post-medieval colonialists. The English – when still Anglo-Normans – were busy learning the business after Strongbow arrived in Ireland in 1166. Taken together with their Scottish, Welsh and Continental experiences, the occupation of Ireland for more than seven hundred years, by far the longest in colonial history, gave Britain the best possible manual on colony management.

decisive, especially as competition among European powers escalates. Transport by sea relied on stations to protect trade, communications and other strategic interests.[12] The land masses they controlled translated into wealth. Repatriated to London, it contributed directly, and massively, to Britain's pre-eminence in the hierarchy of nations. They guaranteed raw materials for manufacturers, diamonds and other precious stones, platinum, gold, silver and other metals. Colonies had to be profitable; otherwise, why have them? It helped considerably if they were also markets for British manufacturers. In a cycle of primary (coloniser) and secondary (colonised) prosperity, "time" was marked by the continuous competition among the British, French and Dutch, and, later, the Germans and Italians. Colonised people became second-class citizens, marginalised. They and their leaders had to adjust to the new dispensation that reduced the circumscribing power and operational radius of their cultural universals, by confining it to what was a parallel but contained society, functioning on reduced terms.

Only when they became independent in the late 1940s and early 1950s did the former colonies set about restoring the proper sequence of People, Time and Place.[13] People again provided the primary focus. Time was one of continuing national reconstruction and construction, within an international order dominated by America, Britain and France, the victorious Allies. Place had to adapt its colonial infrastructure to a national, regional, global one. There was a cline rising from underdeveloped, through developing, to developed; the "Third," "Second" and "First" Worlds. Recovery, restoration and development were the key words around which programmes got built. National pride and national identity – sought especially to bridge ethnicities – were the dominant themes. The curious thing about identity is that you do not talk about it – in fact, dismiss it – when it has been absorbed into the national psyche, turned into a conditioned reflex. It is a vital force in the growth of a nation, as Shakespeare knew full well when he wrote the history plays. Identity is not a flat word. It is a complex site. Its DNA, espe-

---

[12] These included Gibraltar, Malta, Cyprus, Port Said, Aden, Bombay, Trincomalee, Rangoon, Penang, Singapore, Hong Kong; Darwin, Perth, Sydney, Wellington, Suva, Western Samoa, the Cook Islands, Pitcairn; Freetown, Accra, Lagos, Cape Town, Dar es Salaam, the Seychelles, Mauritius; the Falklands, Tristan Da Cunha, and St Helena. They established, and preserved, Britain's global interests and kept rival colonial powers out.

[13] That was the vision, the theory, the hope. A decent chance of fulfilment *if* government was clean, intelligent, dedicated, democratic. As revealed by the effects of colonialism, the unity-sequence is diagnostic. Its prioritising power is the basis of the maximum good for the maximum number. Corruption in high places distorted the sequence again, by putting the personal interests of leaders first and last. They exploit time by suspending free elections; manipulate place by pampering their electoral districts with new schools, hospitals, industrial estates, housing etc, by introducing costly, unproductive projects to skim off ten percent of their total cost.

cially if it encodes a colonial history, is a permanent source of attitude, bonding, thinking and behaviour. Whether in capitals or lower case, it often protects its inhabitants from changes that work against their permanent interests, as when colonies become independent and start to construct and pursue their own agendas of recovery and national reassertion, of which the new literatures in English are part. They encode the national recovery from a comprehensive colonialism of considerable duration.

The need for critical preparation, and caution, and re-thinking is extensive – and obvious – if we are to possess the back-, middle and foreground of these literatures. We could start by unpacking labels, including new "literatures in English," which is but one in a series that includes "Commonwealth literature," "contact literature" and "postcolonial literature." The challenge is not so much to take the politics as to see and reflect its sides. Labels should give an immediate sense of what they purport to identify. Hence "E-literatures," "E" for English, the present writer's label.[14] Accuracy apart, Indian E-literature, Nigerian E-literature, Filipino E-literature and Singapore E-literature would call up specificities. Those who know these literatures will call their writers and critics immediately to mind. Those who do not will at least realise the limits of generalities. And the label could easily put the E-literatures in the company of the other national literatures, which are important to each nation, and which are themselves in danger of being overlooked by those chiefly concerned with the life conducted in English. In Malaysia and the Philippines, for instance, the literature in Bahasa and Filipino respectively are far more national in reach than their E-literatures. E-literatures need to live with them, and their other literatures, perhaps as much as, if not more than, with each other.

III

A useful way to look at continuity and change is to move from abstraction to policy, from policy to plans, from plans to substance and facts. But life is rarely, if

[14] In a recent interview/discussion with Norbert Schaffeld which is to appear in *Anglistik*, the present writer said that "we badly need a conference on paradigms, definitions, and concepts – with a section on labels – to identify the problems, assess the limitations of present terminology and the distortion it creates, and try to look for useful answers. In the meantime why not try Indian E-Lit, Nigerian E-lit, Malaysian E-lit, Sri Lankan E-lit, Pakistan E-lit, Singapore E-lit, and so on. If preferred, as I do, E-lit could be spelt out as Singapore E-literature, with our other literatures labelled as Singapore, M-literature, C-literature and I-literature. The strong advantage is clear: immediate identification. The mention of names brings to mind their writers on the instant. Do not these very positive factors outweigh what reservations that may be put forward? And the E-literatures do not have to go through postcolonial, or other, tunnels.

ever, so neat as to allow that. And the topic sits differently in each national context, while in the larger of these, especially America, English studies is subject to wide variations. The main concern here is with the last fifty years or so, seen from an individual point of view formed by life and contacts in Singapore. Both its ethnic profile and its concerted response to the challenges of transformation from colony to a modern, thriving island republic rehearse most of the key issues implicit in the topic. Singapore has four official languages – Bahasa, Chinese, Tamil and English – to meet the needs of the Malays, Chinese, Indians, and the Eurasians who use English.

English has a pivotal place. Apart from bridging the ethnic groups, it is used in administration, education, the press and other mass media, high technology manufacture, regional and international contact and so on. The great majority of Singapore's best young scholars are sent to Berkeley, Cambridge, Harvard, MIT, London, Oxford, Princeton, Stanford and comparable institutions; a few to Beijing, Madras, Tokyo and leading universities in Germany and France.

Given this multi-ethnic profile, Singapore's cultural universals have deep and varied roots, as well as powerful modernising elements. It is enough to show that the "other" is a label of closure that excludes the rich, complicated and thriving worlds of the E-literatures. The matrix for each universal contains head, subheads, sub-subheads, down to minutiae which, given the nature of things, often reflect powerful considerations. When the colours of a Singapore regiment are commissioned – an attractive colonial inheritance – the following share the act of blessing: Catholic, Anglican, Methodist, Hindu, Muslim, Taoist, Buddhist, Sikh, Baha'i priests, and rabbi. This is only one E-literature. Understanding what goes into all the E-literatures and their worlds, in all their complexity, is crucial if we intend to explicate and judge, and want to see how, on the one hand, they belong to the family of literatures in English and, on the other, to the national families which, together, have hundreds of languages. They include some with powerful oral traditions, others with classic texts, like the *Rig-Veda* and *I-Ching*, which go back two to three thousand years.

English was the language of administration. Language shapes sensibilities; it colonises minds. When Queen Isabella of Spain – the tough lady whom Christopher Columbus supplicated for ships – was presented in 1492 with a copy of Antonio de Nebrija's *Gramatica*, she wanted to know its purpose. The Bishop of Ávila's reply is instructive, core: "Your Majesty, language is the perfect instrument of empire."[15] We might add that it remains a potent instrument, well after empire: Spanish, Portuguese, French, with English leading the pack by a long shot. All international languages, they each manage neocolonial possibilities in proportion to their current influence.

In Singapore as it did elsewhere, English followed the Empire. Schools were started to educate the Malays, and the Chinese and Indians, chiefly the children of immigrants, to produce a local source of manpower. There were two more groups, the Eurasians and the Perenakans. The Eurasians used English even if they spoke Portuguese or some other European language. Their surnames suggest a fascinating history.[16] The Perenakans were Chinese, mainly from Fukien, who had settled in Malacca and intermarried with the Malays, adopting elements of Malay culture including language, but retaining their traditional religion and unique identity across many generations.[17] To say that the colonial "other" is complicated runs the risk of understatement.

---

[15] Quoted by Peter Farb, *Word Play: What Happens When People Talk* (New York: Bantam Books, 1974) 157.

[16] Eurasian surnames: Aeria, Albuquerque (D'), Almeida (D'), Alloy, Alphonso, Aroozoo, Augustine, Cardoza, Carlos, Coelho, Conceicao, Consigliere, Cordeiro, Costellou, D'Aranjo, D'Costa, D'Cruz, D'Rosario, Da Cotta, Da Cunha, De Britto, De Castro, De Conceicao, De Cruz, De Mello, De Rosario, De Roza, De Souza, Dias, Fernandez, Fernando, Ferreira, Francisco, Galistan, Gomes, Gomez, Gonzales, Lazaroo, Lobo, Lopez, Machado, Martinez, Mayo, Miranda, Monteiro, Morais, Morales, Netto, Nonis, Nunis, Oliveiro (D'), Olivera, Oliveras, Paglar, Pasqual, Pereira, Pestana, Pinto, Rodrigues, Rosario (D'), Santa Maria, Sequerah, Sta Maria, Texeira, and Theseira. — Abbas, Aitken, Anderson, Andrews, Archer, Armstrong, Arnold, Ash, Augustine–Reed, Bachelor, Bain, Balhetchet, Baptist, Barker, Barnabas, Bartlett, Bateman, Bates, Beins, Bennett, Bersu, Branson, Broughton, Brown, Campbell, Carnegie, Carson, Clarke, Clement, Clunies–Ross, Cockburn, Collins, Crawford, Davenport, Davidson, Donough, Dragon, Drysdale, Dunstan, Dyson, Ferguson, Fitzpatrick, Fox, Francis, Garvin, Glass, Goddard, Hamilton, Hardy, Harris, Hawkins, Henderson, Higgs, Hobson, Hogan, Hubbard, Hughes, Hutchinson, Jackson, James, Jeremiah, Johnson, Jones, Joseph, Kelly, Leicester, Lewis, Logan, Lowe, Lowry, Macintire, Macmahon, Marcus, Marshall, Martin, Matthews, McClelland, McIntyre, Merlin, Miles, Mitchell, Moss, Murphy, Neighbour, Neville, Newton, Norris, O'Hara, Parker, Paterson, Pennyfather, Pierce, Ramsay, Rankine, Richards, Richmond, Ross, Ryan, Sanderson, Saunders, Savage, Sculy, Shelley, Shepherdson, Siddons, Simmons, Sims, Sinclare, Snodgrass, Sweeney, Tanner, Taylor, Thomas, Thompson, Walters, Watson, Watts, Webb, White, Williams, Wilson, Winters, Woodford, Wright, Wyatt, and Yeoman. — Boudville, Jacques, Lambert, Le Blond, Le Mercier, Misson, Papineau, and Xavier. — Bogaars, Danker, De Vries, De Witt, Desker, Esperkerman, Ess, Grosse, Hansen, Hendricks, Hochstadt, Hoeden, Holmberg, Jansen, Kessler, Klass, Klyne, Koenig, Koenitz, Kraal, Krempl, Martens, Martinus, Minjoot, Mosbergen, Neubronner, Oehlers, Olsen, Philipps, Reutens, Rodyk, Schelkis, Skadiang, Skading, Tessensohn, Van Der Beek, Van Der Straaten, Van Der Van, Vanderput, and Zehnder. — Hoy, Jalleh, Masang, and Rappa.

[17] They responded positively to the British who saw them as enterprising and natural economic allies. As Straits Chinese – a label with a history and agenda – they were to be distinguished from recent arrivals, mainly indentured labourers, clan-centred and hedged by triads.

A solid grounding in English that included studying literature produced the teachers and clerks. Students took the Senior Cambridge Certificate and the London Matriculation, both qualifications for admission to university. In time came colleges, then universities that invariably had English departments. In Singapore, Raffles College (1929) offered a Diploma, requiring two subjects selected from Economics, Education, English, Geography, History and Mathematics for Arts, and Chemistry, Education, Mathematics and Physics for Science. A select few were allowed to specialise in a single subject in the final year.

The history of English studies in Britain is well known. Parts of it, especially the debate and manoeuvres to establish it in Oxford and in Cambridge, make fascinating reading.[18] Below is the initial Oxford English syllabus approved in 1894:

1. Old English Texts (*Beowulf* and Sweet's *Anglo-Saxon Reader*).
2. Middle English Texts (*King Horn, Havelok, Laurence Minot, Sir Gawayne*).
3. Chaucer (selections) and *Piers Plowman* (selections).
4. Shakespeare (about six plays).
5. History of the English Language.
6. History of English Literature to 1800.
7. Gothic (*Gospel of St Mark*) and unseen translations from Old and Middle English.
8. Critical Paper.

9. and 10. Special Subjects.[19]

The Raffles College English syllabus for the academic year 1928–1929 was:

Year 1. a. The history of English Literature from 1780 to the present day;
b. English Language (Composition and Prose Style), with instruction in précis writing.

Year 2. a. The Elizabethan era with some reference to the beginnings of literature in England;
b. English Language with particular attention to the development of Meter.

Year 3 a. Milton, and extending to the close of the 18th Century;
b. English Language including a series dealing with the principles of criticism.

This syllabus, introduced thirty-five years after that first proposed for Oxford, is comparatively impoverished. Himself an Oxford man, E.W. Gillett, the first Pro-

[18] See E.M.W. Tillyard, *The Muse Unchained* (London: Bowes & Bowes, 1958); D.J. Palmer, *The Rise of English Studies* (London: Oxford University Press, 1965); Gerald Graff and Michael Warner, ed. *The Origins of Literary Studies in America* (London & New York: Routledge, 1989).

[19] Palmer, *The Rise of English Studies* 113.

fessor, must have been familiar with the scene in Britain at the time. To be fair, he was the only member of staff before Graham Hough joined him in 1931.

Ronald Bottrall's arrival in 1934 led to a considerable strengthening of the whole syllabus. He was one of the group gathered around F.R. Leavis who had singled him out, with William Empson, as promising poets.[20] The changes he made were far-reaching, though not all survived his departure three years later. Bottrall moved language work to Michaelmas of the First Year. Hilary and Trinity were taken up with an outline of literature from Chaucer to "the present," anchored by "A plan of reading based on set books [of which] detailed knowledge of certain specified books will be required." The Second and Third Years were devoted to "Chaucer to the year 1750" and "1750 to the present day."[21] A major development was the detailed analysis of prose and poetry in class, including unseen passages. Inspired by I.A. Richards, Leavis himself, and Empson, whose *Seven Types of Ambiguity* had appeared in 1930, these Practical Criticism sessions were invaluable. They took the student into the workings of language at a level of imaginative reach and power to be found in one of the world's great literatures. It equipped the student with the tools of close reading, very much a Leavis prescription.[22] The foundation for that kind of work was a strong command of English. The schools were to provide it.

Entering British CUs through its literature had its benefits. You understood the coloniser better, which some thought was of dubious value. Close reading made the text yield more, and sharpened one's language, refined one's sensibility. There are lessons in Mark Antony's "Friends, Romans, countrymen…," especially in how carefully calculated verbal management of language as gesture, and gesture as language, most potent when coming together, turns the mob against Brutus and his fellow-conspirators. Think of the soliloquies of Hamlet, Macbeth and Othello; of poems from William Dunbar to W.B. Yeats. Passages and poems we have explicated; read and/or recited with that fullness of attention that combines the giving of mind and feeling and a simultaneous sense of detachment. Here are lines from the third section of "The Tower":

---

[20] See F.R. Leavis, *New Bearings in English Poetry* (1932; London: Chatto & Windus, 1971) 201–11.

[21] The year seems arbitrary: Thomas Grey's "Elegy" was published, a bill prohibiting colonial manufactures was before Parliament, and Benjamin Huntsman made steel by the Bessemer process, all probably in the same year.

[22] See "Judgement and Analysis: Notes on the Analysis of Poetry," *A Selection from Scrutiny* (Cambridge: Cambridge University Press, 1968) vol. 1 211–57. A footnote explains that the three essays, "'Thought' and Emotional Quality" (vol. 13, 1945), "Imagery and Movement" (vol. 13, 1945), "Reality and Sincerity" (vol. 14, 1952–53), constitute part of a book.

I mock Plotinus' thought
And cry in Plato's teeth,
Death and life were not
Till man made up the whole
Made lock, stock and barrel
Out of his bitter soul,
Aye, sun and moon and star, all,
And further add to that
That, being dead, we rise,
Dream and so create
Translunar Paradise.[23]

Consider the rhythm. It supports every curve and loop of the thought. A set of strong verbs frame the dialectical movement of Yeats's push for release from bare intellect into the poised perfection of paradise. The choice of nouns is equally careful. Apart from their importance to Yeats's system enunciated in *A Vision*, and his general thought, Plato and Plotinus sum up the two main strands of ancient Mediterranean philosophy. It is part of the poetry's careful organisation that the celestial nouns bespeak light, life and immensity. Reading aloud, one notices how the regular beat of the lines takes meaning on a powerful march. The preponderance of monosyllabic words, the unhesitating, repetitive use of "and," the confident alternation of stress, gives each line, literally, the stamp of authority that in turn strengthens Yeats's argument. Perhaps the boldest part of an already bold undertaking is how he shifts the flow. By bracketing "sun and moon and star" with "Aye" and "all," he lifts them above the poem's flow to stress their importance. They are the only physical sources of light in the universe. The other instance of a double "that": "…further add to that / That being dead…." All this creates a rhythmic authority that charges each word in a cliché like "lock, stock and barrel" with unexpected life.

Discussions focused on "core courses," often associated with the "Great Tradition," the "canon," concentrate on only half the question. And that half concerns texts, picked to provide entry into the essential spirit and content of the cumulative literary tradition. The other half, comprising analytical and conceptual skills, was generally assumed because students did Practical Criticism every week. The serious business of studying – on any given level – a text to the fullest extent possible required the development of approaches and various instruments. From the time teaching resumed after the Japanese Occupation (1942–1945) when Graham Hough returned from internment leave to 1969 when D.J. Enright left, courses were built around major figures such as Chaucer, Shakespeare (two full courses at

[23] W.B. Yeats, *The Poems*, ed. Richard J. Finneran (London: Macmillan, 1984) 198.

times), Spenser, Milton, Dryden, Pope, Yeats and Eliot. Course listings over the period included Shakespeare and his Contemporaries, Elizabethan and Jacobean Drama, The Metaphysical Poets, The Augustans, The Eighteenth Century Novel, The Romantics, and The Victorians. For a number of years Anglo-Saxon was offered. The First-Year compulsory course on language was kept. English Language as a full major lay in the future, despite graduates having to teach it in schools.

We studied English literature, achieving a fair degree of inwardness with it. What was missing, and in an especially serious sense, was that essential and extensive sharing of the content, shape and spirit of cultural universals; the societal experience out of which the literature grew. Helpful and comprehensive as they were, the introduction to and extensive notes of the Arden Shakespeare took the student so far but no further.

> Now is the winter of our discontent
> Made glorious summer by this son of York;
> And all the clouds that lowered upon our house
> In the deep bosom of the ocean buried.[24]

Unless the instruction is available in their own cultural universals, not all will see that the play on "son," made possible by the "sun" of "glorious summer," gains deeper reach through the theory of, and belief in, correspondences. The mind understands; the imagination sets to work; feelings stir. Many will spot that clever use of vowels in line three to suggest a dark, sky-wide oppressiveness. But the crucial link that makes winter shiver, and summer vowelly stretched into glory, is the actual experience of the four seasons that the tropics do not offer. Moreover, direct experience apart, the images and metaphors of the literatures in English differ in their meaning-making, their meaning-potential. Herein lies the central challenge: the reorientation of English – what Braj Kachru calls its "nativisation."[25] The object, experience and idea, and the calculus of meaning and implication, the connotative layering described by literature and environment within that literature, however rich and memorable, was not on all fours with the cultural universals of the colonised.

Colonialism changed the equations of contact. There were the colonisers and the colonised. A substantial part of the coloniser's universals – administrative

---

[24] *The Tragedy of King Richard the Third*, William Shakespeare, *The Complete Works*, ed. Alfred Harbage (Harmondsworth: Penguin Books, 1969) 554.

[25] See his *The Indianisation of English* (New Delhi: Oxford University Press, 1983) and *The Alchemy of English* (London: Pergamon Press, 1986).

practice, language, law, religion, custom, social structure, the economy, education – arrive. Where there had been one set of universals, now there were two. Some were imposed; some introduced as alternatives the colonised accepted, ignored or took to in part. The centres of power, especially related to the branches of government, shift from local to colonial hands. The contact invariably led to irrevocable change, sometimes deep and fundamental; the beginnings of multiplicity, you might say. There were two sets of cultural universals, the second the indigenous and immigrant-imported ones: Malay, Chinese and Indian.

IV

Nationalism and independence sought to restore the unity-sequence of people, time and place, and to repair and modify cultural universals. To have been colonised before or when the industrial revolution was not yet in full swing, and to be released into the mid-twentieth century of jet aircraft and nuclear power stations, made national renovation imperative. The idea of a national identity is a vital necessity during key formative periods of a people's history – when they are yet to become a people, when there is yet to be sufficient binding for them to be justifiably seen as a nation rather than a country. It is pursued on all levels, on all occasions. Not to recognise that this identity is a condition, a commodity, an instrument, a major pervasive theme, is to miss an essential force in the formation of literature and the other key institutions that define and sustain society and nation. Broad-based, it is often passionate, a potent source of political, cultural, social and economic will and doing. It is idea, ambition and substance.

At the time Singapore became independent in 1965, students in the Faculty of Arts and Social Science majored in either one or two subjects, graduating with a Class based on performance. The final examination for the one-subject course had eight three-hour papers based on two years' work. These were

(i) Practical Criticism, and Readings in Criticism
(ii) Chaucer
(iii) Shakespeare
(iv) Spenser, Milton and Pope
(v) Literature 1578–1700 (excluding Spenser and Milton)
(vi) Literature 1700–1798 (excluding Pope)
(vii) Literature 1798–1880
(viii) Literature 1880 to the Present.

Based on the major texts of the Great Tradition, the courses were demanding. Training in close reading, based on a representative selection of poetry, fiction and drama, was central. The question was whether, in their existing form, such studies, vigorous though they were, were ultimately appropriate, given the time and the place. More than any other subject, English studies *per se* took students into cultural universals of the literature, which, in some instances, exerted a powerful influence, taking them away from their immediate environment. That generally happened when a student was absorbed both into the literature and the criticism, and into that larger culture. If their own cultural universals were insufficiently empowered, then sensibilities, values, assumptions, attitudes, ways of thinking, and expectations were changed markedly.

It was inevitable for disciplines in the humanities and social sciences to confront the fundamental question of their postcolonial relevance. Apart from the basic concepts, theories, hypotheses and principles – themselves in need of inspection – there is the question of content. For instance, history in the mid-1950s meant, chiefly, "European Expansion Overseas," starting with the Portuguese, and progressing through English, Dutch, French, and brought up by the American occupation of the Philippines. Labour economics started to look at local problems. Geography was getting tropicalised. English studies kept a steady course.

But the times had started changing. Nationalism was in the air, gathering strength and direction, first among student intellectuals studying in London, then at the University of Malaya (located in Singapore at the time), which had been formed in 1948. The editors and associates of *Fajar*, published by the University Socialist Club, were arrested in May 1954, during the Final Examinations, and tried for sedition in August. They were acquitted: perhaps the intention had been to scare. Nor were they the first to be arrested. The serious desire in the late 1940s and early 1950s to create a Malayan literature in English, one reflecting the cultural matrix of Malaya and Singapore, was part of that nationalism.

The recognition of the need for that literature was beginning to spread. This is from an editorial in a magazine edited by, and for, secondary schools in Singapore:

> "YOUTH" therefore appeals to you, the young men and women of this country, to help STIMULATE INTEREST IN THE CREATION OF A GENUINELY ORIGINAL MALAYAN LITERATURE. This is especially urgent in view of the efforts being made towards the creation of a MALAYAN NATION. Or, are we to be a nation without our own literature?[26]

Malayan literature in English started at the University. Goh Sin Tub, Wang Gung–wu, Lim Thean Soo, James Puthucheary and Beda Lim were the pioneers.

---

[26] Edwin Thumboo, Editorial in *YOUTH* 4.1 (Singapore 1953) 3–4.

Ee Tiang Hong went up to read English, in 1951; the present writer in 1953; Lloyd Fernando in 1954; Wong Phui Nam in 1956. While the language was English, and the sources of technical instruction its literature, the sentiments, the imagery, the metaphors were increasingly ours. A few of us knew the works of Raja Rao, Mulk Raj Anand, R.K. Narayan, the modern founders of Indian E-literature, Amos Tutuola and Wilson Harris. This was entirely "unofficial" reading. The enterprising, forward-looking proprietor of Orient Star News, a leading bookshop in the 1950s, brought in their novels. English literature was gradually broadening into literatures in English. What struck the reader immediately was the environment of the fiction, and how Rao and Tutuola especially used English. This awareness led to interest in the literatures of the CUs defining Singapore's multiracial inheritance. Apart from reading translations, some of the poets themselves worked with Indian and Chinese friends on translations; Dollah Majid on a collection of Malay poems that included sharply nationalistic ones.

The interest in writing our literature – the division between Singapore and Malaysia was formalised only in 1965 – into existence did not directly affect the syllabus. What it did, though, was create an increasingly energetic awareness that other literatures in English were already in existence, and growing. A thesis on African poetry in English that examined the relationship between intention and idiom in Lenrie Peters, Kofi Awoonor, Gabriel Okara, Christopher Okigbo, Wole Soyinka and Denis Brutus was completed in 1969. In the same year, a course in Commonwealth Literature comprising a selection of African and Australian texts was offered for the first time. Other doctoral dissertations were "An Authentic Idiom: A Study of Australian Literature" (1976), "Vain Empires: the response of some British writers to the East" (1978), and "Identity in contemporary literatures in English from the Philippines, Malaysia and Singapore" (1986). Successful MA theses included "The Asian novel in English expression (including translation): change, responsibility, direction" (1978) and "Post-War Indian poetry in English: a study of themes and techniques in selected poets" (1986).

The role of the English department was systematically reconsidered in 1970. Like all other sectors of the educational system, it served subject and national needs; these were not incompatible. Singapore's survival and, later, her progress included training and educating her young to the highest level they were capable of attaining. A small population made this an imperative, especially as we moved into high-tech industries and finance, and sought maximum efficiency in service and other sectors of the economy. The more sophisticated the infrastructure, the greater the chances of success, the higher the demand for trained minds. Characteristically, graduates were required in both the public and the private sectors as administrators, teachers, editors, journalists, TV and radio producers, advertising copywriters, public relations executives, and personnel officers. A small number went into banking. The Department had to ensure that graduates were both well-grounded in the subject and able to bring the premium of their language skills to whatever work they chose. That work was not only varied. At this level, whatever the profession or vocation, it opened into a society very much on the move. It was not a matter of ripening, of maturity. Development, consolidation and growth were far more basic forty years ago. When it became independent in 1965, Singapore had no armed forces to speak of; it now has F–16s. The point made earlier about the different circumstances in which changes in society are evolutionary or revolutionary certainly applies, given the aggregate of rapid changes in a relative period of time, and, moreover, compacted in an island republic of about 250 square miles. Professionalism functioned in a larger constructive context that sought independence and viability in a number of key areas vital to national interests.

Given time and place, English studies had to expand, reorientate and place themselves strategically. While maintaining a strong, sufficient interest in the historically mainstream English literature, the E-literatures needed to be brought in. That move, it could be said, combined a diachronic inheritance with a synchronic, contemporary challenge and opportunity. Based on a broadly common set of themes, E-literatures were especially close in spirit and thrust to the local, national and regional experience. These themes arose from the continuities and ruptures of pre- and postcolonial life. E-literatures were closer to home. Their wrestle to indigenise English by inserting new rhythms, playing with its syntax, adding images and metaphors and so on, was and is instructive.

But there had to be balance, secured by combining compulsory and elective courses in a specialist, fourth-year Honours degree good enough to give entry to leading universities in America and Britain for postgraduate work. This meant strong programmes covering the literature from Shakespeare down to what was virtually contemporary. In 1971 "Special Topics" was introduced. Students had a chance to do more detailed, demanding work, often in an area where staff had special teaching and research strengths. Two courses, "Asian Literature in Translation" and "Style and Stylistics," were also offered for the first time. The latter signalled the need for work in language. Significant numbers of graduates took up teaching each year. They had no formal training in language. For various reasons, the standard of English was declining in the schools, to the extent that some students had to take, and pass, "Remedial English" in addition to their degree work. Poor language exacts a high cost in personal development, in social intercourse, in education, in administration and other areas where good language meant good work. Something had to be done. For the BA, students took two subjects, selected from Chinese Studies, Economics, English Literature, Geography, History, Malay Studies, Philosophy, Political Science, Social Work, Sociology, and Statistics, as majors, and a minor consisting of two courses offered by other departments.

In 1972 the department was renamed "English Language and Literature," signalling a major shift in focus. Staff were seriously concerned about the inroads a full-fledged language programme would make into the number of students – on which teaching posts depended – taking literature. Fortunately, intake of students into the Faculty of Arts and Social Sciences rose gradually from about 300 in 1975 to 500. That and the introduction of Modern Drama, Modern American Literature, and Modern European Literature in translation as Honours courses when the department was renamed, helped to allay fears. English Language became a full major in 1980, when the University of Singapore and Nanyang University (whose medium of instruction was Chinese) were merged to form the National University of Singapore. By then literature and language staff saw the benefits of joint courses and joint research.

This fundamental broadening created the base for necessary refinements reflecting developments in English studies. It was a part of the wider movement within the faculty that has led to the introduction of Chinese Language – for virtually the same reasons that led to the introduction of English Language – European Studies, Information and Communications Management, Japanese Studies, Psychology, South Asian Studies, Theatre Studies, and American Studies. Both the extent and the direction of English studies are rapidly indicated by courses listed in the Faculty handbook.

Language: Level 1000 – Analysing English, Studying English in Context;
Level 2000 – English Sounds and Words, English Structure and Meaning;

Level 3000 – Semantic and Pragmatic Analysis, Language Development, Professional Writing: Theory and Practice, Literary Stylistics, Discourse Analysis, Special Topic, Writing Film Criticism, Oral Communication Skills for Professionals, Practical and Experimental Phonetics, Language Planning and Policy, Phonetic and Phonological Analysis, Syntactic Analysis, Language Development, Language and Society, Writing in the Electronic Era, Critical Reading-Persuasive Writing, Critical Discourse Analysis, Feminist Theory and Feminist Discourse;

Level 4000 – Phonological Theory, Syntactic Theory, Interactional Discourse, Functional Theories, English as a World Language, Lexicology and

Lexicography, Computational Linguistics, Semantic and Pragmatic Theory, Language Education, Narrative Structures, History of English, Special Honours Topic.

Literature: Level 1000 – Foundations of Literary Studies I – The Novel, Foundations of Literary Studies II – Drama and Poetry;

Level 2000 – Seventeenth Century, Topics in the Eighteenth Century, Film and Drama I, Post-Independent Literature: Malaysia and Singapore, Professional Writing, Writing Film Criticism, Introduction to Filmic Narratives, Topics in the Seventeenth Century, The Eighteenth Century, American Literature I, History of Criticism, Teaching of Literature, Backgrounds to English Literature, Literature and Identity;

Level 3000 – Nineteenth Century, Topics in the Twentieth Century, American Literature II, Literature and the Other Arts, Creative Writing, European Literature, The Sociology of Literature, Film and Drama II, Modern Drama, Asian American Literature, Literature and Rhetoric, Gender and Literature, Feminist Theory and Feminine Discourse, Notions of Postcoloniality;

Level 4000 – Honours Thesis (equivalent to two modules); American Literature III, Critical Theory, Topics in Film, The Literature of the Imaginary Journey, Topics in Cultural Studies, Recent Developments in Literary Thinking, Utopian Fiction, Research Methodology, Metafictions of the Novel, Discourses of the Early Twentieth-Century Novel.

To compare the syllabi of the 1930s, 1960s and this reveals the enormous developments that have transformed English studies. The changes come from a number of sources. First there is the general evolutionary, at times dramatic, growth of the subject. That expansion rested on fields opened up by feminist studies, E-literatures and other specialist areas. The interest in theory is perhaps the main revolution, one that not all approve of when it takes us away from the texts of fiction, drama and poetry, when it puts itself forward as the only proper study. But that is the extreme case. The influence of the mass media has led to the integration of film studies, with considerable all-round benefit.

In all this richness and variety, in the excitement of constantly permutating opportunities that now include Internet sites, the one permanent concern remains: the development of critical powers, discrimination, independence of judgement and the other benefits a solid literary education provides. That may be too conservative for some. The question is: what are the alternatives? Only time will unfold what forces the new machinery hides.

"Innovation and continuity": they are still among the major driving forces. And the subtleties are such that switching these key words can mean a wholly fresh undertaking. What has changed, and is changing, in response to time and place is the relationship between them. In the form of tradition, continuity took longer to change before innovation gathered momentum. The unprecedented pace of invention contributes to, and therefore affects, every level of individual, family, community and national life. Today, a powerful consumerism based on goods, and on style, fad and fashion as culture, working together with mass media giving access to a vast network of information sites, are among the current locations of debate. They alter the way we live, the young especially. It is something that those seriously interested in literature – readers, educators, politicians, teachers, critics, and writers themselves – cannot afford to ignore. In an important sense, the substance of literature, the experience that makes it, is the collective substance and experience of both individual and nation. There is no conclusion except to say that, so long as there is interest in words – for their own sake, as instruments, as beginnings, and as ends – English studies will flourish, shaping and reshaping itself for people, time and place.

"The times they are a-changing," even in an LDC: Musings on English Studies from Dhaka

KAISER HAQ

AS THE HORSEMEN OF THE APOCALYPSE trample English studies (by which, of course, I mean the academic study of English literature) underhoof and we are inundated by the muddy prose of a global horde of theorists, it is an imaginative writer – unsurprisingly enough – who, for me at least, offers the most graphic and poignant account of the situation. J.M. Coetzee's latest novel, *Disgrace*, has been portrayed, accurately enough, as a searing drama of the brutalities attending changing power relations in post-apartheid South Africa, but as far as I know reviewers have ignored the full significance of the protagonist David Lurie's professional debacle. True, his sordid sex life and the pathetic affair with a pupil that precipitates his disgrace have titillated ordinary readers and reviewers alike, but before this fall lies another.

When the novel opens he has for some time been quietly smarting from the dispossession wrought by "the great rationalization." His institution, Cape Town University College, has been rechristened Cape Technical University; his department, "Classics and Modern Languages," has been closed down. He used to be a professor of Modern Languages; now, one of the "rationalized personnel," he is an adjunct professor of Communications. He teaches, mandatorily, "'Communications 101,' 'Communication Skills, and Communications 201,' 'Advanced Communication Skills'." The new terminology, needless to say, is presented in a manner calculated to evoke anything from sober amusement to Orwellian disgust. One can easily guess Lurie's attitude to the new academic order. He finds "preposterous" the basic premise of the Communications courses, that "Human society has created language in order that we may communicate our thoughts, feelings and intuitions to each other"[1] and has to hide his alternative view like a dirty secret: "His own opinion, which he does not air, is

[1] J.M. Coetzee, *Disgrace* (London: Secker & Warburg, 1999) 3–4.

that the origins of speech lie in song, and the origin of song in the need to fill out with sound the overlarge and rather empty human soul."[2] This unfashionable and unscientific view has long been the mainstay of literary appreciation, though perhaps not necessarily of literary scholarship or criticism. It chimes in well with several contemporary pronouncements that have drawn my attention. Frank Lentricchia, confessing his past sins as the "Dirty Harry of literary theory," reveals in the "Last Will and Testament of an Ex-Literary Critic" that he has all along led a double life in which "me-the-reader" "engaged in the act of reading: an experience in which the words of someone else filled me up and made it irrelevant to talk about my reading."[3] Martin Amis, in his recent autobiography, *Experience*, declares, apropos of Saul Bellow:

> He is on the shelves, on the desk, he is all over the house, and always in a mood to talk. That's what writing is, not communication but a means of communion. And here are the other writers who swirl around you, like friends, patient, intimate, sleeplessly accessible, over centuries. This is the definition of literature.[4]

Finally, and most pertinently, there is Harold Bloom's claim that the Common Reader – as she has been identified by Dr Johnson and Virginia Woolf – "does not read for easy pleasure or to expiate social guilt, but to enlarge a solitary existence."[5]

Bloom's Kaddish for the canon makes an interesting comparison with Coetzee's novel, for both strike a note of loss and lament. It is worth pointing out that both Bloom and the fictional David Lurie are specialists in the Romantics, the latter's three books being all in this area. "Allowed to offer one special-field course a year, irrespective of enrolments, because that is good for morale," Lurie "is offering a course in the Romantic Poetry."[6] The commissars of cultural politics, Bloom's *bête noire*, sit in judgment on Lurie. I would not rule out the possibility of Bloom's direct influence on the novel. Coetzee's protagonist is a near-namesake of one of Bloom's heroes, the kabbalist Isaac Luria, whose revisionary account of Creation shaped Bloom's theory of misprision. Perhaps part of

---

[2] Coetzee 4.

[3] Lentricchia, "Last Will and Testament of an Ex-Literary Critic," *ALSC Newsletter* 2.4 (Fall 1996): 1.

[4] Quoted in David Hughes, "A Difficult Birth," *London Magazine* 40.7 (October–November 2000): 121.

[5] Bloom, *The Western Canon: The Books and School of the Ages* (1994; London: Macmillan, 1995) 518.

[6] Coetzee 3.

David Lurie's problem is that he is what Bloom would call a weak reader; but I will not press the point.

Lurie's situation is not identical with Bloom's though. While Bloom feels threatened by the School of Resentment – feminists, postcolonialists, New Historicists, et al. – Lurie is supplanted by a young man, S. Otto, who has specialised in "Applied Language Studies." "A right little prick," is Lurie's private opinion of Otto, who divests Lurie's former office of its books and pictures and puts up instead "a poster-size blowup of a comic-book panel: Superman hanging his head, as he is berated by Lois Lane."[7]

Lurie's situation is more of a Third-World situation, rather than a global one; hence it is akin to my situation in Bangladesh, one of the LDCs or "Least Developed Countries" – a monstrous euphemism. My place of work is still known as the Department of English, and my tenured professorship is safe till I retire, but I am witness to changes similar to the ones that so distress David Lurie.

Time was when "department of English" meant "department of English literature"; it was understood and did not require explicit expression. The BA Honours syllabus, demanding three years of full-time study, together with a one-year MA covered the entire range of English literature "from *Beowulf* to Virginia Woolf," with an optional paper on American Literature, covering the classics of the American Renaissance and of High Modernism. Eighty percent of the student's marks depended on a gruelling four-hour examination for each paper; and there were eight such papers for the BA (in addition to three three-hour papers on each of two subsidiary subjects, taken at the end of the second year), four for the MA. This was the system I went through, before going to Britain for a PhD. This system lasted till the late 1970s, since when various changes have crept in.

In an attempt to 'americanize' the system (it had been originally modelled on the British system), the "papers" were rechristened "courses," and instead of a marathon of examinations at the end of three years students were allowed to sit for examinations on a few courses at the end of each year. Full-scale americanisation, with teachers individually designing courses and grading students at the end of a semester, was not introduced, though. Courses were still designed by the department's faculty collectively, and these had to be ratified by the university's Academic Council. But efforts were made to offer more course options, especially at MA level. Conspicuous new entrants were a course in Asian, African and Caribbean Literature in English, and, a little later, another offering a smattering of the new theory. While these courses tried to enlarge the canon and introduce students

[7] Coetzee 177.

to new styles of analysis, a very different kind of change came with the introduction of language teaching and linguistics.

The first signs of this change were noticed in the early 1970s, when a number of the younger members of the English faculty in my university and in other institutions in the country went on British Council scholarships to the UK to study for diplomas in ELT or English Language Teaching. Soon enough there were others on their way to study for the MA or PhD in areas designated by a variety of acronyms: TEFL, TESOL, ESP, etc. When the first batch of these language specialists returned home they quietly went back to teaching literature, which was all that university English departments then taught. Clearly this could not go on.

Before long, opportunities were created for the language specialists to use their newly acquired know-how. At the undergraduate level, remedial courses in English language were introduced when it was discovered that educational standards at lower levels had dropped so far that students coming to university often did not have enough English to deal with the literature in the language. At the graduate level a new MA was introduced in "Applied Linguistics and ELT."

A general restructuring recently introduced a four-year BA Honours, with "Foundation Courses" in English and Bengali (language, not literature, needless to say) that are compulsory for first-year students in all disciplines. The syllabus of the English department has been expanded to include composition, English for professional purposes and linguistics. In their fourth year, students concentrate on either literature or linguistics. Graduate study leads to an MA in either English Literature or Applied Linguistics and ELT.

Now, where does David Lurie come in here? No literature specialist in Dhaka University has been sacked to make room for language specialists; instead, fresh positions have been created to accommodate the latter. Still, it cannot be denied that the situation at Dhaka University (and at other universities in Bangladesh) and that in the fictional Cape Technical University are part of the same syndrome. A David Lurie in Dhaka would no doubt have bemoaned the seduction of students by the upstart discipline of "Applied Linguistics and ELT." Scholarships for higher studies abroad (in the UK, North America and, latterly, Australia) are easier to come by in this new area than in literature. A professional qualification in ELT from a Western university then makes one eligible for jobs for English teachers in schools, colleges and universities in countries (in the Middle East, for instance) that pay in hard currency; such lucrative positions for literature specialists, needless to say, are relatively few. As a result, more and more of the brighter students are opting for "Applied Linguistics and ELT," and even young faculty members who have done their MA in literature may become dispirited by the dwindling number of foreign scholarships in the subject and apply instead for a scholarship to study for a graduate degree in ELT.

My response to the rise of ELT is partly like David Lurie's, partly one of resignation. After all, one cannot argue against the market, at least not these days, and ELT is clearly a worldwide growth industry. Like many of my colleagues, I do a bit of language teaching myself, to eke out a miserable salary. As in the case of most industries, academic and otherwise, the West leads in the area. Western universities started the whole business, and so profitable has it been that they regularly advertise their ELT courses even in newspapers in Dhaka. With no foreseeable challenge to the role of English as a global language, individuals and institutions who have invested in the ELT industry can expect undiminished prosperity. One result of growing globalisation has been a dramatic increase in the number of foreign students at Western universities, many of whom need to bone up on their English; hence the growth of remedial language courses. A friend of mine, a poet and comparative literature specialist who is an adjunct faculty at the City University of New York, told me that she was quite happy to teach these courses. They require more teaching hours and bring her more money, and are also more satisfying than the literature courses she teaches. Why? Because the language students are eager to do well, as a better command of English enables them to cope better with the subjects they are studying for their degree, and for the teacher it is gratifying to note steady improvement in their performance. But the literature students nowadays, my friend said, tend to be increasingly ill-prepared to deal with the subtleties of literary appreciation and analysis.

This has also been my experience at Dhaka University, and that of David Lurie, who is not only the protagonist of Coetzee's novel but so far has also been the protagonist of this essay (if we allow essays to have protagonists – and why not?). "Post-Christian, posthistorical, postliterate," Lurie describes his students at his poetry lectures,[8] and thinks of himself and others like him "in this transformed and, to his mind, emasculated institution of learning" as "clerks in a post-religious age."[9] But, granted that there is cause for lament, it is also true that we have more literary research and criticism than even before. Isn't that ground for hope? Or is it another source of disquiet? Turning again to Lurie, we find that in the novel he grows tired of literary criticism and tries instead to write a chamber opera centred on one of Byron's Italian amours, with indifferent results, as far as one can make

[8] Coetzee 32.

[9] Coetzee 4.

out, though the experience of working on it is absorbing and even, in a strange and intense manner, emotionally satisfying.

Somewhat surprisingly, Coetzee's novel does not take on board the new schools of criticism that gained worldwide prominence concomitantly with ELT and Applied Linguistics – structuralist, deconstructionist, New-Historicist, feminist, postcolonialist. In his situation (and Lurie's) and mine, the last-named is the one that can – and indeed has – laid claim to special relevance. It is both convenient and logical to regard Edward Said as the founding father of postcolonial criticism through his application of the Foucauldian notion of the complicity of knowledge and power to Western writings about the East. A veritable horde of researchers in his wake have been uncovering signs of collusion with imperialism in virtually every Western writer. In the context of my region – the Indian subcontinent or South Asia – the Saidian exercise has been extended to English studies, which of course turns out to be impregnated with imperialism. *Masks of Conquest* (1989) by Gauri Viswanathan, a student of Said's, is generally regarded as a magisterial contribution in this area, and is often cited as having definitively established certain crucial facts. Thus Sara Suleri confidently notes: "As Gauri Viswanathan's work has meticulously demonstrated, the issue of the canonicity of English literature was primarily formulated in the laboratory provided by colonial terrain."[10] Let us ignore the mixed metaphor in the final phrase and consider the claim about canonicity. What does it mean to formulate "the issue of the canonicity of English literature?" To ask whether English literature is worthy of being canonical? To ask which English works are canonical? In either case, was the question first posed in India? Or, indeed, in British academia? Despite the general view that the canon is a list of texts and authors considered worthy of academic study, I incline to the position of Bloom, which is that it is created by writers and readers/critics on the basis of their agonistic encounters with other writers and readers/critics. Long before English literature became an academic subject, the question of canonicity relating to it was a part of its warp and woof, and the most obvious evidence of this is in the great critics, from Sidney, through Dryden and Dr Johnson, to Wordsworth, Coleridge and Shelley.

Viswanathan "sets out to demonstrate in part that the discipline of English came into its own in the age of colonialism" – heaven knows why this should require demonstration, since it is an historical fact –

---

[10] Sara Suleri, *The Rhetoric of English India* (Chicago and London: University of Chicago Press, 1992) 22.

> as well as to argue that no serious account of its growth and development can afford to ignore the imperial mission of educating and civilized colonial subjects in the literature and thought of England, a mission that in the long run served to strengthen Western cultural hegemony in enormously complex ways.[11]

Fair enough. The writer then goes on to claim that

> English literature appeared as a subject in the curriculum of the colonies long before it was institutionalized in the home country. As early as the 1820s [...] English as the study of culture and not simply the study of language had already found a secure place in the British Indian curriculum.[12]

The first claim is ambiguous, and on examination loses its dramatic quality. The "curriculum" was followed in two or three schools in and around Calcutta, e.g. Drummond's Academy, where Derozio, the first Indo-Anglian poet and, later, literature master at the Hindu College (established 1816), was educated; the Hindu College, the most famous institution of the time; and the Serampore College, run by missionaries. By the institutionalising of English literature in Britain, on the other hand, is meant (as an endnote makes explicit) its introduction in the entire school system of the country, a massive undertaking that was accomplished in the 1870s. But long before that, a chair in English had been instituted at London University; Viswanathan cites 1848 as the date of the event, but Bernard Bergonzi's *Exploding English*, perhaps the finest account of the state of the discipline, mentions 1828. It is an ineluctable aspect of being an academic in an LDC (one of the Least Developed Countries, in case the reader has forgotten) that the libraries in the country are no help in settling the question, and I must ask the reader, if she is happily located close to a good library, to settle it for herself. Bergonzi also mentions that "an important figure in its prehistory, well before the concept of 'English' had emerged, was Hugh Blair, professor of rhetoric and *belles-lettres* at Edinburgh University in the late eighteenth century."[13] Still, it is true that the classroom study of English literature began remarkably early in India, and its growth was attended by a vigorous tussle between the rival approaches of missionaries on the one hand, and the East India Company authorities on the other; and the history of this dialectic is integral to the history of the growth of English literature as an academic discipline in Britain.

More crucial, though, are Viswanathan's

---

[11] Gauri Viswanathan, *Masks of Conquest: Literary Study and British Rule in India* (London: Faber & Faber 1989) 2.

[12] Viswanathan, *Masks of Conquest* 3

[13] Bernard Bergonzi, *Exploding English: Criticism, Theory, Culture* (Oxford: Oxford University Press, 1990) 28.

> two general aims in writing [her] book: the first is to study the adaptation of the content of English literary education to the administrative and political imperatives of British rule; and the other is to examine the ways in which these imperatives in turn changed that content with a radically altered significance, enabling the humanistic ideals of enlightenment to coexist with and indeed even support education for social and political control.[14]

Her pronouncements clearly imply, as Aijaz Ahmad sums up, "that English literature was assembled in Bengal as a mode of constructing colonialist consent."[15] Viswanathan's entire approach is stymied by her resolute refusal (on flimsy grounds that I will not go into here) to take into account the role of the Indians themselves in the promotion of the study of English. The outcome is a bizarre mechanistic picture in which colonial power manipulates literary studies to shape a passive "colonial subject." It's a pleasant irony that the Marxist Ahmad offers a far more perspicacious account of the origins of English studies in India. "My own sense is that English language and literature, both of which grew in tandem as certain forms of modern knowledge in India, came out of three quite different pressures," he notes:

> One is the pressure that was contested, I believe, between Ram Mohan [Roy] and Macaulay. Ram Mohan who wanted English very much, as a window of [sic] the world, as a window on modernity, on modern forms of knowledge, especially scientific and technical knowledge; but in order to gain that knowledge you [...] had to have a very high, sophisticated level of knowledge of English which, in nineteenth century pedagogy, was understood as meaning that language and literature must be taught in tandem with each other.[16]

As Ahmad goes on to point out, the desire to learn English "is actually much prior to Macaulay's decision that we should do so. And that desire was deeply connected with class mobility and caste consolidation." Regarding the role of English as a window on the world, Ahmad thinks, rightly, that it

> continued to persist and get elaborated in successive phases. And to this day, I think that one of the central roles that English has played in the formation of intelligence across South Asia is precisely this, so that even in the limited field of literature, English has been an instrument for us, not only for an encounter with what Leavis might call 'The Great Tradition' [...] but for our encounter even with

[14] Viswanathan, *Masks of Conquest* 3

[15] Aijaz Ahmad, "The Future of English Studies in South Asia," *Colonial and Post-Colonial Encounters*, ed. Niaz Zaman et al. (Dhaka: University Press, 1999) 48.

[16] Ahmad, "The Future of English Studies" 49.

> literatures that were [not] written in the English languages [sic], whether of European, African, Latin American, or even South Asian origin.[17]

With devastating consequences for studies like Viswanathan's, Ahmad rounds off:

> Thus posing the question of English Literature Departments purely in relation to English syllabi structured during the colonial period somewhat misses the point, because knowledge of English literature has always served a much wider function for the literary intelligentsia throughout India. Associated with that has been [...] the well-known, historical role of the English teacher. English teachers teach English and English literature in the classrooms but, by and large, historically, the majority of them have written in their own languages, so that the development of modern, vernacular literatures, across India, has been historically deeply connected with this double role of the English teacher.[18]

Ahmad's Marxist view, interestingly, is in consonance with that of the "reactionary" Nirad Chaudhuri, whose monumental *Autobiography of an Unknown Indian* (1951) is an eloquent testimony to the enriching impact of English education on the colonial Indian. "The truth was that the Indian mind had become dependent on the English language for all its highest functioning," Chaudhuri once declared in a lecture.[19] He went on to provide a succinct account of his English education "in one of the backwaters of East Bengal [present-day Bangladesh]." It began at the age of five, and at ten his textbooks were Kipling's *Jungle Book*, Andrew Lang's *Animal Story Book*, and Palgrave's *Children's Treasury of Lyrical Poetry*: "What we got from those books was as much English life as the English language."[20] Then came the kind of change in language teaching that we still see being introduced with much fanfare:

> Soon after our time the English educational authorities in Bengal introduced a change in regard to the textbooks for English in our schools. They said that a foreign language was difficult enough, and if in addition utterly foreign ideas and feelings were introduced that would create insuperable difficulties for our boys and girls. That was nonsense, because no language can be learnt for any purpose above the crudely utilitarian unless some idea of the life and civilization which have their voice in it is also communicated. The unfamiliar life or ideas do not create any difficulty whatever, if the writing is real writing.[21]

---

[17] Ahmad, "The Future of English Studies" 49.

[18] Ahmad, "The Future of English Studies" 49–50.

[19] Nirad C. Chaudhuri, "Opening Address," *The Eye of the Beholder: Indian Writing in English*, ed. Maggie Butcher (London: Commonwealth Institute, 1983) 10.

[20] Chaudhuri 11.

[21] Chaudhuri 12.

I believe the debate between the two sides represented here is an ongoing one, and the focus on Communication Skills is the latest strategy proposed by the anti-literature side. In Bangladesh high schools, it is worth mentioning in this context, the English course has been redesigned and rechristened "Communicative Skills," but as is usual in such cases it's more a matter of old wine in a new bottle.

In the attitude of Ahmad and Chaudhuri to colonial education in English, one gets a welcome sense of real persons trying to make the most of their historical situation, whereas in Viswanathan's account there is a suffocating air of abstraction. By confining her attention to colonial agencies alone, she ends up by dehumanising the colonial subjects, who are merely acquiescent abstractions. She belongs squarely in what Bloom has dubbed "The School of Resentment," notorious for their weak psychology and weak logic. I will give a couple of illustrative examples. In an essay titled "English in a Literate Society," Viswanathan describes as "yet another colonial legacy" a kind of corruption that crept into Indian education with the establishment of universities:

> University education bore little continuity with the aims of secondary education, and university degrees, linked as they so closely were with employment, acquired an autonomous value. Learning, knowledge, inquiry: these were no longer the motivating principles in the education of Indian youth.[22]

Now, isn't that terrible! Here was a land whose young people were dedicated to "learning, knowledge, inquiry," and along came colonialism and turned them into mercenaries selling their degrees for jobs! Of course the truth is that precolonial Indians, too, acquired an education (in Persian) because it got them jobs. Viswanathan, in the book already mentioned, quotes Ram Mohan Roy on the subject:

> In former times Native fathers were anxious to educate their children according to the usages of those days, to qualify them for such offices under government [...] and young men had the most powerful motives for sedulously cultivating their minds in laudable ambition of rising by their merits to an honourable rank in society; but under the present system, so trifling are the rewards held out to Native talent that hardly any stimulus to intellectual improvement remains.[23]

Quite a different story, isn't it? To go back to Viswanathan's essay: it is rounded off with an anecdote illustrating the association of knowledge of English with af-

---

[22] Gauri Viswanathan, "English in a Literate Society," *The Lie of the Land: English Literary Studies in India*, ed. Niaz Zaman et al. (Delhi: Oxford University Press, 1992) 31.

[23] Viswanathan, *Masks of Conquest* 148.

fluence. Viswanathan was walking home in Madras, her arms laden with books, when a young woman construction worker called out to her:

> "Akka, do you know English?" I turned around, startled by the question, and replied that I did. She then excitedly asked, "Can you teach me English?" This time I was visibly astonished and asked her why she wanted to learn English so badly. Her answer shook me up then, and continues to do so even now when I recall it: "Because I want to live in these houses rather than help build them."[24]

Poor postcolonial critic. Being shaken up every now and then by something every Indian knows, a piece of colonial and postcolonial folk mythology that does have a correlation with reality: that in the subcontinent those who know English tend to be well-off. Why is Viswanathan's reaction so extravagant? Does it manifest her social guilt because she happens to be one of the English-knowing, affluent minority? If so, does she think that melodramatising her guilt in this fashion amounts to expiation? In that case it is yet another instance of what a conservative think-tank in Britain has tellingly described as the sentimentalisation of society. Or is it an extension of what Aijaz Ahmad has dubbed "metropolitan theory's inflationary rhetoric"?[25]

But no matter how powerful or extensive the criticism levelled against critics like Viswanathan (and I have singled her out quite arbitrarily; I could have dealt with one or more of a dozen representative postcolonial critics), the fact remains that this is the moment of postcolonial criticism, especially among academics in and from the Third World. Indeed, it is widely assumed that the Third-World intellectual can find her authentic voice through the rhetoric of postcolonial criticism. We should therefore remind ourselves of the relationship between the Third World and postcolonial rhetoric. Aijaz Ahmad points out:

> So fundamental and even generic is the Indian university's relation with – indeed, dependence on – its British and American counterparts that knowledges produced there become immediately effective here, in a relation of imperial dominance, shaping even the way we think of ourselves.[26]

Postcolonial theory, like applied linguistics and ELT, not to mention older modes of linguistic and literary study, reached the Third World from metropolitan centres. This is an inevitability, given the distribution of knowledge, power and wealth. There is no point in kicking against the pricks, but the situation does place on us the responsibility of assiduously exercising our critical faculties.

---

24 Viswanathan, "English in a Literate Society" 41.

25 Ahmad, *In Theory: Classes, Nations, Literatures* (Delhi: Oxford University Press, 1992) 69.

26 Ahmad, *In Theory* 44.

Postcolonial criticism and a number of allied critical modes may eventually be subsumed under cultural studies, whose champions are like fanatical converts to a new faith. "There won't be any more literature," one of them said to me. "There will only be cultural studies." Such extremism augurs ill for the future of English studies, but then it may remain confined to a lunatic fringe, and saner voices may prevail. Aijaz Ahmad, for instance, acknowledges that "there is one absolutely intractable thing, a form of study which is specific to literature, which is how aesthetic effects are created through language, and how densities of social and historical experience come to us in the form of these aesthetic effects." It is only in addition to this that "literary study becomes a part" of "a much broader sense of historical/cultural studies."[27]

What happens when the aesthetic dimension is ignored can be gauged from a glance at a piece of postcolonial criticism in a postcolonial journal, *Wasafiri*. Funded by Britain's Arts Council, it comes out from Queen Mary and Westfield College, under the auspices of the University of London, and is edited by Susheila Nasta, who is on the college faculty and is quite well known as a postcolonial critic. Sharing the masthead with her is a whole battalion of writers and critics, a number of luminaries among them. Among the thirteen Contributing Editors are Angus Calder, Abdulrazak Gurnah and Alastair Niven, and the thirteen-member Advisory Board includes Nadine Gordimer, Lisa Jardine, Michael Ondaatje, Caryl Phillips and Ngugi wa Thiong'o. "Star-studded," is how a friend described the masthead. I do not keep up with the journal, but recently received a contributor's copy containing a couple of poems of mine that had been solicited some time back by one of the associate editors. My poems take up less than a two-column page and contain half a dozen typos. I mention this only in passing, as incidental evidence of slapdash proofreading. The piece of postcolonial criticism that caught my attention (I haven't yet read the other pieces) is a review of Coetzee's novel. Coetzee "is one of the most persistent commentators of the meandering lines of postcolonialism." In him one recognises "the professional handyman and word architect." The novel's laconic style portrays "daily occurrences in an important as well as threatening manner. The dialogues [...] appear self-evident even when abstract, political or psychological issues are discussed." The author's choice of the present tense is "a decision of which the novel itself and the reader profit." The novel "appears like a unified, whole realistic novel, an impression that is verifying and deceptive at the same time." The reviewer notes "the reversibility as well as the irrevocability of the master/servant relationship," and ob-

[27] Ahmad, "The Future of English Studies" 52.

serves that "violence has sought after different perpetrators and has chosen different victims." The novelist is said to believe "that the world is narratable, again and still."[28] The bizarre diction and bad grammar remind me of the relevance of George Steiner's warnings about the erosion of literacy. One wonders if the reviewer has strayed from a course in remedial English to set himself up as a commentator on serious literature. Only in an intellectual climate vitiated by denigration of such concepts as "the aesthetic" or "the purely literary" or, indeed, of clarity (which is condemned as a sympathy of bourgeois ideology), could someone with his paltry linguistic equipment dare – or be encouraged – to do so.

But am I making too much of literature? Salutarily, Ihab Hassan reminds us that "literature certainly enjoys no ontological privilege. Its boundaries, like the 'numberless wonders' of Sophocles' world or of our own transhumanized earth, dissolve repeatedly before the critical gaze" – that is, the critical gaze when it is sharply focused and accompanied by effective powers of expression, both missing in our postcolonial reviewer. "But," Hassan continues, "literature, however unmargined, still grips our passional, our imaginative life."[29] The fragmentation of literary studies may continue indefinitely, and new disciplines may continue to crop up amidst its crumbling edifice, but there will always be those who will value literature above everything else. As the reformed Lentricchia notes, "The authentic literary type believes with Oscar Wilde that life is an imitation of art. Sociologists don't believe that; philosophers don't either. Why should they? They're sociologists and philosophers, who know that life is an imitation of sociology and philosophy."[30]

---

[28] Harold Leusmann, review of *Disgrace*, *Wasafiri* 32 (Autumn 2000): 69–70.

[29] Hassan, *Rumors of Change: Essays of Five Decades* (Tuscaloosa and London: University of Alabama Press, 1995) 164.

[30] Lentricchia 6.

The Creative Circle in the Intercultural Literary Process

OKIFUMI KOMESU

I

THE OPENING LINE OF THE NOVEL *Snow Country* by Yasunari Kawabata, a Nobel Prize-winning Japanese writer, depicts a scene in which someone or something crosses the "border" through a tunnel into the snow country.[1] My near-literal English translation is as follows: *When you crossed the border through the tunnel, you were in the snow country.* The subject "you" here is a 'generic person.' My choice of the word is deliberate: It leaves the identity of the person unspecified. The choice also precludes an object, such as a train, which may be easily imagined to have come through the tunnel into the snow country. In fact, Kawabata's original sentence does not specify who or what is in motion in this scene, as the sentence lacks a subject.

In a Japanese sentence, a subject may be implicitly understood unless its specification is necessary or desirable. The meaning of such a subjectless sentence is context-bound[2] and is usually self-evident. However, Kawabata has a specific artistic aim in the use of this structure: i.e. to produce a blurred or uncertain im-

---

[1] Yasunari Kawabata, *Yukiguni* (1937; Tokyo: Shinchosha, 1999) 5.

[2] Yoshihiko Ikegami contends that the subjectless structure of Japanese is due to the language's "event-oriented" rather than "thing-oriented" turn in its descriptive discourse, whereas the subject–predicate structure of English reflects its thing-oriented mode of conception; Yoshihiko Ikegami, *Shigaku to Bunkakigoron* [Poetics and Cultural Semiotics] (Tokyo: Chikuma Shobo, 1983) 255–57. For more detailed and percipient discussion of this topic, see his latest book, *Nippongo-ron eno Shotai* [An Invitation to the Study of the Japanese Language] (Tokyo: Kodansha, 2000) 239–310.

Hiroyuki Araki, a comparative ethnographer, attributes this grammatical difference to the contrastive cultural traits arising from the nomadic origin of the Indo-European cultures, on the one hand, and from the communalism of the rice-growing Japanese culture, on the other. Araki maintains that in the former a strong sense of individualism and uncertainty of life contributed to the formation of the I–THOU distinction, which in turn found its linguistic expression in the subject-centred syntactic structure, while in the latter the communal nature of consciousness tended to blur the I–THOU distinction, drowning the pair in the all-embracing crucible of verbal exchange in the community; Hiroyuki Araki, *Yamatokotoba no Jinruigaku* [An Anthropology of the Primeval Forms of Japanese Speech] (Tokyo: Asahi Shobo, 1985) 16ff.

pression of this movement by not specifying its agent, as if it were absorbed into the universal whiteness of the snow country. The sentence immediately following reinforces this impression. Again my literal translation goes: *The bottom of the night turned white.*

The reader does not become aware of the fact that the subject of the movement is indeed the train until the third sentence. Still, the impression of the train is suppressed, for the sentence begins with an adverbial phrase: *In the siding the train came to a stand.* Thus, the snow country, the expected setting of the story, is brought to the fore and the reader's attention is drawn to the whole scene in which the train occupies only an ancillary part.

Now, Kawabata could have specified the subject (the train for instance) in the opening sentence, if his artistic aim were to give the reader information rather than experience. But his aim is to create a sensation in the reader's mind as though he or she were part of the scene and not an objective observer of the train steaming into the snowy panorama spreading beyond the long, dark tunnel.

In Edward G. Seidensticker's translation the sentences read as follows: "The train came out of a long tunnel into the snow country. The earth lay white under the night sky. The train pulled up at the signal stop."[3] Notice the objective tone of the depiction. Of course, these are natural English sentences, a far cry from crude 'translationese,' and would no doubt win an unperturbed reception from English-speaking readers. But they are not a literal translation. A verbatim rendering of the subjectless Japanese sentence into English is obviously impossible, for English lacks, except for special cases, the subjectless structure for a declarative sentence. Thus, Seidensticker had to introduce a subject, "the train," into the first sentence of his version. He also changed the subject of the second sentence to a more concrete "the earth." The result is an utterly different aesthetic world.

The opening portion of *Snow Country*, then, shows us diverse aesthetic worlds when viewed from the perspectives of the source (hereinafter S) and the target (hereinafter T) texts. Kawabata's original creates a monistic–experiential world where the scene and the reader are united and affords the latter an aesthetic experience rather than information. Seidensticker's translation, by contrast, offers the reader a dualistic–cognitive world in which the reader gains information from the scene as an observer. Put more plainly, Kawabata wants the reader to *feel* the opening scene, while Seidensticker expects the reader to *know* what is going on. Seidensticker is hardly to blame for deviating from the original sentences, since the cause is in the structure of the language itself; but there is the rub, for it is ob-

[3] Seidensticker, trans. *Snow Country* by Yasunari Kawabata (Tokyo: Charles E. Tuttle, 1957) 3.

vious that Kawabata capitalises on the subjectless structure of the Japanese language to achieve his artistic aim. Thus, the linguistic question is inseparable from the artistic.

There is an optimistic claim that the translator, freed from the onus of linguistic fidelity to the original text, will turn into a masterful huntsman on the happy hunting ground of creative art. And, ironically, the higher the barrier between the source language (hereinafter SL) and the target language (hereinafter TL), the more advantageous will he be in his artistic endeavour.[4] But whether the translator is truly a happy game hunter in the intercultural literary forest is a moot question. The example of *Snow Country* foreshadows various hazards and pitfalls awaiting the translator on the trek. Seidensticker negotiated the terrain to rework Kawabata's uncanny woods into a garden agreeable to Western taste. Seidensticker's dilemma and his solution shed much light on what happens in the act of literary translation, which is largely ignored or left unexplained in most translation theories, though the translator's act is a long, involved process of intercultural communication. In fact, this act is a complex, circular process beginning with a *receptive stance* towards the SL text, which passes into a *destructive act* against the meaning of the same text, which is none other than a *creative act* vis-à-vis the TL, which finally reconciles itself in a *receptive stance* with the norm of the TL. This essay intends to probe part of the terrain through which the translator proceeds along this precarious track of intercultural literary process.

II

One of the *causes célèbres* relative to literary translation is the quarrel over the question of fidelity to the SL text. With the exception perhaps of Vladimir Nabokov, the call for perfect fidelity to the letter is now generally discredited as unrealistic in the light of the disparity of languages. At the other end of the pole of fidelity are the dogma of untranslatability and the myth of translation as art. The former flatly denies to the TL the capacity to rearticulate artistic texts, while the latter ennobles it to the state of original art. The dogma of untranslatability is as unrealistic as the call for perfect fidelity, for literary translation has always flourished in spite of this dogma, though its advocates are impatient to cut the Gordian knot of translation. It also precludes discussions of the interlingual literary process from being pursued in any constructive way. I shall discuss the myth of translation as art later. Suffice it to say for the moment that this creed, like the dogma

4 George Steiner, *After Babel: Aspects of Language and Translation* (New York and London: Oxford University Press, 1975) 380.

of untranslatability, omits or avoids coming to grips with the complicated, yet interesting, interactions of cultural forces in the interlingual literary process, as if all were well that ended well. At any rate, linguistic inequality ceases to be a problem for those who hold this view.

Nevertheless, theorists are perennially plagued by the question of the inequality of the SL and the TL, because theory must deal squarely with the dogma of untranslatability and justify the ways of the translator to men. One attempt to clear this tight impasse is to introduce the idea of equivalence. Where a perfect mimesis of the letter is impracticable, the translator's next task turns out to be to produce an equivalence of literary meaning in the TL text. Eugene Nida's "dynamic equivalence" and Anton Popovic's "stylistic equivalence" are among the well-known propositions. The idea of equivalence is based on the view of translation as a language-to-language or text-to-text process in which the existence of a firm common ground can be posited for apparently disparate languages. This belief is inspired by a wide range of thinkers varying from the nineteenth-century German linguist Wilhelm von Humboldt and the Victorian Matthew Arnold to modern linguists such as Roman Jakobson and Noam Chomsky.

The belief in equivalence now faces new challenges, however. The identity of meaning and of context in the translingual process, which underlies the idea of equivalence, is seriously contested, for instance, by the contributors to a volume of essays edited by Joseph Graham, who offer common resistance to the deterministic notion of meaning and context. However, their own conceptions of translation are so divergent that they perplex the editor himself, for he asks: "If and when it is possible to say so many things about translation, how can we ever know that we are all talking about one and the same thing?"[5]

Another challenge comes from a collection of essays edited by Susan Bassnett and André Lefevere.[6] This volume was a significant landmark in the theory of translation, in that it moved the arena of translation debate from text to culture. It neutralised at once the tenacious bastions of fidelity and equivalence. Regrettably, as with Joseph Graham's book, the contributors' "cultural turn" flanks out on all sides with no concerted strategic plans. The cultural forces affecting translation which they discuss are as various as the power struggle of society, feminist writing, history, media culture, and editorial authoritarianism, among other things.

[5] Joseph F. Graham, "Introduction" to *Difference in Translation*, ed. Joseph F. Graham (Ithaca, NY, and London: Cornell University Press, 1990) 13–30 (22).

[6] Basnett and Lefevere, ed. *Translation, History and Culture* (London: Pinter Publishers, 1990).

The essays that appear in *Between Languages and Cultures*, edited by Anuradha Dingwaney and Carol Maier, also move beyond the questions of fidelity and equivalence to probe into forces operating between source and target cultures. They are mainly concerned, however, with an ideology of translating between Western and non-Western cultures, an ideology which one of the editors defines as "a politics of translating ('Third World') cultures."[7]

A unique answer to the question of the inequality of languages is offered by Walter Benjamin, who takes a mystical view of linguistic disparities. These he turns into constitutive fragments for the restoration of the pre-Babel sacred vessel of the pure language, *die reine Sprache*. Through translation, Benjamin believes, the languages of suprahistorical kinship can achieve the totality of meaning, or *intentio*, "which no single language can attain by itself but which is realised only by the totality of their intentions supplementing each other."[8]

With Ezra Pound, the process is reversed. He is not a knight in quest of the Holy Grail of the lost language; he is a *fabbro*, as T.S. Eliot rightly characterised him, who fashions, rather, a contemporary sacred shrine of artistic creation through the act of translation. "A great age of literature is perhaps always a great age of translation; or follows it," says Pound.[9] Translation, however, must be artistically rendered in a manner such as that of Arthur Golding, who brought the meaning of the original "most germane, familiar, homely, to his hearers."[10] By contrast, Milton "tried to turn English into Latin [...] neglecting the genius of English, distorting its fibrous manner, making schoolboy translation of Latin phrases: 'Him who disobeys me disobeys'."[11] Here Pound clearly favours Golding's stance, which is receptive to the TL norm, over Milton's, which is receptive to the SL norm.

In his own translations of Chinese and Japanese texts, Pound even garbles the original work to achieve his artistic effect. *Cathay*, which is reputed to have immensely enriched twentieth-century poetry, deviates considerably from the original poems and from the notes furnished by Ernest Fenollosa. Pound's howlers have suffered fastidious comments from the scholars of comparative literature,[12]

---

[7] Dingwaney & Maier, eds. *Between Languages and Cultures: Translations and Cross-Cultural Texts* (Pittsburgh, PA, and London: University of Pittsburgh Press, 1995) 3.

[8] Benjamin, "The Task of the Translator," *Illuminations: Essays and Reflections*, ed. Hannah Arendt, trans. Harry Zohn (New York: Schocken, 1968) 69–82 (74).

[9] Pound, *Literary Essays*, ed. T.S. Eliot (1954; New York: New Directions, 1968) 239.

[10] Pound, *Literary Essays* 239.

[11] Pound, *Literary Essays* 238.

[12] After painstaking comparison of *Cathay* and Li Po's poems together with Fenollosa's notes, Saneide Kodama shows various disparities between Li Po's original and Pound's rendition; Sanehide

though it is generally acknowledged that nothing can take away from Pound's brilliant artistic achievement in his creative translations. Such critical assessments aside, Pound's translations invite some crucial observations about the intercultural literary process, which I shall discuss presently.

The Poundian translation was later eulogised by George Steiner and Willis Barnstone, both of whom assert that his ignorance of the SL is by no means detrimental so long as his translated texts are masterpieces. In his provocative book on the theory, history and practice of translation, which he ambitiously entitles *Poetics of Translation*, Barnstone complains that there is a fundamental misconception in the linguistic approach to translation about the aims of literary translation, for linguists fail to see that "art must be translated as art."[13] From this point of view, Ezra Pound is the epitome of a literary translator: "His translation passes into the sacred sphere of originality. We hear perhaps Odysseus or Homer or Pound. We don't hear Pound translating."[14] Thus, Pound gave birth to another ideology for the severance of the Gordian knot: the myth of translation as art.

III

In the Poundian translation à la Barnstone, then, the ideal translator *qua* translator becomes invisible, approaching the condition of an original creator. It seems a mistake, however, to weigh the translator with the creative author on the same scale. In the examples of Pound himself and Seidensticker already cited, we find the translator working in a situation that is quite different from that of an intralingual literary artist, struggling with severe intercultural constraints, which makes him anything but invisible or inaudible. His cries of pain can be heard interlinearly by anyone conversant with both languages. Even when his work is successful in blending two languages and cultures, his presence is clearly visible in the unique sphere of art where two cultures converge, melt into each other, yet never perish, each re-creating the other as a new life.[15] We hear a unique

---

Kodama, *American Poetry and Japanese Culture* (Hamden, CT: Shoestring Press, 1984) 58–99. Christine Brooke–Rose, too, points out Pound's deviations from the original meaning by comparing his version of the Confucian *Analects* with Arthur Waley's, but she applauds Pound for creating poetry out of the Chinese ideograms where Waley remains pedestrian; Brooke–Rose, *A ZBC of Ezra Pound* (Berkeley and Los Angeles: University of California Press, 1971) 105.

[13] Barnstone, *The Poetics of Translation: History, Theory, Practice* (New Haven, CT, and London: Yale University Press, 1993) 47.

[14] Barnstone 112.

[15] New or modified metaphors provide an interesting case study of the meeting of cultures. For instance, the Japanese metaphor of 'love' has undergone a drastic change since the introduction of the English expression 'to fall in love.' The Japanese have responded sensitively to the idea of verticality

voice reverberating from his work, with a cadence hitherto unknown and sounds unheard; through his process of translation, we gain a new awareness of various aspects of intercultural communication which may otherwise lie hidden, for literature involves the whole range of intra/intercultural communication with which information-oriented texts such as business and legal documents are only partly concerned.

But to return to the constraints on the translator: I have already cited Seidensticker's English version of *Snow Country* as an example of linguistic constraint encroaching upon the artistic sphere. A similar example can be found in Pound's translation of Li Po's poem "Changkan Hang." In the original poem, there is an allusion – which Pound expunges from his version – to a legendary Chinese episode: it is about the strong bond of love epitomised by a young lover, Weisheng, who waits for his sweetheart at the tryst under a bridge until he is caught by a flood and drowns clinging to the pillar of the bridge. The allusion is made succinctly in the three Chinese ideograms 'embrace–pillar–trust,' about which Fenollosa expends dozens of words in his explanatory notes. The conciseness of Chinese expressions derives from a unique feature of the language, the functional shift. The collocation of the verb 'to embrace' and the noun 'the pillar' (V+O) functionally shifts to an adjectival phrase, thereby forming, together with two other ideograms, a five-ideogram line embedding an allusion to a rich literary legacy. Thus the line can be read: "Your affection always promised such a trust in love as was shown by Weisheng, who is said to have been drowned clinging to the pillar."[16] It is easy to imagine Pound's perplexity. Obviously it was difficult even for such a skilled *fabbro* to translate so richly allusive a line and not crowd the translated version with learned exegesis. Pound's solution was to delete the whole line and put in its place his own: "Forever and forever and forever."[17]

---

expressed by the verb 'to fall' as opposed to horizontality implied in the traditional Japanese metaphor as exemplified in the expression 'love path' (*koiji* meaning 'love affair'). The appropriation of the English metaphor resulted in a verbatim translation of the expression 'to fall in love' (*koi ni ochiru*) and the birth of such a figure of speech as 'love deeper than the sea,' among others. The Japanese failed, however, to respond to the idea of *love as container* implied by the preposition in the phrase 'in love' and therefore could not produce a Japanese equivalent of 'to be *out of* love,' for which another metaphoric structure, '*love as heat*,' has been appropriated. Thus, we have the Japanese expression 'Love has cooled.' In the new Japanese metaphor of love, then, we see the cultures of the East and the West blend through the destructive/creative process.

16 Tomohisa Matsuura, *Rihaku: Shi to Shinsho* [Li Po: Poetry and Imagery], (Tokyo: Shakaishisosha, 1970) 105.

17 Pound, "The River Merchant's Wife: A Letter," *Personae: The Shorter Poems*, ed. Lea Baechler & A. Walton Litz (1926; New York: New Directions, 1990) 134.

In both Seidensticker and Pound, then, we have a case in which the translator is faced with a linguistic barrier that has artistic rather than purely linguistic implications. Problems involved here transcend the levels that have been highlighted by linguists and communication theorists. It is too insouciant of William Frawley, for instance, to explain away this linguistic–artistic dilemma as a matter of a translator's semantic choice, a choice to be incorporated into a third code that he builds on top of the 'matrix' (source) and the 'target' codes.[18]

The translator's predicament is exacerbated further when he confronts the vast domain of intellectual and spiritual traditions that inspire creative artists. Various complications arise in the intercultural literary process when the intellectual and spiritual backgrounds are so diverse as Japanese and English. Two examples will illustrate the nature of the problem.

The first example comes from Shakespeare's *Hamlet* and its translation into Japanese. The passage is from Act I, Scene ii, where Hamlet agonises over his mother's hasty marriage to his uncle Claudius: "O God! A beast that wants discourse of reason, Would have mourned longer – married with my uncle ...."[19] Hamlet here places his mother on the moral scale below the beast that lacks the faculty of reason. In the tradition of the Great Chain of Being, man is found above the beast precisely because he is endowed with the power of reason. Hamlet's censure of his mother derives from this intellectual tradition. We are given to know not only Hamlet's personal agony and anger but also a Western view of man held by Hamlet and Shakespeare's contemporaries.

Hamlet was translated into Japanese by Koya Tozawa in 1905. For those of his audience who were unconversant with Western literature, Tozawa used as the medium of translation a rather archaic Japanese, one informed by classical Chinese and Japanese literary lore. As a result, his version became quite readable to the Japanese audience of his time, who found in it familiar vocabulary and tropes. In translating Hamlet's words, Tozawa resorts to two Chinese terms, *Li* and *Qing*.[20] *Li* means the essential principle that sustains all existing things according to the Zhuzi school of Confucianism, while *Qing* is a Buddhist term for the 'sense' or 'emotion' with which all sentient beings are imbued. Thus, a beast in Tozawa's *Hamlet* is represented as a being which violates the principle of the

[18] Frawley, ed. *Translation: Literary, Linguistic and Philosophical Perspectives* (London and Toronto: Associated University Presses, 1984) 172.

[19] William Shakespeare, *Hamlet, Prince of Denmark*, trans. Koya Tozawa, *Saogeki Zenshu Dai Ikkan* [The Collected Plays of William Shakespeare, vol. I] (1905; Tokyo: Dai Nippon Tosho Kabushiki Kaisha, 1909) 150–51.

[20] Tozawa 26.

universe and which is insentient like stone and wood. To reverse the formula, we have a man endowed with *Li* and *Qing*.

In Tozawa's version, then, the Western image of idealised man is perverted. Man is ennobled for a reason contrary to the Western ideal, for having a faculty attributed mainly to the beast: namely, passion. But the Eastern image of humanity in possession of the universal principle and emotion is clearly articulated. Thus, Hamlet's woe gained access to the Japanese imagination through Tozawa's translation, for the terms *Li* and *Qing* (*ri* and *jo* in Japanese) readily evoke in the Japanese reader's mind banal literary ideas about humanity which abound in the Japanese classics. But Tozawa had to warp Hamlet's and the Westerner's *Weltanschauung* in transplanting this Western play onto Japanese soil. This warping was inevitable, for he had to use the vocabulary and tropes derived from the Japanese intellectual tradition; and this in turn made his translation palatable to the Japanese audience.

Another example comes again from Pound. From Fenollosa's notes on Japanese Noh plays, Pound translated fourteen pieces. Among them was *Hagoromo*, based on a Japanese legend of a *Tennyo*, a heavenly beauty, who descended to the sands of Udo and had her feather mantle stolen by a fisherman while she was bathing in a nearby spring. Without the mantle she could not fly back to *Ten*, the Chinese Kingdom of Heaven. The *Tennyo*'s chagrin over her loss and her yearning for her heavenly home are expressed by the voices of the supernatural birds, which she is accustomed to hearing but which are now becoming fainter and fainter, and by the sight of the terrestrial birds flying homewards with ease and in freedom, the latter emphasising a sense of forlornness that the hapless *Tennyo* feels. Pound's translation is as follows: "... hearing the sky-bird, accustomed, and well accustomed, hearing the voices grow fewer and fewer, along the highways of air, how deep her longing to return! Plover and seagull are on the waves in the offing. Do they go or do they return?"[21] Note that the birds here are earthly creatures. In the original Noh play, the first bird is *Karyobinga*, a mythical bird of the Buddhist Paradise. This means that the Buddhist concept of heaven is superposed upon the Chinese, thereby creating an aesthetic world, characteristic of the Japanese imagination, in which things Chinese and Indian are often blended. Pound's translation falls short of this artistic effect – but, not having similar contextual resources out of which he could produce an appropriate aesthetic equivalence, this is nearly unavoidable.

---

[21] Ezra Pound and Ernest Fenollosa, *The Classic Noh Theatre of Japan: 'Noh' or Accomplishment* (1917; New York: New Directions, 1959) 101.

IV

Pound's dilemma shows that a literary translation means a dialogue between whole cultures. Even linguistic difficulties are found to be culturally rooted, as the example of *Snow Country* bears out. There are thus many facets to literary translation vis-à-vis the literary process in which various cultural strands are woven together to produce meaning. A translator must cope with the whole network of such strands in his work.

A dialogue between the Rev. and Mrs Davidson in W. Somerset Maugham's novella "Rain" will illustrate my point. The zealous preacher makes desperate efforts to reform Sadie Thompson, a harlot who sets up her trade at the hostelry in rainy Pago Pago where they are all staying. Mrs Davidson is sceptical about the success of her husband's efforts and tries to dissuade him from going to see her:

> "You don't know what she is. She'll insult you."
> "Let her insult me. [...] She has an immortal soul, and I must do all that is in my power to save it."
> Mrs Davidson's ears rang still with the harlot's mocking laughter. "She's gone too far."
> "Too far for the mercy of God?" [...] "Never. The sinner may be deeper in sin than the depth of hell itself, but the love of Lord Jesus can reach him still."[22]

The main strands of this dialogue are: (1) on the thematic level, a Christian morality (sin and salvation) and (2) on the expressive level, a familiar trope to cover the Christian idea of sin and salvation: the Lord's hands reaching out to the sinner. Mrs Davidson thinks Sadie the sinner is "gone too far" to be saved, but her husband believes no sinner can sink deeper than the reach of God's mercy. Mrs Davidson's metaphor is based on a horizontal distance, the preacher's on a vertical depth. In either case, the sinner is an object of God's reaching.

To these I want to add a third strand: the dualistic–cognitive perspective of narrative discourse, which I discussed earlier. The sinner is posited as a cognitive object in a dualistic frame of reference: "She's gone too far," etc. The first two strands are familiar to anyone born into Western culture. The last one may not be so, but it is latent in the linguistic structure and ready to serve as a vehicle for intended meaning, whether one is aware of it or not. These strands are part of the contextual resources with which Stanley Fish's "informed reader" is familiar and which enable him to comprehend the meaning of the discourse.[23] They are also "a

---

[22] Maugham, "Rain," *The Complete Short Stories* (Garden City, NY: Doubleday, 1934) vol. 1 1–39 (19).

[23] Fish, *Is There a Text in This Class? The Authority of Interpretive Communities* (Cambridge, MA: Harvard University Press, 1980) 48.

network of response-inviting structures" which impel Wolfgang Iser's "implied reader" to grasp the text.[24]

The translator's task is presumably to transfer the meaning of the SL text thus created to the TL. However, he frequently deviates from these constitutive elements of the original discourse and replaces them with components of his own invention. This he does from choice as a creative artist, or because compelled by unfavourable circumstances: i.e. the absence of these elements in the TL. In either case, the result will be a warping of the original text. In the case of the former, it will be a Bloomian misreading by a strong poet; if the latter, it will be an interesting case of a hermeneutical process.

In Yoshio Nakano's Japanese version, the second and the third strands of the passage quoted are modified. Thus Mrs Davidson's statement "She's gone too far" ceases to be her assessment of Sadie; it becomes instead an articulation of her own disgust towards the harlot. My crib version would be: *But [it is] intolerable indeed.* Nakano eliminates the subject, turning his version into a subjectless sentence.[25]

Another effect of Nakano's rendering is that the metaphoric structure of the original discourse is destroyed. Thus the dialogue between the preacher and his wife loses much of its original tension, since the contrary opinions of the couple hinge on this metaphor. The crucial meaning of sin and salvation becomes vague as well, as it is also sustained by the metaphor. And, most of all, the logical chain of the dialogue based on this metaphor is broken and the sharp contours of the discourse as well as the characters lose their edges.

Nakano had to compose a new dialogue, however, at the expense of all these losses in order to create dramatic tension in Japanese and to make his translated version natural and readable to his audience. With a view to preserving the monistic–experiential tenor of the Japanese discourse and the unfamiliar trope (to the Japanese readers) of the Christian idea of sin and salvation, he chose to sacrifice the Western cultural strands of logic and metaphor which were woven into the discourse of the original work.

---

[24] Iser, *The Act of Reading: A Theory of Aesthetic Response* (Baltimore, MD, and London: Johns Hopkins University Press, 1980) 34.

[25] Yoshio Nakano, trans. "Rain," by W. Somerset Maugham, *Mohmu Tanpenshu I* [The Short Stories of Maugham I] (Tokyo: Shincho Bunko, 1959) 9–74 (40).

V

The constraints encountered by the translator are intrinsic to the intercultural process – intrinsic because they derive from the basic imbalance of cultures. Yet they have received insufficient attention compared to those relating to the question of linguistic disparity. They are also bypassed in discussions of translation as art, for the proponents of this theory are mainly concerned with the artistry of the end-product of translation, hence tend to gloss over, in their fervent exaltation of artistic translation, these dilemmas and their consequences in the intercultural literary process.

Whether he likes it or not, the translator must work under those constraints in order to produce his version in the TL. After all, he is an interpreter working between two cultures, an interpreter, withal, situated in one culture or the other, not a transcendental divinity or a pre-Babel speaker of the pure language. He is an historical being born into one or the other culture and is obliged to work under certain cultural constraints. His interpretation can never attain perfect transparency;[26] it is clouded with the preconceptions and presuppositions of the culture to which he or she belongs. Such is the intercultural literary process.

But what is an intercultural literary process and what is, above all, a cultural process? A culture, I submit, is a system of symbolic forms and meanings that presupposes a set of previous forms out of which it grew, perpetually surrendering itself to new forms as it passes from one generation to the next. It is continually re-created and regenerated while being inherited from previous generations. No culture is created out of nothing or by a single generation at one stroke. It is in a perpetual state of flux, time-bound, continuing and changing at the same time in this state.

In this process of continuity and change, a generation of people plays the double role of preserver and creator, or of learner within and interpreter of the cultural system into which it is born. The learner finds a set of symbolic forms and mean-

---

[26] Ethnographers have now abandoned an ideology claiming transparency of representation. In his introduction to a volume of essays by contemporary American ethnographers, James Clifford declares: "The essays collected here assert that this ideology has crumbled"; *Writing Culture: The Poetics and Politics of Ethnography*, ed. James Clifford and George E. Marcus (Berkeley, Los Angeles and London: University of California Press, 1986) 2.

A similar situation is found between the texts of cognate languages as testified by a translator of Jacques Derrida, who comments on the opacity of the TL vis-à-vis the SL text: "When English re-articulates a French utterance, it puts an interpretation on that utterance that is built into English; it simply cannot let the original say what it says in French"; quoted in Philip E. Lewis, "The Measure of Translation Effects," *Difference in Translation*, ed. Joseph F. Graham (Ithaca, NY, and London: Cornell University Press, 1985) 31–62 (36).

ings imposed on him, which he must acquire. From birth, he is exposed to an endless bombardment of linguistic forms, for example, from the people around him. In fact, at the start of his life he is forced into a receptive stance towards the total system of symbolic forms and meanings afforded by the culture.

However, the learner's receptive phase passes imperceptibly into the interpreter's active phase,[27] because he is situated in an historical context which is different from that of the parent generation and which therefore gives rise to symbolic forms and meanings distinct from those handed down to him. The system of symbolic forms thus interpreted becomes a newly created system, which, in turn, is forced upon the next generation for it to learn and interpret. A culture thus exists in a circular process of being learned and interpreted, or of continuity and change; it is on the premise of this circularity that a culture is possible.

The circularity of continuity and change, of understanding and interpretation, of reception and creation, constitutes the basic cultural process. For lack of a better term, I call it "the creative circle." The circularity refers to the human creative process as having no "in the beginning" or "day of judgment."[28] The process is as circular as the hermeneutical circle is, having neither an absolute point of departure nor a destination. It designates, furthermore, no clear line of distinction between the subject and the object of creation: the circularity of the creative process gives rise to a unique relationship between culture and people[29] in which each is

---

[27] Hans–Georg Gadamer contends that understanding is identical with interpretation; Gadamer, *Truth and Method*, trans. Garrett Barden and John Cumming (New York: Seabury Press, 1975). The historicity of meaning, however, would seem to be grounded in the conflicting ontological modes of continuity and change: understanding has to do with continuity while interpretation causes change. Transferred to the cultural context, the dichotomy expresses the learner's receptive stance versus the interpreter's destructive stance vis-à-vis the cultural heritage, the former being superseded by the latter but never identical with it. The changeover takes place when the meaning understood by the learner is given his own expression and symbolisation, or when, to follow Paul Ricœur, the subject appropriates the meaning in order to gain "a new capacity of knowing himself"; Ricœur, *The Philosophy of Paul Ricœur*, ed. Charles E. Reagan and David Stewart (Boston, MA: Beacon Press, 1978) 145.

[28] Of course, I am not concerned here with the creative act of a single individual that takes place during his lifetime with a temporal beginning and end, or with a temporal or a conceptual beginning in the broad area of man's symbolic behaviour in the sense that Edward Said calls "transitive" and "intransitive"; Edward Said, *Beginnings* (Baltimore, MD, and London: Johns Hopkins University Press, 1975); my interest is in man's symbolic behaviour in a transindividual and non-conscious sense as seen by Lucien Goldmann in his *Methodology in the Sociology of Literature*, trans. and ed. William Q. Boelhower (Oxford: Blackwell, 1981) 97.

[29] This curious relationship between culture and people is recognised by a wide variety of thinkers and academics:

Wilhelm von Humboldt: "By the same process whereby he spins language out of his own being, he ensnares himself in it"; quoted by Ernst Cassirer, *Language and Myth* (New York: Dover, 1953) 9;

both the creator and the created. But the circle is not a vicious circle; it is the living circle of human existence in which the Miltonic oxymoron "Man was created free" has real meaning.

The creative act of the literary artist is subject to this circularity, with a difference that involves highly individual and conscious efforts on the part of the artist. The creative act in the broad area of man's symbolic behaviour is, on the whole, communal and non-conscious, as seen by Lucien Goldmann:[30] no one claims authorship or copyright on what has been added to the culture. Even in the literary sphere, ancient storytellers rest content in anonymity. The modern literary artist, by contrast, asserts his individuality and makes conscious efforts to create a new aesthetic world of his own. But he, too, is subject to the circularity of the creative act. By the time he starts his literary work, he has learned his language well or less well and is proficient in the literary conventions of his culture. These cultural forms and systems are the given which he inherits from his predecessors, and it is by these forms and systems that he launches himself into the literary universe. In other words, the literary artist cannot create a literary world out of nothing, nor can he create an entirely new world of his own. He is condemned to work within the confines of the literary and cultural given. In this sense, his creative act is the "process of depersonalisation" posited by T.S. Eliot, though it does not lead to the timeless realm of the transcendental mind of the culture. This depersonalising process of the literary artist guarantees the continuity of the literary heritage.

The literary heritage takes its concrete form, however, from nothing other than the symbolic representations by succeeding generations of literary artists, to whose interpretations the heritage is subjected and by whom it is given ever new expressions. These expressions are not exact replicas of what has been handed

---

Lucien Goldmann: "An object exists, is worn down and transformed, but it does not transform itself. Man, on the other hand, is not only the object of transformations but also the subject of them"; Goldmann 118;

Richard Shweder: "The basic idea of cultural psychology is that, on the one hand, no sociocultural environment exists or has identity independently of the way human beings seize meanings and resources from it, while, on the other hand, every human being's subjectivity and mental life are altered through the process of seizing meanings and resources from some sociocultural environment and using them"; Shweder, *Thinking Through Cultures: Expeditions in Cultural Psychology* (Cambridge, MA and London: Harvard University Press, 1991) 74;

Ron Scollon and Suzanne Wong Scollon: "History, worldview, beliefs, values, religions, and social organizations may all be reflected through different languages and linguistic varieties in a culture. At the same time, language may be a directly defining aspect of a culture, rather than simply a reflection of other, more basic structures"; Scollon & Scollon, *Intercultural Communications: A Discourse Approach* (Oxford and Cambridge, MA: Blackwell, 1995) 137.

[30] Goldmann 97.

down to the new artists by their predecessors. They are instead a new form of the literary heritage appropriated by the new artists, a new form which is bound to express the identity of the new generation. The new expressions thus bring change to the literary tradition, while at the same time ensuring its continuity. Hence the receptive act of the literary artist contains within itself the potentiality for a destructive act. Of course, there will be differences of degree in destructiveness between the artist whose main artistic concern is to preserve the norm and the one whose controlling artistic urge is to reshape it or innovate. But the difference cannot be one of quality, for any artist is bound to act at once receptively and destructively in his creative activity. He is condemned to enter a creative circle in which there is no escaping bondage to the literary tradition, no matter how revolutionary he may be, and no way of expressing the tradition without interpreting it, no matter how slavishly he may try to adhere to it. Thus, we see the double nature of the literary artist, who is at once the learner and interpreter of meaning, the inheritor and creator of a literary tradition, and the chronicler and prophet of a culture.

The literary artist who goes to a foreign literature for a new source of inspiration finds himself in a creative circle similar to the one explained above. His artistic process, however, is more complicated than that of the artist engaged in an intracultural, creative activity, since there are two literary norms to which he reacts both receptively and destructively. He becomes engaged in a double circle, so to speak, of preserving and destroying the aesthetic ideals of his own culture as well as those of the foreign one. The two operations are intimately interrelated, like Yeats's interlocking gyres: the receptive phase in one circle is a reversal of the destructive in the other, and vice versa. That is, the artist's receptive attitude to the foreign aesthetic ideals is directly motivated by a negative estimation of his own aesthetic heritage; conversely, his interpretation of a foreign art reflects the preconceptions that were imposed on him by his own literary tradition.[31] To this extent, his interpretative act becomes destructive vis-à-vis the foreign text.

The literary translator finds himself in the same double circle of creative process. He assumes a receptive stance towards the SL text before him when preparing to translate it. However, he cannot maintain this receptive stance very long,

---

[31] W.B. Yeats thought he had found in the Japanese Noh drama a revolutionary dramatic form. However, his adaptations of the Noh drama proved to be essentially Aristotelian, for dramatic conflict of the characters' actions forms the main part of the play, whereas, in the Japanese Noh drama of dream vision, the plot is meagre and the whole play is constructed around the dance of the *shite* (the main performer). Yeats's interpretation of the Noh aesthetic was strongly conditioned by the Western literary norm. Thus, his dance plays proved to be destructive/receptive to the Western drama.

for the SL meaning will soon start to strain the tolerance of the symbolic forms (vocabulary and grammar) of the TL and will be obliged to undergo metamorphosis in order to remain intelligible in the TL's meshwork of meaning.[32] This happens against or at the translator's will, as is exemplified by Tozawa's version of *Hamlet* and Nakano's rendering of Maugham's dialogue in "Rain." Needless to say, the destructive dynamism is inherent in the translator's act of reading, too. The SL text accepted into the TL will in turn work as an innovative force on its host, transforming and enriching, in other words, creating it anew. Thus, the creative circle in the intercultural literary process completes itself.

Having dwelt at length upon the destructive phase of the intercultural literary process, it behooves me to emphasise in conclusion that the creative and innovative phase is a coequal feature with the destructive in what is, after all, the "creative" circle of the literary process. The truth about and mystery of literary translation, in the final analysis, lie between the two blades held by the would-be King of Macedon: the SL-oriented dogma of untranslatability and the TL-oriented myth of translation as art. Neither blade could successfully sever the knot.

[32] Willis Barnstone argues: "The translator must be a traitor to the letter to be loyal to the meaning and spirit of the source text"; Barnstone 260. Granted, but the vassals with whom the translator travels in loyal homage to the source text, alas, are often found to be traitors to him, perverting or subverting the pristine essence of the source text.

Between Language and Literature, Philology and Linguistics: An Historical Review of English Studies in Japan

YOSHIHIKO IKEGAMI

THE PRESENT CONTRIBUTION is intended as a concise review of English studies in Japan at the university level, both in their initial stages and over the past fifty years. The focus will be on the linguistic rather than the literary side of the problem.[1] The reason for this choice is personal – it is simply that the former is the field of my speciality, on which I hopefully can offer a fairer picture. Before addressing the specifically linguistic side of the problem, however, I propose to offer some account of the "prehistory" of the problem – how the new non-native discipline was introduced into Japanese universities, and what the initial reaction was before it became established as an integral part of foreign studies in this country.

I.1

The first English department in Japan was founded in 1889 at the University of Tokyo, the oldest university in the country. As was to be expected, the earliest staff members to be appointed were foreign teachers who were native speakers of English. Lafcadio Hearn (1850–1904), the second of two teachers initially appointed, is a well-known figure in Japan. He was born in 1850 of an Irish father and a Greek mother, spent his childhood in Ireland, worked as a journalist in the USA and came to Japan in 1890 as a correspondent for *Harper's Magazine*. He soon found himself fascinated by the alien culture he encountered in the Far East. (One might suspect that he found in the indigenous culture of Japan something congenial to his own Irish mentality.) Resolving to stay in Japan, he worked as a teacher of English, married a Japanese woman, and became

[1] For relevant biographical information, I have relied on Tokyo Daigaku Hyakunenshi Henshu Iinkai [Editorial Committee of the Hundred-Year History of Tokyo University], ed. *Tokyo Daigaku Hyakunenshi* [One Hundred-Year History of Tokyo University]: *Bukyokushi* [History of the Faculties and Institutes], vol. 1 (Tokyo: Tokyo University Press, 1986).

naturalised in 1896. In the same year, he was appointed lecturer in the English Department of the University of Tokyo, remaining in the post until 1903, shortly before his death in 1904.

We have a sizable amount of evidence which suggests that the series of lectures by this foreign (but later naturalised) teacher were very popular among the students. Letters and memoirs written and left by some of these students (not a few of whom were later to become eminent figures themselves) clearly show that the students were enthusiastic about Hearn's lectures (in striking contrast, as I will presently show, to those of his successor).

The general tenor of Hearn's lectures can be divined from the titles of some of his later published books, written on the basis of his lectures at the University of Tokyo: *Interpretations of Literature*, *Appreciations of Poetry* and *Life and Literature*, among others.[2] In a word, his approach is appreciative, appealing to the heart and imagination of his students. In his diary, one of his former students, Tetsuo Kawasumi (who was later to become one of Japan's early specialists in English philology), quoted his teacher as saying:

> I teach literature as expression of emotion, as description of human life. When I talk about a poet, I try to explain the impact and quality of emotion which he conveys. In other words, the foundation of my teaching method is to appeal to the students' imagination and emotion.

This quotation is followed by a passage describing Hearn's teaching method:

> After paraphrasing the text and explaining the meanings of difficult words and phrases, he commented on the beautiful lines of the poem in his no less beautiful words and told us where the artistic significance of the work lay. Instead of giving us too much of logical argument and factual information, he went straight to an interpretation which struck a responsive chord in the hearts of the audience. There was a world of difference between him and a self-styled scholar who, relying on the annotations by Western researchers, spent as many as two or three hours in explaining the etymology of just a single word without letting us get even a single glimpse of the true meaning of art. At the end of the lecture, our teacher often uttered, as if to himself, "Wonderfully beautiful!" The words touched a chord in our hearts.[3]

It is interesting to compare student response to Hearn's lectures with the reception given the lectures of Sōseki Natsume (1867–1916). The novelist Natsume, an

---

[2] Lafcadio Hearn, *Interpretations of Literature*, 3 vols. (New York: Dodd, Mead, 1915), *Appreciations of Poetry* (New York: Dodd, Mead, 1916), and *Life and Literature* (New York: Dodd, Mead, 1916).

[3] Tetsuo Kawasumi, ed. *Shiryo: Nihon Eigakushi* [Data Book: History of English Studies in Japan] (Tokyo: Taishukan, 1998) vol. 1.2 987.

even better-known figure in Japan than Hearn, was one of the earliest graduates of the Tokyo English Department and the first native scholar to hold a chair of English Literature in Japan. He was sent to London by the Ministry of Education to undertake further study of English. After attending the classes of W.P. Ker for some time, he chose to conduct his studies by himself, except for occasional visits to his private tutor, W.J. Craig. Returning to Japan two years later, he was appointed Hearn's successor. Two of the courses that he taught in the English Department in his earliest years were "Forms of English Literature" and "Theory of Literature."

As is suggested by the titles of the courses he offered, Natsume's approach was analytical – reminiscent of that adopted in scientific research. He apparently addressed the same question with which Roman Jakobson was later to be concerned: "What makes a verbal message a work of art?" He proposed to approach the question from the viewpoint of form, on the one hand, and from that of content, on the other. In his lectures on "Forms of English Literature," he showed how different arrangements of words could produce special effects either by manipulating meaning or by manipulating the sounds of words. In the lecture series entitled "Theory of Literature," he attempted to characterise literature in terms of the content being conveyed by forms of verbal expression: "In general, the form of the literary content needs to be (F + f). F means the focal impression or idea; f means the emotion which attaches to it."[4]

It is not hard to imagine the reaction to his lectures. Again we have the testimony of Tetsuo Kawasumi:

> Too sharp, too cold. He dissects the soft flesh of the beautiful works of English literature, so much so that our pride as students of literature is sorely hurt. [...] Today he talked mainly about the forms of literature in terms of psychological theories. I doubted if such an observation was really right and I discussed it critically with some classmates of mine. I concluded that if we looked at literature in the way he did, we would never come to appreciate the real charm of literature.[5]

In order to bring the difference between the approaches of the two teachers into sharper relief, we can compare Hearn saying "the highest form of art must necessarily be such art as produces upon the beholder the same moral effect that the passion of love produces in a generous lover"[6] (from an essay, "The Question of the Highest Art") and Natsume explaining his notion of "F" ("focal impression or

---

[4] Sōseki Natsume, *Sōseki Zenshu* [Collected Works of Sōseki], vol. 9: *Bungakuron* [Theory of Literature] (1907; Tokyo: Iwanami, 1966) 27.

[5] Kawasumi 1341.

[6] Lafcadio Hearn, "The Question of the Highest Art," *Interpretation of Literature*, vol. 1, 7–10 (9).

idea"): "When focal consciousness A shifts to B, A turns into peripheral consciousness a; when B then turns into C, a and b constitute the two peripheries of the wave of consciousness."[7]

Hearn was a foreign teacher, but he was able to talk about literature in a way more congenial to the Japanese students at the time than Natsume's approach. Just as Hearn himself found something congenial to him in Japanese culture and was strongly attracted to it, so his Japanese students found in his essentially appreciative approach to literature much charm and appeal.

It may sound a little ironical that Natsume, a native teacher who had done two years' research in London, was not so successful with the students who attended his lectures on the theory of literature. It was not at all the case that the students were unhappy because the lecturer was just offering them the doctrines of Western scholars. On the contrary, his theory of literature was of his very own making. As he himself writes in the preface to *Bungakuron* (A Theory of Literature), he found in English literature a conception of literature somewhat dissimilar to that prevalent in either Japanese or Chinese literature (both of which were quite familiar to him), and this led him to address the fundamental question of the psychological and sociological *raison d'être* of what is called literature. He was also known to be often critical of his colleagues, who were content to convey Western ideas. Thus it was his characteristically "analytical" approach *per se* to literature that the students found off-putting. It must also be added that Natsume also offered courses on Shakespeare's plays for non-majoring students and we have ample testimony to the effect that he was extremely popular in these courses: "There wasn't even standing room left in the hall," wrote Kawasumi in his diary.[8]

I.2

The contrasting evaluations given to Hearn's appreciative and Natsume's analytical approach betoken the way in which literature is traditionally conceived of in Japan, and this in turn derives from the way language – the stuff of literature – is traditionally regarded.[9] This last point concerns the question of the "ideology of

---

[7] Natsume 31.

[8] Kawasumi 1344.

[9] Yoshihiko Ikegami, "Sign Conceptions in Japan," *Semiotik: Ein Handbuch zu den zeichentheoretischen Grundlagen von Natur und Kultur*, 2. Teilband, ed. Roland Posner, Klaus Robering and Thomas A. Sebeok (Berlin: Mouton de Gruyter, 1998) 1898–910, and "Sprachliche Ideologie und sprachlicher Mythos: im Fall des Japanischen," *Bericht des III. Ost–West Kolloquium für Sprachwissenschaft, März 2000* (forthcoming).

language" recently discussed by some anthropologists,[10] a term used in several different, but mutually related, senses. What concerns us in the present context is its most broad and neutral sense – "shared bodies of common sense notions about the nature of language in the world."[11]

The particular point about the different conceptualisation of language I have in mind concerns the way in which language is either correlated or contrasted with something else. It seems to me that there are largely two different types of conceptualisation in this respect. In one type, language is contrasted with something extralinguistic – entities in the "real" world. From this orientation there naturally arises an interest in the possible match or mismatch between the words and the objects they refer to or between the sentences and the situations they encode. As can be expected, cases of mismatching will be found to predominate by far over cases of a close match. Language is then branded "imperfect" – an imperfect instrument for unmistakable reference and precise communication. It is well known that this conviction has led some to start a painstaking search for a "perfect language,"[12] often motivated by missionary zeal and culminating in the construction of an artificial sign system based on the ideology of logical positivism. Thus, as John Lyons writes in an article on subjectivity in language, the mainstream of Western preoccupation with language seems to have been "dominated by the intellectual prejudice that language is essentially, if not solely, an instrument for the expression of propositional thought."[13]

The line of thinking that has dominated in Japanese is rather different from this. It is more clearly oriented towards the speaking subject. Thus, if in the Western tradition the basic contrast is between "language" and "referent" (whether object or situation) and the two entities are conceived as being related to each other in terms of the former "referring to" the latter, the basic contrast in the Japanese tradition is between "language" and "heart/mind" (i.e. something which the speaker has to say) and the two entities are conceived as being related to each other in terms of the former "expressing" (i.e. externalising) the latter. (It may be added in passing that the contrast in question is rendered in Japanese as one between *kotoba* ["word/speech/language"] and *kokoro* ["heart/mind"], the word

---

[10] Bambi B. Schieffelin, Kathryn A. Woolard and Paul V. Kroskrity, ed. *Language Ideologies: Practice and Theory* (Oxford: Oxford University Press, 1998).

[11] Kathryn A. Woolard and Bambi B. Schieffelin, "Language Ideologies," *Annual Review of Anthropology* 23 (1994): 55–82 (57).

[12] Umberto Eco, *The Search for a Perfect Language* (1993; Oxford: Blackwell, 1995).

[13] Lyons, "Deixis and Subjectivity: Loquor, ergo sum?" *Speech, Place, and Action*, ed. R.J. Jarvella and W. Klein (New York: John Wiley, 1982) 101–23 (103).

kokoro covering both the intellectual and the emotive aspects of the psychological process – a symbolic indication, incidentally, that the distinction between the objective and the subjective is not rigidly insisted on in the Japanese tradition.) One important point that derives from the Japanese conceptualisation of "language" in relation to "heart/mind" as described above is that these two entities are, unlike the corresponding two entities "language" and "referent" in the West, not so much contrasted with each other as integrated with each other. There is, in fact, an essential continuity between the two. They differ only in that one is something internalised (hence not directly perceivable) and the other something externalised (hence perceivable): the former is "expressed" (in the etymological sense of the word) as the latter. A Japanese way of capturing this process is to say that the former ("heart/mind") "spontaneously becomes" the latter ("word/speech/language"). It is assumed here, again, that this process can never be perfect – there is, in fact, always a mismatch between "heart/mind" and "word/speech/language." But the way in which this inadequacy of language is coped with takes a different form in Japan. Quite in contrast to what happened in the West, Japanese speakers did not necessarily address themselves to rectifying the imperfect language. Instead, they were encouraged to rectify their hearts/minds. The idea here is that proper language derives naturally from a proper heart/mind: if the heart/mind is right, language will follow suit. Quite characteristically, rhetoric did not thrive in Japanese culture. The emphasis was on spiritual discipline – on how one should hold true to one's heart/mind.

II

That was how English studies in Japan started at the university level. The English Department of Tokyo University served as an example for the English departments in other universities that were subsequently established in major cities of the country. The typical image associated with the graduates of the English department of a prestigious university was that they aspired to be either authors or translators (of literary works), if not scholars. It is significant that the first two native Japanese professors of English ended up becoming far more famous as an author and a translator respectively than as scholars. Sōseki Natsume resigned from his professorship in the English Department of Tokyo University after four years of teaching to concentrate on writing novels. In this he was immensely successful; he is regarded as one of the most popular novelists ever in Japan. Natsume's earliest local colleague, Bin Ueda (1874–1916), who later left to become the first professor of English at Japan's second-oldest university, Kyoto, is now remembered as an excellent translator of Western poetry rather than as a professor of English.

It may be added in this connection that in Japan the translation of literary works has traditionally enjoyed especially high esteem. The idea was that the translation of Western literature required both sufficient linguistic proficiency and a full understanding of the cultural background, and access to these was for a long time limited to a select few. I once heard someone say sarcastically that the translator's name was printed as large as the author's in the Japanese versions of Shakespeare's plays.

The predominantly literary orientation continued to be characteristic of the English Department of the University of Tokyo and, for that matter, of other English departments in the country. Among those foreigners appointed to visiting professorships at Tokyo University, one finds such names as Edmund Blunden (from 1924 to 1927 and again visiting and staying in Japan from 1947 to 1950), William Empson (from 1931 to 1934) and G.S. Fraser (from 1950 to 1951 and often visiting Japan afterwards). Presumably there was an implicit understanding that the purely academic study of English was a task to be undertaken in the Department of Linguistics. The appointment of a professor of English who specialised in linguistic rather than literary study did not take place until 1916, nearly thirty years after the Department was established. The appointee, Sanki Ichikawa (1986–1970), was in fact a graduate of the Department of Linguistics. He had spent four years as a research scholar in England and, on coming back to Japan, was appointed to the chair of English. His work was generally in the line of Otto Jespersen, predominantly empirical rather than theoretical, and philological rather than linguistic. He also published some annotations and translations of Shakespeare's works as well as a textbook on Old English and thus belonged to a generation of English philologists.

His successor, Fumio Nakajima (1904–1999), was actually my mentor. He was a student of Ichikawa's and spent two years from 1929 studying in Europe (during which time he attended R.W. Chambers's class on Old English and A.H. Smith's on Middle English). I remember him once mentioning as one of the books that influenced him most A. Boekh's *Encyclopädia und Methodologie der philologischen Wissenschaften* (1932). He was, however, more theoretically oriented than his predecessor. He was interested in Anton Marty's theory of language as well as Franz Brentano's psychological theory; in his later years he also became interested in the theory of transformational grammar.

III

We now come to the 1950s, and from this point on I can speak from the viewpoint of a participant observer. I was an undergraduate student in the Department of English, University of Tokyo, from 1954 to 1956 and a graduate student there from 1956 to 1961. The number of students in the undergraduate course per year was around forty, but only a handful of them chose to go on to the graduate course. (By this time it had become quite common for students to choose professions connected with journalism after they finished the undergraduate course.) The number of graduate students admitted to the MA course was around a dozen each year, and after finishing this two-year course only a very few (between zero and three at most) were allowed to go on to the three-year PhD course. At that time, however, the students in the PhD course were not expected to submit a dissertation. They were supposed to take the prescribed number of credits in three years and then find a teaching position at a university. In the case of the humanities, this system persisted until the early 1990s.

Out of the dozen or so students who entered graduate school every year, most majored in literature. The percentage of those who majored in language studies was normally one or two in ten. In view of the heavily literature-oriented tradition of the English Department, those majoring in language tended to be regarded as heretics.

The language-related courses offered at graduate school concerned Old or Middle English exclusively – a brief survey of the grammar followed by the reading of selected texts. The orientation was thus essentially philological rather than linguistic. In fact, it was obligatory for students majoring in language to take some courses on literature as well (but not vice versa). It was not until the 1970s that the situation began to change.

IV

Since the early 1950s and through to the 1970s, an ever-increasing number of young Japanese university teachers and graduate students were sent to the USA under the programme sponsored by the Japan–USA Educational Commissions (also called the Fulbright Commission). Among them were a limited number of people who majored in linguistics. I was one of the grantees for the year 1965 and was enrolled as a graduate student in the Department of Linguistics at Yale.

I recall being pleased to find the department of linguistics in the USA rather different from its counterpart in Japan. The traditional image of the Japanese linguistics department was that it was a place where people worked assiduously on details of little-known languages – each student devoted almost exclusively to a particular language of his choice. By contrast, the linguistics department in the USA had a solid programme in linguistic theory, and the general atmosphere was very "open." On the other hand, the Department at Yale was characteristically and exclusively "linguistic." When I talked with the Head of Department, Bernard Bloch, about the courses I was to take and mentioned that I was also interested in taking courses on Old and Middle English offered in the English Department, he dismissed my suggestion: "No. That's literature."

That was a period of transition, both for American linguistics generally and for linguistics at Yale. Yale had for years been the centre of structural linguistics, but by that time the discipline had apparently reached a dead end. On the other hand, after the publication of Noam Chomsky's *Syntactic Structures* in 1957, the newly emerging transformational grammar had been making its presence increasingly felt; it was probably as a potential rival that Sydney Lamb, with his theory of stratificational grammar, was appointed to the chair of general linguistics at Yale. I was thus to become one of the few students to write a dissertation in stratification theory.[14]

V

Back in Japan, the impact of American linguistics was becoming apparent as the number of young scholars studying in the USA increased. We can distinguish three phases here.

In the earliest period, the returnees had been trained in structural linguistics, which they started to teach in their courses in the English departments. They were still few in number, however, and the impact they had was limited. Through the 1950s and still to a considerable degree in the early 1960s, the language-oriented courses offered by Japan's English departments were largely traditional – either courses on Old and Middle English or courses on traditional grammar in the line of Jespersen.

By the end of the 1960s, the new Chomskyan paradigm in linguistics had become predominant in the USA. With a considerable increase in the number of scholarships and fellowships offered for study in the USA, more and more young students and researchers had the opportunity to study linguistics at American universities, by far the greater part being trained in transformational grammar. Thus, throughout the 1960s and 1970s, staff and students in Japan were largely divided

[14] Yoshihiko Ikegami, *The Semiological Structure of the English Verbs of Motion: A Stratificational Approach* (Tokyo: Sanseido, 1970).

into two groups: those specialising in transformational grammar and those specialising in Old and Middle English. Those working outside these two main groups – those engaged either in non-transformational theory (e.g. stratificational grammar, systemic grammar) or in areas of linguistics other than syntax (e.g. semantics, discourse analysis) – formed a decided minority. The interests of the two main groups, one called "linguistics" people and the other "philology" people, diverged in time, to the extent that students in the former group were sometimes accused of being interested solely in theory without adequate linguistic proficiency and those in the latter of being concerned with detail with no theoretical underpinnings. For quite some time, the "philology" group held their position well against the surge of the "linguistics" group, but through the 1980s and 1990s there was a slow but steady decrease in the number of those who chose the "philology" line. The "literature" people in the English department, who were naturally more sympathetic towards the "philology" people, deplored the tendency in which the good old tradition of "close reading" – undoubtedly a German legacy in the Japanese university – came to be lost. Thus, in quite a number of English departments one often found two groups of staff and students whose interests and orientation were so different from each other that they might have belonged to different faculties. The situation led to the establishment of the English Linguistics Society of Japan in 1982 independently of the English Literary Society of Japan, which had been established as early as 1928 and had at that time been the only nation-wide society for those affiliated with English departments. As of autumn 2000, the English Linguistic Society had a membership of around 1700.

All this while, there were indeed scholarships and fellowships offered for study in the UK, especially those sponsored by the British Council, but the number of candidates in linguistics selected was much lower than that studying in the USA. Thus, coupled with their sharper theoretical orientation, returnees from the USA, mostly trained in transformational grammar, constituted the mainstream of linguistic study in the English departments, a situation that persisted until the beginning of the 1990s.

In the 1990s, the opportunities for studying English abroad increased more rapidly. Quite a large number of researchers and students found it possible to spend some months abroad on their own. Some chose to spend time in such countries as Canada, Australia and New Zealand. The themes they worked on abroad also became more diversified: many were encouraged to write theses and dissertations on Japanese rather than English. Now, Japanese is known as a language with an eminently pragmatic orientation which functions in relatively heavy dependence on contextual factors (as manifested by the large extent to which ellipsis is tolerated in discourse, on the one hand, and by the popularity of that extremely short traditional poetic form called *haiku*, on the other). Working on Japanese certainly helped develop a special interest in such disciplines as pragmatics, sociolinguistics and discourse analysis, and the year 1998 saw the establishment of the Japanese Association for Pragmatics.

In the meantime, a paradigm shift was taking place in the USA. The newly emerging new direction of cognitive linguistics was making its presence increasingly felt. The new paradigm was welcomed in Japan, especially by those who intuited that the predominantly syntactic-formalistic orientation of transformational-generative grammar was not quite in agreement with the genius of the Japanese language. With the rise of interest in the new paradigm, the Japanese Association for Cognitive Linguistics was established in 2000 with a membership of around four hundred already at its inauguration.

VI

There remain a few comments to be added. First, English departments in Japan have been very much academically oriented. Training students as potential English teachers has occupied only a marginal position in the curriculum. Traditionally, language teacher training has been left to the Department of Education or to teacher's colleges. It was generally only after the nation-wide reform of the university system since the late 1980s that faculty members specialising in English education were to be found in the English departments alongside scholars of literature and linguistics.

Second, people in the linguistics departments have not been involved centrally in the linguistic study of English. Their departments are generally much smaller than the English departments and their orientation has been empirical rather than theoretical.

Third, people specialising in the Japanese language in Japanese departments have also been in the minority. As in English, these departments have traditionally been dominated by scholars of literature. With their background in Japanese, a typologically different language from English, however, they could have played an important role in evaluating linguistic theories whose illustration was based, above all, on English. Unfortunately, their orientation was traditionally philological and this, coupled with their general lack of proficiency in English, has caused their contribution to be only fragmentary.

Finally, at the turn of the millennium, we are now witnessing a phase of rapid change and transition. To cope with the ever-growing need for interdisciplinary research, and in response to the increase in those entering tertiary institutions and the concomitant diversification of interests, the Japanese university system has for some years been undergoing a process of reshuffling. Reorganised departments like those of human sciences and of language and information have been set up alongside departments of international communication and of language and culture, and researchers and teachers who would formerly have been accommodated in English departments are now widely distributed across these new departments. English studies in the new millennium will certainly be conducted in a more integrated way than before, with a better balance between theory and practice, research and teaching. There will be more cooperation between specialists in English and specialists in Japanese, and English, in both its linguistic and its cultural aspect, will be increasingly studied on a comparative basis in relation to Japanese, leading, hopefully, to substantial contributions to a real understanding of human language.

The History of the English Language

NORMAN F. BLAKE

I WANT TO OPEN THIS PAPER by considering the publication history of the *Cambridge History of English Literature*[1] and the *Cambridge History of the English Language*.[2] The former, most volumes of which were published in the first two decades of the twentieth century, consisted of fourteen volumes devoted to literature from the Anglo-Saxon till the end of the Victorian period. These volumes are largely descriptive with some literary evaluation. The first volumes of the latter were published in 1992; when this *History* is complete, for one volume has yet to appear, it will consist of six volumes, two of which will be devoted to North American English and to varieties of English outside England. The second of these two volumes, which is already published, contains descriptions of varieties of English in Scotland, Wales and Ireland as well as those in Africa, India and Australasia. The English language in this *History* is thought to embrace all varieties of English throughout the world, and although one may distinguish them by titles such as British English, Australian English and American English they are still considered varieties of English. Although literature throughout the world may be written in English, it is often not thought of as English literature in the same way.[3] Scholars refer to American literature rather than to American English literature. This is in part because it is not considered appropriate to separate in any country the literature produced in English from that written in other indigenous or adopted languages. Canadian literature can embrace works written in English, French or native Indian or Eskimo languages. Literature written in English in former British colonies may be referred to as postcolonial literature without reference to a specific language. However, multiple volumes of the history of English

[1] Sir Adolphus William Ward and Alfred Rayney Waller, ed. *The Cambridge History of English Literature*, 14 vols. (Cambridge: Cambridge University Press, 1907–32).

[2] Richard Hogg, ed. *The Cambridge History of the English Language*, 6 vols. (Cambridge: Cambridge University Press, 1992–).

[3] Cf. Ton Hoenselaars and Marius Buning, ed. *English Literature and Other Languages* (Studies in Literature 24; Amsterdam and Atlanta, GA: Rodopi, 1999).

literature continue to appear, and it seemed in the second half of the twentieth century as though no publishing house could be considered respectable until it had produced its own multi-volume history. This is not true of the English language. Oxford University Press, for example, has its own multi-volume history of English literature, albeit still incomplete,[4] but, despite its tradition of publishing dictionaries and other works about the English language, the press has not yet, as far as I am aware, made any plans to publish a corresponding history of the English language.

Why is it that the only multi-volume history of the English language yet produced was issued so long after its sister history of literature, and why is it still the only one to appear at all? There seem to be several possible reasons for this state of affairs. The first is doubtless linked with the history of the teaching of English in Britain.[5] The study of the classics, which was the mainstay of education until well into the twentieth century, was regarded as both intellectually challenging and laying a solid foundation for moral behaviour. At first English literature was taught as a subsidiary subject in colleges and universities as the poor man's or, more usually, woman's classics, and it was given a strong historical bias. As a subject it was deemed too easy and one which could easily be crammed to pass examinations. On the other hand, philology, especially in Germany, was a more established discipline which was regarded as demanding. When English literature emerged as a possible subject to be studied to degree level, its supporters had to convince others of its intellectual fitness and toughness. It could have been linked with history, but it was at Oxford linked with philology in England's first school of English. To compete with classical literature, the study of English literature had to have backbone, and that meant a dose of early language and literature. When they were instituted, degree courses in English at university level usually included the study of Old and Middle English as languages and required familiarity with some of the literature in these varieties. *Beowulf* and Chaucer were part of English. Hence, for many lecturers, "English language" was identified with Old and Middle English, since one had to be a specialist in language to teach early English literature. The corollary of this was that language was hardly ever taught for post-medieval periods, so that students of English could read Shakespeare with little or no formal instruction in his language; to this day it remains unusual for a teacher

[4] F.P. Wilson et al., ed. *The Oxford History of English Literature*, 11 vols. (Oxford: Clarendon Press, 1947–).

[5] D.J. Palmer, *The Rise of English Studies: An Account of the Study of English Language and Literature from its Origins to the Making of the Oxford English School* (London, New York and Toronto: Oxford University Press for University of Hull, 1965).

of English language to be an editor of a Shakespearean text or act as a consultant for a major series of Shakespearean editions.[6] For many, the history of the English language stopped at about 1500, and even some recent histories of the English language devote far more space to the period prior to 1500 than to the period after, as witness the history by Charles Barber,[7] which devotes 174 pages to the Old and Middle English periods out of its 299 pages (including index etc.).

The second reason for the absence of multi-volume histories of the English language has to do with the development of English as a language. It was long thought that there was no standard English before 1500, for before then there were competing varieties but no standardised one. Hence Old and Middle English often seemed the most interesting periods in the language's history because one could study all varieties on a more or less equal footing. There were also records from many parts of the country which allowed the scholar to trace the language's development in different areas. No one variety was necessarily better than another. The post-medieval period was one that witnessed the gradual emergence and triumph of the standard language, which by the eighteenth century was established and accepted as the norm for English. Other varieties were increasingly regarded as substandard forms of the language which were hardly worth studying within the same framework as standard English. The development of English was seen rather like Whig history: a gradual progression to an ideal form of the language, which was then taught through grammatical rules formulated largely on the model of classical languages, especially Latin. D.J. Palmer notes that Thomas Dale, the first Professor of English at University College, London, included in his proposals for the study of English language this item: "The History of Language: comprehending a view of its origin, formation, progress, and perfection."[8] This perfect language to which Dale refers was taught in all corners of the British Empire, and even when countries like the USA achieved their independence, they still continued for a long time to see standard British English as the model they should emulate, as though it was the only variety acceptable in civilised society.

This attitude did not prevent people from taking an interest in other varieties, such as local British dialects. But this study was considered antiquarian, and from the sixteenth to the nineteenth century it focused largely on lexis. Collections of words associated with local varieties or with certain classes, such as vagabonds,

[6] Cf. N.F. Blake, "Editing Shakespeare: the Role of Language Studies," *European Journal of English Studies* 1 (1997): 329–53.

[7] Charles Barber, *The English Language: A Historical Introduction* (Cambridge Approaches to Linguistics; Cambridge: Cambridge University Press, 1993).

[8] Palmer 19.

were compiled. But for many people this activity was not directly related to the study of the history of the language. Such collections were interesting curios or relics of those who had failed to be part of the mainstream of the English language. Those who used standard English were the guardians of the language, and to study dialects on the same footing as the standard would have been regarded almost as heretical. Multi-volume grammars of the English language did appear, and some of these had an historical dimension. Thus Otto Jespersen produced his seven-volume *Modern English Grammar on Historical Principles*, which was started in 1909 and finished after his death.[9] This illustrated how the language had developed, but its focal point was the usage of modern standard English. Dialects were not a source for comparison, though Old and Middle English forms and usage were invoked. Nevertheless, language was and remains an interesting subject of occasional enquiry among many people, though this interest is largely focused on words, their etymology and meaning. People continue to write to newspapers to enquire about the origin of words or to find out what is the correct usage of a particular item in grammar, and for their part newspapers respond by including small items on language and its use.[10] It is widely accepted that there is a correct way of writing and speaking, and books offering guidance on how to speak and write remain very popular. For many, these books are especially associated with Fowler,[11] whose dictionary of usage was frequently reprinted and has many imitators.[12]

A final reason for the absence of multi-volume histories of the language in the early twentieth century was the dominant position of phonology in the nineteenth century and its role in establishing the theoretical background to language study. Starting from the discovery at the end of the eighteenth century by Sir William Jones that Sanskrit was related to Latin and Greek, nineteenth-century scholars gradually built up a picture of the development of the Indo-European languages from what is now usually known as Proto-Indo-European, and their relationship.[13] The basis of this relationship was the study of sound changes which were characteristic of branches of the languages. Thus Jakob Grimm was able to show the relationship between the classical and the Germanic languages and the distinc-

[9] Otto Jespersen, *A Modern English Grammar on Historical Principles*, 7 vols. (Copenhagen: Munksgaard, 1909–49).

[10] Philip Howard, *A Word in Time* (London: Sinclair–Stevenson, 1990).

[11] H.W. Fowler, *A Dictionary of Modern English Usage* (Oxford: Clarendon Press, 1926).

[12] For example, Sidney Greenbaum and Janet Whitcut, *Guide to English Usage* (Harlow: Longman, 1988).

[13] Holger Pedersen, *The Discovery of Language: Linguistic Science in the Nineteenth Century*, trans. John W. Spargo (Cambridge, MA: Harvard University Press, 1959).

tions within the Germanic languages in what has since become known as Grimm's Law. This was later refined by Karl Verner in what is now known as Verner's Law. The precise details of these laws are not relevant here. What is significant is that they were based on changes in the sounds of the various languages and that they were known as "laws." This promoted the view, which came to be known as the Neo-Grammarian position, that changes in a language are universal and consistent: that is, all speakers of that language adopt the changes enshrined in a law such as Grimm's Law. Not to have done so would imply that some speakers of the language were not really German if they failed to observe the sound changes which were characteristic of the German language. A law does not admit exceptions and it was possible to accept this for languages because languages were usually studied through written texts that had gone through a process of standardisation or, if they were older varieties, were often edited in a standard spelling and punctuation. The classical languages were usually edited in a standardised spelling, and even today editions of older English authors such as Shakespeare are frequently edited with modern spelling and punctuation. And it was the language of literary authors that was mostly studied and used as evidence, partly because their texts were more readily available and partly because they had written texts which were still worth reading as part of the highest form of expression in a given language.

It follows from this that there was little or no discussion of what was meant by "English" or "German" or "Latin" other than that each exhibited certain phonological developments which created that language. It was accepted that the standardised version of each language was the language, and "substandard" varieties of a given language were simply ignored as not being the proper language. Other features of language such as syntax were given little attention, because the study of syntax is more complicated, for, whereas there are a finite number of sounds in any language, this is not true of syntax. Even vocabulary was not invoked for the establishment of any historical laws, though it could be used to determine when the different branches of Indo-European separated, usually indicated by different words for the same common concepts, and which languages had contributed loanwords to a given language. Nevertheless, some attention was paid to non-standard varieties, and Wyld even wrote a history of colloquial English.[14] But this history dealt with colloquial Modern English as a separate subject which had little bearing on or reference to the development of standard English.

---

[14] H.C. Wyld, *A History of Modern Colloquial English* (1920; Oxford: Blackwell, 3rd ed. 1936).

The Neo-Grammarian approach to the historical study of language was for many identified with philology, and that was certainly the dominant tradition within English departments. One-volume histories of the English language which were produced in the early twentieth century were basically philological, though they also gave space to the historical and social background. Their emphasis was on the development of sounds as interpreted through written sources and vocabulary within a discursive framework which embraced attitudes to language. A good example of this type of history is that by A.C. Baugh,[15] which, with revision, is still used in classrooms today. Two developments, which are both opposed and complementary to each other, began to undermine this approach to the history of English. The first was the development of linguistics, whose origin is associated with Ferdinand de Saussure and the book reconstructed from his lectures after his death by some of his pupils as *Cours de linguistique générale*.[16] This book undermined the preeminent position which the written language had had and retained until well into the twentieth century and emphasised the importance of the spoken language and its primacy in communication. It also looked at language from a theoretical point of view, so that language was no longer a collection of isolated facts but a method of communication which could be studied by understanding of certain general principles. The influence of this book took some time to percolate through to the study of the history of the English language; an English translation did not appear until 1959. In part this was because the teaching of historical English was part of the study of Old and Middle English and was subsumed under English degree courses which were largely literary in their orientation. The study of Modern English language was hardly, if ever, a part of such degrees. Hence the influence of Saussure was principally felt in those institutions where the study of Modern English language was a significant element, and it often led to the separation of the teaching of language and literature, with the former increasingly being studied in newly created departments of linguistics. In such departments, English was merely one of the languages studied; it was simply one of the forms communication could take. This development tended at first to relegate historical linguistics to a less important position in academia, because it could not be studied from a living language, since its sources were inevitably written. Attention was centred on modern living languages, especially those which had hardly been studied before, such as American Indian languages and other so-called "primitive" languages.

---

[15] Albert C. Baugh, *A History of the English Language* (New York: Appleton–Century, 1935).

[16] Ferdinand de Saussure, *Cours de linguistique générale* (Lausanne: Payot, 1916).

The second development was the increased attention given to the whole matter of standard, or perhaps standardised, forms of English. In the 1930s, C.L. Wrenn delivered a paper on "Standard" Old English[17] to the Philological Society. This was a novel concept to many philologists, who had been brought up on the idea that Standard English was the culmination of a long development in the language and as such existed only in the post-medieval period. Even for Wrenn, this may have been a daring suggestion, as the inverted commas around "Standard" suggest. He saw Standard Old English as based on that variety known as West Saxon, which had been standardised under King Alfred and re-emerged in the tenth century in a slightly different form and was especially linked with the Benedictine monastery at Winchester. This suggestion was followed up by Helmut Gneuss in his article "The Origin of Standard Old English,"[18] but by the time Gneuss wrote there was no longer any need to put inverted commas around Standard, for the concept was well established by then. The significance of this idea of a standard Old English was that West Saxon, whether in its Alfredian or in its Winchester form, was not that form of Old English which was the ancestor of the modern standard. Hence a standard was seen as no more than a dialect which was thrown into prominence through political circumstances, and because of this a standard could revert to being merely another dialect when political conditions changed. This was the fate of the West Saxon dialect in Old English, which ceased to be a standard as political power moved further to the east. The standard was no longer the culmination of a natural development like evolution, by which the best form of the language became predominant. Later studies began to chart the development of other regularised varieties of English. Michael Samuels[19] showed that there were four standardised varieties of English in and around London at the end of the Middle English period. One of those varieties, now usually known as Chancery English, formed the basis for the spelling system of the future standard.[20] However, this development was partly arbitrary and partly the result of the role of the Chancery in issuing public documents that were sent throughout the kingdom. It was only later that the development of dictionaries and grammars in the seventeenth and eighteenth centuries helped to establish what were the

---

[17] C.L. Wrenn, " 'Standard' Old English," *Transactions of the Philological Society* (1933): 65–88.

[18] Gneuss, "The Origin of Standard Old English," *Anglo-Saxon England* 1 (1972): 63–83.

[19] M.L. Samuels, "Some Applications of Middle English Dialectology," *English Studies* 44 (1963): 81–94.

[20] John H. Fisher, "Chancery and the Emergence of Standard Written English in the Fifteenth Century," *Speculum* 52 (1977): 870–99, and *The Emergence of Standard English* (Lexington: University of Kentucky Press, 1996).

proper words and grammatical systems for the standard. Increasingly it was realised that the standard had no inherent advantage over other forms of the language as a tool of communication and that its position was the result of political and educational support. This enabled serious attention to be devoted to other forms of the language, which were less and less considered to be corrupt varieties. The culmination of this trend exhibited two complementary outcomes: some single-volume histories of the language took the growth and history of the standard language or languages in England as their point of reference without taking account of other varieties of the language,[21] and other histories concentrated on the growth of other varieties of the language, either dialects in England or varieties of English outside England, without feeling constrained to take standard British English as their point of reference. Studies of how other varieties have developed, such as Scots,[22] became more frequent.

The development of linguistics as a scholarly subject has exercised different influences on the study of the history of the language. Its most important benefit has been the introduction of theory into the study of language change. It was no longer possible to consider the history of a language as a list of apparently arbitrary and haphazard changes. Linguistics studied how languages changed, and produced theoretical explanations for such changes, which in turn led scholars to look for the data to illustrate these theoretical positions in the language they were studying. But linguistics also spawned a whole host of different theoretical approaches to the study of living languages, transformational grammar and functional grammar being two of the most widespread. Although these were in the main developed for the study of contemporary speech, it was inevitable that they would gradually be applied to the study of historical change, either theoretically or to a given language, and books based on one theory or another appeared. For the most part, when books of this nature were applied to a comprehensive history of the English language, they did not have much impact or remain standard textbooks for courses. In many cases this may have been because the wider readership of books on the history of English were not sufficiently familiar with the theory behind the books, and many felt that the authors were more interested in justifying the theory than in illuminating the history of the language. Unlike the *Cambridge History of the English Language*, most histories of the English language continue to be single-volume works that appeal to a general and educational read-

[21] N.F. Blake, *A History of the English Language* (Basingstoke: Macmillan, 1996).

[22] Amy J. Devitt, *Standardizing Written English: Diffusion in the Case of Scotland 1520–1659* (Cambridge: Cambridge University Press, 1989).

ership. Theoretical approaches tended to have greater influence when a particular theory was employed to explain a significant feature of the language's history, such as the development of modal verbs[23] or the origins of the Great Vowel Shift in English.[24] Applications of new theoretical approaches did put the study of English language within a more theoretical framework and increasingly saw the history of English against this theoretical background and in comparison with the development of other languages.[25] Historical linguistics became a topic in its own right within linguistics, and it sought to show how languages change. Books detailing what changes in languages were likely and how they were motivated appeared.[26] This allowed historians of the English language to think of changes in English as either external or internal. Whereas previously it was often implied or even stated that changes in language were largely due to migration, conquest or immigration which had arisen from political or external factors, it was increasingly accepted that many changes in the history of a language arise within a language itself and with no external input.

The various linguistic theories that have been promoted within modern linguistics have never individually commanded universal assent. Different schools have arisen and each has tried to convince others of the benefits of their own theory. Another problem with them has been that they have been developed to explain modern language use, and it is always possible to decide through empirical observation what the modern language allows. If a claim is made that a particular usage or pronunciation is not acceptable in Modern English, it is perfectly possible to test that claim by trying to find examples of it among the speakers of the language. This is not possible for the study of earlier periods of the language where the evidence is fragmentary and often survives in only specialised varieties, usually literary or administrative. Access to records of the spoken language of a previous period is restricted. Nevertheless, change in a modern language serves as a guide to how change operates in language generally, and this can influence the way scholars see change in earlier periods of the language. Since many of the

---

23 David W. Lightfoot, *Principles of Diachronic Syntax* (Cambridge Studies in Linguistics 23; Cambridge: Cambridge University Press, 1979).

24 J.J. Smith, "Dialectal Variation in Middle English and the Actuation of the Great Vowel Shift," *Neuphilologische Mitteilungen* 94 (1993): 259–77.

25 M.L. Samuels, *Linguistic Evolution with Special Reference to English* (Cambridge Studies in Linguistics 5; Cambridge: Cambridge University Press, 1972); William Labov, *Principles of Linguistic Change*, vol. 1: *Internal Factors* (Language in Society 20; Oxford and Cambridge, MA: Blackwell, 1994).

26 H.H. Hock, *Principles of Historical Linguistics* (Trends in Linguistics 34; Berlin: Mouton de Gruyter, 1986).

theoretical approaches are grammar-based, it was natural that both transformational and functional grammar have been applied to the history of English syntax.[27] Although both have aided in a greater understanding of the development of various features of English syntax, neither has become the major approach. Greater theoretical advances have been made in phonology, probably because the number of variables is so restricted. Phonetics was able to map the complete inventory of the sounds that can be made in human languages and, equally importantly for historical language study, to show which changes are possible and which are improbable for a human speaker, so that changes proposed for English could be measured against this theoretical background. A number of more exotic theories within phonology have been proposed, but they have not been incorporated into mainstream histories; the reason for this has been essentially the demands of publishers, who wish to sell their books to as wide a market as possible, for this maximises their returns. The knowledge of most theoretical approaches and their implications for the history of English is limited to a small band of scholars. Most readers of histories of English are not familiar with these theories and not generally concerned with their application to English. Hence histories of the language increasingly indicate that their work is informed by advances in historical linguistics, but assure their readers that theoretical linguistics has been kept to an absolute minimum. The learned journals may devote many pages to the discussion of some disputed point in the phonological development of English, such as open-syllable lengthening in Middle English, and how this phenomenon can best be explained, but in most general histories this type of change is more often simply described than explained theoretically. Even the general acceptance of the principle that a change once made in a language cannot be reversed is hardly likely to be mentioned, any more than the apparent exceptions to this principle, such as the merger of the diphthongs /ay/ and /oy/ in the late-seventeenth and eighteenth centuries in English (line~loin, vice~voice), which was reversed in the nineteenth century.

Antiquarian interest in other varieties of English than the standard had been manifest since the sixteenth century, though this largely consisted in collections of vocabulary items which were different from the lexis of the standard variety. The language of vagabonds was of particular interest in the late-sixteenth and early-seventeenth centuries, though interest in rustic dialects became much more pre-

[27] Elizabeth C. Traugott, *A History of English Syntax: A Transformational Approach to the History of English Sentence Structure* (New York: Holt, Rinehart & Winston, 1972).

dominant in the eighteenth century.[28] At first this interest was somewhat condescending, though with the interest in nature and rural life associated with the Romantic Revival, it became tinged with a hint of regret for the passing of a more innocent life-style. During the nineteenth century, developments in the understanding of phonetics and the ability to record speech on paper more precisely led to the more accurate recording of dialect speech.[29] The spoken language of those unfamiliar with standard English had been represented in literature and other writings for many centuries,[30] but usually in a stereotypical way and normally for purposes of poking fun at such speakers. Their language was thought to represent lack of education, hence of intelligence. Now the speech of such speakers could be given proper attention in a scholarly way.

The twentieth century saw many new technological inventions, two of which came to have considerable relevance for the study of the English language: tape recorders and computers. Although machines to record sound were first produced in the nineteenth century, it took many years to fashion instruments which were sufficiently portable that they could be taken around by fieldworkers. It is hardly surprising that, when this possibility arose, it was first used to record the speech of rural speakers in a comprehensive survey. *The Survey of English Dialects* built on the work of Ellis and others in its attempt to record the language of elderly rustic speakers in all corners of the country. The survey attempted to record both the vocabulary and the pronunciation of speakers who lived in areas where it was thought the language had been least influenced by the standard. The reason for this approach was that it was assumed that all rural varieties of speech were gradually disappearing under the advance of education, radio and television, and population migration from the countryside to the towns. The results were published in book form,[31] although these results were later used for analysing the geographical distribution of lexical items and sounds in the form of word maps[32] as well tracing some syntactic[33] and grammatical forms.[34] The widespread assump-

[28] Maurizio Gotti, *The Language of Thieves and Vagabonds: 17th and 18th Century Canting Lexicography in England* (Lexicographica Series Maior 94; Tübingen: Max Niemeyer, 1999).

[29] Alexander J. Ellis, *On Early English Pronunciation, with Especial Reference to Shakespeare and Chaucer*, 6 vols. (London and Berlin: Asher & Co for Philological Society, 1869–89).

[30] N.F. Blake, *Non-Standard Language in English Literature* (The Language Library; London: André Deutsch, 1981).

[31] Harold Orton and Eugen Dieth, *Survey of English Dialects*, 4 vols. [13 parts] (Leeds: E.J. Arnold for the University of Leeds, 1962–71).

[32] Clive Upton, Stewart Sanderson and J.D.A. Widdowson, *Word Maps: A Dialect Atlas of England* (London: Croom Helm, 1987).

[33] John M. Kirk, Stewart Sanderson and J.D.A. Widdowson, ed. *Studies in Linguistic Geography: The Dialects of English in Britain and Ireland* (London: Croom Helm, 1985).

tion that these forms had to be recorded before they disappeared was only partly true, though the whole ethos behind the survey was to trace the gradual disappearance of these varieties of the language before they were lost for ever, as though these varieties represented the diverse nature of the language which was soon to become more or less uniform among all speakers. But the significant feature of this survey was that it and other dialect surveys in Europe and the USA were the first major collections of different varieties of a language based on fieldwork. They inspired other corpora of linguistic items.

The second half of the twentieth century saw the growth of fieldwork among different speakers and the creation of numerous corpora, of both written and spoken language. At the spoken level, the fieldwork concentrated on what in the past might have been considered non-standard or regional varieties, especially those used by speakers in towns rather than those in the country. Much of this work was published as studies rather than as corpora. Among some of the more familiar studies are those by Labov on Black English[35] and by Trudgill on the language of Norwich.[36] The fieldwork using tape recorders meant that the speech of those being studied could be recorded directly without the researcher having to ask the informant how he or she pronounced a word or which words were familiar to them, since we all like to pretend that our language is "better" than it is. With tape recorders, the data could be stored and new research at a later date could see whether and in what ways the variety had changed over a period of time. This type of fieldwork and the collection of data that was produced also encouraged other forms of collection. Corpora of both written and spoken varieties were amassed. At first these were of Modern English varieties, but they relied on a diversity of sources. They were by no means restricted to what one might describe as literary or correct English; every type of language could be investigated. Some corpora, such as the Survey of English Usage based at University College London, were intended as data for the production of grammars of Modern English, which were to be based on real language rather than the presumption of what was correct based on the norms of Latin grammar.[37] Their data included newspapers of all types as well as different genres of writing and speech. Indeed, it could be

---

[34] Clive Upton, David Parry and J.D.A. Widdowson, *Survey of English Dialects: The Dictionary and Grammar* (London and New York: Routledge, 1994).

[35] William Labov, *Language in the Inner City: Studies in the Black English Vernacular* (Philadelphia: University of Pennsylvania Press, 1972).

[36] Peter Trudgill, *The Social Differentiation of English in Norwich* (Cambridge Studies in Linguistics 13; Cambridge: Cambridge University Press, 1974).

[37] Randolph Quirk et al., *A Grammar of Contemporary English* (London: Longman, 1972).

said that many of these corpora turned their back on the standard language, which had dominated the whole study of language for so long. A new corpus, the Cambridge and Nottingham Corpus of Discourse in English or CANCODE, has been compiled at Nottingham under Ron Carter, and it is specifically devoted to spoken language so that the research team can in due course produce a grammar of spoken British English. However, this may mean introducing a completely new approach and theory of grammar, since there are so many features which cannot be described using those grammatical categories associated with more traditional grammars. When this grammar is complete, its approach and categories may have significant implications for the study of historical grammar, for there are many features of historical English which cannot easily be shovelled into traditional categories.

The compiling of corpora and wide-ranging collections of data spread to historical language study. Angus McIntosh instituted a collection of Late Middle English texts, which could be localised on non-linguistic grounds, to construct a linguistic atlas of Late Middle English.[38] This work used spelling forms of individual scribes in key words to produce an inventory of spelling systems which could be localised within quite narrow boundaries. Such spellings could often be used to indicate the sounds behind them. When the pattern for the country as a whole was established, other texts which could not be localised on external grounds could be matched against the criteria of the atlas to determine where they had been written. Using these tools, it was possible to start compiling a record of different sounds, lexical items and grammar in different parts of the country. A Helsinki research group under Matti Rissanen started to compile a computer collection of texts in English from the beginning of the language to the seventeenth century, which were already edited and published.[39] This collection contains excerpts of texts chosen to illustrate various genres and to cover as wide a range of dates as possible. With various search tools, this allows the study of syntax and other aspects of language to be carried out on a more coherent basis. The Helsinki Corpus has encouraged the formation of other corpora, both in Helsinki and other parts of the world. It is computers that now allow the scholar to access and manipulate large amounts of data very quickly and conveniently so that certain syntactic topics, which had hitherto been studied using a restricted database and some

[38] Angus McIntosh et al., *A Linguistic Atlas of Late Medieval English*, 4 vols. (Aberdeen: Aberdeen University Press, 1986).

[39] Merja Kytö, *Manual to the Diachronic Part of the Helsinki Corpus of English Texts: Coding Conventions and Lists of Source Texts* (Helsinki: Department of English, University of Helsinki, 3rd ed. 1996).

guesswork, can be researched more scientifically. It may be assumed that corpora for all periods of English, both in England and abroad, will be compiled to make historical developments more easily traceable.

Of the various branches of linguistics, the one that has been most significant after phonetics is probably sociolinguistics, which aims to study language in relation to social factors like class, environment, situation and the interaction of speakers who can use more than one language. The studies by Trudgill[40] mentioned earlier, and by Labov of New York speech,[41] are sociolinguistic, for they studied a range of speakers of different social backgrounds within a given geographical area. An important finding of such studies is that no one uses only a single form of their language. We all adapt our speech to the situation in which we find ourselves. One may use a slower and more careful pronunciation and a more considered choice of words if one is giving a lecture or sermon; when speaking within one's family, one will use a more informal choice of vocabulary and grammatical structures; and when in the pub with one's peers one may well choose a highly colloquial register including slang and swear words. It is not only vocabulary that changes, but also sounds and grammatical structures. This adaptation of language to the environment in which it is used is now known as code-switching, and not to know the appropriate code for a given environment may lead a speaker to be ridiculed or even ostracised. The same must have happened at all stages of the language. It is well known that in Shakespeare the personal pronouns 'he' and 'them' can appear as 'a' and 'em/'em' respectively, and these forms are used by both low- and high-class characters. The form 'a' represents the fall of initial /h/ and the survival of a different vowel, the form 'em/'em' represents the older dative plural form 'hem/heom' with loss of initial /h/. We today are often surprised that someone like the Princess of France in *Love's Labour's Lost* uses these forms as readily as some of the low-born characters, but the existence of code-switching makes this variation in her usage perfectly understandable.

The implication of much of what sociolinguistics has told us is that there is no such thing as a uniform and consistent form of the language used by the speakers of that language on all occasions. The idea that there was a standard language which was used by educated speakers in all social environments is simply not true. This discovery naturally placed the whole matter of the development of the

---

40 Trudgill, *Social Differentiation.*

41 William Labov, *The Social Stratification of Language in New York City* (Washington, DC: Center for Applied Linguistics, 1966).

language and the reasons for change in it within a different framework. Some scholars produced single-volume histories of the language which were based on the findings of sociolinguistics.[42] In the past it was often thought that change may have originated at a colloquial level of the language, but how this happened was difficult to explain, given the stranglehold of the standard as the norm of linguistic utterance. Sociolinguistics made an explanation for a socially upward movement of linguistic features comprehensible. But it is not simply change showing the acceptance of more colloquial usage into the mainstream that can happen. The reverse tendency is also apparent. Speakers often wish to distinguish themselves from others, whose accent or general usage they regard as vulgar. It is well known that in earlier drama upper-class speakers often use what those in other classes regard as an affected pronunciation of their vowels; Alexander Gil[43] in the early-seventeenth century referred to such affected speakers as the *Mopsae*. Restoration drama, for example, is full of upper-class characters who use forms like 'Gad' instead of 'God.' It is important for people to have their own social code, including both pronunciation and form of words, which enables them to freeze out those who are not familiar with that code. The concepts "U" and "non-U" were very popular in the 1950s and 1960s.[44] It has been suggested that some changes in the history of English were motivated by this desire to keep one's language different from that of others. The Great Vowel Shift may be an example of this tendency. As a knowledge of French ceased to be available as a distinguishing factor between educated and less educated speakers, because knowledge of French had ceased to be a social distinction, those who wanted to maintain a linguistic as well as a social distance between themselves and others like the immigrants into London from the provinces may have changed their pronunciation of certain vowels. Educated London speakers raised the height at which they pronounced certain vowels to produce those changes which we now know as the Great Vowel Shift so as to maintain this status difference between themselves and those they considered socially inferior.[45]

All of these factors changed the approach to and study of the history of the English language during the second half of the twentieth century. It was, there-

---

[42] Dick Leith, *A Social History of English* (Language and Society Series; London: Routledge & Kegan Paul, 1983).

[43] Bror Danielsson and Arvid Gabrielsson, ed. *Alexander Gill's Logonomia Anglica, 1619*, 2 vols. (Stockholm Studies in English 26 & 27; Stockholm: Almquist & Wiksell, 1972).

[44] A.S.C. Ross, *Noblesse Oblige: An Enquiry into the Identifiable Characteristics of the English Aristocracy* (London: Hamish Hamilton, 1956).

[45] Smith 259–77.

fore, not unnatural that towards the end of that century scholars began to think the time had come to prepare a major history of the English language taking all these new developments into account. Hence, the first multi-volume history of the language started to appear in 1992 and was able to build on the discoveries and new approaches that had arisen over the previous half century or so.

Variation, Change and New Evidence in the Study of the History of English

MATTI RISSANEN

AT THE BEGINNING OF THE NEW MILLENNIUM the future of research on the history of English seems promising and inspiring. This is to a considerable extent due to the variationist approach to the analysis and interpretation of language, which defines language as a dynamic entity consisting of variant fields: i.e. alternative ways of "saying the same thing." Linguistic development is inseparably connected with variation; it is the result of the changing shape and tensions within variant fields, be they phonological, morphological, syntactic or lexical. This dynamism and movement is caused both by language-internal processes of change and language-external factors, the most important of which can be grouped under the following headings:

1. Sociolinguistic variation: i.e. the influence of social change and mobility on the development of language, including participant relationship and level of formality.
2. Textual variation: i.e. the interrelation between the genre or topic of a text and linguistic expression, including discourse situation and medium.
3. Regional variation: i.e. the differentiation and amalgamation of dialects and other regional varieties, including contact phenomena.

The competition between variant forms in the course of time naturally results in the loss of forms and creation of new ones. Equally often, however, it results in the reshaping of the variant field in regard to the relative frequency of the competing forms.[1]

[1] An early formalisation of the variationist approach in the 1960s was Uriel Weinreich, William Labov and Marvin Herzog, "Empirical Foundations for a Theory of Language Change," *Directions for Historical Linguistics*, ed. W.P. Lehmann and Yakov Malkiel (Austin: University of Texas Press, 1968) 95–189. See also M.A.K. Halliday, "Language in a Social Perspective," *Explorations in the Functions of Language* (London: Edward Arnold, 1972) 48–71; Suzanne Romaine, *Socio-Historical Linguistics: Its Status and Methodology* (Cambridge: Cambridge University Press, 1982).

The variationist approach has been given more depth and significance by recent developments in linguistic analysis, particularly in the fields of sociolinguistics, pragmatics, text linguistics and discourse analysis. Furthermore, a more profound understanding of such morphosyntactic and semantic processes as grammaticalisation and shifts in prototypical meaning(s) has improved our capacity to analyse and explain the paths of change.

As is the case with so many scholarly innovations, the study of change through variation is solidly based on earlier research in dialectology, philology, stylistics, history and sociology. The last decades of the twentieth century, however, introduced new ways of formalising the earlier approaches to communication-based linguistic analysis and thus offered a welcome counterweight to the highly abstract theoretical models of analysis and description prevailing in the late 1950s and in the 1960s, models which emphasised the autonomous character of linguistics and paid little attention to the function of language as a means of communication between people.

The variationist approach has obvious advantages in opening up new paths for linguistic research in the new millennium. First of all, it combines the past development of language with its present-day variability and, by emphasising the dynamic character of language, even allows cautious predictions of future developments. It would be impossible to explain adequately the differences between the various regional varieties of English (British, American, Indian, Australian, African, etc.), except from a diachronic starting point which pays due attention to cultural and social factors, contact phenomena, etc. An awareness of the changing character of language is also essential for the study of present-day registers, genre-specific styles, spoken and written mediums and standard and non-standard expressions. Overlooking the possibilities offered by the diachronic perspective for the analysis of present-day language can be compared to an attempt to describe the essence of the sea by observing only its surface.

Another advantage of the variationist approach is its focus on both literary and non-literary texts. Text-type or genre-based studies of language provide a natural link between linguistic and literary analysis. Nuances of literary styles and themes can be productively approached through semantic and syntactic variation. This link is, of course, particularly relevant for the analysis of earlier literature but can be applied to present-day literature as well. One of the central topics in literary analysis is still the play with multiple meanings; this is closely related to cognitive semantics, with its particular focus on the metaphor as a core concept in change of meaning.

As mentioned above, the variationist model meant a new opening for linguistic analysis after a period of heavy emphasis on abstract theoretical methods of description. This does not mean, however, that these two models should be mutually exclusive or hostile to each other. On the contrary, variationist scholars should be well aware of the fact that their micro-level, often highly detailed analyses of variant fields gain enormously in importance when combined with a more generalised and more abstract theoretical framework of change, with due reference made to the interrelation and co-occurrence of changes and to the overall typological development of language. Conversely, theoretical descriptions and discussions are valuable only if, where possible, their validity and correctness are carefully tested against existing linguistic evidence. Thus, for the first time in years, it seems that linguists using different analytic models find each other's methods and results useful and productive, although, quite naturally, a great diversity of bias and focus of interest still exists among research centres and between individual scholars. Topics in which various methodologies in historical linguistics support each other include grammaticalisation, word-order typology, changes in the system of inflectional endings and derivative affixes, semantic developments in terms of prototypical and peripheral meanings, phonological change as reflected by spelling, and so on.[2]

Textual evidence plays a major role in the study of variation, either present or past. The restrictions of relying only on one's intuition or introspection[3] even in the study of present-day variation – sociolinguistic, regional or generic – are very noticeable; in historical linguistics, the application of introspection or "native speaker competence" is, of course, impossible.

Thus it is not surprising that the end of the millennium also meant a break-through in new methods for storing, sorting and analysing vast amounts of linguistic evidence in the form of computerised corpora ranging from fairly small but carefully structured ones to huge but less systematically collected databanks.[4]

2 It would be a hopeless task to try to list even the most central works successfully combining theory with textual evidence in diachronic research into English. Reference may be made to the volumes of the *Cambridge History of the English Language* and to such recent studies as those of Douglas Biber, David Denison, Olga Fischer, Ans van Kemenade, Terttu Nevalainen, Jeremy Smith and Elizabeth Closs Traugott. See also Dieter Kastovsky's paper in this volume.

3 For so-called armchair linguistics, see Charles J. Fillmore, " ' Corpus Linguistics' or 'Computer-Aided Armchair Linguistics'," *Directions in Corpus Linguistics: Proceedings of Nobel Symposium 82, Stockholm, 4–8 August 1991*, ed. Jan Svartvik (Berlin and New York: Mouton de Gruyter, 1992) 35–60.

4 See, for example, Stig Johansson, "Mens Sana in Corpore Sano: On the Role of Corpora in Linguistic Research," *The European English Messenger* 4 (1995): 19–25; Matti Rissanen, "The World of English Historical Corpora: From Cædmon to the Computer Age," *Journal of English Linguistics* 28 (2000): 7–20.

Both written and spoken English can be found in these electronic resources. The ICE (*International Corpus of English*) project has expanded and will expand the coverage of corpora from British and American English to other regional varieties. The written standard of the 1960s (the *Brown* and *Lancaster–Oslo/Bergen* corpora) can be compared with that of the 1990s (the *FROWN* and *FLOB* corpora, compiled at the University of Freiburg). The *British National Corpus* provides access to one hundred million words of late-twentieth-century English.

The compilation of present-day English corpora is facilitated by the constant flow of electronically produced text material from printing houses and other sources. In the study of the history of English, the situation is completely different. Extant written texts, in manuscript or printed form, are practically the only source of evidence for earlier periods of the language, which is precisely why computerised corpora have revolutionised the methodology of historical linguistics. Although historical corpora are much more laborious to compile and although their total coverage is small compared to present-day English corpora, they have opened up quite new vistas for language historians, both for those concentrating on a particular period of English and those interested in long-term diachrony. Surveys of evidence that used to demand months or years of patient plodding through texts can now be completed in a few days. Even more importantly, the results are much more easily verifiable or falsifiable than before, and new corpus material generates observations on details and developments which improve the hazy and chaotic but nevertheless fascinating story of the English language.

The first structured historical corpus of English covering a long time-span was the *Helsinki Corpus of English Texts*, which has been available to scholars all over the world since the early 1990s. Despite its relatively small size (c.1.7 million words), it gives a surprisingly reliable picture of morphological, syntactic and lexical development of high-frequency forms in the earlier periods of English up to the beginning of the eighteenth century. The *ARCHER Corpus*,[5] approximately the same size as the *Helsinki Corpus*, covers the period from the seventeenth to the second half of the twentieth century, thus forming a bridge between the *Helsinki Corpus* and present-day corpora. This backbone formed by the two long-diachrony corpora is strengthened by a number of others, more

[5] This corpus is available in a few research centres in Europe and the USA. Unfortunately, for copyright reasons its public distribution is not possible.

The electronic version of the *Oxford English Dictionary* also offers masses of useful information on the entire history of English, although in a differently structured form than the *Helsinki* and *ARCHER* corpora.

focused in regard to time or genre. Practically all Old English texts can be found in the *Dictionary of Old English Corpus*; the *Middle English Compendium* consists of a large number of Middle English texts and all the material of the *Middle English Dictionary*. These corpora are supplemented by the *Innsbruck Computer Archive of Middle English Texts*, and an extensive project concentrates on Chaucer manuscripts.

Moving to Modern English, it is possible to consult a corpus of private letters from the fifteenth to the end of the seventeenth century, a corpus of sixteenth- and seventeenth-century argumentative prose, and corpora of early forms of Scots and Irish English. Corpora in preparation include medical language from Late Middle to Modern English, newspaper language from the seventeenth century onwards and early modern speech-based prose (e.g., drama, fictitious dialogue and records of examinations in court trials).[6] Commercially produced corpora cover a very large number of writings, from Old English onwards.[7]

The usefulness of many of these corpora has been and will be greatly enhanced by a coding system which enables the scholar to search for evidence not only on the basis of words or phrases but also by word class or syntactic category. Another recent development which has greatly contributed to corpus-based research is the possibility of accessing corpora through the Internet. In addition to some of the corpora mentioned above, many literary texts can be found on the Internet either for free or for a moderate licence payment.

Thus, at the beginning of the third millennium historical linguists can base their research on the concept of a varying language, understood as a dynamic process rather than a static lump. They can concentrate on changes relating to both language-internal tendencies and language-external factors, combine detailed observation and analysis of individual linguistic features with generalising theoretical considerations and thus aim at an integrated overall view of the English language, its development and present-day variability. The scholar's work has been enhanced by the explosive growth in the amount of evidence provided by

---

[6] *Corpus of Early English Correspondence* (Helsinki, Terttu Nevalainen and Helena Raumolin–Brunberg); *Lampeter Corpus of Early Modern English Tracts* (Chemnitz/Zwickau, Josef Schmied); *Helsinki Corpus of Older Scots* (Anneli Meurman–Solin); *Edinburgh Corpus of Older Scots* (Keith Williamson); *Corpus of Irish English* (Essen, Raymond Hickey). In preparation: *Corpus of Early English Medical Writing* (Helsinki, Irma Taavitsainen and Päivi Pahta); *Zurich English Newspaper Corpus* (Udo Fries); *A Corpus of English Dialogues* (Lancaster and Uppsala, Jonathan Culpeper and Merja Kytö); *Early American English Corpus* (Uppsala, Merja Kytö). For information on other corpora, completed or in preparation, see the articles mentioned in fn. 4 above.

[7] Particularly those produced by Chadwyck–Healey.

computerised corpora. The time of worn-out examples copied from earlier studies, historical grammars and dictionaries is over.

It must be emphasised, however, that the ease of assembling evidence should not tempt scholars and students of the history of English to overlook the importance of a profound, "near-native-speaker" knowledge of the earlier stages of the language, from Old English onwards. The corpora enable the scholar to direct his energy and creativeness to analyses, syntheses and new visions of language development, but if these are not based on a solid mastery of the language form studied, the results are bound to be of little value.

It is important to keep this in mind in planning syllabuses and course programmes in English departments. But even here the computer may turn out to be a great help. Easy computer-supported access to evidence increases the students' interest in and enthusiasm for the older forms of English. This enthusiasm is further enhanced by the possibility of compiling useful and well-motivated seminar papers and master's theses on topics that would previously have been impossible because of the sheer difficulty of finding sufficient evidence in a reasonable time.

It is no wonder that, at the turn of the millennium, the promising new openings outlined above have given impetus and coherence to the work of research groups and individual scholars. One of the groups inspired by the principles of the variationist approach is the Research Unit for Variation and Change in English at the English Department of the University of Helsinki.

This Research Unit started as a group of young and senior scholars of English at Helsinki in the mid-1980s. Their intention was to create a diachronic corpus which would cover the first thousand years of the English language, the most important centuries from the point of view of its typological development. The *Helsinki Corpus of English Texts* was followed by other projects concentrating on English historical linguistics and corpus building, carried out either by individual members of the group or by smaller teams, until, at the end of the century, the time was ripe for the restructuring of the group and its teams into a research unit. The Unit is divided into five teams working in the fields of historical sociolinguistics, dialectology and regional variation, text conventions and genre evolution, pragmatic variability, and internal processes of linguistic change. At present, the total number of scholars and postgraduate students is around fifty.

Each team on the Unit defines its goals and work methods individually, and all scholars from the most senior to postgraduate students have the freedom to work independently on their research topics; at the same time, they relate their work to the more general overall goals of the teams and the Unit. The ultimate goal will consist in an attempt to create an integrated model of linguistic variation, with special focus on change, a model which could at least to a certain extent be applied to other languages as well. The Unit also works actively in the field of corpus building and corpus-based research methodology and hopes to become an international clearing-house for English historical corpus studies.[8]

Let me end with a personal note on my debt of gratitude to IAUPE. My 25-year membership coincides fairly closely with my gradually developing awareness of the significance of variation in linguistic development. I have been allowed to talk about these ideas at IAUPE conferences, most extensively in Copenhagen in 1995, when, by the kind invitation of Arne Zettersten and Dieter Kastovsky, I both read a paper in the historical linguistics section and directed a workshop on historical corpus study. I am grateful to the IAUPE conferences for stimulating discussions with internationally renowned scholars, for learning about linguistic and literary topics far removed from my own field of specialisation, and for making life-long friends.

[8] The Unit was fortunate to be selected as one of the twenty-six National Centres of Excellence for six years from 2000 on.

Local and Global-Typological Changes in the History of English: Two Complementary Perspectives[1]

DIETER KASTOVSKY

I.1

THE STUDY OF THE HISTORY of the English language has been thoroughly transformed over the past hundred years, and, at the beginning of the new millennium, is undergoing a further transformation, thanks to the great advances in the creation and processing of huge electronic corpora (see Matti Rissanen's paper in this volume). At the beginning of the twentieth century, historical linguistics was dominated by the Neo-Grammarian paradigm, originating in the nineteenth century primarily in connection with the attempt to account for sound changes in terms of exceptionless sound laws. Each sound change was usually treated individually, except in instances such as the Germanic Sound Shift (Grimm's Law) or the Great Vowel Shift, where a set of sounds underwent parallel changes: i.e. in instances of chain shifts affecting whole systems. This basically atomistic approach was extended to other domains such as morphology, syntax and semantics, but the attempt to establish "laws" at these linguistic levels comparable to sound laws proved even more difficult than at the phonological level. Too many exceptions had to be explained, and analogy or dialect mixture, the two most frequent escape-hatches, were not really appealing to a generation which was on the lookout for mechanistic explanations of linguistic change, where the actual speakers of the language did not really play a role. It was this approach that provided us with excellent, detailed and comprehensive handbooks such as Brunner, Campbell, Luick[2] and others which are still widely in use, but

---

[1] Some of the material included in this paper was presented at a workshop on "Typological Aspects of the History of English" at the ESSE Conference in Helsinki, August 2000, and engendered a lively discussion, which will hopefully result in a collective volume on this topic.

[2] Karl Brunner, *Die englische Sprache: Ihre geschichtliche Entwicklung*, 2 vols. (1950; Tübingen: Max Niemeyer, 2nd ed. 1960–1962); Karl Brunner, *Altenglische Grammatik* (Tübingen: Max Niemeyer,

which, from today's point of view, are somewhat deficient. They are full of data, but there is no attempt at explaining what is actually going on; the various linguistic levels – phonology, morphology, syntax, semantics – are treated without relation to each other, and the social aspect is usually not addressed at all.

When, in the 1930s and 1940s, and especially after the Second World War, structuralism gradually became the dominant linguistic framework, this had little impact on historical linguistics, at least outside phonology, and certainly not on the writing of handbooks. The work of Twaddell, Moulton, Penzl[3] and other American structuralists (partly of European origin) was known to very few in Europe until the late 1960s, when it was already overshadowed by the generative paradigm. Thus I recall that in a class on Gothic at the German Department of the University of Tübingen in 1961, when I wanted to know whether the spellings <i> = [i] and <aí> = [e] (cf. *bindan* vs. *waírþan*) represented phonemes or allophones, since they seemed to occur in complementary distribution, I was told that phonemes and allophones only existed in English but not in Gothic. This does not mean, of course, that no individual studies on historical phonology and morphology were carried out in this framework. But their results never made it into the classical handbooks. Brunner, in the second edition of his *Die englische Sprache: Ihre geschichtliche Entwicklung*,[4] introduced slashes to indicate a phonemic notation, but this was a superficial cosmetic change without any thoroughgoing phonemic analysis. Research within the generative paradigm, which began to dominate linguistics in the 1960s both in the USA and in Europe, also did not really make it into large-scale descriptions of the history of English. This is not surprising, of course, since generativism had always been a theory-oriented enterprise, which was not really interested in a full-scale description of a particular language or an investigation of its history. There were attempts to implement transformational-generative grammar in introductions to the history of English;[5] however, they were nothing but a reformulation of some known facts using a new technical

3rd rev. ed. 1965); Alistair Campbell, *Old English Grammar* (Oxford: Clarendon Press, 1959); Karl Luick, *Historische Grammatik der englischen Sprache* (Stuttgart and Oxford: Tauchnitz and Oxford University Press, 1914–40, repr. 1964).

[3] Freeman W. Twaddell, "A Note on Old High German Umlaut," *Monatshefte für den deutschen Unterricht* 30 (1938): 177–81; William G. Moulton, "The Stops and Spirants in Early Germanic," *Language* 30 (1954): 1–42; Herbert Penzl, "The Phonemic Split of Germanic *k* in Old English," *Language* 23 (1947): 34–42, and "Umlaut and Secondary Umlaut in Old High German," *Language* 25 (1949): 223–40.

[4] Brunner, *Die englische Sprache* (see fn 2 above).

[5] John C. McLaughlin, *Aspects of the History of English* (New York: Holt, Rinehart & Winston, 1970).

framework, and did not really bring any new insights into the mechanisms of language change. Again, however, a lot of individual work has been, and is still being, carried out in this framework on specific problems, especially in syntax, but also in morphology and phonology, but there is as yet no attempt at integrating these investigations into a more comprehensive history of English. It is not surprising, therefore, that the respective chapters in the *Cambridge History of English*[6] are informed by generative insights, but not couched in a generative framework.

I.2

Another turning point, and one that has left a much more noticeable mark on the discipline, is the (re-)discovery of the speaker/listener as the key to historical changes in connection with the development of sociolinguistics in the late-1960s, especially in connection with the work of Labov and Weinreich. Sociolinguistics started out as a purely synchronic enterprise and was a reaction to Chomsky's notion of the "ideal native speaker," who would never make a mistake. Every deviation from this ideal was ascribed to performance, thus was of no interest to generativists, who were interested solely in competence. Unfortunately (or fortunately), ideal native speakers do not exist – otherwise language would not change, and consequently we are always confronted with a lot of variation – regional, social, stylistic – in every speech community. And it soon became clear that it is this variation which is the germ of linguistic change: one variant in the long run becomes dominant and ousts the other(s), the factors for its success having to do with social status, gender, prestige, and so on. This was also recognised by historical linguists,[7] but they did not yet have the tools to plot variation and variation-induced changes through social space in sufficient detail. In a synchronic investigation, one could ask informants and do quantitative studies using social status, gender, education, region and other factors as parameters. But in historical linguistics, all we have are texts, whose authors can no longer be questioned about these parameters. Thus it seemed that historical linguistics was barred from using quantitative methods based on extensive empirical data in the same way as synchronic sociolinguistic studies did. The only way out would be the collection of large corpora that could be investigated for certain variations over time, and that in turn could be measured for their frequency in correlation with sociolinguisti-

[6] Richard Hogg, ed. *Cambridge History of the English Language*, 5 vols. (Cambridge: Cambridge University Press, 1991–99).

[7] Suzanne Romaine, *Socio-Historical Linguistics: Its Status and Methodology* (Cambridge: Cambridge University Press, 1982).

cally relevant properties of the authors of the texts in question as well as genres and text types. In order to do this, one needed a technical tool to handle a large amount of data, and this became available in the form of the personal computer in the 1980s. Looking back now, it seems obvious that this was the way to do things, but at that time this was by no means so obvious. But, fortunately, there was someone who put two and two together and immediately realised the potential of this new technology – Matti Rissanen, a brilliant historical linguist, computer freak and gifted and energetic organiser, who, with a group of dedicated co-workers, created the first tool for this type of research: the *Helsinki Corpus*,[8] which crops up in almost every empirical historical study today, and which in the meantime has fathered many other electronic corpora making this type of research possible on a larger and larger scale. Now it has become possible to trace individual changes over several decades in social space, isolating the factors that have promoted or retarded a change in progress, which has to be interpreted as a process of selection from competing variants. In a way, this might also be regarded in genetic terms as the survival of the (sociolinguistically) fittest. This approach can also be interpreted as a more empirically oriented version of Keller's "invisible hand" principle,[9] according to which random variation on the part of the speakers may gradually start moving in a specific direction, since certain variants may be favoured over others. And it is precisely the variationist approach as developed by Rissanen and others that attempts to discover the factors responsible for a random variation becoming a directed one. This approach has also made it possible to include text-linguistic, pragmatic and discourse-analytic aspects in historical linguistics; historical pragmatics in particular – as evidenced in issues of the *Journal of Historical Pragmatics* – has, alongside historical sociolinguistics,[10] become one of the most promising research domains in recent years.

I.3

All these approaches to the study of the history of a language, in this case English, deal with language change from a basically local perspective: i.e. history is treated

[8] Matti Rissanen, *The Helsinki Corpus of English Texts* (Diachronic part) (Helsinki: Department of English, University of Helsinki, 1991).

[9] Rudi Keller, *Sprachwandel: Von der unsichtbaren Hand in der Sprache* (Tübingen: Francke, 1990).

[10] See, in particular, Helena Raumolin–Brunberg, "Historical Sociolinguistics," *Sociolinguistics and Language History: Studies Based on the Corpus of Early English Correspondence*, ed. Terttu Nevalainen and Helena Raumolin–Brunbert (Amsterdam and Atlanta, GA: Rodopi, 1996) 11–37, and Dieter Kastovsky and Arthur Mettinger, ed. *The History of English in a Social Context* (Trends in Linguistics: Studies and Monographs 129; Berlin and New York: Mouton de Gruyter, 2000).

as a series of individual, local changes, which follow each other, or which sometimes interact with each other (although this interaction between levels is more often than not disregarded). This is, incidentally, also true of the *Cambridge History of the English Language*,[11] where we do not find any systematic discussion of morphophonemic alternations: i.e. the interaction of phonology and morphology. But there is also a more general perspective: such individual, local changes sometimes move in the same direction over centuries with far-reaching consequences, which in the long run affect the general *Gestalt* of certain parts of the structure of the language. These are what I call "global" or "typological changes."[12] Of course, certain changes of this kind have been noticed because they are so obvious, such as the movement from a basically synthetic to an analytic language, the replacement of inflection as a signal of syntactic function by fixed word order (i.e. SVO) in order to compensate for this loss, or the development of an etymologically mixed vocabulary due to massive borrowing from French and Latin, with consequences for the phonology and morphology. But such observations have usually been very general and one has not really looked systematically at what these changes mean for the overall typological make-up of English, when one compares Old English, Middle English and Modern English in this respect. Such changes would constitute what Sapir called a "drift," which he defined as follows: "The drift of a language is constituted by the unconscious selection on the part of its speakers of those individual variations that are cumulative in some special direction. This direction may be inferred in the main from the past history of the language."[13] This means that independent local changes may share a directionality which cannot be explained simply by recourse to the random behaviour of individual speakers, as in the case of Keller's "invisible hand." On the contrary, it is the momentum developed by the accumulation of certain changes in a specific direction that prompts the speakers/listeners to follow a path that is already there: i.e. to favour certain variants that go in this direction rather than another. In other words, it would seem that "drift" in Sapir's sense is a kind

[11] Hogg, ed. *Cambridge History of the English Language*.

[12] Dieter Kastovsky, "Typological Reorientation as a Result of Level Interaction: The Case of English Morphology," *Diachrony Within Synchrony: Language History and Cognition*, ed. Günter Kellermann and Michael D. Morrissey (Duisburger Arbeiten zur Sprach- und Kulturwissenschaft 14; Frankfurt am Main: Peter Lang, 1992) 411–28; Dieter Kastovsky, "On Writing a History of English: The 'Local' and the 'Global'," *European English Messenger* 8.1 (1999): 13–15; Terttu Nevalainen and Helena Raumolin–Brunberg, "The Changing Role of London on the Linguistic Map of Tudor and Stuart England," *The History of English in a Social Context*, ed. Kastovsky and Mettinger 279–337 (281ff.).

[13] Edward Sapir, *Language: An Introduction to the Study of Speech* (New York: Harcourt, Brace, 1921) 165–66.

of feedback mechanism: once a certain number of changes happen to go in the same direction, it is the direction (and the resulting incipient restructuring) that triggers further changes (or at least favours the selection of variants supporting this direction).

This view of linguistic change is related to Coseriu's concept of language change: he also sees linguistic change as a cumulative process, starting at the level of speech (*parole*), where individual speakers introduce more or less random variation.[14] If, however, such variants increase in number and become directional, they will eventually lead to changes in the norm of the language: i.e. to a change in the preferred realisation of rivalling forms or constructions. This, by the way, is the main domain of variationist research discussed above: the interaction of the social forces with the changing preferences for variants and the sorting-out of preferred variants. If in this process one variant finally wins out and the other variants disappear, we have a systematic grammatical change: i.e. a change at the level of the linguistic system (*langue*). And if several such systematic changes on the same linguistic level (e.g. phonology, morphology, syntax) happen to go in the same direction, or interact with each other in the form of an "inter-level conspiracy" producing a combined cumulative effect, the final result may be an incipient typological change, a drift. This in turn may have a reinforcing feedback effect: i.e. it may contribute to the selection of those changes that conform better to the emerging new type, which, eventually, may replace the older type. Thus, drift interpreted as typological shift can also be regarded as a triggering factor for long-range global linguistic changes, which in turn may affect local changes: i.e. the selection of a variant that conforms to the ongoing long-range change better than another. This perspective is largely missing in the existing histories of the English language, and is complementary to the variationist approach. The more we know about local changes, the better we can assess whether there is a cumulative effect. On the other hand, once we know that there is a feedback effect, we can look for its origin. There is thus a clear feedback between these two perspectives, the local and the global, which, I hope, will direct future research into the history of English. Let me illustrate this with a few examples from various domains of the history of English.

---

[14] Eugenio Coseriu, *Sistema, norma y habla* (Montevideo: Facultad de Humanidades y Ciencias, 1952), repr. in *Teoría de lenguaje y lingüística general: Cinco Estudios* (Madrid: Gredos, 1962) 11–113; in German as *Synchronie, Diachronie und Geschichte: Das Problem des Sprachwandels*, trans. Helga Sohre (Internationale Bibliothek für Allgemeine Linguistik 3; Munich: Wilhelm Fink, 1974).

II.1

In the Early Middle English period, pairs such as *consume* : *consumption* or *deceive* : *deception* became English loan-words. This is, if seen as an isolated phenomenon, a purely local change in the vocabulary: some lexical items were added to it; sometimes this was a genuine addition, and sometimes it was just a replacement of some already existing item, as in the case of OE *swican*, *swice*, which were replaced by *deceive*, *deception*. This would cause a minor restructuring of a lexical field in the case of a genuine addition (compare also, for example, items like *close* [vs. *shut*], *enter* [vs. *go in*]), but would not have had any further consequences for the lexicon or the language as a whole. However, such borrowings did not remain isolated instances but became a flood in later Middle English. The borrowing process continued in Early Modern English with loans from Latin as an additional source. The reasons for this phenomenon are not relevant in this connection, although they are of course important for the explanation of the local change (the borrowing process) itself: they were partly linguistic (language death: i.e. the shift of French speakers to English), and cultural (the effect of the Renaissance and its Latin background). Individual speakers apparently preferred a non-native lexeme to a native one, either because they did not know the former, or it did not exist, or because the speakers wanted to sound more educated, etc.

The ultimate (i.e. global) consequences of these many local changes (i.e. individual borrowings), however, were far-reaching, because they triggered a structural-typological change in phonology, morphology and morphonology, which can justifiably be called global. This change, first of all, consists in the shift from a basically monostratal (Germanic) vocabulary to a lexicon with two strata, a native-Germanic and a non-native Romance/Latinate one.[15] This in itself would still have to be regarded as basically a local change, in the sense that it only affects the level of lexis as such and its lexical–semantic structure. But the implementation of this second lexical stratum had far-reaching repercussions on other domains, viz. the phonology and the morphology of the language.[16] First of all, the loans introduced a new, variable stress-pattern into the language, cf. series such as *hístory* : *históric* : *historícity*; *Japán* : *Jàpanése*, whereas the original (Germanic) system had basically been characterised by initial stress except for verbal prefixes as in *befáll*, *untíe* vs. nominal *óutcome*, *íncome*, *únderpass*, etc. Some linguists – Lass,

[15] Dieter Kastovsky, "Historical English Word-Formation: From a Monostratal to a Polystratal System," *Historical English Word-Formation: Papers Read at the Sixth National Conference of the History of English*, ed. Rolando Bacchielli (Urbino: Quattro Venti, 1994) 17–31.

[16] Note that the consequences of the borrowing process are treated rather controversially in the literature – if they are treated at all systematically.

for example[17] – even argue that this resulted in a general change from Germanic rightward to Romance leftward stress assignment, which I find somewhat problematical in view of the many stress doublets in Modern English. But, as a minimal assumption, borrowing introduced a second type of stress assignment (perhaps as a combination of leftward assignment and lexical government), which would mean that, generally, stress assignment shifted from an automatic to a lexically governed system.

The lexical restructuring also had morphological and morphophonemic consequences: it introduced new derivational patterns with specific non-native properties into the language. While native word-formation is word-based throughout,[18] many borrowed patterns are stem-based, cf. *drama* : *dramat-ic*, *electr-ic* : *electr-ify*, *electr-ific-ation*, *science* : *scient-ist*, *scient-ific*. Moreover, in contradistinction to native or nativised suffixes, the non-native suffixes are stress-sensitive in two respects: either they are stressed themselves (cf. *Jàpan-ése*, *èmploy-ée*, *pròfit-éer*, *elèctrific-átion*), or they assign stress to some non-initial part of the base (cf. *hístory* : *histór-ic* : *hìstor-íc-ity*, *légal* : *lègál-ity*). As a side-effect, such stress shifts introduce into the system morphophonemic alternations between a full vowel and schwa, which are absent in the native word-formation patterns, since these are invariant. Non-native word-formation patterns are also characterised by morphophonemic alternations such as /k/ ~ /s/ as in *historic* : *historicity* and others. Thus, the various local changes triggered by the massive borrowing of foreign lexical items have produced a typological change from a morphologically and phonologically monostratal system to a polystratal one.

II.2

The same phenomenon can be illustrated with examples drawn from the development of the English vowel system. All classic handbooks mention the operation of certain lengthening and shortening processes in Old English and Middle English, viz. the shortening of long vowels in trisyllabic words (e.g. *suþerne* > *suþerne*) or obstruent clusters (e.g. *cepte* > *cepte*), or the lengthening of short vowels before voiced homorganic clusters, i.e. liquids and nasals + homorganic voiced stops (e.g. *findan* > *findan*, cf. also Mod. English *child* : *children*) or in open syllables (e.g. *nama* > *name*). Usually, these sound changes are treated as independent, wholly unrelated phenomena. That this is not the case has been

---

[17] Roger Lass, "Phonology and Morphology," *Cambridge History of the English Language*, vol. 2: *1066–1476*, ed. Norman Blake (Cambridge: Cambridge University Press, 1992) 23–155 (85ff.).

[18] Kastovsky, "Typological Reorientation."

clearly demonstrated by Ritt[19] and others. What tends to be overlooked, however, is that the combined effect of these changes eventually led to a complete restructuring of the phonemic system: originally, vowel length was phonemic (at least in certain interpretations), but this contrast was given up in favour of a basically qualitative opposition, with vowel length being predictable on the basis of the environment: long before voiced consonants, short before voiceless consonants.

This development is, in fact, somewhat more complex and is connected with the general interpretation of the English vowel system, especially the subsystem of long vowels and diphthongs and the role of length. This, in turn, highlights another aspect affecting long-range developments. It seems that languages sometimes have certain built-in tendencies which trigger cyclical developments: i.e. developments that recur in the history of the language once the appropriate conditions arise. This assumption underlies the interpretation by Stockwell and Stockwell–Minkova of the so-called "Great Vowel Shift," which seems to repeat itself in Modern English.[20] The Great Vowel Shift is usually described as a general raising of long vowels and the diphthongisation of the highest vowels, because these cannot be raised any further. This process is accompanied by diphthong-maximisation, i.e. the distance between diphthong components is increased: /Iy/ > /2y/ > /ay/ or /Uw/ > /7w/ > /aw/, etc. The same process is observable in Modern Southern English today (as a spread from Cockney-influenced London English). At the same time we observe progressive monophthongisation of diphthongs and triphthongs: cf. > /ay7/ > /a7/ > /a:/ (= /ah/) as in *fire*, or /aw7/ > /a7/ > /a:/ (= /ah/) as in *power*. Since similar developments have happened repeatedly in the history of England, Stockwell and Stockwell–Minkova conclude that long vowels in English always had some underlying diphthongal quality: i.e. had always consisted of a vocalic nucleus and a glide, and that the cyclical development merely involved diphthong maximisation with subsequent diphthong minimisation (monophthongisation), accompanied by glide vocalisation.[21] Since similar developments occur in other Germanic languages, e.g. German, this seems to be a built-in tendency of these tongues. Treating Old English vowels as primarily based on a quantitative contrast, where length is realised as a sequence of two identical

---

19 Nikolaus Ritt, *Quantity Adjustment: Vowel Lengthening and Shortening in Early Middle English* (Cambridge: Cambridge University Press, 1994).

20 Robert P. Stockwell, "Perseverance in the English Vowel Shift," *Recent Developments in Historical Phonology*, ed. Jacek Fisiak (The Hague: Mouton, 1978) 337–48; Robert P. Stockwell and Donka Minkova, "The English Vowel Shift: Problems of Coherence and Explanation," *Luick Revisited: Papers Read at the Luick-Symposium at Schloss Liechtenstein, 15.–18.9.1885*, ed. Dieter Kastovsky and Gero Bauer (Tübinger Beiträge zur Linguistik 288; Tübingen: Gunter Narr, 1988) 355–94.

21 Stockwell 337–48; Stockwell and Minkova 355–94.

vowels instead of as vowel + glide, thus involves a structural change. Nevertheless, in both interpretations we are faced with a long-range phenomenon that is not restricted to the period usually dubbed "The Great Vowel Shift."

Another peculiar inherent property of the English phonological system seems to be its aversion to rounded front vowels in contradistinction to other Germanic languages like German or the Scandinavian languages. Thus, at several stages in its history English acquired the front rounded vowels /ü/, /œ/ etc. (through i-umlaut in pre-OE, through borrowing in Middle English), however, somehow these sounds never survived for long, but were unrounded again in contradistinction to German, which even exploits the contrast for morphological purposes like plural formation (cf. *Mutter* 'mother': *Mütter* 'mothers').

II.3

My final example is one that goes even further back in time than that involved in the previous examples; it starts out with a prosodic change. One of the characteristic features of the Germanic language family is the fixed stress on the first syllable, which is normally also the stem,[22] in contradistinction to variable stress in Indo-European. In view of the subsequent reduction of unstressed syllables in the Germanic group, we might also speculate about the phonetic character of this initial stress pattern. It was probably expiratory, and prosody in general was stress- rather than syllable-timed, since with the latter type of prosody vowel reductions seem to be less common: cf. Finnish or German as compared with English (cf. *Japán* : *Jàpanése* with vowel reduction as against *Jápan* : *Japáner* without vowel reduction).[23] At this stage, this is a local change, affecting only a certain part of the phonology of the language. The consequences, however, did not remain local, but became global. The first direct consequence of this change was a progressive weakening and eventual loss of unstressed syllables. Again, seen as a purely phonological process, it was a local one. But it had morphological consequences, which gradually began to affect the morphological type of the language.

The typical noun and verb structure of Early Germanic morphology was

base		stem-formative		inflectional ending		
stem						
**naz*	+	*j* (= /i/)	+	*d*	+	*a*
**dag*	+	*a*			+	*z*

22 Prefixations are somewhat more complicated and will be disregarded here.

23 Note that in Finnish, despite initial stress, vowels do not seem to be reduced, and that Finnish also does not have expiratory stress.

Thus, the base was always followed by a stem-formative or thematic element which, however, could also be zero – for example, with strong verbs or a small group of athematic nouns. Stem-formatives had a dual role: they acted as derivational elements producing denominal verbs or deverbal nouns in the absence of other derivational suffixes, and they acted as inflectional markers characterising the stem as a member of a specific inflectional class with class-specific inflectional endings: cf. terms such as nominal *-o-*, *-a-*, or *-n-*stems, or *-jan-*, *-on-*verbs. Thus, the domains of derivation and inflection were not neatly separated, as they are today, but formed a continuum, as they did in Indo-European and, to a certain degree, still do in the Slavonic languages.[24] Moreover, inflection was stem-based, since no paradigm had an uninflected base form. Also, each paradigm had an overt class marker (the absence of one, i.e. zero, also counted as a marker), so that each inflectional form could unambiguously indicate class membership.[25]

The weakening and eventual loss of unstressed syllables – a purely phonological process – had the following morphological side-effects. In certain inflectional paradigms, e.g. the strong masculines of the type OE *cyning*, the nominative singular ending was lost together with the stem-formative. In other inflectional paradigms, the stem-formative was also either lost completely, in accordance with Siever's Law (High Vowel Deletion), or at least it changed its phonetic quality, merging with other stem-formatives. It therefore lost its class-marking function and must synchronically be reinterpreted as part of the remaining inflectional ending, or as an integral part of the stem (a re-analysis that is not reflected in many handbooks, by the way). The consequences of this morphological development are:

1. The inflectional class characterisation is no longer overt, but covert–implicational: i.e. it now is an invisible, inherent property of the lexical item in question and can only be predicted on the basis of the overall shape of the inflectional paradigm.[26] As a consequence, class shifts become frequent.

---

[24] Dieter Kastovsky, "Verbal Derivation in English: A Historical Survey; Or: Much Ado About Nothing," *English Historical Linguistics 1994*, ed. Derek Britton (Current Issues in Linguistic Theory 135; Amsterdam and Philadelphia, PA: John Benjamins, 1996) 93–117.

[25] Dieter Kastovsky, "Morphological Classification in English Historical Linguistics: The Interplay of Diachrony, Synchrony and Morphological Theory," *To Explain the Present: Studies in the Changing English Language in Honour of Matti Rissanen*, ed. Terttu Nevalainen and Leena Kahlas–Tarkka (Mémoires de la Société Néophilologique de Helsinki 52; Helsinki: Société Néophilologique, 1997) 63–75.

[26] Kastovsky, "Morphological Classification."

2. The loss and/or reinterpretation of the stem-formative brings about a strict separation of inflection and derivation and the rise of affixless derivation (zero-derivation).[27]
3. The total loss of inflection in some forms – notably the nominative singular, the morpho-semantically least marked form – introduces word-based inflection into nominal inflection. This signals a beginning typological reorientation from stem-based to word-based morphology.

This situation characterises Old English, which, moreover, exhibited extremely widespread stem-variability due to pervasive morphophonemic alternations (ablaut, umlaut, palatalisation, etc.) which, however, had lost their phonological conditioning and were therefore no longer phonologically predictable. By the end of the Old English period, further weakening of the unstressed syllables resulted in a general merger of most unstressed vowels in schwa, which obliterated most class and case distinction. As a consequence, number (plural formation) emerged as the dominant, class-defining feature with nouns. At first, there were four rivalling classes, *-s*-plurals, *-n*-plurals, zero plurals and irregular nouns, with *-s*-plurals being numerically dominant. The latter eventually became the norm (the unmarked case), whereas all other types of plural formations ended up as being irregular. In other words, the system shifted from one having various inflectional classes to a default system with regular and irregular nouns. The former is the default case, where the plural allomorphs /ɪz/, /s/, /z/ are chosen on the basis of the phonetic properties of the base-final phoneme, whereas the irregular formations are morphologically determined. A similar development took place in the verbal system, where past-tense and past-participle formation became the class-defining features, with regular verbs having phonologically predictable forms (/id/, /d/, /t/), and irregular verbs having morphologically conditioned allomorphs of the respective inflectional endings, including stem allomorphy. Another consequence of this development, by the way, is the loss of grammatical gender.[28]

There are some further consequences related to these developments. Word-based morphology spreads from nouns to verbs due to the loss of the infinitive ending, but this can no longer be attributed to purely phonological developments (i.e. the loss of final syllables including final *-n*), since *-n* was preserved as plural marker. This is where the drift factor seems to have played a role in eliminating the formal marker of the semantically least-marked category (nominative and

[27] Kastovsky, "Verbal Derivation in English."

[28] Dieter Kastovsky, "Inflectional Classes, Morphological Restructuring, and the Dissolution of Old English Grammatical Gender," *Gender in Grammar and Cognition*, vol. 2: *Manifestations of Gender*, ed. Barbara Unterbeck and Matti Rissanen (Berlin: Mouton de Gruyter, 1999).

infinitive), especially since the infinitive was also marked by the preposition *to*. It would seem that the generalisation of word-based morphology also made the pervasive morphophonemic alternations unsuitable, especially since almost all of them had lost their predictability. Thus they were levelled out in the Middle English period, and those that remain, e.g. *keep* : *kept*, *deal* : *dealt*, *sing* : *sang* : *sung*, *louse* : *lice*, *goose* : *geese*, count as irregular in Modern English. The emerging tendency to stem-invariancy in morphology is corroborated by the fact that almost all the nouns and adjectives related to strong verbs and exhibiting ablaut alternations were lost (in contradistinction to German), *song*, *writ*, *batch* being rare exceptions.[29]

The change in the prosodic system thus had far-reaching consequences at the morphological level as well, and brought about a total reorientation of the morphology. Many of these changes were originally local, but they eventually developed a directionality, a drift, and resulted in an overall typological reorientation of the language.

III

Similar long-range phenomena can be observed in syntax, e.g. the development of relative pronouns and the restructuring of relative clauses, the development of infinitival constructions, or the gradual emergence of sentence adverbs from various other types of adverb. Another domain is the creation of the category of the modal verb, which in turn was instrumental in grammaticalising the *do*-periphrasis. A further area that should be investigated from this typological point of view is the gradual restructuring of the tense and aspect system of English, with the spread of the progressive from tense to tense, and the emergence and systematisation of the present perfect and the pluperfect. And it would seem that such considerations can also be applied to the level of text types or genres.

At the beginning of the third millennium, we thus witness a renewed interest in historical linguistics after a certain decline in the second half of the previous century. The interaction of the investigation of local changes in the variationist framework and their localisation in long-term developments will, I hope, produce a feedback effect which will give historical studies a new direction and impetus.

---

[29] Note, however, that this development was not unidirectional, since in the derivational system morphophonemic/allomorphic alternations were reintroduced in the non-native stratum (see II.1. above).

The Old English Suffix *-el* / *-il* / *-ol* / *-ul* / *-l* (> ModE *-le*, cf. *beetle*, *girdle*, *thistle*) as Attested in the *Épinal–Erfurt Glossary*

HANS SAUER

I Introduction: Research on Old English word-formation

THERE ARE MANY DETAILED AND SPECIALISED STUDIES of Old English (OE) word-formation, but no comprehensive treatment exists.[1] The best current survey is Kastovsky's,[2] which provides many examples but also addresses theoretical and methodological questions throughout and tries to analyse OE word-formation within a consistent framework. I cannot, of course, give a complete survey of OE word-formation here; instead, I shall concentrate on one pattern as exhibited in one text – the noun-forming suffix *-el* / *-il* / *-ol* / *-ul* / *-l* (and *-ils*) as attested in the *Épinal–Erfurt Glossary* (ÉpErf). This suffix, which "is a difficult and complicated ending,"[3] was inherited from Germanic (and, ultimately, from Indo-European), where it was certainly productive. It seems to have still been somewhat productive in Old English, but it lost its productivity later. It survives in Modern English (ModE), however, mainly in the form *-le* /l/, e.g. in *beetle*, *girdle*, *thistle* etc., and also as *-el* /l/, for example, in *hazel*.[4]

[1] For bibliographical information, see, for example, Alistair Campbell, *Old English Grammar* (Oxford: Clarendon Press, 1959) 368–69, Herbert Koziol, *Handbuch der englischen Wortbildungslehre* (Heidelberg: Carl Winter, 1972), and Gabriele Stein, *English Word Formation over Two Centuries: In Honour of Hans Marchand on the Occasion of his Sixty-Fifth Birthday* (Tübingen: Gunter Narr, 1973). I hope to write such a treatment eventually. For help with the present article, I thank Renate Bauer, Sabine Gieszinger, Zora Gnädig, Claudia Lechner, Ursula Lenker and Ulrike Manta.

[2] Dieter Kastovsky, "Semantics and Vocabulary," *The Cambridge History of the English Language* [CHEL], vol. 1, ed. Richard M. Hogg (Cambridge: Cambridge University Press, 1992) 290–408.

[3] Zung–Fung Wei Koo, "Old English Living Noun-Suffixes Exclusive of Personal and Place-Names" (unpublished doctoral dissertation, Radcliffe College, Cambridge, MA, 1946) 3.

[4] See, for example, *The Oxford Dictionary of English Etymology* [ODEE], ed. C.T. Onions et al. (Oxford: Oxford University Press, 1966) s.v. *-le*[1] and *–el*[1]; Koziol 198–99 (§468 = *-le*[1]); cf. Hans Mar-

II The *Épinal–Erfurt Glossary*

The *Épinal–Erfurt Glossary* is the earliest written record of the English language of any length. It is transmitted in two manuscripts:

1) Épinal, Bibliothèque municipale 72 (2), fols. 94–107, written in England by an English scribe in the late seventh or early eighth century (Ép);
2) Erfurt, Wissenschaftliche Allgemeinbibliothek, Codex Amplonianus F.42, fols. 1ar1–14va33, written in Cologne by a German scribe in the late eighth or early ninth century (Erf).[5]

There have been several editions as well as facsimiles of both manuscripts. The most recent critical edition is the one edited by Pheifer, and all quotations in this article are taken from this edition.[6] The most recent facsimile is that edited by Bischoff et al.[7] Both manuscripts go back to a common ancestor, which has been dated c.670–680 (Pheifer lxxxix).

Épinal–Erfurt is a Latin glossary in rough alphabetical order (mostly in a-order). Many lemmata have Latin glosses, but about 1,100 have OE glosses.[8] The nouns are mostly given in the nom. sing., but sometimes also in inflected cases, and this is normally reproduced in the OE gloss, e.g. *instites* (506) – *suedilas* (L & OE: nom./acc. pl.); *cuniculos* (199) – *smigilas / smygilas* (L: acc. pl. – OE: nom./ acc. pl.); *blat(t)is* (145) – *bitulin / bitulum* (L: dat./abl. pl. – OE: dat. pl.); *temonibus* (1043) – *dislum*, *dixlum* (L: dat./abl. pl. – OE: dat. pl.); *aere alieno* (115) – *gaebuli* (L: dat./abl. sing. – OE: dat. sing.); *amiculo* (84) – *hraecli* (L: dat./abl. sing. – OE: instr. sing.), etc.[9]

The Latin of ÉpErf contains many difficult and rare words (some of which are of Greek origin). Moreover, the scribes made a number of mistakes. The German scribe of Erfurt (working in Cologne), for example, did not recognise the OE

chand, *The Categories and Types of Present-Day English Word-Formation: A Synchronic–Diachronic Approach* (Munich: C.H. Beck, 1969) 324.

[5] See, for example, Neil R. Ker, *Catalogue of Manuscripts Containing Anglo-Saxon* (Oxford: Clarendon Press, 1957) no.114 & Appendix 10; J.D. Pheifer, *Old English Glosses in the Épinal–Erfurt Glossary* (Oxford: Clarendon Press, 1974) xxi ff.; Hans Sauer, "The Earliest Layer of English Word-Formation: A Sketch of Word-Formation Patterns in the *Épinal–Erfurt Glossary*," *Anglistentag 1999 Mainz: Proceedings*, ed. Bernhard Reitz and Sigrid Rieuwerts (Trier: Wissenschaftlicher Verlag Trier, 2000) 77–90 (77–78).

[6] Pheifer, *Old English Glosses*.

[7] Bernhard Bischoff et al., *The Épinal, Erfurt, Werden, and Corpus Glossaries* (Early English Manuscripts in Facsimile 22; Copenhagen: Rosenkilde & Bagger, 1988).

[8] Pheifer edits only the OE glosses.

[9] See also V.8 below. For further examples, see Hans Sauer, "Animal Names in the *Épinal–Erfurt Glossary*," *Text and Gloss: Studies in Insular Learning and Literature Presented to Joseph Donovan Pheifer*, ed. Helen Conrad O'Briain et al. (Dublin: Four Courts, 1999) 128–58 (139–40); Sauer, "English Word-Formation" 77. For *hraecli*, see Campbell 224, 398.

letter wynn <ƿ> (for /w/) and reproduced it as <p>, cf., for example, 173 Ép *windil*, but Erf *pindil* instead of [*w*]*indil*.[10] On the other hand, the German scribe of Erfurt sometimes retains a correct or an earlier spelling, where the scribe of Épinal has made a mistake or uses a later spelling (reflecting a change in pronunciation), e.g. 50 Ép *aesil* (with h-dropping), but Erf *haesil* 'HAZEL'; 127 Ép *bridils* (with loss of <g> /g/), but Erf *brigdils* 'BRIDLE' (the word is derived from *bregdan* 'to pull' etc.); 1043 Ép *dislum* (dat. pl. of *disl* 'pole'), but Erf *dixlum* (the word is probably derived from a Gmc **þīhslō* < **þenhslō*, i.e. Erf has retained the [hs] as [ks] <x>; G 'DEICHSEL').

Furthermore, OE spelling was not yet standardised. On the one hand, the same word is sometimes spelled in different ways (cf. also the examples just given), e.g. 199 Ép *smigilas* – Erf *smygilas*; 572 Ép *haecilae* – Erf *hecile*; 461 Ép *cisil* – Erf *cisal* (for L *glarea*; both are early forms of later OE *ceosol* 'pebble,' G 'KIESEL'). On the other hand, forms that look similar may belong to different words: thus, 457 and 1054 *cesol* (ÉpErf) is not another spelling of *cisil*, *cisal*, *ceosol*, but a loan-word from the Latin *casula*, *casella*, here with the meaning 'gullet' (see IV.2 below). 2 *rysil*, *risil* is not a form of 851 *hrisil*, *hrisl* with h-dropping (cf. *aesil* – *haesil* above), but a different word: *hrisil* 'radius, shuttle' etc. (L *radium*) – *rysil*, *risil* 'lard, fat' etc. (L *axiunga*). This kind of variation makes it also difficult to tell how many different words are attested in ÉpErf. A further example is 326 *thuachl* 'soap' (Erf) and 1060 *thuelan* 'fillets, head-bands' (ÉpErf), glossing L 326 *delumentem* 'soap,' 1060 *uit(t)as* 'fillets, head-bands (towels).' *Thuachl* and *thuelan* go back to the same (West)Germanic (Gmc) form **þwahilō* (from **þwah-* > OE *þwēan* 'to wash') and are here regarded as instances (tokens) of the same word (type), although they may have been viewed as different words by the scribes of ÉpErf, especially since the two occurrences seem to have different meanings and gloss different Latin words.[11] Another question is whether and how far such spelling differences reflect differences in pronunciation. As far as the suffix *-el* / *-il* / *-ol* is concerned, I shall deal with its form in section V below.

[10] This presupposes that the common exemplar of ÉpErf sometimes used the wynn <ƿ>. The scribes of ÉpErf, however, often do not use the wynn, they use the double-u <uu> instead. Reading <p> instead of <ƿ> is something our students still often do when they begin to learn Old English. See also Sauer, "English Word-Formation" 78.

[11] But both refer to instruments used in connection with the body (and with washing).

III Productivity and analysability of Old English word-formation

One problem in analysing OE word-formation is where to draw the borderline between Germanic word-formation, from which OE word-formation developed and from which it inherited a number of formations, and OE word-formation proper. Related to this problem is the question of productivity and analysability.[12] Since we have no speakers who can form new OE words for us, we can only estimate from the written material which has come down to us that frequently attested patterns were probably productive, whereas rarely attested patterns were probably less productive or even unproductive. It has to be checked, of course, which of the words containing these patterns were inherited from Germanic (or West-Germanic) and which were newly formed in Old English – once more a question which is not always easy to answer, and which in any case leads us from word-formation in the stricter sense into the area of etymology (i.e. the origin and development of words) and of comparative Germanic philology. Compounding, especially the formation of noun+noun compounds, was certainly highly productive in Old English, as were, for example, the prefix *un-* (*unboren* 'unborn') or the suffixes *-ere* (*bæcere* 'baker'), *-ing*/*-ung* (*offrung* 'offering') and *-nes(s)* (*beorhtness* 'brightness'). The tree-name suffix *-dor*/*-dur*, on the other hand, is attested very rarely (*apuldor* 'apple tree,' *mapuldor* 'maple[tree]' and one or two other words) and it may have been unproductive even in Old English.[13] Since Old English spans a period of roughly 600 years (c.450–c.1100, with the earliest written material from c.700; see section II above), there may, of course, have been changes in productivity within the OE period and also differences according to text-type. Thus, the suffix *-ere* (> ModE *-er*), which forms mainly agent nouns, seems to have acquired its productivity only gradually[14] and it remained rare in OE poetry.

But even if we do not emphasise productivity and concentrate on analysability instead, we run into problems. Although many complex words are analysable on a synchronic OE basis (regardless of whether they were inherited from Germanic or newly formed in Old English), others can only be analysed on an historical (dia-

---

[12] See also Sauer, "English Word-Formation" 79.

[13] See, for example, Sauer, "Old English Plant Names in the *Épinal–Erfurt Glossary*: Etymology, Word-Formation and Semantics," *Words, Lexemes, Concepts: Approaches to the Lexicon; Studies in Honour of Leonhard Lipka*, ed. Wolfgang Falkner and Hans-Jörg Schmid (Tübingen: Gunter Narr, 1999) 23–28 (28); Sauer, "English Word-Formation" 85.

[14] Whereas almost fifty formations with *-el*/*-il* are attested in ÉpErf (excluding Latin loan-words etc.), there are only two examples of formations with *-ere*, namely *flitere* 854 and *teblere* 7.

chronic) basis. Kastovsky cites, for example, *ǣs* 'food, meat' (cf. G *Aas*), and *blǣs* 'blowing, blast.'[15] They may look like simplexes, but originally they were formed from *etan* 'EAT' and *blāwan* 'BLOW.'[16] Kastovsky suggests that formations like these should be excluded from a survey of OE word-formation, because such derivations are no longer obviously connected with their (original) bases. Unfortunately, borderline cases abound, and since we have to start from a corpus, all instances which may be examples of a certain pattern have to be collected first and then forms or words which do not belong to the pattern in question have to be eliminated.[17]

Moreover, in many complex words one constituent seems to be analysable whereas the other is not. Thus, *haesil*, *mistil* and *thistil* (ModE *hazel*, *mistle*, *thistle*) apparently contain the suffix *-el* / *-il* etc. (ModE *-le*, *-el*), but their bases no longer existed even in Old English. Nevertheless, they are here regarded as instances of formations with the suffix *-el* / *-il*. If only those combinations were included where all constituents can be accounted for, a lot of material would have to be disregarded.

IV The material: Inclusions, exclusions and Latin influence

There are some seventy different words in ÉpErf that end in *-el* / *-il* etc. (see section X below). Because some of these words occur twice or even three times, the number of actual occurrences (tokens) is even larger than the number of different words (types). Most of these words occur independently, but some occur in ÉpErf additionally or exclusively as a part of a compound, mainly as the second element, e.g. *-ādl* in *lenctinadl* (see section X.5 below).

Not all of the approx. seventy words can be analysed as containing the OE noun-forming suffix *-el* / *-il*, however. There are at least three groups of words which have to be excluded. Four words contain the homonymous adjective-forming suffix *-el* / *-il* (see IV.3. and X.4), eleven are Latin loan-words that contain the Latin suffix (rather, suffix family) *-el(l)us*, *-illus*, *-ul(l)us* (*-a*, *-um*) (see IV.2.

---

[15] Dieter Kastovsky, "Semantics and Vocabulary," CHEL, ed. Hogg 290–408 (358).

[16] Rather, the earlier forms of these verbs – see, for example, Kluge and Seebold s.v. *Aas*.

[17] There is one group of authors, including Kastovsky, who tend to concentrate on productive patterns (i.e. patterns which were synchronically productive in Old English) and analysable formations, and another, earlier group of authors, such as Karl Best, *Die persönlichen Konkreta des Altenglischen nach ihren Suffixen geordnet* (dissertation, Strassburg, 1905), Martin Both, *Die konsonantischen Suffixe altenglischer Konkreta und Kollektiva* (dissertation, Kiel, 1909), and Otto Thiele, *Die konsonantischen Suffixe der Abstrakta des Altenglischen* (Darmstadt: dissertation, Strassburg, 1902), who collect material and then try to describe it entire, whether productive and analysable or not.

and X.3), and another nine are native nouns which are either very difficult to analyse or which do not seem to have been derived with the suffix under discussion here (see IV.1. and X.2). This still leaves about forty-six nouns which certainly or probably show the suffix *-el* / *-il* (see X.1). Since ÉpErf has approx. 1,100 OE entries, about seven percent of these end in *-el* / *-il* / *-ul*, and about four percent have the OE noun-forming suffix *-el* / *-il*. The following groups do not contain the OE noun-forming suffix *-el* / *-il*:

1. Native words such as *-aepl*, *-fel* (*blecthrustfel*), *-bil (wudubil)*, *edwalla*, *eola*, *gecilae* / *gicela*, *innifli*, *maethlae* / *medlae*, *spelli*. I have excluded them because they do not seem to consist of a base to which the suffix *-el* / *-il* etc. was added, or because the base is no longer analysable in Old English.

2. Latin loan-words: ca. eleven loan-words from Latin end in *-el* / *-il* etc.:[18]

1. *candel* 'CANDLE' < *candela*: *candelthuist* 'candle-trimmers' Erf 382 (hapax legomenon); glossing L *emunctoria*. ClH *candel*.
2. *cesol* (2x) 'gullet, maw' < *casula*, *casella* (lit. 'little cottage, little house'): (a) *cesol* 457, glossing L *gurgustium* (lit. 'small dwelling'); (b) *cesol* 1054, glossing L *uentriculus stomachus auis uel cesol*. ClH *ceosol* I. *Cesol* thus shows an interesting semantic development, from 'small house' to 'gullet, maw' (G *Magen*, *Schlund*), the common semantic element being 'small, narrow.'
3. *cetil* (2x) 'KETTLE' < *catillus*: (a) *cetil* 168; glossing L *caccabum* (< Gk *kakkabos* 'cooking-pot'); (b) *cetil* Erf 350; glossing L *enunum*. ClH *cetel*, *cetil*, *citel*. *Cetil* < Gmc **katila*- m. < L *catillus* < dim. of *catinus*, i.e. *cetil* goes back to a common Gmc word, which in its turn is an early loan-word from Latin, cf. EWDS (Kluge/Seebold), s.v. *Kessel*. ModE *kettle* is a ME loan from ON *ketill* < L *catillus*, cf. ODEE, s.v. *kettle*.
4. *couel* 'basket' (for *ca[u]uel* or *cawel*; Pheifer 79) < *cauellum*: *couel* 305; glossing L *coruis*. ClH *cawl* I 'basket.'
5. *cunillae* 'wild thyme' (ClH 'a plant, species of oregano') < *cunila*: *cunillae* 246; glossing L *cerefolium*. Cf. G *Quendel*. ClH *cunel(l)e*, *cunille*.
6. *faecilae* '(little) torch' < *facula* (dim. of fax 'torch'): *fæcilae* Ép 407, *faecile* Erf; glossing L *fax*. Cf. G *Fackel*. ClH *fæcele*.
7. *fibulae* < *fibula* 'clasp, buckle, brace': *fibulae* Ép 3a, *fibulæ* Erf, glossing L *ansa* 'handle, brace.' Cf. G *Fibel*, which is a later loan. ClH *fifele*.
8. *finugl* 'FENNEL' < *fenuculum* etc. 'fennel' (dim. of *fenum*, *faenum* 'hay'): *finugl* 451; glossing L *finiculus*. Cf. G *Fenchel*.[19] ClH *finu(g)l*, *finol*.

---

[18] Mary S. Serjeantson, *A History of Foreign Words in English* (London: Routledge & Kegan Paul, 1935) 16–18, lists only some of these.

[19] See Alfred Wollmann, *Untersuchungen zu den frühen lateinischen Lehnwörtern im Altenglischen: Phonologie und Datierung* (TUEPh 15; Munich: Wilhelm Fink, 1990) 484–507.

9. *lebil* 'cup, bowl' etc. (2x) < *labellum* 'small water-vessel' (dim. of *labrum* 'basin, tub'): (a) *lebil* 633; glossing L *manile*; (b) *lebil* 995; glossing L *triplia* (Ép) / *triblia* (Erf). ClH *læfel*.
10. *sigil* (3x) 'buckle, brooch' etc. < *sigillum* (which, in its turn, is a diminutive of *signum*): (a) *sigil* 134; glossing L *bulla*; (b) *sigil* 408; glossing L *fibula*; (c) *sigil* 882; glossing L *sibba*.[20] ClH *sigil, sigl, sigle* (?).
11. *teb(e)l* (2x) 'cube, die, game with dice or tables' < *tabula*: (a) *teblae* Ép 6, *tefil* Erf; glossing L *alea*; (b) *tebelstan* 'die, gambling-stone' Ép 172, *tebiltan* Erf (for *tebil[s]tan*); glossing L *calculus ratio uel sententia uel tebelstan uel lapillus*; cf. also (c) *teblere* 7; glossing L *aleator* (Ép); (d) *teblith* 178; glossing *cotizat*. ClH *tæfl*.

Strictly speaking, these loan-words have to be excluded from an analysis of the OE suffix *-el / -il*, since they are not products of OE word-formation (nor of Gmc word-formation) but of Latin word-formation.[21] They are nevertheless mentioned here, because many of them contain the Latin suffix (or suffix family) *-el(l)- / -ill- / -ul-* (as in *-ella*, *-illus*, *-ula*, *-ulus*, *-ulum* etc.), which is etymologically related to the OE suffix. In Latin, it mainly has diminutive function and forms desubstantival nouns; among the eleven Latin lemmata given above (at least) six are diminutives or were originally such:[22] *casa* 'house, hut' > *casula / casella* 'small house,' *catinus* 'vessel, bowl' > *catillus* 'small bowl,' *fax* 'torch' > *facula* 'little torch,' *fenum* 'hay' > *fenuculum / faeniculum / finiculus* etc. 'fennel' (lit. 'little hay'), *labrum* 'basin, tub' > *labellum* 'small water-vessel,' *signum* 'sign' > *sigillum* 'little image.' Further examples from ÉpErf are, e.g., *auriculum* (44); *carduus*, 'thistle' (271) > *cardella* (266); *fiscilla*, *fiscella* 'small basket' (403) < *fiscina*; *mergulus* (647) < *mergus* 'diver, kind of water-fowl' (662); *munusculorum* (346); *mustella* 'weasel' (diminutive?) (650) < *mus* 'mouse'; *turdella* (1011) < *turdus* 'thrush,' etc. In OE, the diminutive function plays only a minor role and desubstantival formations are rarer than deverbal ones (see VI.6 below). It is impossible to tell, however, whether and how far the OE speakers nevertheless felt that the loan-words somehow contained the OE suffix *-el / -il* etc.

It is also interesting to note that loan-words, once borrowed, lead an independent life in the receiving language. Most of the loan-words mentioned above gloss not their Latin etymon, but quite different Latin words: e.g. *cetil* glosses *caccabum*, *enunum* (and not *catillus*); *fibulae* 3a glosses *ansa* (not *fibula*), whereas *sigil* 408 glosses *fibula*. An exception is *finugl*, which glosses its etymon *finiculus*; *fæcilae* glosses *fax*, from which *faculum* was derived. The suffix *-el(l)- / -ill- / -ul-*

[20] See Wollmann 263–323.
[21] *Mugil* 660 is a Latin word (and not a loan-word into OE).
[22] Later, the diminutive meaning was lost in a number of formations, e.g. in *fenuculum*.

was quite productive in Latin, at least in later Latin, as seen in the examples from ÉpErf given above.[23]

3. There was also a suffix *-il*, *-ol* which formed adjectives. This has to be regarded as a different, homonymous suffix.[24] It is no longer productive in ModE, but it survives in, for example, *nimble*. Some examples from ÉpErf are:

1. *aedil*: *aedilra* (gen.pl.) 479; L *gregariorum*. ClH *aeðelre* 'noble, splendid' etc.[25]
2. *nihol* 'precipitous, prone' 799; L *pronus*. ClH *neowol*.
3. *sinuurbul* 'round' Ép 1047, *sinuulfur* Erf; L *teres* 'round.' ClH *sinhwyrfel*.
4. *staegil* 'steep': *staegilrae* Ép 747, *stegelrae* Erf;[26] L *praerupta*. ClH *staegel*.

None of these formations is extant in ModE.

V The form and etymology of the suffix *-el* / *-il* / *-ol* / *-ul* / *-l* (and *-ils*)

1. *Old English spellings*

The suffix appears in a number of different spellings in ÉpErf: as <l> (e.g. *dislum*, *eglae*, *-scofl*), as <el> (e.g. *auuel*), as <il> (e.g. *gecilae*, *mistil*), as <ol> (e.g. *sadol*), and as <ul> (e.g. *bitulin*, *uuapul*). The literature also lists a variety of spellings: The *Oxford Dictionary of English Etymology* (ODEE), s.v. *-le*[1], gives as OE forms *-el*, *-els*, *-la*, *-le*, *-ol* and *–l*, Kastovsky (384–85) gives as OE forms *-ele(e)*[sic]/*-l(a)* / *-ol*; Voyles lists *-el-*, *-els-*, *-ell-*, *-isl-*:[27] i.e. *-il* and *-ul* are often

[23] Further examples from ÉpErf are: 22 *aesculus*; 33 *acerabulus*/*acterabulus*; 39/44 *auriculum*; 59 *actula*/*accitula*; 60 *acitelum, accitullum*; 63 *acitulium*; 84 *amiculo* (< *amiculus*); 101 *adsaeculam*/ *adsexulam*; 120 *Buccula* (< *bucca*); 127 *bagula*; 153 *buculus, bacculus*; 164 *contribulus*; 165/172 *calculus* (< *calx*); 175 *carbunculus* (< *carbo*); 199 *cuniculos*; 218 *crepacula, tabula*; 221 *cerula* (< *cera*); 240 *cornicula* (< *cornix*); 241 *cornacula*; 263 *calciculium*; 265 *cuculus*; 288 *crustulla*; 391 *esculus*; 393 *ebulum*; 408 *fibula*; 422 *ficetula*; 450 *ferula*/*ferola*; 462 *glumula*; 469a *genisculas*/ *genisculae*; 518 *intula*; 553 *caenaculi*/*caenaculo*; 569 *larbula*; 570 *lunules*; 582 *legula*; 665 *merula*; 763 *perpendiculum*; 770 *pustula*; 771/791 *papula*; 792 *populus*; 806 *parrula*; 816/838 *pendulus*; 850 *Renunculus*; 854 *rabulus*; 877 *ridimiculae*/*ridimiculi*; 887 *sarculum*/*surculum*; 896 *stabula*; 898 *sagulum*; 919 *simbulum*/ *symbulum*; 923 *situla*/*situlae*; 936 *spiculis* (?< *spicum*); 943 *scindulis*; 959 *stabulum*; 963 *scapula*; 971 *spatula*; 1006 *tremulus*; 1008 *toculus*/*taculus*; 1009 *trifulus*; 1009a *tabula*; 1028 *titule*/*titulae*; 1052 *uenabula*/*venabula*; 1054 *uentriculus* (< *venter*); 1057 *uestibulum*; 1093 *oculo*.

[24] On this suffix, see, for example, ODEE s.v. *-le*[2]; Koziol 199 (§ 469). Marchand does not mention it, as it is no longer productive.

[25] The gloss is striking: whereas Latin *gregarius* normally means 'belonging to a herd, common' etc., OE *æðele* means the opposite: namely, 'noble, excellent' etc. For an attempt to explain this discrepancy, see Pheifer 91.

[26] The form in *-rae* was perhaps regarded as a fem.gen./dat. sing. or as a gen.pl., cf. Campbell 263.

[27] Joseph B. Voyles, *West Germanic Inflection, Derivation and Compounding* (Janua Linguarum, ser. pract. 145; The Hague: Mouton, 1974) 115.

omitted in the literature, but for a description of ÉpErf, *-il* and *-ul* certainly have to be added. Of course, the question arises whether these forms should be regarded as different suffixes or as variants of the same suffix.

2. *One suffix or several?*

Koo relegates *-el* etc. to an appendix and doubts whether it should be regarded as one specific and coherent suffix. Koo (340–49) points out that *-el* etc. (1) "forms words of all genders," (2) appears in a great variety of spellings (see above) "without any pronounced distinction in function or source of formation," (3) forms several semantic groups (see sections 6 and 8 below); furthermore (4) several *-el* words are clearly derivatives, but many are not analysable on a synchronic OE basis and were probably no longer recognised as derivations from a particular base even by OE speakers (e.g. *adl*, *æppel* etc.).

But since the different forms cannot be assigned to different functions (nor even always to different origins), it would also be impracticable to regard all these forms (*-el* / *-il* etc.) as different suffixes. It seems best to follow Kastovsky's suggestion (360, 384) and to group them together as a suffix family. They can be assigned a fairly general basic function, mainly to derive concrete nouns, especially from verbs.

3. *Reasons for variation*

The bewildering array of variant spellings can be attributed to the influence of at least three different factors: (1) partly it is due to the fact that there was no fixed spelling in OE (see p. 291 above), (2) partly it is due to the fact that the OE suffix goes back to a Gmc and ultimately a Proto-Indo-European (PIE) suffix family which showed a certain amount of variation already in Gmc and PIE, (3) and partly it is due to the operation of certain phonological processes.

As to the Gmc and PIE origins of the suffix family: the ODEE, s.v. *-le*[1], for example, reconstructs the PIE forms as **-(i)lo-*, **-(u)lo-*, **-(e)la-*;[28] Meid reconstructs the Gmc forms as *-la-*, *-el-*, *-lo-*, *-ila-*, *-ala-*, *-ula-* etc., < IE *-lo-*, *-ila-*, *-el-*, *-ol-*, *-l-* etc.;[29] Kärre reconstructs as Gmc forms *- lo*, *-ilo*, *-ilō(n)*, *-alo*, *-ulo*, *-lōn*, *-alōn*, *-ulōn*.[30]

[28] See also Friedrich Kluge, *Etymologisches Wörterbuch der deutschen Sprache* [EWDS], ed. Elmar Seebold (Berlin: de Gruyter, 1989) s.v. *-el*. A much longer list of PIE "Formantia" with *-l-* is given by Karl Brugmann and Berthold Delbrück, *Grundriss der vergleichenden Grammatik der indogermanischen Sprache*, vol. 2, part 1 (Strassburg: Trübner, 2nd ed. 1906) 360ff.

[29] Wolfgang Meid, *Wortbildungslehre* = Hans Krahe, *Germanische Sprachwissenschaft*, vol. 3 (Sammlung Göschen 1218; Berlin: de Gruyter, 1967) 84–88.

[30] Karl Kärre, *Nomina agentis in Old English*, part I (Uppsala: Uppsala University Press, 1915) 44ff.

4. *Pheifer's analysis*

An interesting analysis is offered by Pheifer, who points out that phonological processes played a role.[31] However, Pheifer regards words containing an <l> mainly from a phonological and less from a morphological point of view: i.e. he does not always take into consideration the fact that they contain a suffix or variant forms of this suffix (*-l*, *-el*, *-il* etc.).[32] It would appear that Pheifer takes as the basic forms *-il*, *-ul* and *-l*: *-il* as in *haecilae*, *suedilas*, and loan-words such as *faecilae*; *-ul* as in *gaebuli*, *bitulin*, *uuesulae*, and loan-words such as *fibulae*; *-l* as a syllabic consonant, as in ÉpErf *-aepl* 830, *-adl* 999, *scofl* 1022 & 1065, and Erf *haesl* 50 & 236, *hraegl* 84, *uuefl* 300, *thuachl* 326, *hrisl* 851. This system was, however, disturbed by at least three processes (according to Pheifer) – syncope, on the one hand; a secondary vowel which developed before syllabic *–l*, on the other; and suffix-ablaut.

1. Syncope took place, for example, in *scybla* 627 (OHG *scubil*), Ép *teblae* 6 (but Erf *tebil*), Ép *eglae* (but Erf *egila*; OHG *ahil*). Syncope also sometimes happened in inflected forms such as *sneglas* (OHG *snegil*), *gebles* Erf 394, but not always, e.g. not in *smigilas*.
2. A secondary vowel sometimes developed, according to Pheifer,[33] before syllabic *-l*, e.g. in ÉpErf *segil-* 111, *thistil* 266, *þistil* 601 (OS *thisla*), Ép *(h)aesil* 50, 236 (but not in Erf *haesl* 50, 236, where the syllabic *l* remained), *hrisil* 851. Other authorities, however, give different reconstructions: The ODEE posits PIE **kosolos*, **koselos* > Gmc **χasalaz* > OE *hæsel* > ModE *hazel*, and Gmc **þistilaz*, *-ilo* > OE *þistel* > ModE *thistle*, i.e. according to the ODEE there was a vowel before the /l/ in Gmc and PIE;[34] cf. also EWDS, s.v. *Distel*, *Hasel*.
3. An *-il* has to be assumed in formations whose stem vowel shows i-mutation.[35] If, for example, *thyfel* is derived from *ðuf* (see VI.6 below), then the i-umlaut in the stem should be due to an original form **ðuf-il*. But even this *-il* does not have to be the original form; it can be a later substitute. Pheifer posits a "suffix ablaut" (interchange between *æ*, *i*, *u*) in some cases, i.e. a change of the stem vowel which can only be explained by a change in the suffix.[36] Thus *teblae* etc. with i-umlaut in the stem vowel cannot be derived from the classical Latin *tabula*, but only from a later form **tabil-*. Cf. *gecilae*/*gicela* (< **jakil-* < **ja-kul*); *cesol* (< **kasil-* < *casula*).

[31] Pheifer lxxvii–lxxx (esp. §§ 66–68).

[32] It is not always clear to me whether he starts his analysis from OE or from Germanic.

[33] With reference to Campbell § 363, etc.

[34] The ModE pronunciation is /heɪz(ə)l/ and /θisl/.

[35] Eduard Eckhardt, "Die angelsächsischen Deminutivbildungen," *Englische Studien* 32 (1903): 325–66 (335).

[36] Pheifer lxxix–xxx (§ 68).

The amount of variation that exists is also illustrated by *gaebuli* (dat. or instr. sing.; ÉpErf 115), *gebil* (nom.sing.; Erf 336; Ép –), and *gebles* (gen. sing.; Erf 394; Ép –): *gebles* can be explained as a case of syncope,[37] but whether *-ul* as in *gaebul* or *-il* as in *gebil* was the original form of the suffix, is more difficult to decide.

5. *Further considerations*

A fourth factor to keep in mind is that the suffix formed an unstressed final syllable. Originally, the different spellings probably represented different pronunciations, but in later OE, the suffix was weakened to /əl/, which is reflected in the preponderance of <el> spellings in later OE. In ÉpErf, however, the <el> spelling is rare (*auuel*; loan-words such as *tebelstan*), and the <il> spelling is much more frequent.

6. *The variant* -els / -ils

Furthermore, there is a variant <ils>, attested in ÉpErf in *bridils*, *gyrdils*. Kastovsky treats the latter as a separate suffix *-els* (immediately after *-el* etc.), but he states that it forms "deverbal nouns of the same semantic types as the preceding suffix group" (385) (i.e. *-el* etc.). Moreover, a number of words apparently occurred with and without the <s>; ClH lists, for example, *bridel / bridels*, *gyrdel / gyrdels*, *smygel / smygels*. Therefore, <ils> is here regarded as a variant of *-el / -il* etc. The origin of the *-ils / -els* is explained as secretion plus ensuing metathesis, i.e. when a word (word-stem) ended in *-s* and had the suffix *-l*, then *-sl* was regarded as the suffix, and this was then metathesised to *–ls*.[38]

7. *A suffix family*

From the morphological and word-formational point of view it probably suffices to say that *-el / -il / -ol / -ul / -l* and *-els / -ils* are members (or variants) of a suffix family. Other letters/sounds following the <l>, e.g. *-lae*, *-ilae*, *-lum*, *-ulin*, have to be regarded as inflexional endings (see p. 290 above and V.8 below).

8. *Gender and inflexional class*

Kastovsky points out that the suffix family "includes several subgroups distinguished as to gender and/or inflectional class" (384). Since nouns in ÉpErf are, however, mostly given in the nom.sing. and without an accompanying article, pronoun or adjective, gender and inflectional class often cannot be determined on

---

[37] Cf. also *fuglum* Ép 1067, *fluglum* Erf 1067, *fuglaes* Ép 1085, *flugles* Erf 1085.

[38] See, for example, Sievers and Brunner = Karl Brunner, *Altenglische Grammatik: Nach der angelsächsischen Grammatik von Eduard Sievers* (Tübingen: Max Niemeyer, 3rd ed. 1965) §183.2.; Campbell §460 (7).

the evidence offered by ÉpErf. Forms where gender and inflectional class can be clearly determined are (cf. p. 290 above):

1. those with the nom./acc. pl. in *-as*, which are inflected as strong masculines = masc. a-stems: *smigilas*, *sneglas*, *suedilas*;
2. forms in *-ae* (*-ilae*, *-lae*), which in later texts appear as *-e* (*-ile*, *-le*); these represent the nom.sing. of the weak feminines[39] = fem. n-stems: *-bindlae* in *uudubindlae*, *eglae*, *gecilae*, *-gristlae* in *naesgristlae*, *haecilae*, *oslae*, *throstlae*, *uuesulae*, *-uistlae* in *uuodaeuistlae*, and probably also *scybla*; further, Latin loan-words such as *cunillae*, *faecilae*, *fibulae*, *teblae*.

This seems to confirm Kastovsky's observation that "masculines and neuters mainly belong to the strong declension, feminines mainly follow the weak declension" (384).

VI Function and derivational processes of *-el* / *-il* in Old English

The suffix family *-el* / *-il* etc. forms concrete nouns, mostly from verbs; in other words, it mainly forms deverbal nouns (see 1–5 below). These formations are also usually easiest to analyse. They can therefore be regarded as the core group. Denominal (desubstantival) nouns are rarer, at least in ÉpErf (see 6 below), and there are also a number of unclear or disputed cases (see 7 below).[40]

Apart from the fairly general function of forming concrete nouns, the suffix family *-el* / *-il* etc. does not seem to have a specific meaning. Most of the underlying verbs are strong verbs, and it has to be kept in mind that derivation was not always made from the present stem, but sometimes also from one of the past stems (see X.6 below). A number of subtypes can be distinguished.[41]

1. *Action nouns*

This group is listed by Kastovsky (384), but there are no clear examples in ÉpErf. *Thuachl* (from *ðwēan* < **ðwahan* str.VI 'wash') can mean 'washing,' but in ÉpErf it means 'soap' (cf. Bammesberger):[42] i.e. it belongs to the instrument type ('instrument for washing'). In Marchand's model, action nouns correspond to the predication type.

---

[39] Cf. Campbell 249 (§617).

[40] Kärre (72–73) says that most of the *-el* formations (at least as far as they form agent nouns) are "denominational" and are "connected with denominational meaning" – but apparently by "denominational" he does not mean denominal, because most of the *-el* formations are deverbal.

[41] Kastovsky 384.

[42] Alfred Bammesberger, *Die Morphologie des urgermanischen Nomens* (Heidelberg: Carl Winter, 1990) 76.

2. *Agent nouns*

These are also rare in ÉpErf. An example is probably *bitul* 'BEETLE' (from the short base of *bītan* str. I 'to bite'), i.e. originally 'an insect that bites.' Another example may be *uuidubindlae* 'WOODBINE' (from *bindan* str. III 'to bind'): i.e. 'a plant which binds the wood, the trees,' but this is only a variant form of the more frequent *uuidubinde* etc. For *sprindil*, see 4 below. In Marchand's model, agent nouns correspond to the subject type. For other formations which may originally have been agent nouns, see sections 7 and X.1 below (*aemil*, *earendil*, *thistil*, *uuibil*).

3. *Result or object of the action*

This is probably expressed by *uuindil* 'basket' (from *windan* str. III 'to wind'): i.e. 'something which has been wound,'[43] and by *gaebul* (*gafol*) (from *giefan* str.V 'to give'): i.e. 'something which is given (by someone to someone).' In Marchand's model, those belong to the object type ('something which is given' < 'someone gives something'). Formations expressing the result or the object of the action are not always easy to distinguish from formations expressing the instrument used for an action.[44]

4. *Instrument*

At least in ÉpErf, the instrument nouns, i.e. nouns expressing the instrument used for an action, form the largest group.[45] An example is *spinil* 'SPINDLE' (G *Spindel*, from *spinnan* str. III 'to spin'): i.e. 'an instrument with which one spins.' In Marchand's model, these belong to the adverbial complement type ("someone spins with it/this instrument'). To this group belong:[46]

1. *bridils* 'BRIDLE' < **brigdel*, from *bregdan* str. III 'to pull': i.e. 'instrument used for pulling.'
2. *disl*, *dixl* (*dislum*, *dixlum*) 'waggon-pole' from Gmc **þīhsl-* (**þiuhsl*) < **þenh-slō-* 'instrument for drawing, pulling' < PIE verbal root **teng-* 'to draw'; cf. G *Deichsel*.
3. *gyrdils* 'GIRDLE' (Gmc **gurd-ila*) from *gyrdan* wk.1 'to gird' (Gmc **gurd-ja*): i.e. 'an instrument to gird someone with,' cf. G *gürten* and *Gürtel*.

---

[43] The German *Windel* is a parallel formation (derived from the same strong verb, G *winden*), but it has taken on a different meaning ('diaper') and belongs to the instrument-class: 'something which is used to wind around babies.'

[44] Some of Kastovsky's examples for the object/result group should perhaps be put in the instrument group instead, e.g. *scytel* 'dart, missile' and *bitol* 'bridle.'

[45] They seem to be the most typical (prototypical) group among the OE *-el/-il* derivations; Voyles (115) lists only the instrumental function, and (159–60) adds the agent function ("Subject [human, masculine]").

[46] For all of these, see ODEE and EWDS, and, for some, also Pheifer.

4. *naeðl* 'NEEDLE' from Gmc **nēþlō* / **nǣþlō* (G *Nadel*), derived from a verb **nǣ-ja* (<**nē-*) (G *nähen*) 'sew': i.e. 'an instrument for sewing.'
5. *scofl* 'SHOVEL' (Gmc **skuf-lō* < **skuf-*) from *scūfan* str. II 'to SHOVE, push, thrust': i.e. 'an instrument to shove with,' cf. G *Schaufel* and *schieben*.
6. *scybla* possibly also from *scūfan* (see section 7. below).
7. *scytil* 'SHUTTLE' (Gmc **skut-ila-*< * *skut-*) from *scēotan* str.II 'to SHOOT': i.e. 'an instrument for shooting, moving quickly.'[47]
8. *snaedil* 'great gut, rectum' was possibly derived from OE *snǣdan* wk. 1 'to cut, slice, eat.'
9. *spinil* 'SPINDLE' (WGmc **spenn-ilō-* < **spin-*) from *spinnan* str.III: i.e. 'instrument for spinning,' cf. G *spinnen* – *Spindel*.
10. *sprindil* 'spring-snare' either from a Gmc **sprend-* (which is unattested in OE) (Kärre 46–47) or a derivation from *springan* str. III 'to SPRING,'[48] this is an instrument which is also an agent: 'a snare which springs.'
11. *stricel* 'STRICKLE, pulley' was probably derived from *strīcan* str. I 'move, go, stroke, rub': i.e. 'an instrument which moves,' which would make it also a combination of instrument and agent.
12. *suedil* 'swaddling band, bandage' is related to *besweðian* wk. 2 'to swathe, wrap up, wind round,' cf. ODEE s.v. *swathe*; AEW s.v. *swěðel*.
13. a) *thuachl* 'soap' from *ðwēan* str. VI 'to wash' (<**þwahan*): i.e. 'instrument for washing' (Gmc **þwah-la*); b) *thuelan* 'fillets, head-bands.'
14. *uuefl* 'woof, warp' from *wefan* str. V 'to WEAVE': i.e. 'instrument for weaving.' Gmc **web-la*.

Other possible examples of original instrument nouns are *auuel*, *sadol*, *scybla*.

5. *Locative nouns*

These refer to the place of or for an action; they are rare in ÉpErf. A probable example is *smygil* (*smygilas*) 'retreat, burrow' from *smūgan* str.II 'to creep': i.e. 'place where an animal creeps to.' In Marchand's model, this group belongs to the adverbial-complement type ("someone creeps to this place or hides at this place').

6. *Denominal (desubstantival) formations and diminutives*

Kastovsky (384–85) only mentions deverbal formations with the suffix *-el* / *-il*, but a few formations seem to have been derived from nouns. The ODEE (s.v. *-le*[1]) also says that no diminutives with *-el* / *-il* existed in Old English, which is somewhat surprising, because in Latin the main function of the corresponding and etymologically related suffix *-illus* / *-ellus* / *-ullus* etc. was to form diminutives (see IV.2 above). Some of the following desubstantival formations, however, may

[47] The German *Schüssel* is a different word.

[48] In the latter case it has to be assumed that the *g* was replaced by *d*, which would be quite unusual.

have been diminutives, at least originally (*cisil*, *coecil*, *hrisil*, *þȳfel*).[49] Usually it is also more difficult to give a syntactic paraphrase for the desubstantival nouns. To this group belong probably or possibly:

1. *cisil*, *cisal* 'gravel': this corresponds to the German *Kiesel(stein)*, which has been derived from *Kies*, and it may therefore be a WGmc formation, but in OE, the base was apparently no longer attested independently.
2. *coecil* 'little cake': an OE derivation from WGmc **kōkōn* 'cake' (> G *Kuchen*), but once again, the base was no longer attested independently in OE – ModE *cake* was apparently only introduced later as a loan-word from Old Norse.
3. *hrisil* 'shuttle, radius,' was derived either from *hrīs* 'twig, branch' (G *Reis*), or from *hrisian* vb. weak 2 'to shake, move.'[50]
4. *taenil* 'TEANEL, wicker basket,' was probably derived from *tān* 'twig, rod'; a ModE reflex is the second element of *mistletoe* < OE *mistiltān*.
5. *thyfel* 'shrub, bush' may have been derived from *ðūf* 'tuft, banner, crest, bush.'

VII Difficult and disputed cases

There is a fairly large group of nouns ending in *-el* / *-il* which are problematic for some reason or other. Generally they seem to contain the suffix *-el* / *-il*, but the base of the derivation no longer existed independently even in Old English, or the connection with the underlying verb was no longer felt by the speakers. Sometimes an earlier root or base can be reconstructed, but it is isolated and cannot be assigned a meaning, or the putative root and its original meaning is disputed by scholars. Here we also move from an attempt to present a basically synchronic analysis of OE word-formation into the area of etymology. Nevertheless, the formations concerned cannot be simply ignored. Since they are unclear or disputed, their discussion often takes up more space than the analysis of regular forms. To this group belong, for example:[51]

1. *earendil*, *oerendil* 'dawn, light' has been much discussed. It is is probably an example of an obscured compound. *Earendil* perhaps goes back to a Gmc **auz(a)wandilaz*; *oerendil* (if for *eorendil*) may go back to its ablaut-variation **euz(a)wandilaz*.[52] The second element is probably derived from the strong verb OE *windan* – *wand* – *wundon* – *gewunden* (III), the first element perhaps

[49] On the diminutives, see Eckhardt 334ff. (§§16ff.). That *-el* formed diminutives in Old English is also confirmed by the *Middle English Dictionary* [*MED*], ed. Hans Kurath et al. (Ann Arbor: University of Michigan Press, 1952–) s.v. *-el* (1).

[50] Cf. Kärre (65–66), who favours the derivation from the verb.

[51] See, further, X.1 below. On these formations see, for example, Ferdinand Holthausen, *Altenglisches etymologisches Wörterbuch* [AEW], 2nd ed. with a bibliography by H.C. Matthes (Heidelberg: Carl Winter, 1963), ODEE, and EWDS.

[52] See Kärre 55–56; Pheifer 95.

corresponds to **auz-*, **euz-* 'dawn, aurora,' so perhaps the original meaning was 'ray of light announcing the arrival of the day' (Kärre 55–56): i.e. it was an agent formation.[53]

2. *fugel-* 'FOWL, bird' can be reconstructed as Gmc **foglaz*, **fuglaz (*fug-la-)*. Some (e.g., the ODEE, s.v. *fowl*)[54] have taken this as a dissimilation of **flug-laz*, thus connecting it with the verb OE *flēogan* str. II 'fly' (OE *flēogan – flēah – flugon – geflogen* < Gmc **fleugan*), but this view has not been generally accepted. Since, however, Erf has the form with *fl-* even twice (*fluglum*, *flugles* 1067, 1085, where Ép has *fuglum*, *fuglaes*), this may represent the preservation of an archaic form rather than a scribal mistake, and it may indeed point to a derivation from *flēogan*. This would make *fugel* an agent formation 'the animal which flies.' For a different view, see EWDS, s.v. *Vogel*.

3. *[h]aesil*, *haesl* 'HASEL' (G *Hasel*[*nuss*]) has been derived via a Gmc **hasla-*, **χasalaz* from an IE **kosolos*, but the basis no longer existed in Old English, and the original meaning of **kos-* is also unclear.

4. *hraecl(i)*, *hraegl* (OHG [*h*]*regil*) 'garment, RAIL' can be traced back to a WGmc **χragil-*, the origin and meaning of which is unknown, however.

5. *mistil* 'MISTLEtoe' (G *Mistel*) can be traced back to a Gmc **mistilō*, f. < **mihs-tlō*. Holthausen[55] connects it with the German *Mist* 'dung, excrement,' because there seems to have been a belief that the seeds were spread through birds' dung – if so, *mistil* would be a desubstantival formation.

6. *oslae* 'OUZEL, blackbird' (G *Amsel*) developed from a WGmc **amslōn*, but the meaning of **ams-* and its further origin is unclear. *Oslae* is apparently a hapax legomenon in OE and only attested in ÉpErf, but that it must have been a relatively common word is shown by its survival in ModE *ouzel*, *ousel*.[56]

7. *sadol* 'SADDLE' 283 (G *Sattel*): the Gmc etymon is reconstructed as **saðulaz* by the ODEE and tentatively connected with *sit* (OE *sittan* str.V; G *sitzen*); thus it would fit nicely into the instrument group ('instrument on which to sit'), cf. VI.4 above – but according to the EWDS this is uncertain; EWDS prefers to regard *sadol* as a loan into Germanic.

8. *scybla* 'woman's headdress or veil or hood (hiding the face)' 627 is connected by Holthausen in AEW with the verb *scūfan* (str. II; > *to SHOVE*; G *schieben*), which would make it a member of the instrument group.

---

[53] Apparently not listed by Charles Carr, *Nominal Compounds in Germanic* (London: Humphrey Milford for Oxford University Press, 1939).

[54] Cf. Bammesberger 75.

[55] Holthausen in AEW s.v. *mistel*.

[56] Some of the hapax legomena or very rare words which occur only in the glossaries seem to have been made up by the glossators and some may also be due to scribal mistakes, but the occurrence of *ouzel* shows that glossaries sometimes also preserve common words which are preserved neither in OE poetry nor in prose due to the fragmentary nature of the transmission; see also Hans Sauer, "Angelsächsische Glossen und Glossare und ihr Fachwortschatz," *Fachsprachen/Languages for Special Purposes*, ed. L. Hoffmann et al. (Berlin: de Gruyter, 1999) 2452–58.

9. *snegl(as)* 'SNAIL(S)' 217, 651: the Gmc root can be reconstructed as **snag-*, **sneg-*. The EWDS, s.v. *Schnecke*, connects it with the vb OHG *snahhan* 'crawl,' which would make it an agent formation 'animal which crawls.'
10. *thistil* 'THISTLE' (G *Distel*): the Gmc form can be reconstructed as **þistilaz* (-*ilō*). According to the ODEE the further origin is unclear, but according to the EWDS this is a development from *þihstila-*, which the EWDS tentatively derives from **(s)teig-* 'sting' (with loss of the initial *s*), which would make it an agent-derivation 'plant which stings' (the EWDS states that **þihstilaz* has an instrumental suffix, but an interpretation as an original agent noun seems preferable to me).
11. *uuesulae* 'WEASEL' (G *Wiesel*) comes from a WGmc **wisulōn*, which is, however, of unknown origin (Kärre 52).
12. *uuibil* 'WEEVIL, beetle' (G *Wiebel*): the (W)Gmc form has been reconstructed as **webilaz.* At least two explanations have been offered:[57] namely, (1) derivation from the vb *weave* / G *weben* (OE *wefan*), or (2) derivation from a verb **web-* 'to move briskly.' The latter explanation seems more convincing. In either case, *uuibil* would be an agent-formation 'insect which weaves or which moves around briskly.'[58]

VIII Word-fields

The formations with the suffix *-el* / *-il* cannot only be classified according to semantic groups such as action, agent, instrument etc., but also according to word-fields. Here even those words whose origin and etymology is unclear find a place. At least five groups can be distinguished, four of which are attested (Koziol 198–99) in the material from ÉpErf:

1. Persons: Although *-el* / *-il* derived names for persons (e.g. *bȳdel* 'beadle'), no such formations are attested in ÉpErf.
2. Animals:[59] some eight animal names in *-el* are attested in ÉpErf: *aemil*, *bitul* (*bitulin*), *fugel*, *oslae*, *snegl* (*sneglas*), *throstlae*, *uuesulae*, *uuibil.*[60] *Bitul* was probably the only formation that was still motivated for OE speakers: i.e. connected to its base.[61]
3. Plants:[62] some six plant names in *-el* are attested in ÉpErf: *-bindlae* (*uuidubindlae*), *(h)aesil*, *mistil*, *thistil*, *thyfel*, *-uistlae* (*uuodaeuistlae*). *Eglae* refers

[57] See ODEE s.v. *weave*[1] and *weave*[2], *weevil*; EWDS s.v. *Wiebel*; Kärre 47–48.

[58] According to the ODEE, s.v. *weevil*, ModE *weevil* is not a direct continuation of OE *wifel*, but a late ME loan-word from MLG.

[59] See Sauer, "Animal Names."

[60] According to Pheifer 77 (see Sauer, "Animal Names" 150–51), *thistil* 266 is elliptical for *þisteltwige* 'goldfinch, thistlefinch': i.e. this instance refers also to an animal, not to a plant.

[61] On the question of which *-el* formations were obscured in OE and which were still motivated for the speakers, see also Kärre 74–75.

[62] See Sauer, "Old English Plant Names."

to a part of a plant. Again, probably just one of these formations (*-bindlae*) was still motivated for OE speakers.

4. Minerals: there is just one formation in ÉpErf, *cesol.*
5. Things: this is the largest group, with some twenty-five formations. It can be subdivided into the following:
   (i) Instruments, which form the largest subgroup (cf. VI.3 above) with approx. nineteen formations in ÉpErf: *auuel, bridils, disl/dixl, naeðl, sadol, scofl, scytil, sprindil, stricel, taenil, thuachl* and *thuelan, uuindil*; to the subsection clothing belong *gyrdils, haecilae, hraecli, scybla, suedil*; to the subsection spinning and weaving belong *spinil, uuefl.*
   (ii) Other things: *coecil, earendil, gaebul, hrisil, rysil, smigilas, uuapul.*
   (iii) Parts of the body and bodily functions: *-gristlae, snaedil*; *-adl.*

IX Chronological layers: Etymology and survival

As indicated above, several chronological layers can be distinguished among the formations with *-el/il*, which touches not only upon the question of etymology, but also of productivity. It is not always easy to assign a given formation to a certain layer, one of the reasons being that the root may come from an earlier period, but the actual derivation may have been formed later. The dating of a formation should be according to the period when the form was derived.

As the examples show, the suffix was quite productive in Gmc and in WGmc. It is disputed whether it was still productive in OE. Koo (340) claims that *-el/-il* etc. had "ceased to be a living suffix in OE," whereas Kastovsky (385) says that "it is quite likely that the pattern was still productive in OE." Kastovsky founds his judgement mainly on the basis of the derivations. He suggests that the derivations from strong verbs, which form the large majority, are generally quite old, whereas the derivations from weak verbs tend to be younger (since weak verbs are generally younger than strong verbs).[63] From the evidence offered by the formations attested in ÉpErf, Kastovsky is right, and the suffix still had a certain amount of productivity in OE. The *-el/-il* formations attested in ÉpErf can be assigned to the following strata:

[63] Two or three formations in ÉpErf are derived from weak verbs: *gyrdils*, a Gmc formation (from *gyrdan*, which may have been a strong verb originally, but which was certainly weak in OE), *snædil*, probably an OE formation (from *snǣdan*), and probably also *suedil*, possibly a WGmc formation (cf VI.4 above).

1. Indo-European (PIE): Only one of the formations attested in ÉpErf can be traced back to IE with any certainty, namely *(h)aesil*. *Eglae* may be of PIE origin, if the connection with the Latin *acus* > *aculeus* is correct.
2. Germanic (Gmc): More formations go back to Gmc (ca. 21), especially *aemil, auuel, disl / dixl, earendil, eglae, fugel, gecilae, gyrdils, haecilae, mistil, naeðl, rysil, sadol, -scofl, scytil, segil, snegl, thistil, thuachl / thuelan, uuapul, windil.*
3. West Germanic (WGmc): Of WGmc origin are probably about fourteen formations: *bridils / brigdils, cisil, gaebul, gristle, hraegl, oslae, scybla* (?), *spinil, suedil, taenil, throstlae, uuefl, uuesulae, uuibil.*
4. Old English (OE): Around twelve formations were apparently formed in OE: *-ādl, auuel, -bindlae (uuidubindlae)*,[64] *bitul, coecil, hrisil, smigil, snaedil, sprindil, stricil, thyfel, -uistlae (uuodaeuistlae)*. At least as far as I can see at the moment, these words have no related forms in other Gmc or WGmc languages.[65]
5. Survival: Many of the OE *-el / -il* formations died out later, but a fair number live on in ModE, several in the standard language, and a few others in archaic or dialectal use. The suffix itself is no longer productive, however. Among the survivals in ModE are: *BEETLE, BRIDLE, FOWL, GRISTLE, GIRDLE, HAZEL, MISTLE- (mistletoe), NEEDLE, OUZEL, SADDLE, SHOVEL, SHUTTLE, SNAIL, SPINDLE, THISTLE, THROSTLE, WEASEL, WEEVIL*. The variant form *uuidubindlae* did not live on, but the more frequent form *wudubinde* survives as ModE *woodbine*.

X The material

1 *Words certainly or probably showing the OE suffix* -el / -il *etc.*

1. *-adl* 'disease': *lenctinadl* Erf 999, *lectinadl* Ép (for *le[n]ctinadl*); L *tertiana*. ClH *lenctenadl* 'spring fever' etc. Probably an OE formation; origin unclear.
2. *aemil* 'weevil, corn-worm' (2x): (a) *ǣmil* Erf 257; L *cuculio* (for *cu[r]culio*); (b) *aemil* 484; L *gurgulio*; ClH *ymel*. According to Kärre (74), this can be traced to a Gmc **amil-* with the original meaning 'injurer, damager,' and would thus be an agent formation.

2a. *-aesil* → *haesil*

3. *auuel* 'awl, hook, fork' 29; L *arpago auuel uel clauuo*. ClH *awel*. According to Kärre (51), from a Gmc **agwala-* (*a*χwala-*) 'something which stings' (further connected with L *aculeus*).
4. *-bindlae*: *uuidubindlae* 'WOODBINE' 559 (a variant of *wudubinde, wuduwinde*, cf. 348, 1059, 1082); L *inuoluco*. ClH *wudubinde, -bindle*. Apparently an OE formation. From *bindan* 'to bind.'

[64] But the original form *wudubinde* is perhaps a Gmc compound. See Carr 53 on the complicated relations between the variant forms.

[65] I have excluded the question of when the Latin loan-words ending in *-el/il* (see IV.2 above) were borrowed.

5. *bitul* 'BEETLE': *bitulin* Ép 145 (dat.pl.), *bitulum* Erf (dat.pl.) 145; L *blattis* (dat.pl.; n.sg. *blatta*). ClH *bitela*. Probably an OE formation (parallel formations in other Gmc languages have different meanings[66]). From *bītan* 'to bite.'

6. *bridils* 'BRIDLE' Ép 127, *brigdils* Erf; L *bagula*. ClH *bridel, bridels*. A WGmc formation. From *bregdan* 'to pull.'

7. *cisil* 'gravel, sand' Ép 461, *cisal* Erf; L *glarea*. Cf. G *Kiesel*. ClH *ceosol, ceosel*. A WGmc formation; see section VI.6 above.

8. *coecil* 'little cake' 993; L *tortum*. ClH *cecel*. Probably an OE formation; see section VI.6 above.

9. *disl* 'waggon-pole': *dislum* (dat.pl.) Ép 1043, *dixlum* (dat.pl.) Erf . L *temonibus*. Cf. G *Deichsel*. ClH *ðisl*. Probably a Gmc formation. See section VI.4 above.

10. *earendil* 'day-star, day-spring' Ép 554, *oerendil* Erf ; L *iuuar leoma uel earendil*. ClH *earendel*. A Gmc formation. See section VII above.

11. *eglae* 'AIL, mote, beard, ear of grain' Ép 470, *egilae* Erf; L *glis*. ClH *egl*. From a Gmc **agilō(n)* 'something which stings' (cf. OHG *ahil*) (Kärre 49). Possibly further connected with L *acus* > *aculeus*.

12. *fugel-* 'FOWL, bird' (2x): (a) *fuglum* (dat.pl.) Ép 1067, *fluglum* Erf; L *unibrellas* (acc.pl.) *stalu to fuglum/fluglum*; (b) *fuglaes bean* 'vetch' Ép 1085, *flugles bean* Erf; L *uicium*. ClH *fugel*; *fuglesbēan*. A Gmc formation. Perhaps from *flēogan* 'to fly.'

13. *gaebul, gebil* 'GAVEL, tribute, tax, debt' etc. (3x): (a) *gaebuli* (dat.sg.) 115; L *aere alieno*; (b) *gedæbin gebil* Erf 336; L *debita pensio*; (c) *gebles monung* Erf 394; L *exactio*. ClH *gafol*. Possibly an OE formation.[67] From *giefan* 'to give.'

14. *-gristle* 'GRISTLE, cartilage': *naesgristlae* 'nose-gristle' 174; L *cartilago* Ép, *cartalago* Erf. ClH *gristle, næsgristle*. Probably from a WGmc **gristle*; the further origin is unknown.

15. *gyrdils* 'GIRDLE, belt' (2x): (a) *gyrdils* Ép 573, Erf 573a; L *lumbare gyrdils uel broec*; (b) *gyrdislrhingae* Ép 582, *gyrdilshringe* Erf; L *legula* Ép, *legu* Erf. Cf. G *Gürtel*. ClH *gyrdel*; *gyrdelhring*. A Gmc formation. From *gyrdan* 'to gird.' See section VI.4 above.

16. *haecilae* 'HACKLE, cloak, coat' (2x): (a) *haecilae* Ép 572, *hecile* Erf; L *lacerna haecilae uel lotha*; (b) *haecilae* Ép 740, *hecæli* Erf; L *paludamentum genus uestimenti bellici idest haecilae*. ClH *hacele*. Cf. OHG *hahhul*. A Gmc formation.

17. *[h]aesil* 'HAZEL' (2x): (a) *aesil* Ép 50 (for *[h]aesil*), *haesl* Erf ; L *auellanus*; (b) *haesil* Ép 236, *haesl* Erf; L *corylus*. Cf. G *Hasel(nuß)*. ClH *haesel*. An IE formation. See section VII above.

18. *hraecl, hraegl* 'RAIL, dress, clothing': *hraecli* (dat.sg.) Ép 84, *hraegl* Erf; L *amiculo*. ClH *hraegl*. A WGmc formation; base unknown (see section VII above).

---

66 See Elmar Seebold, *Vergleichendes und etymologisches Wörterbuch der germanischen starken Verben* (The Hague: Mouton, 1970) 97.

67 But see Seebold 218.

19. *hrisil* 'shuttle, radius' Ép 851, *hrisl* Erf; L *radium*. ClH *hrisel*. Probably an OE formation. On the basis of the derivation, see section VI.6 above.

20. *mistil* 'MISTLEtoe' 1083; L *uiscus*. ClH *mistel*. Cf. G *Mistel*. A Gmc formation; see section VII above.

21. *naeðl* 'NEEDLE': *naeðlae* Ép 796 (dat. sing.), *nedlæ* Erf; L *pictus acu mið naeðlae asiuuid* Ép, *pictis acu mid nedlæ asiuuid* Erf. ClH *nǣdl*. From Gmc **nēþlō/nǣþlō* (G *Nadel*) < *nē-* (**nǣ-ja*) 'sew' (G *nähen*): i.e. a deverbal formation. The underlying verb survives in German, but it is no longer attested in OE.

22. *oslae* 'OUZEL, OUSEL, blackbird' 665 (hap.leg. in OE); L *merula*. ClH *ōsle*. Cf. G *Amsel*. A WGmc formation; see section VII above.

23. *rysil* 'lard, fat, abdomen' Ép 2, *risil* Erf; L *axungia*. ClH *rysel*. A Gmc formation. Base unknown.

24. *sadol* 'SADDLE' (2x): (a) *sadol* Ép 926, *satul* Erf; L *sella*; (b) *sadulbogo* 'saddle-bow' 283, L *carpella*. ClH *sadol*, *sadolbogo*. Cf. G *Sattel*. A Gmc formation; see section VII above.

25. *-scofl* 'SHOVEL' (2x): (a) *scofl* Ép 1022, *scolf* Erf; L *trulla*; (b) *gloedscofl* 'fire-shovel' 1065, L *uatilla*. ClH *scofl*, *gledscofl*. Cf. G *Schaufel*. A Gmc formation, see section VI.4 above.

26. *scybla* 'woman's hood, veil, head-dress etc.' 627; L *mafort(a)e*. ClH *scyfel(e)*. A WGmc formation (?).

27. *scytil* 'SHUTTLE, lever or beam or bar or tongue of a balance' 632; L *momentum*. ClH *scytel*. A Gmc formation; see section VI.4 above.

28. *segil* 'SAIL': *segilgaerd* 111; L *antempna* Ép, *antemna* Erf. ClH *seglgyrd* 'sail-yard, cross-pole.' From Gmc **segla(m)* (G *Segel*). According to the ODEE, its further origin is unknown; according to the EWDS, it was possibly derived from **sek-* 'to cut,' i.e. 'a piece of cloth which has been cut off.'

29. *smigil* 'retreat, burrow': *smigilas* (nom./acc. pl.) Ép 199, *smygilas* Erf 199; L *cuniculos* (acc.pl.). ClH *smygel*, *smygels*. Probably an OE formation; from *smūgan* 'to creep.'

30. *snaedil* 'gut, bowels, rectum' Erf 381; L *extale snaedil uel thearm*. ClH *snædel* = *snæðeldearm* 'great gut' (Pheifer: "rectum"). Probably an OE formation, from *snǣdan* 'to cut, eat.'

31. *snegl* 'SNAIL' (3x): (a) *sneglas* (nom./acc. pl.) 217, L *cocleae lytlae sneglas*; (b) *snel* Ép 611, *snegl* Erf; L *limax*; (c) *snegl* Ép 651(Erf-), L *maruca*. ClH *snægl*, *snægel*. A Gmc formation (**snagil-*, **snegil-*); see section VII above.

32. *spinil* 'SPINDLE' 967, L *stilium uel fusa spinil*. ClH *spinel* f. A WGmc formation. From *spinnan* 'to spin,' cf. G *Spindel*.

33. *sprindil* 'spring, snare (for catching birds), basket-snare' 1025 (hap. leg.), L *tenticum*. Cf. ClH *sprincel*. Probably an OE formation. See VI.4 above.

34. *stricil* 'pulley' ('fount, breast'): *stricilum* (dat.pl.) 994; L *trocleis rotis modicis uel stricilum*. ClH *stricel*. Probably an OE formation from *strīcan* vb str.I 'move, go' etc.

35. *suedil* 'swaddling band, bandage': *suedilas* (nom. acc. pl.) 506; L *instites*. ClH *sweðel*. A WGmc formation.

36. *taenil* 'TEANEL, wicker basket' Ép 403, *tenil* Erf. L *fiscilla* Ép, *fiscella* Erf. ClH *tænel* m. Probably a WGmc formation.

37. *thistil* 'THISTLE' (3x): (a) *thistil* Erf 266; L *cardella*; (b) *thistil* Erf 271; L *carduus*; (c) *þuþistil* Ép 601, *popistil* Erf; L *lactuca*. ClH *ðistel*. A Gmc formation; see section VII above.

38. *throstlae* 'THROSTLE, thrush' 1011; L *turdella*. ClH *ðrostle*. Can be traced back to a WGmc *þrust-lō* f.; the further origin is complicated (WestIE **tr(o)zdo-*) and originally perhaps onomatopoeic.

39a. *thuachl* 'soap (washing)' Erf 326; L *delumentem*. ClH *ðweal*. A Gmc formation, see 39b.

39b *thuelan* 'fillets, headbands (towels)' 1060; L *uittas* Ép, *uitas* Erf (for *uit[t]as*). From Gmc **þwahilo* (cf. OHG *duahila/duehila*).

40. *-thyfel* 'shrub, bush' (2x): (a) *scaldthyflas* (nom.acc.pl.) 'thicket' (Pheifer: lit. "plants growing in shallow water") Ép 58, *scaldthyblas* Erf; L *alga* Ép, *alge* Erf; (b) *riscthyfil* 'rush-bed' Ép 517, *rycthyfil* Erf (for *ry[s]cthyfil*); L *iungetum*. ClH *scealdðyfel*, *riscðyfel*. Probably an OE formation.

41. *uuapul* 'bubble, froth,' or 'lie' 447; L *famfaluca* Ép, *fanfaluca* Erf (cf. 426: *famfaluca leasung uel faam*). ClH *wapul*. A Gmc formation. The base is unclear (cf. Kärre 52).

42. *uuefl* 'woof, warp' 300; L *caldica*. ClH *wefl*. Probably a WGmc formation (cf. OHG *weval*). From *wefan* 'to weave.'

43. *uuesulae* 'WEASEL' 650; L *mustella*. ClH *wesle*. A WGmc formation; see section VII above.

44. *uuibil* 'WEEVIL' 310; L *cantarus*. A WGmc formation; see section VII above.

45. *windil* 'WINDLE, basket' Ép 173, *pindil* Erf (for *[w]indil*); L *cartellus*. ClH *windel*. From *windan* vb. 'WIND' (cf. G *Windel*, with different semantic development). A WGmc formation.

46. *-uistlae*: *uuodaeuistlae* 'hemlock' (Pheifer 76) Ép 248, *uuodeuuislae* Erf (both for *uuodae [th]istlae*?).

2 *Words excluded as not containing the suffix* -el / -il *(see* IV.1 *above)*

47. *-aepl* 'APPLE' (G *APFEL*): *hunaegaepl* Ép 830, *caenegaepl* Erf 'lozenge, pastille of honey'; L *pastellas* Ép, *pastellus* Erf. ClH *æppel*. From a Gmc **apli-*, **aplu-*; ultimately perhaps the name of the town *Abella* (ODEE). For other views, see EWDS, s.v. *Apfel*.

48. *blecthrustfel* or *blec thrustfel* 'leprosy' 139; L *bitiligo*. ClH *blæcðrustfel*, *ðrustfell*. It is difficult to decide whether this is a compound *blec-thrustfel* or a syntactic group *blec thrustfel*. In any case *ðrustfell* is a Gmc formation (Gothic *þrūts-fill*), a compound of *þrūts* (OE *ðrust* shows metathesis) 'swollen' etc. and

fill, OE *fell* (cf. L *pellis*) 'skin, hide' etc.: i.e. 'swollen skin,' but *þrust* is no longer attested independently in OE.[68]

49. *-bil* 'BILL, chopper, axe, sword': *uudubil* 'hatchet' Ép 430, *uuidubil* Erf. L *falces uudubil sigdi riftr* Ép (*falcis* ... Erf). ClH *bill*. From WGmc **bilja*; the *l* seems to be part of the root. German *Beil* is apparently a different word, see EWDS.
50. *edwalla* 'eddy, vortex, whirlpool' Ép 1068, *edualla* Erf. L *uertigo*. ClH *ed-wielle*. From the verb *weallan* 'to well, bubble' etc.: i.e. the *-ll-* is part of the root.
51. *eola* 'ELK' Erf 346a. L *damina bestia idest eola*. ClH *eolh*. From **eolha* < WGmc **elha-* (G *Elch*) < IE **elk-*: i.e. the *-l-* seems to be part of the root. Cf. EWDS s.v. *Elch*.

51a *-fel*: see *blecthrustfel*.

52. *gecilae* 'icicle, ice' Ép 954, *gecile* Erf; L *stiria*. ClH *gicel(a)*. Probably a Gmc formation. From **jakil(az)* < Gmc **jakul(az)*. The base is unknown, however.
53. *innifli* 'bowels, womb' Ép 504, *inifli* Erf; L *interamen*. ClH *innylfe*; AEW *innelfe*. According to AEW, perhaps derived from *afol* 'power, might': i.e. 'inner might.'
54. *maethlae*, *medlae* 'council, meeting': *in maethlae* Ép 549, *in medlae* Erf; L *in curia*. ClH *maeðel*. The etymology is difficult; see Feist s.v. *maþl*, who reconstructs a PIE form **m↔d-tlo-*, and Bammesberger (89) (Gmc **maþla-*).
55. *Spell* 'SPELL': *spelli* (dat.sing.) 869; L *relatu*. ClH *spell*. From Gmc **spellam* of unknown origin.

3 *Latin loan-words ending in* -el / -il *etc.* *(see* IV.2 *above)*

56. *candel* 'CANDLE' 382
57. *cesol* 'gullet, maw' 457, 1054
58. *cetil* 'KETTLE' 168, 350
59. *couel* 'basket' 305
60. *cunillae* 'wild thyme' 246
61. *fæcilae*, *faecile* 'torch' 407
62. *fibulae* 'clasp, buckle, brace' 3a
63. *finugl* 'FENNEL' 451
64. *lebil* 'cup, bowl' 633, 995
65. *sigil* 'buckle, brooch' 134, 408, 882
66. *teblae, tefil* 6, cf. 7 (*teblere*), 172 (*tebil*[*s*]*tan*)

---

[68] See Sigmund Feist, *Vergleichendes Wörterbuch der Gotischen Sprache* (Leiden: E.J. Brill, 3rd ed. 1939) s.v. *þrūts-fill*. According to Carr 66, *ðrūstfell* was originally a bahuvrihi compound, meaning 'having a swollen skin.'

4 *Adjectives containing the adjective-forming suffix* -el / -il *etc.* *(see* IV.3 *above)*

67. *aedil* 'noble' 479
68. *nihol* 'prone' 799
69. *sinuurbul, sinuulfr* 'round' 1047
70. *staegil* 'steep' 747

5 *Compounds and derivations formed with nouns in* -el / -il *(including loan-words)*

Several formations with the suffix (suffix family) *-el / -il* etc. occur as a part of a compound or, more rarely, as the basis of another derivation (prefix or suffix formation). This illustrates the recursivity of word-formation processes, i.e. after one word-formation process has been completed, another one can be applied to the newly created formation later on. Usually, one process follows another, which of course also shows that the basis is the earlier formation and the compound or derivation the later one.

(i) Compounds:

blec-thrustfel (or a syntactic group *blec thrust-fel*, where *thrust-fel* is the compound)

candel-thuist

earendil (probably an example of a synthetic compound [G *Zusammenbildung*], where compounding and suffixation operate at the same time; also an example of an obscured compound)

fuglaes bean

gebles monung (probably a syntactic group)

gloed-scofl

gyrdils-hringe

hunaeg-aepl (Carr 26)

lenctin-adl

naes-gristlae

risc-thyfil

sadul-bogo (Carr 79)

scald-thyflas

segil-gaerd[69]

tebel-stan (Carr 140)

uudu-bil (Carr 21)

uuidu-bindlae

uuodae-uistlae

[69] A WGmc compound, according to Carr 103.

(ii) Prefix-formations:

innifli (if from *in* and *afol*)
edwalla

(iii) Suffix-formations: Only formations with loan-words are attested in ÉpErf:

teblere
teblith

6 *Verbs used for* -el/-il *derivations*[70]

1) *bindan* 'BIND' (G *binden*) str. III (Gmc **bend-a-*; OE ***bindan*** – *band* – *bundon* – *bunden*) > *uuidu-bindlae.*
2) *bītan* 'BITE' (G *beißen*) str. I (Gmc **beit-a-*; OE *bītan* – *bāt* – ***biton*** – ***biten***) > *bitul.*
3) *bregdan* 'pull' str. III (Gmc **bregd-a-*; OE *bregdan* – *brægd* – ***brugdon*** – *brogden*) > *brigdils* > *bridils.*
4) *flēogan* 'FLY' (G *fliegen*) str. II (Gmc **fleug-a-*; OE *flēogan* – *flēah* – ***flugon*** – *flogen*) > *fugol* (?).
5) *giefan* (G *geben*) str. V (Gmc **geb-a-*; OE *giefan*/*gefan* – *geaf* / ***gæf*** – *gēafon*/ *gēfon* – *giefen*/*gefen*) > *gaebul.*
6) *gyrdan* 'GIRD' (G *gürten*) wk. 1 > *gyrdils* (cf. G *Gürtel*). Gmc **gerd-*a-* (?).
7) *scēotan* 'SHOOT' (G *schießen*) str. II (Gmc **skeut-a-*; OE *scēotan* – *scēat* – ***scuton*** – *scoten*) > *scytil.*
8) *scūfan* 'SHOVE' (G *schieben*) str. II (Gmc **skeub-a-*; OE *scūfan* – *scēaf* – *scufon* – *scofen*) > (1) *scofl* (G *Schaufel*); (2) possibly also *scybla.*
9) *sittan* 'SIT' (G *sitzen*) str. V (Gmc **set-ja-*; OE *sittan* – ***sæt*** – *sǣton* – *seten*) > (?) *sadul* 'SADDLE' (G *Sattel*).
10) *smūgan* 'creep' (G *schmiegen*) str. II (Gmc **smeug-a-*; OE *smūgan* – *smēag* – ***smugon*** – *smogen*) > *smygil.*
11) *snǣdan* 'cut, eat' wk. 1 (derived from *snīðan* str.I 'cut') > *snǣdil.*
12) *spinnan* 'SPIN' (G *spinnen*) str. III (Gmc **spenn-a-*; OE ***spinnan*** – *spann* – *spunnon* – *spunnen*) > *spinil* 'SPINDLE'(G *Spindel*).
13) *strīcan* 'STRIKE, stroke, move, go' (G *streichen*) str. I (Gmc **streik –a-*; OE *strīcan* [–*strāc* – ***stricon*** – *stricen*]) > *stricil* 'STRICKLE' (in ÉpErf: 'pulley').
14) *þwēan* < **þwahan* 'wash' str. VI (Gmc **þwah-a-*; OE ****þwahan*** > *þwēan* – *þwōg*/*þwōh* – *þwōgon* – *þwagen*/*þwegen*) > *thuachl, thuelan.*
15) *wefan* 'WEAVE' (G *weben*) str. V (Gmc **web-a-*; OE ***wefan*** – *wæf* – *wǣfon* – *wefen*) > (a) *uuefl*; (b) (?) *uuibil* (or from **web* 'move briskly').
16) *windan* 'WIND' (G *winden*) str. III (Gmc **wend-a-*; OE ***windan*** – *wand* – *wundon* – *wunden*) > (a) *windil*; (b) *earendel* > **auzwandilaz.*

---

[70] Only the relatively clear cases are listed; the basis of the derivation is printed in ***boldface***. On these verbs and the derivations formed with them, see Seebold.

On English Lexicography at the Turn of the Millennium

ARNE ZETTERSTEN

I Manpower vs. machine power

AMERICAN MURDERER HELPED WRITE Oxford Dictionary" was the staggering headline of an article published in the *Sunday Star*, Washington D.C., in July 1915 by an American journalist called Hayden Church. The story about Dr William Chester Minor, who constantly helped the editors of the *Oxford English Dictionary* for about twenty years with nearly ten thousand definitions during the last few decades of the nineteenth century and the beginning of the twentieth, also appeared in the *Strand* magazine in September 1915.

The close cooperation between Dr James Murray and Dr Minor is well documented through Dr Murray's own letters. Their first meeting is, however, known through the fictionalised account in Hayden Church's story which runs as follows, starting here at the point when Dr Murray first arrived at Broadmoor, Crowthorne, in Berkshire:

> James Murray removed his cap and unbuttoned the Inverness tweed coat that had protected him from the cold. The servant said nothing, but ushered him inside and up a flight of marble stairs. He was swept into a large room with a glowing coal fire and a wall covered with portraits of gaunt-looking men. There was a large oak director's desk, and behind it, a portly man of obvious importance. The servant backed out and closed the door.
>
> Murray advanced toward the great man, who rose. Murray bowed stiffly and extended his hand.
>
> "I, Sir, am Dr. James Murray of the London Philological Society," he said in his finely modulated Scottish voice, "and editor of the *Oxford English Dictionary*."
>
> "And you sir, must be Dr. William Minor. At long last. I am most deeply honoured to meet you."
>
> There was a pause. Then the other man replied:

> "I regret not, sir. I cannot lay claim to that distinction. I am the Superintendent of the Broadmoor Criminal Lunatic Asylum. Dr. Minor is an American, and he is one of our longest-staying inmates. He committed a murder. He is quite insane."
>
> Doctor Murray, as the story continues, was in turn astonished, amazed, and yet filled with sympathetic interest.
>
> He begged to be taken to Doctor Minor, and the meeting between the two men of learning who had corresponded for so long and who now met in such strange circumstances was an extremely impressive one.[1]

The above story, based on a combination of facts and fiction, has created new interest in the fascinating background of the world's probably greatest lexicographical achievement so far, The *Oxford English Dictionary*, published originally between 1884 and 1928 in ten volumes. The renewed interest in the OED these days is due partly to the recent publication of Simon Winchester's *The Professor and the Madman*, published in 1998, and partly to the newest formats of the OED, recently introduced by Oxford University Press.

The history of the OED and its dedicated editors has been well documented, particularly by publications such as K.M. Elisabeth Murray's *Caught in the Web of Words*, Donna Lee Berg's *A Guide to the Oxford English Dictionary*, and John Willinsky's *Empire of Words*.[2] However, it is Winchester's book that brings out best the extraordinary circumstances under which the collection of the vast material was carried out. It also shows us the ways in which Murray as Chief Editor[3] had to improvise and to make unprecedented decisions. Even today, with the use of so much sophisticated computer hardware and software, we must still admit that some dictionary projects are quite impressive. It is still difficult to imagine how such a small team of OED scholars could mastermind so much with so little technology at the time of the first ten volumes.

This brief introduction to the history of the OED is meant to put the latest formats of this dictionary in perspective: namely, the CD-ROM version of 1999 and the online edition of 2000, both examples of how databases of words, expressions and texts can be utilised with new technology, whether for monolingual or for bilingual purposes. The upgraded CD-ROM version of 1999 came with search techniques like the following:

---

[1] Winchester, *The Professor and the Madman: A Tale of Murder, Insanity, and the Making of the Oxford English Dictionary* (New York: HarperCollins, 1998) 169–71.

[2] K.M. Elisabeth Murray, *Caught in the Web of Words: James A.H. Murray and the "Oxford English Dictionary"*, preface by R.W. Burchfield (New Haven, CT: Yale University Press, 1977); Donna Lee Berg, *A Guide to the Oxford English Dictionary* (Oxford: Oxford University Press, 1993); John Willinsky, *Empire of Words: The Reign of the OED* (Princeton, NJ: Princeton University Press, 1994).

[3] Murray, ed. *A New English Dictionary on Historical Principles* (Oxford: Oxford University Press, 1984).

1. Searches for headwords or compounds can be undertaken at any time through the "Find word" function.
2. Search for words or phrases across the entire text or narrow the parameters (e.g. search only quotation text, definition text or etymologies).
3. Search by date, title of work or author of quotation.
4. A powerful new proximity search permits the location of words that occur near, before, or after one another in an entry.
5. Wildcards can be applied to search for any number of unknown characters and to search for any individual character the user is uncertain about.

The OED Online Edition was made available in 2000 by annual subscription. In addition to the Second Edition of the OED (1989) and three additional volumes, there will be quarterly releases and new revised material up to 2010. The dictionary has also advertised the following benefits of OED Online:

1. Select how entries are displayed by turning pronunciations, etymologies, variant spellings, and quotations on and off.
2. Everything from simple word look-ups to proximity searching, using any of the fields in the dictionary, can be done with speed and ease.
3. Find a term when you know the meaning but have forgotten the word.
4. Use wildcards if you are unsure of a spelling, or if you want to search for words with common characteristics.
5. Search for quotations from a specified year, or from a particular author and/or work.
6. Search for words which have come into English via a particular language.
7. Compare revised entries with entries from the Second Edition to see how language has changed and how new scholarship has increased understanding of our linguistic and cultural heritage.

The example of the development from manpower to machine power is only one of many similar developments in the history of lexicography. The reason for using the OED for this exemplification is of course the exceptional bulk of both the original project and the latest venture to double the size of the dictionary by 2010. This plan to bring the OED completely up to date will probably make the revision programme one of the world's largest humanities research projects.

The *Longman Web Dictionary* (1999) is a further example of Internet lexicography, an online dictionary which will be updated regularly. Most major English dictionaries nowadays have CD-ROM versions, like the *Longman Dictionary of Contemporary English*, the *Collins COBUILD English Dictionary* and the *Cambridge International Dictionary of English.*

II From Murray to Sinclair and beyond

Thanks to the rapid development of computer technology towards the end of the twentieth century, corpus linguistics became increasingly important for the production of dictionaries, particularly for English-based bilingual dictionaries. The earliest corpora of English language text came in the 1960s, such as the *Brown University Corpus of Modern American English* (1961) followed by the *Lancaster–Oslo/Bergen Corpus of British English Texts* of 1961. These two corpora contain 1 million running words each, both subdivided into the same fifteen categories of prose. They were therefore useful for linguistic comparison but not large enough to be the basis for dictionary making. As the storage capacity of computers developed during the 1980s and 1990s, it became more meaningful to utilise new scanning techniques and the new storage capacity of computers in order to create large databases of language text (linguistic corpora) for new types of dictionaries.

The real pioneering project in this field was the *Bank of English*, composed at the University of Birmingham under the directorship of Professor John Sinclair. The first corpus, containing 20 million words, formed the basis for the first edition of the *Collins COBUILD English Language Dictionary* of 1987.[4] The *Bank of English* continued to grow in the 1990s and the corpus used for the second edition in 1995 comprised some 200 million words, divided into several subcorpora. The table on page 319 shows the status of the corpus in 1996 with approximately 323 million words. By the beginning of the new millennium, the *Bank of English* had probably grown to well over 500 million words. With such a wealth of material, it is clear that the *COBUILD Dictionary* may provide appropriate examples for even extremely infrequent English words, which will be further evidenced by

[4] *Collins COBUILD English Language Dictionary* (London: Collins, 1987).

the third edition of the *Collins COBUILD English Dictionary*, to appear at the beginning of the new millennium.

COBUILD: *Bank of English*: 323-million-word Corpus: 1996

Subcorpus	*Size (in words)*	*Number of texts*	*Average text size (words)*	*Dates*
BBC (daily transcripts from broadcasts of the BBC World Service, London)	18.52 million	143	130,000	1990–1991
ECON (issues of the *Economist*, London)	12.13 million	178	69,000	1991–1995
GUARD (issues of the *Guardian*, London)	24.26 million	271	88,000	1995
INDY (issues of the *Independent*, London)	19.45 million	185	103,000	1990, 1995
NEWSCI (issues of the *New Scientist*, London)	6.09 million	138	46,000	1992–1995
NPR (daily transcripts from broadcasts of National Public Radio, Washington D.C.)	22.26 million	726	31,000	1990–1993
OZNEWS (issues of the *Courier Mail* and *Sunday Mail*, Brisbane)	33.35 million	370	90,000	1994–1995
TIMES (issues of *The Times* and *Sunday Times*, London)	20.95 million	155	135,000	1995–1996
TODAY (issues of *Today* newspaper, London)	26.61 million	794	64,000	1991–1995
UKBOOKS (384 non-fiction, 188 fiction, 300 male writers, 189 female, 27 joint male/female, 56 other)	42.13 million	572	71,000	post-1990
UKEPHEM (junk mail, brochures, leaflets, newsletters, etc; also personal letters)	4.72 million	2,359	2,000	post-1990
UKMAGS (issues of 66 different periodicals; general and specialist interests)	30.14 million	760	39,000	1992–1993
UKSPOKEN (recordings of mainly spontaneous, informal conversation from all parts of Britain	20.18 million	2,669	7,000	post-1990
USBOOKS (169 male authors, 63 female, 12 joint male/female, 83 other)	32.66 million	327	98,000	post-1990
USEPHEM (junk mail, brochures, leaflets, newsletters, etc; also personal letters)	1 million	939	1,000	post-1995
USNEWS:				
WSJ (issues of the *Wall Street Journal*, New York)	6 million	75	81,000	1989
PALO ALTO (issues of the *Palo Alto Weekly*, Palo Alto, California)	2.58 million	84	33,000	1994

According to Douglas Biber et al.,[5] the best-known commercially available corpora at the end of the last century were the following:

Corpora

Written

ACI/DCI (Association of Computational Linguistics/Data Collection Initiative): includes 63 million words written AmE; 40 million words from the *Wall Street Journal*; 23 million words from scientific abstracts.

Brown: c.1 million words of written AmE; many registers.

Freiburg: c.1 million words written BrE; parallel to the LOB, but from material published in 1991.

Lancaster–Oslo/Bergen (LOB): c.1 million words written BrE; many registers; all published in 1961.

Longman–Lancaster: c.30 million words written BrE and AmE; many registers from the early 1900s to the 1980s.

Spoken

IBM–Lancaster Spoken English Corpus: 52,000 words spoken BrE, mostly from BBC recordings.

London–Lund: c. half a million words spoken BrE.

Corpus of Spoken American English (CSAE): goal of 200,000 words of spoken AmE – under construction.

Written and spoken

British National Corpus (BNC): c.100 million words BrE; 90 million written; 10 million spoken; many registers.

CHILDES Project: corpora of children's spoken and written language.

COBUILD/Birmingham Corpus: 200+ million words BrE; constantly growing, mostly written.

Survey of English Usage Corpus (SEU): c. 1 million words of BrE collected from 1953 to 1987 divided evenly into spoken and written. The spoken texts make up the London–Lund Corpus.

Historical

ARCHER Corpus: c.2 million words BrE and AmE, 1650–1990; written and speech-based registers.

Helsinki Corpus: c.1.5 million words 850–1710; many registers.

Helsinki Corpus of Older Scots: 830, 000 words from 15 registers, 1450–1700.

Innsbruck Computer Archive of Middle English Texts (ICAMET): c.2 million words of Middle English prose, 1100–1500; texts arranged alphabetically.

---

[5] Douglas Biber, Susan Conrad and Randi Reppen, *Corpus Linguistics* (Cambridge: Cambridge University Press, 1998) 281–82.

Newdigate Newsletter: 750,000 words of manuscript newsletters, 1674–1692.

Zurich Corpus of English Newspapers (ZEN): London newspapers from the mid 1660s to the beginning of the twentieth century.

Varieties of English

Hong Kong University of Science and Technology (HKUST) Learner Corpus: c.6 million words (with on-going collection) of written undergraduate assignments and "A" level Use of English scripts from the Hong Kong Examination Authority.

International Corpus of English (ICE): A collection of corpora, each representing spoken and written registers from a national variety of English.

International Corpus of Learner English (ICLE): c.1 million words of written English texts from nine different language backgrounds.

Kolhapur: 1 million words of written Indian English from 1978.

Melbourne–Surrey Corpus: 100,000 words from Australian newspapers.

Northern Ireland Transcribed Corpus: c.400,000 words of spoken material from 42 locations and over three age groups.

In the new millennium, it will be more and more obvious that many areas of linguistics can be addressed with corpus-based studies, for example grammar, sociolinguistics, stylistic studies, language acquisition, historical linguistics, and particularly lexicography. Biber et al.[6] have identified six major types of research questions addressed with corpus-based lexicographic investigations:

1. What are the meanings associated with a particular word?
2. What is the frequency of a word relative to other related words?
3. What non-linguistic association patterns does a particular word have (e.g., to registers, historical periods, or dialects)?
4. What words commonly co-occur with a particular word, and what is the distribution of these "collocational" sequences across registers?
5. How are the senses and uses of a word distributed?
6. How are seemingly synonymous words used and distributed in different ways?[7]

We may all recognise the fact that James Murray was the pioneer of English lexicography towards the end of the nineteenth century, just as John Sinclair was towards the end of the twentieth. As the new millennium proceeds, we realise that the consistent development of the COBUILD Corpus in the 1980s and 1990s had an immediate impact on other similar dictionary products in the English-speaking

[6] Biber et al. 11–12, 23–24.

[7] See Biber et al. 11–12, 23–24.

world and beyond. It became clear in 1995, the great year of four major English learners' dictionaries:

The Collins COBUILD English Dictionary (COBUILD 2)[8]
The Longman Dictionary of Contemporary English (LDOCE 3)[9]
The Oxford Advanced Learner's Dictionary (OALD 5)[10]
The Cambridge International Dictionary of English (CIDE).[11]

In addition to COBUILD, LDOCE stresses the importance of electronic corpora being essential for the production of modern dictionaries, and from this year onwards this has been obvious in all kinds of dictionary production.[12]

III From monolingual to bilingual dictionaries and beyond

In his discussion of "Tomorrow's dictionaries" in *Living Words*,[13] Tom McArthur presents a series of eight processes in dictionary making, all terms ending in "-isation."

1. The first is *globalisation*, meaning dictionaries showing English as an international language for all people and places. McArthur maintains that the emergence of learners' dictionaries in the 1930s was a cardinal development for English lexicography. Particularly the *Advanced Learner's Dictionary of Current English* in all its editions has had, according to McArthur, a vast impact on perceptions of English as an international language.
2. The term *localisation* means that international dictionaries may be customised for one country or one group of countries. For example, the *Times–Chambers Essential Dictionary*, published by Federal Publications, Singapore (1997), contains the "core English" (standard British and American), English words specific to Singapore and Malaysia (called "SME") and regional words adopted into SME.

---

[8] *Collins COBUILD English Dictionary* (London: HarperCollins, 2nd ed. 1995).

[9] *The Longman Dictionary of Contemporary English* (Harlow: Longman, 3rd ed. 1995).

[10] *The Oxford Advanced Learner's Dictionary of Current English* (Oxford: Oxford University Press, 5th ed. 1995).

[11] *The Cambridge International Dictionary of English* (Cambridge: Cambridge University Press, 1995).

[12] On the background of ELT learners' dictionaries, see esp. Tom McArthur, *Living Words* (Exeter: Exeter University Press, 1998) 133–48.

[13] McArthur 206–11.

3. *Bilingualisation* indicates that a major dictionary is translated into another language and made available to users in that language. McArthur explains how this has been a success with Chinese learners in the case of the *Longman Dictionary of Contemporary English* (1976 onward) and the *Longman Lexicon of Contemporary English* (1981).
4. *Semibilingualisation* is a process whereby the main principle is that all translation equivalents are inserted for all dictionary headwords. Examples can be provided by the pioneer in this field, the Kernerman Semi-Bilingual Dictionaries, for example, *Passport: English Hebrew Learner's Dictionary* (1996), based on *Passport English Learner's Dictionary.*
5. The fifth process is called *nationalisation*, indicating that major English-speaking countries like Australia and Canada have produced indigenous Australian or Canadian dictionaries, such as the *Macquarie Dictionaries* and the *Canadian Oxford Dictionary*, respectively. There are now also special national style guides, such as the *Cambridge Australian English Style Guide* (1995), and the *Guide to Canadian English Usage* (1997).
6. The next process is *regionalisation*, referring to regions larger than a single state, such as South and East Asia. McArthur suggests that a native-speaker-style dictionary for this area may be foreseen, as well as one fitting Australian English more firmly into the Asian context. Whether this means that "the middle classes are welcoming English into work and home as an Asian Language"[14] is too soon to tell.
7. The next process, *thematisation*, indicates formats like that of *Roget's Thesaurus*, in which words and meanings are presented thematically, not alphabetically. Further examples are the *Longman Essential Activator: Put Your Ideas into Words* (1997) and the *Oxford Learner's Wordfinder Dictionary* (1997).
8. The last process could be called *electronicisation*, including all varieties of electronic tools for dictionary making and electronic media for presenting dictionary items and complete dictionaries.

[14] McArthur 209.

In all these eight categories, one would hope that dictionary producers always bear in mind the wishes and attitudes of potential users.[15]

The new English–Danish Dictionary[16] is an example of a project in which a comprehensive evaluation was carried out by one of the commercial assessment companies in Copenhagen. Thanks to this careful needs-analysis, the producers believed that they would meet the needs of the users as closely as possible. This type of English-based bilingual dictionary is the closest one can get to a combination of a monolingual English dictionary and a bilingual dictionary.

The new English–Danish Dictionary contains several features which contribute to making it markedly different from most English-based bilingual dictionaries. A few of these characteristic features will be summarised here.[17]

1. The dictionary is based on the entries, definitions and authentic examples of the second edition of the *Collins COBUILD English Dictionary* of 1995.
2. The *Bank of English* at Cobuild, Birmingham, contributed about 200 million words of English text for the work on the second edition.
3. By courtesy of HarperCollins, London and Cobuild, Birmingham, the 1995 database was brought over to Copenhagen, where the editors set up a new bilingual database of their own at Politikens Forlag (the publishing house owned by *Politiken*, one of the leading Danish newspapers).
4. Owing to the fact that the COBUILD dictionary was corpus-based, the editors were able to draw on the vast collection of complete sentences. This bilingual dictionary thus contains c.100,000 examples, illustrating the meanings and submeanings of the headwords.
5. For each meaning and submeaning, Danish equivalents were provided, sometimes up to six.
6. One other major feature of the dictionary is the fact that the definitions of all meanings of each head-word are written in the character-

[15] Cf. here Gabriele Stein, *The English Dictionary: Past, Present and Future* (Exeter: Exeter University Press, 1984) 6, and R.R.K. Hartmann, "Dictionaries of English: The User's Perspective," *Dictionaries of English*, ed. Richard W. Bailey (Cambridge: Cambridge University Press, 1987) 121–35.

[16] *Politikens Engelsk–Dansk med betydningsforklaringer*, ed. Arne Zettersten and Hanne Lauridsen (Copenhagen: Politikens forlag, 1999).

[17] I have also presented this with further exemplification in "Aspects on the Future of Lexicography Within Interdisciplinary Research," *Artefakte/Artefiktionen: Für Christian W. Thomsen zum 60. Geburtstag*, ed. Angela Krewani (Heidelberg: Carl Winter, 2000) 325–35.

istic interactive COBUILD style in full English sentences. One reason for keeping the COBUILD definitions in English in the new English–Danish Dictionary is that the level of English proficiency in Denmark is generally rather high, especially for understanding typical COBUILD definitions, which are composed in a style that is quite easy to follow. The defining vocabulary is normally about 2,500 words in COBUILD. This is fairly normal for the new monolingual dictionaries, the *Longman Dictionary of Contemporary English*, for example, having a defining vocabulary of c.2,000 words. Another reason for keeping the definition in English is the fact that important collocations can be studied by the user both in the whole-sentence definitions and in the complete examples, which are usually two or three in number.

7. After the *Collins COBUILD English Dictionary* was published in 1995, the COBUILD database, The *Bank of English*, continued to grow. By 1996 it had reached 323 million words.
8. From 1995 on, the COBUILD vocabulary has been supplemented with new data, particularly within areas like electronics, new media, business and politics.
9. All the 100,000 examples in the *Collins COBUILD English Dictionary* (1995) were equipped with grammar tags indicating the grammatical build-up of most examples. The editors translated all these word-classes and grammar patterns into Danish, which means that all of the 100,000 examples in English can be used as model sentences which are all grammatically analysed in Danish codes. This information provides the user with a new English grammar in the format of complete model sentences, all grammatically coded and equipped with relevant word definitions and equivalents.
10. Since a complete set of equivalents has been given as well as a complete analysis of syntactic constructions expressed in Danish, the editors believe that maximum information on all Danish equivalents of all English entries has been obtained. This is even more obvious from the fact that ample indication of pragmatics is included in Danish.

Bearing in mind the fact that some typologists discuss dictionaries in terms of whether they are "active" or "passive," meaning that the former are "encoding" (writing and speaking) and the latter "decoding" (reading and listening), this monolingual–bilingual English–Danish Dictionary is certainly more "active" than most standard bilingual dictionaries.[18]

With such a wealth of information on definitions, meanings, examples, collocations, synonyms, antonyms and pragmatics, the user is in a good position to select the most satisfactory equivalent in Danish. This is also made clear by the CD-ROM version published in 2000. In addition, the user's knowledge of English for productive purposes will – provided he or she reads and absorbs everything under an entry – increase considerably.

IV The web of words: Multimedia and beyond

In April 1879, Dr James Murray published his famous appeal for volunteers to work on the new dictionary, which eventually became the *Oxford English Dictionary*. Two thousand copies were printed and circulated by booksellers. At the start of the new millennium readers are invited to contribute to the development of OED Online and to submit new material by searching the Internet under www.oed.com. Readers and scholars are invited to participate in a dialogue with the editors and researchers of the dictionary and to receive the latest OED News by e-mail up to the completion of the project in 2010. The only thing we cannot foresee now is what new technologies will have entered the market by that time.

It was already possible at the end of the last century to access language corpora for research on the Internet. For example, the Linguistic Data Consortium (LDC), University of Pennsylvania, is a collection of online multilingual sources which can be accessed via the World Wide Web:

Lexicon corpora

Microphone lexicon:
LDC99L23 American English Spoken Lexicon

Pronunciation lexicon:
LDC97L20 CALLHOME American English Lexicon (PRONLEX)
LDC97L19 CALLHOME Egyptian Arabic Lexicon
LDC97L18 CALLHOME German Lexicon
LDC96L17 CALLHOME Japanese Lexicon
LDC96 L15 CALLHOME Mandarin Chinese Lexicon
LDC96L16 CALLHOME Spanish Lexicon
LDC99L22 Egyptian Colloquial Arabic Lexicon

[18] Cf. Bo Svensén, *Practical Lexicography* (Oxford: Oxford University Press, 1993) 10–12.

Speech corpora

Broadcast speech:
LDC97S66 1996 English Broadcast News Dev & Eval (Hub-4)
LDC97S44 1996 English Broadcast News Speech (Hub-4)
LDC98S71 1997 English Broadcast News Speech (Hub-4)

Mobile-radio speech:
LDC94S14B Air Traffic Control BOS
LDC94S14A Air Traffic Control Complete
LDC94S14C Air Traffic Control DCA
LDC94S14D Air Traffic Control DFW
LDC99S83 Tactical Speaker Identification Speech Corpus (TSID)

Telephone speech:
LDC93S7 *SWITCHBOARD
LDC96S61 1996 Speaker Recognition Benchmark
LDC99S80 1997 Speaker Recognition Benchmark
LDC98S76 1998 Speaker Recognition Benchmark
LDC99S81 1999 Speaker Recognition Benchmark
LDC96S46 CALLFRIEND American English – Non-Southern Dialect
LDC96S47 CALLFRIEND American English – Southern Dialect
LDC96S48 CALLFRIEND Canadian French
LDC96S49 CALLFRIEND Egyptian Arabic
LDC96S50 CALLFRIEND Farsi
LDC96S51 CALLFRIEND German
LDC96S52 CALLFRIEND Hindi
LDC96S53 CALLFRIEND Japanese

Text corpora

Broadcast text:
LDC98T31 1996 CSR Hub-4 Language Model
LDC97T22 1996 English Broadcast News Transcripts (Hub-4)
LDC98T28 1997 English Broadcast News Transcripts (Hub-4)
LDC98T24 1997 Mandarin Broadcast News Transcripts (Hub-4NE)
LDC98T29 1997 Spanish Broadcast News Transcripts (Hub-4NE)
LDC99T36 USC Marketplace Broadcast News Transcripts

Conversation text:
LDC97T14 CALLHOME American English Transcripts
LDC97T19 CALLHOME Egyptian Arabic Transcripts
LDC97T15 CALLHOME German Transcripts
LDC96T18 CALLHOME Japanese Transcripts
LDC96T16 CALLHOME Mandarin Chinese Transcripts
LDC96T17 CALLHOME Spanish Transcripts
LDC98T26 Hub-5 Mandarin Transcripts
LDC98T27 Hub-5 Spanish Transcripts
LDC99T33 SUSAS Transcripts
LDC93S7-T SWITCHBOARD-1 Transcripts

Newswire text:
LDC2000T43 BLLIP 1987–89 WSJ Corpus Release 1
LDC95T6 CSR-III Text
LDC2000T48 Chinese Treebank (preliminary release)
LDC95T11 European Language Newspaper Text
LDC99T34 Japanese Business News Text Supplement
LDC95T8 Japanese Business News Text
LDC2000T45 Korean Newswire
LDC96T10 MUC-VI Text Collection
LDC95T13 Mandarin Chinese News Text
LDC95T21 North American News Text Corpus
LDC98T30 North American News Text Supplement
LDC99T40 Portuguese Newswire text
LDC95T9 Spanish News Text
LDC99T41 Spanish Newswire Text, Volume 2

Some further sources that can be accessed[19] via the World Wide Web are the following: ALEX: A Catalogue of Electronic Texts on the Internet, the British National Corpus, COBUILD Direct World Wide Web Service, and the International Computer Archive of English (ICAME).

Within the field of dictionaries and encyclopaedias, the Internet offers innumerable possibilities. For example, the *Literary Dictionary*, to be released in 2001, is a free Internet reference work which will provide biographical profiles for English-language literary writers, critical profiles of all major texts, articles on important theories – in fact, a portal to all valuable Internet resources in the humanities.[20]

Ten years ago we knew about videodisks, viewdata and satellite communication, but we were not yet familiar with the CD-ROM or the Internet. Synthetic speech was known for computer-assisted pronouncing dictionaries, but artificial intelligence was just as enigmatic as it is today. Videoconferencing and digital television were known, but took a long time to develop. Multimedia did not mean the same as it does now.

Since the Internet has developed at such extraordinary speed, it is most likely that multimedia techniques and online services will change so much over the next ten years that the technical presentation of dictionaries will look astoundingly different on computers or TV screens. The *Encarta World English Dictionary*[21] is an example of how an Internet concept (by Microsoft) is presented in a traditional

---

19 Biber et al. 286.

20 See Robert Clark, "Literacy, the Book and the Internet: Retrospects and Prospects," *European English Messenger* 9.2 (2000): 57–61.

21 *Encarta World English Dictionary* (New York: St. Martin's Press, 1999).

book format. On the Internet one can now find a number of Encarta activities – the Microsoft Encarta 98 Encyclopedia, the Encarta World English Dictionary Online, and the Encarta Schoolhouse with Internet sites for teachers. There is also the CD-ROM version of the Encarta World English Dictionary 2001. The Encarta Reference Suite 2001 is an example of multimedia information.

At the PC EXPO 2000 at the Jacob K. Jarits Convention Centre, New York, in June 2000, it was made clear that PCs and hand-held computers are becoming smaller and smaller. Computers and human beings are getting closer and closer, and the most futuristic view is that computer-like implants in the human brain may be a reality within the next twenty-five years. When will artificial intelligence have a breakthrough, when will automatic translation or interpreting be completed, when will multimedia techniques integrate all necessary lexical linguistic and cultural information in our intelligent and productive work-stations? When will we get automatic lexicography?[22] May we eventually produce written texts just by thinking in the environment of our work-station? With what dictionaries will we be assisted? Will the techniques of OED Online, the *Longman Web Dictionary* or Microsoft's Encarta appear outdated by 2010? How will the papers of IAUPE 2010 be presented?

[22] Cf. John Sinclair, "Prospects for Automatic Lexicography," *Symposium on Lexicography VII* (Lexicographica Series Maior 76; Tübingen: Max Niemeyer, 1996) 1–10.

International Association of University Professors of English (IAUPE)

Constitution

Article 1 – *Purposes of the Association*

The aim and purpose of the Association shall be to promote international understanding and exchange among scholars of English at a high academic level. To further this aim the Association shall:

(a) make accessible to all its members, by means of the *Bulletin* and other publications, information of common interest, in particular information relating to English studies and to the teaching of English in universities;

(b) hold international conferences at regular intervals.

Article 2 – *Affiliations of the Association*

The Association will foster contact at an international level, as appropriate, with other relevant bodies, such as the *Fédération Internationale des Langues et Littératures Modernes* (FILLM), UNESCO, the *European Society for the Study of English* (ESSE) and the British Council.

Article 3 – *Membership*

Membership of the Association may be conferred on university professors of English Language and/or Literature and on other scholars of distinction in these and related fields. Admission to membership is determined by the International Committee, on the basis of a simple majority decision.

Article 4 – *Subscription*

A subscription, the sum from time to time determined, shall become due on 1 January in each year. From 1 January following a member's retirement, the subscription shall be reduced by half. The funds of the Association shall be devoted to furthering the purposes of the Association.

Article 5 – *Committees*

Overall responsibility for the activities of the Association shall be held by the International Committee. This Committee (which shall meet at least once every three years) shall consist of:

(a) the President (whose role is defined below) for three years preceding the conference he or she hosts and for a further three years afterwards;

(b) twelve ordinary members;

(c) the Secretary-General and Treasurer;

(d) the Editor of the *Bulletin*.

The International Committee shall elect a chairman from among its members.

The functions of the International Committee are:

(a) to promote and sustain the aims of the Association as defined above;

(b) to secure adequate funding to sustain these aims;

(c) to promote and monitor membership in all parts of the world;

(d) to prepare an agenda and reports for each General Meeting, normally held at the triennial conference;

(e) to arrange elections to the Association's committees as they fall due;

(f) to recommend to each General Meeting venues for future conferences.

The International Committee shall elect from its members an *Executive Sub-Committee* to be responsible for the conduct of the Association's activities between conferences. This Sub-Committee shall consist of the Chairman of the International Committee and four other members, together with the Secretary-General and Treasurer. It shall ordinarily meet twice between conferences.

ARTICLE 6 – *Elections*

Election to the International Committee shall be by postal ballot of all members of the Association. Nominations, in writing, shall require a proposer and a seconder and be accompanied by a statement of no more than 300 words on the qualifications of the candidate.

The International Committee will be responsible for drawing up a list of not more than thirty names, having regard to

(a) the candidate's scholarly distinction;

(b) his or her active commitment to IAUPE;

(c) geographical distribution.

The twelve ordinary members of the International Committee shall be elected for a period of six years and shall not be eligible for re-election until a period of three years has elapsed following that term of office. To ensure continuity, no more than half the Committee shall be elected at any one time. Elections will be held every three years, with every member entitled to vote for up to six candidates in order of preference.

The Secretary-General and Treasurer and the Editor of the *Bulletin* shall both be elected for six years and shall be eligible for re-election.

ARTICLE 7 – *Conferences*

An Intenational Conference shall be held at regular intervals, normally every third year, as far as possible alternately in an English-speaking and non-English-speaking country.

Admission to any conference shall be open to all members of the Association, subject to the payment of a fee.

The Executive Committee shall have power to admit non-members to a conference on payment of a fee or by invitation, provided that accommodation and other circumstances so permit.

ARTICLE 8 – *President*

For the purpose of organizing the conference, the International Committee shall appoint a President from among the members of the Association in the country where the next conference is to be held. The President may appoint his or her own Conference Committee and shall be accountable to the membership of the Association through the International Committee.

ARTICLE 9 – *Revision of the Constitution*

The International Committee shall have power to recommend changing the articles of the Constitution. All such changes shall require the approval of a majority of the members of the Association ascertained by postal ballot.

PRESIDENT

W. Viereck (Bamberg)

INTERNATIONAL COMMITTEE

A. Breeze (Pamplona)
C. Butler (Oxford)
H. Grabes (Giessen)
I. Hassan (Chairman, Wisconsin–Milwaukee)
W. Speed Hill (CUNY)
I. Iwamoto (Tsukuba)
I.J. Kirby (Lausanne)
M.–M. Martinet (Paris)
P.G. Stanwood (Vancouver)
S. Ter–Minasova (Moscow)
W. Viereck (Bamberg)
J.R. Watson (Durham)
I. Wright (Australian National)

EXECUTIVE SUB-COMMITTEE

C. Butler, H. Grabes, I. Hassan, I.J. Kirby, P.G. Stanwood, I. Wright

SECRETARY-GENERAL AND TREASURER

I.J. Kirby
University of Lausanne, BFSH 2
CH–1015 Lausanne, Switzerland

December 2000

International Association of University Professors of English (IAUPE)

List of Current Members

NOTE: "R" = emeritus status. The year = entry into the Association.

Abádi–Nagy, Zoltán (Kossuth Lajos University, Debrecen) 2000

Adams, Hazard (R; University of Washington, Seattle) 1985

Adamska–Salaciak, Arleta (Technical University of Pozna□) 1999

Adone, Dany (Heinrich Heine University, Düsseldorf) 2001

Ahrens, Rüdiger (Julius Maximilian University, Würzburg) 1981

Aijmer, Karin (University of Göteborg) 1998

Alexander, Michael (University of St. Andrews) 1986

Algeo, John (R; Georgia State University, Atlanta) 1979

Allentuck, Marcia (R; City University of New York) 1977

Allott, Miriam (R; University of Liverpool) 1974

Amalric, J.C. (R; Paul Valéry University, Montpellier) 1983

Anderson, David D. (R; Michigan State University, East Lansing) 1999

Anderson, John M. (University of Edinburgh) 1989

Ando, Shinsuke (Keio University, Tokyo) 1986

Andrew, Malcolm (Queen's University, Belfast) 1987

Antor, Heinz (Cologne University) 2000

ApRoberts, R.P. (R; California State University, Northridge) 1972

ApRoberts, Ruth (R; University of California at Riverside) 1980

Arac, Jonathan (Pittsburgh University, Pennsylvania) 1999

Armens, S.M. (R; University of Iowa, Iowa City) 1971

Ashton, Rosemary (R; University College, London) 1995

Asselineau, Roger (R; University of Paris IV–Sorbonne) 1954

Assmann, Aleida (University of Konstanz) 2000

Axelrod, Rise B. (California State University, Northridge) 1999

Axelrod, Steven O. (University of California at Riverside) 1999

Bailey, Richard W. (University of Michigan, Ann Arbor) 1999

Bald, W.D. (Cologne University) 1977

Bammesberger, Alfred (Catholic University of Eichstätt) 1991

Banerjee, A. (Kobe College / Kobe Jogakuin Daigaku, Nishinomiya) 1999

Barrat, Alain (University of Lyon III) 1995

Bassnett, Susan (University of Warwick, Coventry) 1996

Batchelor, John (University of Newcastle upon Tyne) 1990

Bately, Janet (R; King's College, London) 1980

Battestin, Martin C. (R; University of Virginia, Charlottesville) 1976

Beer, John B. (R; Peterhouse College, Cambridge) 1989

Bell, Michael (University of Warwick, Coventry) 1998

Bell, Millicent (R; Boston University, Massachusetts) 1979

Bender, John (Stanford University, Stanford, California) 2000

Bender, Todd K. (University of Wisconsin, Madison) 1980

Bennett, B.H. (University College, University of New South Wales, Sydney) 1999

Bentley, O.E., Jr. (R; University of Toronto, Ontario) 1968

Beppu, Keiko (Kobe College / Kobe Jogakuin Daigaku, Nishinomiya) 1994

Berger, Thomas L. (St. Lawrence University, Canton, New York) 1986

Bergner, Heinz (Justus Liebig University, Giessen) 1977

Berry, Francis (R; Royal Holloway College, London) 1968

Bertens, Hans (State University of Utrecht) 1988

Berthoud, J.A. (University of York, Heslington) 1980

Besses, Pierre (R; University of Toulouse–Le Mirail) 1995

Bignami, Marialuisa (University of Milan) 1989

Birrell, T.A. (R; Catholic University of Nijmegen) 1956

Bischoff, Volker (Philipps University, Marburg) 2000

Björk, Lennart A. (University of Göteborg) 1981

Bjork, Robert E. (Arizona State University, Tempe) 1999

Blackall, Jean Frantz (R; Cornell University, Ithaca, New York) 1999

Blair, John G. (University of Geneva) 1979

Blake, Norman (R; University of Sheffield) 1977

Blewett, David (McMaster University, Hamilton, Ontario) 1995

Blissett, William F. (R; University of Toronto, Ontario) 1962

Boas, Hans Ulrich (Erfurt University) 1995

Bode, Christoph (Otto Friedrich University, Bamberg) 1997

Bonheim, Helmut (R; Cologne University) 1967

Boulton, James T. (R; University of Birmingham) 1998

Breeze, Andrew (University of Navarre) 1993

Breivik, Leiv Egil (Bergen University) 1983

Brink, Jean R. (Arizona State University, Tempe) 2000

Broich, Ulrich (R; Ludwig Maximilian University, Munich) 1971

Brooker, Jewel Spears (Eckerd College, St Petersburg, Florida) 2000

Brown, George H. (Stanford University, Stanford, California) 1993

Brown, Michelle P. (University of London) 2001

Brown, Terence (Trinity College, Dublin) 1996

Brumm, Ursula (R; Free University, Berlin) 1999

Buckley, Jerome (R; Harvard University, Cambridge, Massachusetts) 1967

Burnley, David (University of Sheffield) 1995

Busza, Andrew (University of British Columbia, Vancouver) 1976

Butler, Christopher (Oxford University) 1983

Butters, Ronald R. (Duke University, Durham, North Carolina) 2001

Bystydzienska, Grazyna (Warsaw University) 2000

Carey, John (Merton College, Oxford) 1993

Carroll, David R. (R; University of Lancaster) 1980

Carruthers, Mary (New York University) 1991

Chapman, Raymond (R; University of London) 1982

Chapple, J.A.V. (R; University of Hull) 1986

Chénetier, Marc (Denis Diderot University–Paris VII) 1995

Cheney, Donald (University of Massachusetts at Amherst) 1983

Clark, George (R; Queen's University, Kingston, Ontario) 1999

Clayborough, A. (R; Trondheim University) 1975

Clogan, Paul M. (R; North Texas University, Denton) 1998

Cohn, Dorrit (R; Harvard University, Cambridge, Massachusetts) 2001

Collie, Michael (R; York University, Toronto, Ontario) 1968

Cook, Ann Jennalie (Vanderbilt University, Nashville, Tennessee) 1999

Cook, Eleanor (R; University of Toronto, Ontario) 1999

Cooper, Helen (University College, Oxford) 1999

Cope, Kevin L. (Louisiana State University, Baton Rouge) 1995

Corballis, Richard P. (Massey University, Palmerston North, New Zealand) 1997

Crampton, Georgia R. (R; Portland State University, Portland, Oregon) 1982

Creaser, John (Royal Holloway & Bedford College, London) 1994

D'haen, Theo L. (State University of Leiden) 1989

Daleski, H.M. (R; Hebrew University of Jerusalem) 1978

Danchin, Pierre (R; University of Nancy) 1962

Davidsen–Nielsen, Niels (Copenhagen Business School) 1990

Davidson, Clifford (Western Michigan University, Kalamazoo) 1997

Davis, William V. (Baylor University, Waco, Texas) 1983

Daymond, M.J. (University of Natal, Durban, RSA) 1996

De Almeida, Hermione (University of Tulsa, Oklahoma) 1985

De Logu, Pietro (R; University of Padua) 1979

De Paiva Correia, Maria Helena (Lisbon University) 1982

De Sousa, Maria L.M. (Lisboa Nova University) 1980

Deconinck–Brossard, Françoise (University of Paris X, Nanterre) 2000

Dekeyser, Xavier (State University of Antwerp and Catholic University of Louvain) 1976

Delbaere–Garant, Jeanne (R; Free University, Brussels) 1978

Denisova, Tamara (National University Kyiv–Mohyla Academy, Kiev) 2000

Derolez, R. (R; University of Ghent) 1956

Dickson, Donald R. (Texas A&M University, College Station) 2000

Diller, Hans–Jürgen (R; University of the Ruhr, Bochum) 1976

Doorzycka, Irena (R; University of Warsaw) 1983

Doebler, Bettie Anne (Arizona State University, Tempe) 1999

Doltas, Dilek (Istanbul University) 1992

Downie, J.A. (Goldsmiths College, London) 1998

Downing–Rothwell, Angela (R; Universidad Complutense, Madrid) 1987

Drescher, Horst W. (R; Johannes Gutenberg University, Mainz–Germersheim) 1980

Duarte, João Ferreira (Lisbon University) 2000

Durczak, Jerzy (Maria Curie–Sklodowska University, Lublin) 1999

Duskova, Libuse (R; Charles University, Prague) 2001

Dziubalska–Kolaczyk, Kataryzna (Technical University of Pozna□) 1999

Edwards, Anthony (University of Victoria, British Columbia) 1998

Edwards, John D. (University of Paris VIII, Vincennes) 1988

Edwards, Mary Jane (Carleton College, Northfield, Minnesota) 1992

Edwards, Philip W. (R; University of Liverpool) 1961

Eggert, Paul (Australian Defence Force Academy, Sydney) 1996

Egri, Peter (L. Fötvös University, Budapest) 1979

Eisner, Sigmund (R; Arizona University, Tucson) 1969

Elliott, Emory (University of California at Riverside) 1987

Elliott, R.W.V. (R; Australian National University, Canberra) 1967

Ellrodt, Robert (R; University of Paris I–Panthéon-Sorbonne) 1965

Elsness, Joh (Oslo University) 1994

Emons, Rudo (Passau University) 1982

Enkvist, Nils Erik (R; Åbo Akademi / Swedish University of Åbo) 1959

Erdmann, Peter (Technical University, Berlin) 1977

Erzgräber, Willi (R; Albert Ludwig University, Freiburg) 1980

Escure, Genevieve (University of Minnesota, Minneapolis) 1998

Esser, Jürgen (Rhenish-Westphalian Technical University, Aachen) 1997

Evans, R.O. (R; University of New Mexico, Albuquerque, and University of Kentucky, Lexington) 1967

Ezroura, Mohamed (Mohammed V University, Rabat) 1998

Fanego, Teresa (University of Santiago de Compostela) 1999

Fill, Aalwin (Graz University) 1980

Finlayson, John (Queen's University, Kingston, Ontario) 1979

Finneran, Richard J. (University of Tennessee at Knoxville) 1996

Fisch, Harold (R; Bar–Ilan University, Ramat Gan) 1981

Fischer, Andreas (University of Zürich) 1986

Fischer, Olga C.M. (University of Amsterdam) 2000

Fisiak, Jacek, OBE (Technical University of Poznan) 1967

Fjellestad, Danuta (Blekinge Institute of Technology, Karlskrona) 2000

Fludernik, Monika (Albert Ludwig University, Freiburg) 1995

Foakes, R.A. (R; University of California at Los Angeles) 1965

Folsom, L.E. (University of Iowa, Iowa City) 1998

Forsyth, N. (University of Lausanne) 1989

Fowler, Alastair (R; University of Virginia, Charlottesville) 1972

Frank, Armin Paul (R; Georg August University, Göttingen) 1995

Fraser, Hilary (University of Western Australia, Perth) 2000

Freer, Coburn (University of Georgia, Atlanta) 1987

Fries, Udo (University of Zürich) 1978

Gallet–Blanchard, Liliane (University of Paris IV–Sorbonne) 2000

Galván Reula, Femando (University of Alcalá de Henares) 1994

Gardner, Averil (R; Memorial University of Newfoundland, St John's) 1992

Gardner, Philip (R; Memorial University of Newfoundland, St John's) 1992

Gerritsen, Johan (R; State University of Groningen) 1965

Gill, Stephen (Lincoln College, Oxford) 1997

Gilpin, George (University of Tulsa, Oklahoma) 1985

Giorcelli, Cristina (University of Rome III) 2000

Gneuss, Helmut (R; Ludwig Maximilian University, Munich) 1984

Gnutzmann, Claus (Technical University, Braunschweig) 1995

Göbel, Walter (University of the Saarland, Saarbrücken) 1999

Golden, Arthur (R; City College, City University of New York) 1976

Golden, Marija (Ljubljana University) 1998

Göller, Karl Heinz (R; Regensburg University) 1965

Gooch, Bryan N.S. (University of Victoria, British Columbia) 1995

Goodwin, K.L. (R; Sydney University) 1980

Gooneratne, Yasmine (Macquarie University, Sydney) 1986

Gordon, Jan B. (Tokyo University of Foreign Studies) 1999

Gosseif, Suzanne (Loyola University, Chicago) 1996

Grabes, Herbert (Justus Liebig University, Giessen) 1977

Grabher, Gudrun M. (University of Innsbruck) 1998

Grabo, N.S. (R; University of Tulsa, Oklahoma) 1969

Grace, Sherrill E. (University of British Columbia, Vancouver) 1996

Graham, Kenneth W. (University of Guelph, Ontario) 1991

Green, Geoffrey (San Francisco State University) 1995

Greetham, David (Graduate Center, City University of New York) 1998

Groden, Michael (University of Western Ontario, London, Ontario) 1999

Grosman, Meta (Ljubljana University) 1999

Grundy, Isobel (University of Alberta, Edmonton) 1994

Guo, Jide (Shandong University) 1999

Gupta, R.K. (R; Indian Institute of Technology, Kanpur) 1979

Gysin, Fritz (University of Berne) 1984

Haarder, Andreas (R; Odense University) 1985

Haastrup, Kirsten (Royal Danish School of Educational Studies, Copenhagen) 1994

Hajikova, Eva (Charles University, Prague) 2001

Halloran, William F. (R; University of Wisconsin, Milwaukee) 1982

Halter, Peter (University of Lausanne) 1995

Haq, Kaiser (Jahangirnagar University, Savar, Dhaka) 1996

Harada, Keiichi (R; Josai International University) 1999

Harder, Peter (Copenhagen University) 1999
Harris, Joseph (Harvard University, Cambridge, Massachusetts) 1982
Harris, Margaret (Sydney University) 2000
Hashiguchi, Yasuo (R; Yasuda Women's University, Tokyo) 1999
Hashmi, Alamgir A. (R; Quaid-i-Azam University, Islamabad) 1987
Hassan, Ihab (R; University of Wisconsin, Milwaukee) 1970
Hassel, Chris (Vanderbilt University, Nashville, Tennessee) 2001
Hawan, R.A. (R; Hamburg University) 1983
Hawkes, Carol A. (Western Connecticut State University, Danbury) 1967
Hawthorn, J.M. (Trondheim University) 1982
Henderson, Judith Rice (University of Saskatchewan, Saskatoon) 1999
Herendeen, Wyman H. (University of Windsor, Ontario) 1992
Herz, Judith Scherer (Concordia University, Montreal) 1999
Hickey, Bernard (University of Lecce) 1989
Higashi, Nobuyuki (University of Electrocommunications, Ch□fu) 1995
Hill, Joyce M. (University of Leeds) 1996
Hill, W. Speed (R; City University of New York) 1978
Hiltunen, Risto (Turku University) 1993
Höfele, Andreas (Ludwig Maximilian University, Munich) 2000
Hollington, Michael (University of Toulon–Var, Toulon) 1988
Holloway, Karla F.C. (Duke University, Durham, North Carolina) 2001
Holmesland, Oddvar (Tromsø University) 1992
Höltgen, Karl Josef (R; Friedrich Alexander University, Erlangen–Nuremberg) 1979
Honey, John (University of Botswana, Gaborone) 1989
Hook, Andrew (R; University of Glasgow) 1997
Howe, Nicholas (Ohio State University, Columbus) 1998
Hughes, George (Tokyo University) 1993
Hussey, S.S. (R; University of Lancaster) 1980

Ikegami, Yoshihiko (Showa Women's University, Tokyo) 1997
Imai, Mitsunon (□saka University, Suita) 1994
Imura, Kimie (Meisei University, Tokyo) 1994
Innes, Christopher (York University, Ontario) 1988
Iser, Wolfgang (R; University of Konstanz) 1961
Isernhagen, Hartwig (University of Basel) 1983
Iwamoto, Iwao (Reitaku University, Kashiwa) 1988
Iwasaki, Soji (Tokai Women's College, Tokyo) 1978

Jacobs, Johan U. (University of Natal, Durban, RSA) 1997
Jacobs, Nicolas (Jesus College, Oxford) 2001
Jacobsen, Eric (R; Copenhagen University) 1960
Jambeck, Karen K. (Western Connecticut State University, Danbury) 1997
Jasper, David (University of Glasgow) 1996
Jay, Elisabeth (Oxford Brookes University, Headington) 2000
Jeffares, A. Norman (R; University of Stirling) 1951
Jeffrey, David Lyle (Baylor University, Waco, Texas) 1990
Jin, Ha (Emory University, Atlanta, Georgia) 2000
Johansson, Stig (Oslo University) 1994
Jones–Davies, M.T. (R; University of Paris IV–Sorbonne) 1965
Joseph, John E. (University of Edinburgh) 2000
Josipovici, Gabriel (University of Sussex, Brighton) 2001
Jucker, Andreas (Justus Liebig University, Giessen) 2000

Kaplan, Fred (City University of New York) 1983
Kartiganer, Donald (University of Mississippi, Oxford, Mississippi) 2000
Kaske, Carol V. (Cornell University, Ithaca, New York) 1993
Kastovsky, Dieter (Vienna University) 1980
Kawachi, Yoshiko (Kyorin University) 1983
Kaylor, Noel Harold (University of Northern Iowa, Cedar Falls) 2000

Keefer, Sarah Larratt (University of Trent, Peterborough, Ontario) 1999

Kelley, Theresa M. (University of Texas at Austin) 1998

Kelvin, Norman (City University of New York) 2001

Kerby–Fulton, Kathryn (University of Victoria, British Columbia) 2001

Khattab, Ezzat A. (R; King Saud University, Riyadh) 1989

Kiernan, Kevin S. (University of Kentucky, Lexington) 1999

Kiessling, Nicolas K. (Washington State University, Seattle) 1996

Kim, Joo Hyon (R; Seoul National University) 1980

Kincaid, James R. (University of Southern California, Los Angeles) 1999

King, John N. (Ohio State University, Columbus) 2000

King, Pamela M. (University College of St. Martin, Lancaster) 1998

Kinjo, Seiki (Kobe College / Kobe Jogakuin Daigaku, Nishinomiya) 1997

Kirby, Ian J. (University of Lausanne) 1968

Kjellmer, Göran (R; Göteborg University) 1998

Knight, Stephen (University of Wales at Cardiff) 1995

Knoepflmacher, U.C. (Princeton University, Princeton, New Jersey) 1986

Knowles, Richard (University of Wisconsin, Madison) 1989

Kodama, Sanehide (D□shisha Women's College, Kyoto) 1989

Kohl, Stephan (Bavarian Julius Maximilian University, Würzburg) 1994

Komesu, Okifumi (Okinawa International University, Naha) 1993

Koppenfels, Werner von (Ludwig Maximilian University, Munich) 1997

Korshin, Paul J. (University of Pennsylvania, Philadelphia) 1999

Korte, Barbara (Eberhard Karl University, Tübingen) 1998

Kostic, Veselin (Belgrade University) 1979

Kramer, Dale (R; University of Illinois at Urbana–Champaign) 2000

Kretzschmar, William A., Jr. (University of Georgia, Atlanta) 1998

Kroeber, Karl (University of Wisconsin, Madison) 1999

Kröller, Eva–Marie (University of British Columbia, Vancouver) 2000

Krygier, Marcin (Technical University of Poznan) 1999

Kryk–Kastovsky, Barbara (Technical University of Poznan) 1999

Kytö, Meija (Uppsala University) 1996

Labor, Earle G. (Centenary College of Louisiana, Shreveport) 2000

Labriola, Albert C. (Duquesne University, Pennsylvania) 1999

Lal, Malaslin (University of Delhi) 1996

Lampe, David (State University of New York at Buffalo) 1998

Lancashire, Anne (University of Toronto, Ontario) 1992

Lashkevitch, Anatol V. (Udmurt State University) 1996

Latré, Guido (Catholic University of Louvain) 1990

Lecercle, Ann (University of Paris X, Nanterre) 1992

Lecercle, Jean–Jacques (Cardiff University) 1988

Lee, A. Robert (Nihon University, Tokyo) 1998

Lee, Sangsup (Y□nse University, Seoul) 1999

Leggatt, Alexander (University of Toronto, Ontario) 1983

Lehmann, Elmar (Essen University) 1980

Leisi, Ernst (R; University of Zürich) 1956

Lendinara, Patrizia (University of Palermo) 2000

Lerner, Laurence D. (R; University of Sussex, Brighton, and Vanderbilt University, Nashville, Tennessee) 1974

Lewalski, Barbara K. (Harvard University, Cambridge, Massachusetts) 1974

Lieb, Michael (University of Illinois, Urbana) 1999

Lim, C.S. (University of Malaya, Kuala Lumpur) 2000

Limon, Jerzy (Gdánsk University) 1998

Lindberg, Conrad (R; Trondheim University) 1975

Litin, Michael D. (University of Minnesota at Duluth) 1986

Linton, C.D. (R; George Washington University, Washington, D.C.) 1965

Lipka, Leonhard (Ludwig Maximilian University, Munich) 1979

Ljung, Magnus (University of Stockholm) 1980

Loewenstein, David (University of Wisconsin, Madison) 1999

Loving, Jerome (Texas A&M University, College Station) 1982

Ludwig, H.W. (Eberhard Karl University, Tübingen) 1976

Luyat, Anne (R; University of Avignon) 1990

McCarthy, Patrick J. (R; University of California at Santa Barbara) 1991

McDavid, Virginia (R; Chicago State University) 1978

MacDermott Carnicer, Doireann (R; Barcelona University) 1967

MacDonald, A.A. (University of Groningen) 1988

McDonald, William E. (University of Redlands, California) 1999

Mack, Maynard (R; Yale University, New Haven, Connecticut) 1961

McLeod, Alan L. (R; Rider University, Lawrenceville, New Jersey) 1995

McMaster, R.D. (R; University of Alberta, Edmonton) 1968

Maes-Jelinek, Hena, OBE (R; University of Liège) 1988

Maini, Darshan Singli (R; Punjabi University, Patiala) 1975

Malin, Irving (City College, City University of New York) 1981

Malzalin, Manfred (United Arab Emirates University, Al-Ain) 1996

Manning, Robert J. (University of Wales at Lampeter) 1997

Maiker, Frederick J. (University of Toronto, Ontario) 1983

Marotti, Arthur F. (Wayne State University, Detroit, Michigan) 1999

Martens, Klaus (University of the Saarland, Saarbrücken) 1994

Martin, Graham (R; Open University, Milton Keynes) 1980

Martin, Jay (Claremont McKenna College, Claremont, California) 1977

Martinet, Marie (University of Paris IV-Sorbonne) 1988

Matsumura, Masaie (Otemae University, Tokyo) 1987

Mayer, David R. (Nanzan University, Nagoya) 1995

Maynard, John (New York University) 1999

Megally, Shafik (R; University of Fez, Morocco) 1985

Mehl, Dieter (R; Friedrich Wilhelm University, Bonn) 1998

Meier, H.H. (R; Free University of Amsterdam) 1967

Mellor, Anne K. (University of California at Los Angeles) 1991

Mergenthal, Silvia (University of Konstanz) 1998

Mertens-Fonck, Paule (R; University of Liège) 1970

Middlebrook, Diane Wood (Stanford University, Stanford, California) 1999

Miller, J. Hillis (University of California at Irvine) 1965

Miller, James E. (R; University of Chicago) 1992

Mills, A.D. (University of Liverpool) 1986

Mnthali, Felix W.J. (University of Botswana, Gaborone) 1996

Mohr, H.-U. (Technical University, Dresden) 2000

Moldenhauer, Joseph J. (University of Texas at Austin) 1989

Montgomery, Robert L. (R; University of California at Irvine) 1984

Morris, Mervyn (University of the West Indies, Kingston, Jamaica) 2000

Mroczkowski, Przemys□aw J. (Cracow University) 1959

Müller, Wolfgang G. (Friedrich Schiller University, Jena) 1996

Myerson, Joel (University of South Carolina, Columbia) 1999

Nagel, James (University of Georgia, Atlanta) 2000

Nagucka, Ruta (Jagiellonian University, Prague) 1976

Nakano, Hirozo (Nagoya University) 1994

Nänny, Max (R; University of Zurich) 1973

Ndebele, Njabulo S. (University of the North, Sovenga, RSA) 1997

Neuman, Shirley (University of Michigan, Ann Arbor) 1998

Nevalainen, Terttu (Helsinki University) 1998

Nevanlinna, Saua (R; Helsinki University) 1982

Nevo, Ruth (R; Hebrew University of Jerusalem) 1974

Newman, Judie (University of Newcastle upon Tyne) 1997

Nickel, Gerhard (R; Stuttgart University) 1966

Nicolaisen, W.F.H. (R; Aberdeen University) 1979

Nünning, Ansgar (Justus Liebig University, Giessen) 2000

Nuttall, A.D. (New College, Oxford) 1996

Obiechina, Emmanuel (University of Nigeria, Nsukka) 2000

O'Brien O'Keeffe, Katherine (University of Notre Dame, Indiana) 1991

Ogura, Michiko (Chiba University) 1996

Ojaide, Tanure (University of North Carolina at Charlotte) 2000

Oka, Saburo (R; Aoyama Gakuin University, Tokyo) 1994

Olsen, Stein Haugom (Lingnan College, Hong Kong) 1994

Onega Jaén, Susana (University of Zaragoza) 1995

Ono, Shigeru (Showa Women's University, Tokyo) 1995

Orsten, Elisabeth M. (R; University of Trent, Peterborough, Ontario) 1977

Osselton, N.E. (R; University of Newcastle upon Tyne) 1970

Owen, W.J.B. (R; McMaster University, Hamilton, Ontario) 1967

Parkin, A.T.L. (Chinese University, Hong Kong) 1989

Parry, Graham (York University, Toronto, Ontario) 1998

Pearsall, Derek (R; Harvard University, Cambridge, Massachusetts) 1984

Perosa, Sergio (University of Venice) 1969

Petter, Henri (R; University of Zürich) 1974

Pfeiffer, K. Ludwig (Siegen University) 1987

Pocheptsov, George G. (Kiev Linguistic University) 1994

Post, Jonathan F. (University of California at Los Angeles) 1999

Potter, Lois (University of Delaware, Newark) 1999

Preisler, Bent (Roskilde University) 1992

Prescott, J. (R; Wayne State University, Detroit, Michigan) 1959

Priessnitz, Horst (Wuppertal University) 1988

Punter, David (University of Stirling) 1989

Puppel, Stanis□aw (Technical University of Poznan) 2000

Qian, Qing (Foreign Studies University, Beijing) 1992

Quinones, Ricardo J. (Claremont McKenna College, Claremont, California) 1998

Radzinowicz, Mary Ann (R; Cornell University, Ithaca, New York) 1982

Raimond, Jean (R; University of Reims) 1973

Rao, E. Nageswara (R; Osmania University, Hyderabad) 1999

Redonnet, Jean–Claude (University of Paris IV–Sorbonne) 1999

Reed, Mark L. (R; University of North Carolina at Chapel Hill) 2000

Regard, Frédéric (Ecole Normale, St.–Etienne) 1995

Rehder, Robert M. (University of Fribourg) 1985

Reichl, Karl (Friedrich Wilhelm University, Bonn) 1985

Reinhold, Heinz (R; Free University, Berlin) 1959

Revard, Carter (R; Washington University, St. Louis, Missouri) 1991

Richards, Mary P. (University of Delaware, Newark) 1992

Richetti, John (University of Pennsylvania, Philadelphia) 2000

Ridley, Florence H. (R; University of California at Los Angeles) 1970

Riehle, Wolfgang (Karl Franz University, Graz) 1976

Rimmon–Kenan, Shlomith (Hebrew University of Jerusalem) 1995

Rissanen, Matti (Helsinki University) 1978

Roberts, Jane A. (University of London) 1994

Roberts, M.A.M. (Keele University) 1968

Roberts, Neil (University of Sheffield) 1998

Robinson, Alan (University of St. Gallen) 1990

Rolle, Dietrich (Johannes Gutenberg University, Mainz) 1974

Roscoe, Adrian (University of the North, Sovenga, RSA) 1995

Rosenthal, Bernd (State University of New York at Binghamton) 1990

Rossi, Sergio (Milan State University) 1979

Rousseau, G.S. [George] (De Montfort University, Leicester) 1977

Rubik, Margarete (Vienna University) 1999

Rudnytsky, Peter L. (University of Florida, Gainesville) 2000

Rudrum, Alan (Simon Fraser University, Burnaby, British Columbia) 2000

Ryals, Clyde De L. (Duke University, Durham, North Carolina) 1979

Ryan, Kiernan (Royal Holloway College, London) 1979

Ryden, Mats (Uppsala University) 1987

Saito, Isamu (Doshisha University, Kyoto) 1995

Sanders, Andrew L. (University of Durham) 1996

Sandison, Alan (University of New England, Armidale, New South Wales) 1975

Sato, Hiroko (Tokyo Women's Christian University)

Sato, Shuji (Choe University, Tokyo) 1994

Sauer, Hans (Ludwig Maximilian University, Munich) 1993

Schaar, Claes (Lund University) 1965

Schaefer, Ursula (Technical University, Dresden) 1997

Scheer–Schäzler, Brigitte (Innsbruck University) 1998

Schlaeger, Jürgen (Humboldt University, Berlin) 1994

Schleiner, Winfried (University of California at Davis) 1999

Schlüter, Klaus (Albert Ludwig University, Freiburg) 1965

Schneider, Edgar W. (Regensburg University) 1990

Schoeck, Richard J. (University of Colorado, Boulder, and University of Kansas, Lawrence) 1965

Scholes, Robert (Brown University, Providence, Rhode Island) 1989

Schöpp, Joseph C. (Hamburg University) 1995

Schulze, Fritz W. (Johannes Gutenberg University, Mainz) 1962

Seeber, Hans Ulrich (Stuttgart University) 1987

Seidel, Therese (Heinrich Heine University, Düsseldorf) 2000

Sell, Roger D. (Åbo Akademi / Swedish University of Åbo) 1987

Sessions, William A. (Georgia State University, Atlanta) 2000

Shaffer, Elinor (School of Advanced Study, University of London) 1995

Shillingsburg, Peter L. (North Texas State University, Denton) 2001

Shippey, Thomas A. (St. Louis University, St Louis, Missouri) 1999

Shuger, Debora (University of California at Los Angeles) 2000

Shusterman, Ronald (University of Bordeaux III, Talence) 2001

Shuttleworth, Sally (University of Sheffield) 1998

Sikorska, Liliana (Technical University of Poznan) 1999

Simon, Myron (R; University of California at Irvine) 2000

Simon–Vandenbergen, Anne–Marie (State University of Ghent) 1998

Sinclair, J.M. (R; University of Birmingham) 1967

Skandera–Trombley, Laura E. (Coe College, Cedar Rapids, Iowa) 1998

Skilton, David (University of Wales at Cardiff) 1981

S□awek, Tadeusz (Silesian University of Katowice) 2000

Sledd, James H. (R; University of Texas, Austin) 1965

Smidt, Kristian (R; Oslo University) 1956

Söderlind, Johannes (R; Uppsala University)1968

Solomon, Harry M. (Auburn University, Alabama) 1988

Sorelius, Gunnar (R; Uppsala University) 1974

Spånberg, Sven–Johan (R; Umeå University) 1998

Spearing, A.C. (University of Virginia, Charlottesville) 1989

Spevack, Marvin (R; Wilhelm's University of Westphalia, Münster) 1968

Stanonik, Janez (R; Ljubljana University) 1989

Stanwood, Paul G. (R; University of British Columbia, Vancouver) 1990

Stanzel, Franz K. (R; Graz University) 1960

Stein, Dieter (Heinrich Heine University, Düsseldorf) 1995

Stemmler, Theo (Mannheim University) 1982

Stone, Donald (City University of New York, Queens) 1982

Stone, Harry (R; California State University, Northridge) 1971

Stone, Wilfred (R; Stanford University, Stanford, California) 2000

Strandberg, Victor (Duke University, Durham, North Carolina) 1998

Stribrny, Ždenek (Charles University, Prague) 1969

Sturrock, June (Simon Fraser University, Burnaby, British Columbia) 2001

Suhamy, Henri (R; University of Paris X, Nanterre) 1988

Sussman, Herbert (R; Northeastern University, Boston, Massachusetts) 2000

Svartvik, Jan (R; Lund University) 1971

Swearingen, C. Jan (Texas A&M University, College Station) 2000

Szarmach, Paul F. (Western Michigan University, Kalamazoo) 1987

Szwedek, Aleksander (Nicholas Copernicus University, Torun) 1983

Tajima, Matsuji (Kyushu University, Fukuoka) 1994

Takamiya, Toshiyuki (Kei□ University, Tokyo) 1994

Tannen, Deborah F. (Georgetown University, Washington, D.C.) 2000

Taylor, Gordon O. (University of Tulsa, Oklahoma) 1984

Taylor, P.B. (R; University of Geneva) 1994

Templeton, Joan (Long Island University, New York) 2000

Tennyson, G.B. (R; University of California at Los Angeles) 1974

Ter Minasova, Svetlana (Moscow State University) 1991

Terasawa, Yoshio (Gifu Women's University, Tokyo) 1978

Tetzeli von Rosador, Kurt (Wilhelm's University of Westphalia, Münster) 1981

Thieme, John (South Bank University, London) 1998

Thompson, Ann (King's College, London) 1999

Thormähien, Marianne (Lund University) 1997

Thornton, R.K.R. (R; University of Birmingham) 1986

Thumboo, Edwin (R; University of Singapore) 1988

Titlestad, Peto J.H. (University of Pretoria, RSA) 1991

Todd, William B. (R; University of Texas, Austin) 1967

Torgovnick, Marianna De (Duke University, Durham, North Carolina) 2000

Torti, Anna (University of Perugia) 2001

Tracy, Robert (R; University of California at Berkeley) 1995

Trousdale, Marion (University of Maryland, College Park) 1988

Trudgill, Peter (University of Fribourg) 1993

Tschumi, Raymond (R; University of St. Gallen) 1956

Tsuda, Aoi (□saka University, Suita) 1994

Tysdahl, Bjom (Oslo University) 1985

Uhlig, Claus (Philipps University, Marburg) 1975

Ukaji, Masatomo (Tsurumi University) 1994

Vander Meulen, David L. (University of Virginia, Charlottesville) 1993

Vickers, Brian (Swiss Federal Institute of Technology / EJII, Zurich) 1980

Viereck, Wolfgang (Otto Friedrich University, Bamberg) 1974

Waith, Eugene M. (R; Yale University, New Haven, Connecticut) 1995

Wales, Katie (University of Leeds) 1996

Wallace, David John (University of Pennsylvania, Philadelphia) 2000

Walmsley, John (Bielefeld University) 1993

Warren, Beatrice (Lund University) 1998

Wasser, Henry (R; City University of New York) 1966

Watson, J.R. (R; Durham University) 1979

Watts, Richard J. (University of Berne) 1999

Weimann, Robert (R; Humboldt University, Berlin) 1965

Weinstein, Arnold (Brown University, Providence, Rhode Island) 2000

Weinstock, Horst (R; Rhenish-Westphalian Technical University, Aachen) 1970

Weiss, Wolfgang (Ludwig Maximilian University, Munich) 1970

Wiesenfarth, Jay (University of Wisconsin, Madison) 1983

Wilcox, Helen (State University of Groningen) 1992

Williams, G.W. (R; Duke University, Durham, North Carolina) 1986

Winkgens, Meinhard (Mannheim University) 2000

Winton, Calhoun (University of Maryland, College Park) 1985

Wisenthal, Jonathan (University of British Columbia, Vancouver) 1997

Wittreich, Joseph (Graduate Center, City University of New York) 1974

Wolff, Erwin (R; Friedrich Alexander University, Erlangen–Nuremberg) 1994

Woodring, Carl R (R; Columbia University, New York) 1956

Woods, Susanne (Wheaton College, Norton, Massachusetts) 1991

Worth, G.J. (R; University of Kansas, Lawrence) 1967

Wortham, Thomas (University of California at Los Angeles) 1997

Wright, Iain (Australian National University, Canberra) 1995

Wright, Terence Roy (University of Newcastle upon Tyne) 1997

Yuan, Heh–Hsiang (Soochow University, Taipei) 1993

Yuan, Yuan (California State University at San Marcos) 2000

Zach, Wolfgang (Innsbruck University) 1995

Zacharasiewicz, Waldemar (Vienna University) 1977

Zender, Karl F. (University of California at Davis) 1999

Zettersten, Arne (Copenhagen University) 1977

Ziegler, Heide (International University in Germany, Bruchsal) 1994

List of Contributors

HAZARD ADAMS is Professor Emeritus of English and Comparative Literature at the University of Washington (Seattle). He founded the Department of English & Comparative Literature at the University of California, Irvine, and was later dean and then vice-chancellor there. Among his 25 books are four novels, a book of poems, works on William Blake, W.B. Yeats, Lady Gregory, and Joyce Cary, philosophy of the literary symbolic, and the widely used anthologies *Critical Theory Since Plato* and *Critical Theory Since 1965*. His novel *Home*, to appear in 2001, is the third in his Academic Trilogy.

TODD K. BENDER completed his doctoral studies at Stanford University and has been Professor of English at the University of Madison–Wisconsin since 1973. He has held Fulbright Fellowships to England, Greece and France. He is the editor of a series of concordances to Joseph Conrad, Ford Madox Ford, Henry James, and other writers. He is the author of *Gerard Manley Hopkins: The Classical Background and Critical Reception of His Work* (1966) and *Literary Impressionism* (1997).

NORMAN BLAKE has recently retired as Professor and Head of Department of English Language at Sheffield University, though he still works on the *Canterbury Tales* Project at De Montfort University. He has written extensively on Caxton, Chaucer, Shakespeare's language and the history of the English language. His *History of the English Language* was published in 1996, and he has recently completed a grammar of Shakespeare's language for Palgrave. His other works include an edition of the Hengwrt manuscript of the *Canterbury Tales* (1980), a study of the poem's textual tradition (1985), and a life of Caxton (1996).

ULRICH BROICH has been Professor of English at the Universities of Bochum (1967–76) and Munich (1976–2000). He was Visiting Professor at the Universities of Minnesota and Stanford, and President of the German Association of University Teachers of English (1984–86). OBE 1996. Major publications: *Ironie im Prosawerk Thackerays* (1958); *Studien zum literarischen Patronat* (with Walter Schirmer, 1962); *Science Fiction* (with Ulrich Suerbaum and Raimund Borgmeier, 1981); *The*

Eighteenth-Century Mock-Heroic Poem (1990); *Intertextualität* (ed. with Manfred Pfister, 1985); *Die Zwanziger Jahre in Großbritannien* (ed. with Christoph Bode, 1998); and *Britain at the Turn of the Century* (ed. with Susan Bassnett, 2001).

EMORY ELLIOTT is Distinguished Professor of English at the University of California, Riverside, and the Director of the Center for Ideas and Society. From 1972 to 1989, he was on the faculty of Princeton University, where he chaired the English Department and American Studies Program. His books include *Power and the Pulpit in Puritan New England* (1975), *Revolutionary Writers: Literature and Authority in the New Republic* (1982), and *The Literature of Puritan New England* (1994). He is the editor of the *Columbia Literary History of the United States* (1988), the *Columbia History of the American Novel* (1991) and the *Prentice–Hall Anthology of American Literature*. He has edited the American Novel Series for Cambridge University Press and Penn Studies on Contemporary American Fiction for the University of Pennsylvania Press. He has recently published a new "Introduction" and edition of the Oxford World Classics edition of the *Adventures of Huckleberry Finn*.

KAISER HAQ was born in 1950 in Dhaka, and was educated at the Universities of Dhaka (BA Honours and MA) and Warwick (PhD), where he was a Commonwealth Scholar. He fought in the Bangladesh independence war of 1971. At Dhaka University since 1975, he spent 1986–87 as Senior Fulbright Scholar at the University of Wisconsin, Milwaukee. He is the author of four slim collections of poetry (a fifth is in press), is the editor of the anthology *Contemporary Indian Poetry* (1990), and has translated Shamsur Rahman's *Selected Poems* (1985) from the Bengali, as well as *Quartet*, a novel by Rabindranath Tagore (1993); his translation of *The Wonders of Vilayet* is forthcoming, and he is currently revising a translation of another Tagore novel.

IHAB HASSAN is Emeritus Vilas Professor of English and Comparative Literature at the University of Milwaukee–Wisconsin. He is the author of many books, including *Radical Innocence* (1961), *The Literature of Silence* (1967), *The Dismemberment of Orpheus* (1971, 1982), *Paracriticisms* (1975), *The Postmodern Turn* (1987, 2001 online), *Selves at Risk* (1990), and *Rumors of Change* (1995). He has also written two memoirs, *Out of Egypt* (1986) and *Traces of Japan* (1996), and co-edited, with Sally Hassan, *Liberations* (1971) and *Innovation/Renovation* (1983). Most recently, he has taught at the Universities of Giessen, Gothenburg, Mainz, and South Australia. He is the recipient of many fellowships and teaching awards, including honorary doctorates from Uppsala and Giessen.

YOSHIHIKO IKEGAMI, born 1934, holds BA and MA degrees in English from Tokyo University and an MPhil and a PhD in linguistics from Yale. He is currently Professor Emeritus at Tokyo University and Professor at the Graduate School of Showa Women's University. He has held visiting professorships at the University of Munich, Indiana University, and the Free University of Berlin, and has been a Research Fellow of the Humboldt Foundation (Hamburg and Munich), the British Council (London) and the Fulbright Foundation (University of California at Berkeley), and with Longman (London). His chief areas of interest include semantics, semiotics and poetics. His major publications (in Japanese) include the studies *Grammar of English Poetry*, *Semantics*, *Linguistics of DOING and BECOMING* and *Poetics and Cultural Semiotics*, and he is editor of the collections *The Empire of Signs: Semiotic Essays in Japanese Culture* and *Discourse Analysis in Japan*.

DIETER KASTOVSKY is Professor of English Linguistics at the University of Vienna. He studied English, German, Romance and General Linguistics at Tübingen, Berlin and Besançon, and received his doctorate in 1967. Before coming to Vienna, where, from 1986 to 1990 and since 1994, he has been Head of the Department of Interpreting and Translation, he was a research assistant in the English Department of the University of Tübingen (1967–73), and Full Professor of English Linguistics at the University of Wuppertal (1973–81). Since 1991 he has been Secretary and Treasurer of *Societas Linguistica Europaea*. His publications include *Old English Deverbal Substantives Derived by Means of a Zero Morpheme* (1968), *Studies in Morphology: Aspects of English and German Verb Inflection* (1971), *Wortbildung und Semantik* (1982), and contributions to the *Cambridge History of the English Language: The Beginnings to 1066*, ed. Richard M. Hogg (1992), *Diachrony Within Synchrony: Language History and Cognition*, ed. Günter Kellermann and Michael D. Morrissey (1992), and *English Historical Linguistics 1994*, ed. Derek Britton (1996). He has also edited several Festschrifts and conference volumes.

IAN KIRBY has his doctorate from the University of London. Since 1971 he has been Professor of English Language and Medieval Literature at the University of Lausanne, Switzerland. Earlier, he lectured at Uppsala University, Sweden, and was the first professor of English at the University of Iceland. His publications include *Biblical Quotation in Old Icelandic–Norwegian Religious Literature* (1976–80), *Bible Translation in Old Norse* (1986), and numerous articles on Old Norse, Old and Middle English, and Shakespeare. His current research interests include the preparation of the third volume of the Early English Text Society edition of *Laȝamon's Brut*, and an examination of runic inscriptions in Great Britain and North America. A former president of

IAUPE, he has edited its Bulletin, and is currently its Secretary-General and Treasurer.

OKIFUMI KOMESU studied at Muskingum College, Ohio (BA), and at Michigan State University (MA and PhD). He is Emeritus Professor of English at the University of the Ryukyus, Okinawa, and Professor of English at Okinawa International University. Major publications are *The Double Perspective of Yeats's Aesthetic* (1984) and (in Japanese) *The Literary Work of Art: Studies on the Creative Circle in the Literary Process* (1995).

JEAN–JACQUES LECERCLE is currently Professor of English at the University of Cardiff, after many years as professor at Paris X–Nanterre. He is a specialist in Victorian nonsense literature and in the philosophy of language. Among his books are *The Violence of Language* (1991), *Philosophy of Nonsense* (1994), and *Interpretation as Pragmatics* (1999). He is currently engaged in writing a book on Gilles Deleuze and language.

LAURENCE LERNER studied at the Universities of Cape Town and Cambridge. He taught in West Africa, Belfast, Sussex, France, Germany, Canada and the USA, retiring in 1995; he lives in Sussex. His many books of criticism include *The Truthtellers* (1967), *The Uses of Nostalgia: Studies in Pastoral* (1973), *Love & Marriage: Literature in its Social Context* (1979), *The Frontiers of Literature* (1988), and *Angels & Absences: Child Deaths in the Nineteenth Century* (1997). He has published three novels, and nine volumes of poetry, including his *Selected Poems* (1984), *Chapter & Verse: Bible Poems* (1984) and *Rembrandt's Mirror* (1987). He is a Fellow of the Royal Society of Literature. His most recent publication is *Wandering Professor* (1999), an account and discussion of the experience of university teaching in many countries, which is reviewed in the current IAUPE Bulletin.

In 1963, MURRAY KRIEGER† was appointed the first Carpenter Professor in Literary Criticism at the University of Iowa (the first chair of literary theory to be so designated in the USA). In 1966 he moved to the new campus of the University of California at Irvine, where he initiated a programme in literary criticism and critical theory. In 1974 he was named University Professor and in 1994 University Research Professor. In 1976 he became founding Director of the School of Criticism and Theory, and in 1987 founded the University of California Humanities Research Institute, likewise acting as its first Director. He was awarded the UCI Medal in 1990, the University's highest honour. He was honoured again, in 2000, with the renaming of the Humanities Office Building as Murray Krieger Hall in recognition of his distinguished service and contributions to the UCI campus. He is the author of over a dozen books, including *Theory of Criticism* (1976), *Ekphrasis* (1992), and *The Institution of Theory* (1994).

SERGIO PEROSA is Professor of Anglo-American Literature and Chair of the Department of Anglo-American and Latin-American Studies at the University of Venice, where he also served as Dean of the Faculty of Modern Languages and Chair of the Department. A former President of the European Association for American Studies, he has published, in the USA, *The Art of F.S. Fitzgerald* (1965), *Henry James and the Experimental Novel* (1978), *American Theories of the Novel, 1793–1903* (1984) and *From Islands to Portraits* (2000), and, in Italy, *Vie della narrativa americana* (1980), *Storia del teatro americano* (1982), *Le isole Aran* (1987), *Bagliori dal Commonwealth* (1991) and *L'isola la donna il ritratto* (1996), as well as translations and/or editions of Shakespeare, Virginia Woolf, Henry James, Herman Melville, Robert Penn Warren, John Berryman, and others.

MATTI RISSANEN is Professor of English Philology at the University of Helsinki and Director of the Research Centre for Variation and Change in English. He has been member of IAUPE since the late-1970s and was member of the International Committee in 1992–98. He was the leader of the team preparing the Helsinki Corpus of English Texts. His publications include, apart from some hundred scholarly articles, *The Uses of 'One' in Old and Early Middle English, Problems in the Translation of Shakespeare's Imagery into Finnish, Studies in the Style and Narrative Technique of Edward Hall's Chronicle*, and the section on "Syntax" in the *Cambridge History of the English Language*, vol. 3.

HANS SAUER is Professor of English Language and Medieval Literature at the University of Munich. He is a graduate of Munich University; before returning there, he was a professor at Würzburg and at Dresden, as well as a visiting professor at Eichstätt, Innsbruck, □odz, Palermo, Columbus (Ohio) and Venice International University. His research interests include critical editions of Old and Middle English texts, English word-formation and its history, Medieval English plant names, the history of English studies, and varieties of English (including Black English and advertising language). Some of these are reflected in the following publications: *Theodulfi Capitula in England* (1978); *The Owl and the Nightingale* (1983); *Nominalkomposita im Frühmittelenglischen* (1992), and the chapter on linguistics in *Einführung in das Studium der Anglistik und Amerikanistik*, ed. Böker and Houswitschka (2000).

ROGER D. SELL is J.O.E. Donner Professor of English Language and Literature at Åbo Akademi University. His research interests cover various periods of English literature, the implications of communicative pragmatics for literary theory and criticism, and literature within foreign-language education. His books include *The Shorter Poems of Sir John Beaumont: A Critical Edition* (1974), *Stories for Lesley by Robert Frost* (1984) and *Literature as Communication* (2000), and he is the editor of the critical anthologies *Literary Pragmatics* (1991), *Great Expectations: A New Casebook* (1994) and *Literature Throughout Foreign Language Education: The Implications of Pragmatics* (1995).

EDWIN THUMBOO is Emeritus Professor and Professorial Fellow, Department of English Language and Literature, and Chairman/Director of the Centre for the Arts at the National University of Singapore, where he was Head of the Department of English (1977–93) and Dean of the Faculty of Arts & Social Sciences (1980–91). He has written four collections of poems, *Rib of Earth* (1956), *Gods Can Die* (1977), *Ulysses by the Merlion* (1979) and *A Third Map* (1993), and the nursery-rhyme collections *Child's Delight 1* and *2* (1972). His edited publications include *Seven Poets: Singapore/Malaysia* (1973), *The Second Tongue: An Anthology of Poetry from Malaysia and Singapore* (1979), *Anthology of ASEAN Literatures: The Poetry of Singapore* (1985), and *The Fiction of Singapore* (1990; general editor). He is a consulting editor of *World Englishes Westerly*, and is also on the editorial board of *Solidarity*. His distinctions as creative writer include the National Book Development Council of Singapore Book Award for Poetry in English (1978, 1980 and 1994), the Southeast Asian Writers Award (1979), and the ASEAN Cultural and Communication Award (1987). He has served as Chairman of the Association for Commonwealth Literature and Language Studies (1983–86) and on both the International Advisory Panel, East–West Centre, Hawaii (1987), and the Committee of Jurors, Neustadt International Prize for Literature, Oklahoma (1988). He has held visiting professorships and research fellowships at Penn State University (1979–80), University College, London (1987), the Australian Defence Force Academy (1993), and the Universities of Iowa (1986) and Illinois (1998), and has been writer-in-residence at the Institute of Culture and Communication, Hawaii (1985), and the University of Wollongong (1989).

J.R. WATSON is Emeritus Professor of English, University of Durham, England. He was educated at Oxford, where he won the Matthew Arnold Memorial Prize, and at Glasgow, where he won the Ewing Prize. He was successively Lecturer and Senior Lecturer at Glasgow and at Leicester, before becoming Professor at Durham in 1978. He served as the university's Public Orator from 1989 to 1999. He was Chairman of the Modern Humanities Research Association from 1990 to 1999, and President of IAUPE from 1995 to 1998. His principal interests are in the Romantic and Victorian periods, with special attention to landscape and hymnology. His publications include

Wordsworth's Vital Soul (1982), *English Poetry of the Romantic Period, 1789–1830* (1985, second edition 1992), and *The Poetry of Gerard Manley Hopkins* (1985). His most recent book is *The English Hymn* (1997). He is currently working on an anthology of hymns, and on a book to be entitled *Romanticism and War*.

ARNE ZETTERSTEN, Professor of English Language and Literature at Copenhagen University since 1975, studied English, Nordic languages and history of literature at Lund University (Fil.mag. 1956, Fil.lic. 1961, fil.dr. 1965), where he was Docent in English. He has held visiting professorships and fellowships at a variety of universities in Europe, the USA and Asia. The offices he has held include President of the International Association of University Professors of English (1992–95), President of the Nordic Association for English Studies (1980–92), and member of the Board of the European Association for the Study of English (since 1991). Select publications: *Studies in the Dialect and Vocabulary of the Ancrene Riwle* (1965), *The English of Tristan da Cunha* (1969), *A Statistical Study of the Graphic System of Present-Day American English* (1969), *A Critical Facsimile Edition of Thomas Batchelor* (1974), *The English Text of the Ancrene Riwle* (1976), *Papers on English Language Testing in Scandinavia* (1977), *Waldere* (1979), *An Anthology of East African Literature* (1983), *An English Grammar for Microcomputers* (1983), *New Technologies in Language Learning* (1985), *BrainLearn: An Authoring System for Microcomputers* (1987), *Different Places – Different Voices* (1996), *The Politiken English–Danish Dictionary, I–II* (1999), and *The Vernon Manuscript of the Ancrene Riwle* (2001).

GRAZER BEITRÄGE ZUR ENGLISCHEN PHILOLOGIE

Band 1 Peter Bierbaumer: Der botanische Wortschatz des Altenglischen. 1. Teil: Das Lǣcebōc. 1975.

Band 2 Peter Bierbaumer: Der botanische Wortschatz des Altenglischen. 2. Teil: Lācnunga, Herbarium Apuleii, Peri Didaxeon. 1976.

Band 3 Peter Bierbaumer: Der botanische Wortschatz des Altenglischen: 3. Teil: Der botanische Wortschatz in altenglischen Glossen. 1979.

Band 4 Gerd Sieper: Fachsprachliche Korpusanalyse und Wortschatzauswahl. 1980.

Band 5 Rüdiger Pfeiffer-Rupp: Studien zu Subkategorisierung und semantischen Relationen. 1977.

Band 6 Bernhard Kettemann: Aspekte der natürlichen generativen Phonologie eines amerikanisch-englischen Dialektes. 1978.

BAMBERGER BEITRÄGE ZUR ENGLISCHEN SPRACHWISSENSCHAFT UNIVERSITY OF BAMBERG STUDIES IN ENGLISH LINGUISTICS

(Die Reihe wird unter neuer Reihenbezeichnung ab Band 7 weitergeführt)

Band 7 Günter Radden: Ein Profil soziolinguistischer Variation in einer amerikanischen Kleinstadt. 1979.

Band 8 Karin Viereck: Englisches Wortgut, seine Häufigkeit und Integration in der österreichischen und bundesdeutschen Pressesprache. 1980.

Band 9 John Oakeshott-Taylor: Acoustic Variability and its Perception. The effects of context on selected acoustic parameters of English words and their perceptual consequences. 1980.

Band 10 Edgar W. Schneider: Morphologische und syntaktische Variablen im amerikanischen *Early Black English*. 1981.

Band 11 Val Jones-Sargent: Tyne Bytes. A Computerised Sociolinguistic Study of Tyneside. 1983.

Band 12 Lee Pederson: East Tennessee Folk Speech. A Synopsis. 1983.

Band 13 Cornelia Zelinsky-Wibbelt: Die semantische Belastung von submorphematischen Einheiten im Englischen. Eine empirisch-strukturelle Untersuchung. 1983.

Band 14 Rolf Bremann: Soziolinguistische Untersuchungen zum Englisch von Cornwall. 1984.

Band 15 Wolf-Dietrich Bald and Horst Weinstock (eds.): Medieval Studies Conference Aachen 1983. Language and Literature. 1984.

Band 16 Clausdirk Pollner: Englisch in Livingston. Ausgewählte sprachliche Erscheinungen in einer schottischen New Town. 1985.

Band 17 Adam Jaworski: A linguistic picture of women's position in society. A Polish-English contrastive study. 1986.

Band 18 Mark Newbrook: Sociolinguistic reflexes of dialect interference in West Wirral. 1986.

Band 19 George Townsend Dorrill: Black and White Speech in the Southern United States. Evidence from the Linguistic Atlas of the Middle and South Atlantic States. 1986.

Band 20 Birgit Meseck: Studien zur konservativ-restaurativen Sprachkritik in Amerika. 1987.

Band 21 Barbara Kryk: On Deixis in English and Polish: The Role of Demonstrative Pronouns. 1987.

Band 22 Sándor Rot: On Crucial Problems of the English Verb. 1988.

Band 23 Stephen J. Nagle: Inferential Change and Syntactic Modality in English. 1989.

Band 24 Heinrich Ramisch: The Variation of English in Guernsey/Channel Islands. 1989.

Band 25 Ronald R. Butters: The Death of Black English. Divergence and Convergence in Black and White Vernaculars. 1989.

Band 26 Włodzimierz Sobkowiak: Metaphonology of English Paronomasic Puns. 1991.

Band 27 Robert J. Penhallurick: The Anglo-Welsh Dialects of North Wales. A Survey of Conservative Rural Spoken English in the Counties of Gwynedd and Clwyd. 1991.

Band 28 Merja Kytö: Variation and Diachrony, with Early American English in Focus. Studies on CAN/MAY and SHALL/WILL. 1991.

Band 29 Sándor Rot: Language Contact. 1991.

Band 30 Agnieszka Kiełkiewicz-Janowiak: A Socio-Historical Study in Address: Polish and English. 1992.

Band 31 Stanisław Puppel: The Dynamics of Speech Production. 1992.

Band 32 Anna Zbierska-Sawala: Early Middle English Word Formation. Semantic Aspects of Derivational Affixation in the AB Language. 1993.

Band 33 Nadine Van den Eynden: Syntactic Variation and Unconscious Linguistic Change. A study of adjectival relative clauses in the dialect of Dorset. 1993.

Band 34 Marcin Krygier: The Disintegration of the English Strong Verb System. 1994.

Band 35 Caroline Macafee: Traditional Dialect in the Modern World. A Glasgow Case Study. 1994.

Band 36 Robert Penhallurick: Gowerland and its language. A history of the English speech of the Gower Peninsula, South Wales. 1994.

Band 37 Monika Klages-Kubitzki: Article Usage in English. A Computer-based Self-teaching Programme on the Basis of a Functional Theory of Reference. 1995.

Band 38 Juhani Klemola / Merja Kytö / Matti Rissanen (eds.): Speech Past and Present. Studies in English Dialectology in Memory of Ossi Ihalainen. 1996.

Band 39 Piotr Gąsiorowski: The Phonology of Old English Stress and Metrical Structure. 1997.

Band 40 Marcin Krygier: From Regularity to Anomaly. Inflectional i-Umlaut in Middle English. 1997.

Band 41 Graham Shorrocks: A Grammar of the Dialect of the Bolton Area. Part I. Introduction, Phonology. 1998.

Band 42 Graham Shorrocks: A Grammar of the Dialect of the Bolton Area. Part II. Morphology and Syntax. 1999.

Band 43 Mats Rydén / Ingrid Tieken-Boon van Ostade / Merja Kytö (eds.): A Reader in Early Modern English. 1998.

Band 44 Herbert Grabes (ed.): Innovation and Continuity in English Studies. A Critical Jubilee. 2001.